FRANCOPHONE BELGIAN CINEMA

Traditions in World Cinema

General Editors
Linda Badley (Middle Tennessee State University)
R. Barton Palmer (Clemson University)

Founding Editor
Steven Jay Schneider (New York University)

Titles in the series include:

Traditions in World Cinema
Linda Badley, R. Barton Palmer and Steven Jay Schneider (eds)

Japanese Horror Cinema
Jay McRoy (ed.)

New Punk Cinema
Nicholas Rombes (ed.)

African Filmmaking
Roy Armes

Palestinian Cinema
Nurith Gertz and George Khleifi

Czech and Slovak Cinema
Peter Hames

The New Neapolitan Cinema
Alex Marlow-Mann

American Smart Cinema
Claire Perkins

The International Film Musical
Corey Creekmur and Linda Mokdad (eds)

Italian Neorealist Cinema
Torunn Haaland

Magic Realist Cinema in East Central Europe
Aga Skrodzka

Italian Post-Neorealist Cinema
Luca Barattoni

Spanish Horror Film
Antonio Lázaro-Reboll

Post-beur Cinema
Will Higbee

New Taiwanese Cinema in Focus
Flannery Wilson

International Noir
Homer B. Pettey and R. Barton Palmer (eds)

Films on Ice
Scott MacKenzie and Anna Westerståhl Stenport (eds)

Nordic Genre Film
Tommy Gustafsson and Pietari Kääpä (eds)

Contemporary Japanese Cinema Since Hana-Bi
Adam Bingham

Chinese Martial Arts Cinema (2nd edition)
Stephen Teo

Slow Cinema
Tiago de Luca and Nuno Barradas Jorge

Expressionism in Cinema
Olaf Brill and Gary D. Rhodes (eds)

French Language Road Cinema: Borders, Diasporas, Migration and 'New Europe'
Michael Gott

Transnational Film Remakes
Iain Robert Smith and Constantine Verevis

Coming-of-age Cinema in New Zealand
Alistair Fox

New Transnationalisms in Contemporary Latin American Cinemas
Dolores Tierney

Celluloid Cinema: Cinema, Performance and the National
Edna Lim

Short Films from a Small Nation: Danish Informational Cinema 1935–1965
C. Claire Thomson

B-Movie Gothic: International Perspectives
Justin D. Edwards and Johan Höglund (eds)

Francophone Belgian Cinema
Jamie Steele

edinburghuniversitypress.com/series/tiwc

FRANCOPHONE BELGIAN CINEMA

Jamie Steele

EDINBURGH
University Press

Edinburgh University Press is one of the leading university presses in the UK.
We publish academic books and journals in our selected subject areas across the
humanities and social sciences, combining cutting-edge scholarship with high editorial
and production values to produce academic works of lasting importance. For more
information visit our website: edinburghuniversitypress.com

© Jamie Steele, 2019, 2020

Edinburgh University Press Ltd
The Tun – Holyrood Road
12 (2f) Jackson's Entry
Edinburgh EH8 8PJ

First published in hardback by Edinburgh University Press 2019

Typeset in 10/12.5 pt Sabon by
Servis Filmsetting Ltd, Stockport, Cheshire

A CIP record for this book is available from the British Library

ISBN 978 1 4744 2076 1 (hardback)
ISBN 978 1 4744 5963 1 (paperback)
ISBN 978 1 4744 2077 8 (webready PDF)
ISBN 978 1 4744 2078 5 (epub)

The right of Jamie Steele to be identified as author of this work has been asserted in
accordance with the Copyright, Designs and Patents Act 1988 and the Copyright and
Related Rights Regulations 2003 (SI No. 2498).

CONTENTS

List of Figures   vii
Acknowledgements   ix
Traditions in World Cinema   x

    Introduction: Regional/National/Transnational Debates in
    Francophone Belgian Cinema   1

1. The (Francophone) Belgian Film Ecosystem: Trends in Production,
   Distribution and Exhibition   26

2. 'No Future': Social Marginalisation, Social Precariousness and
   Depictions of Seraing in *Le gamin au vélo* (Jean-Pierre and Luc
   Dardenne, 2011) and *Deux jours, une nuit* (Jean-Pierre and Luc
   Dardenne, 2014)   51

3. 'Stills' and Fragmented Families: Contemplating the Private Sphere
   in Joachim Lafosse's Wallonia   82

4. From Slag Heaps to Cliffs: The 'Marked' Regional Landscape in
   Cages (Olivier Masset-Depasse, 2006)   105

5. The Francophone Belgian Road Movie: *Eldorado* (Bouli Lanners,
   2008) and *Ultranova* (Bouli Lanners, 2005)   130

6. Lucas Belvaux's Return: The Thriller Genre and Heists in Liège   155
    Conclusion   178

Works Cited   186
Films Cited   207
Index   213

FIGURES

2.1 Fabrice and Céline embrace along with their son, dressed as a Gille (a traditional costume) during the local carnival at the conclusion of *Je pense à vous* — 52

2.2 In *Le silence de Lorna*, Lorna and Sokol dance in a *Liégeois* bar, with an image of Seraing in its pomp, hidden in the background — 65

2.3 Sandra meets with Mireille in the reception area of her apartment block in *Deux jours, une nuit* — 71

2.4 In *Deux jours, une nuit*, Sandra takes her Xanax pills as she travels to her next meeting on the bus, with the Meuse glimpsed in the background — 72

2.5 Cyril looks on as a group of children from the Val-Potet estate play a game of five-a-side football — 74

2.6 Cyril and Samantha ride along the banks of the Meuse, with the lateral movement of the camera running by their side — 78

3.1 The camera retreats backwards, revealing the farmhouse before unrolling through a country lane and a series of fields — 89

3.2 The concluding image of *Le grand paysage d'Alexis Droeven* is the sole farmhouse in the Fourons — 90

3.3 Lafosse opts to break free from the focus on the character, adopting a figurative frame as the father (Jan) suffocates his son (Thomas) — 93

3.4 Pascale and her two sons François and Thierry sit around the table — 96

4.1	In *Chambre froide*, Rita stands atop a slag heap on the fringes of the city of Charleroi	114
4.2	In *Déjà s'envole la fleur maigre*, Domenico introduces the young Luigi to the Borinage and its issues of unemployment	115
4.3	The opening image of *Chambre froide* reveals Rita and her mother visiting the grave of her deceased father, with the steel plants in the background	117
4.4	*Cages*' title sequence unrolls on the majestic cliffs of Nord-Pas-de-Calais	120
4.5	Before Eve walks on stage to confront her inability to speak, Masset-Depasse focuses on Eve's eyes through a noirish vertical pattern of lighting	124
4.6	Eve confronts Damien, after realising that he is having an affair with Léa. Rainwater operates as a key motif in the sequence	127
5.1	Dimitri caresses a pair of tights, as he sits alone on the periphery of the city of Liège	135
5.2	In *Ultranova*, the camera dollies forward through the mundane warehouse, full of boxes, but with a limited number of workers	138
5.3	The opening sequence of *Ultranova* ends with an image of Dimitri standing alone next to his upturned car	140
5.4	In *Eldorado*, Lanners fixes the camera on the agricultural fields of Wallonia for twenty-three seconds, leaving the spectator to notice the slight movement of the clouds and the flickering of the wheatgrass in the wind	143
5.5	Yvan finds Elie still standing at the crossroads on the outskirts of the city of Liège	149
6.1	Patrick's family, alongside Marc, Robert and Jean-Pierre, sing 'La p'tite gayole'	162
6.2	Carole's broken-down mobylette is walked back by Patrick	167
6.3	Marc and Robert have a heated discussion against the backdrop of the abstract lights that evoke the recycling and breaking-down of the former steel plant	168

ACKNOWLEDGEMENTS

First of all, I would like to place on record my thanks to the Society of French Studies and their very valuable Small Research Support bursary, which significantly helped research at the Cinémathèque Royale in Brussels during the summer of 2015. I'd also like to thank the archivists and staff at the Cinémathèque Royale for their help and support during my research trips from 2011 to 2017 for this project (and no doubt during research trips to come). A further thank-you to Professor Will Higbee for his guidance, comments and advice on this project throughout my PhD. Thanks are also due to the University of Exeter, University of Bristol and Bath Spa University for employing me over the years (2014–present) during which this book was researched and written. Their employment certainly helped with the continuation of this cinematic journey through Belgium. And last, but not least, a special thanks to my family and partner, Nicole Needham, for all of their unwavering support over the many years it took to eventually realise this project.

TRADITIONS IN WORLD CINEMA

General editors: **Linda Badley and R. Barton Palmer**
Founding editor: **Steven Jay Schneider**

Traditions in World Cinema is a series of textbooks and monographs devoted to the analysis of currently popular and previously underexamined or undervalued film movements from around the globe. Also intended for general interest readers, the textbooks in this series offer undergraduate- and graduate-level film students accessible and comprehensive introductions to diverse traditions in world cinema. The monographs open up for advanced academic study more specialised groups of films, including those that require theoretically oriented approaches. Both textbooks and monographs provide thorough examinations of the industrial, cultural and socio-historical conditions of production and reception.

The flagship textbook for the series includes chapters by noted scholars on traditions of acknowledged importance (the French New Wave, German Expressionism), recent and emergent traditions (New Iranian, post-Cinema Novo), and those whose rightful claim to recognition has yet to be established (the Israeli persecution film, global found footage cinema). Other volumes concentrate on individual national, regional or global cinema traditions. As the introductory chapter to each volume makes clear, the films under discussion form a coherent group on the basis of substantive and relatively transparent, if not always obvious, commonalities. These commonalities may be formal, stylistic or thematic, and the groupings may, although they need not, be popularly identified as genres, cycles or movements (Japanese horror, Chinese martial arts cinema, Italian Neorealism). Indeed, in cases in which a group of films is not already commonly identified as a tradition, one purpose of the volume is to establish its claim to importance and make it visible (East Central European Magical Realist cinema, Palestinian cinema).

Textbooks and monographs include:

- An introduction that clarifies the rationale for the grouping of films under examination
- A concise history of the regional, national or transnational cinema in question
- A summary of previous published work on the tradition
- Contextual analysis of industrial, cultural and socio-historical conditions of production and reception
- Textual analysis of specific and notable films, with clear and judicious application of relevant film theoretical approaches
- Bibliograph(ies)/filmograph(ies)

Monographs may additionally include:

- Discussion of the dynamics of cross-cultural exchange in light of current research and thinking about cultural imperialism and globalisation, as well as issues of regional/national cinema or political/aesthetic movements (such as new waves, postmodernism or identity politics)
- Interview(s) with key filmmakers working within the tradition.

INTRODUCTION: REGIONAL/NATIONAL/ TRANSNATIONAL DEBATES IN FRANCOPHONE BELGIAN CINEMA

'Good evening everyone. It is a critical hour, please excuse us for this interruption [...] Flanders is going to unilaterally proclaim its independence' is the epiphanic and irruptive opening line from the feature-length docudrama *Tout ça (ne nous rendra pas la Belgique/Bye Bye Belgium* (2006).[1] On 13 December 2006, the pre-recorded *Bye Bye Belgium* was broadcast by the television company RTBF (*Radio et Télévision Belge Francophone*) across Belgium. The programme posited the end of Belgium as a sovereign and political entity, drawing on a pervading sense of 'national trauma' (Collard 2014: 544). In the French-language newspaper *La Libre Belgique*, film critic Hubert Heyrendt diachronically noted that, even six years after its initial release, the made-for-television film remained 'in the Belgian collective memory' (Heyrendt 2012).[2] As Frédéric Martel observes, the docudrama was based 'on the model offered by Orson Welles' *War of the Worlds* [radio play]' in which 'programming on RTBF was cut short and interrupted [...by] interviews with real politicians and falsified reports' (Martel 2010: 400). The programme becomes even more prescient given the discourse around the notion of 'fake news', a byword of 2016.[3]

Bye Bye Belgium comprises news bulletins and interviews with prominent figures in politics and the media, examining the political issues (such as national debts, the proposed national border, the new currency, the territoriality of Brussels and the naming of Mechelen/Malines as the Flemish capital) and socio-economic issues (the loss of jobs and the movement of businesses between Belgium's regions). Collard interprets these events as examples of 'subversive remediation', proposing that 'RTBF's spoof newscast effectively *staged* multiple communicative texts simultaneously, and in so doing, stimulated in the minds of interpreting agents the very type of cognitive *procedure* as when presented with an *adaptation*' (2014: 550). In essence, it offers another version of 'ethnic tensions' (ibid.) between francophone and Flemish Belgian speakers. The false presentation of these political concerns and issues on *La Une* (a RTBF-run television channel) contrasts dramatically with Mosley's (2001: 11) analysis of public service broadcasting in Belgium. Mosley posits that 'in times of national crisis [...] informational programming (news bulletins, interviews, panel discussions, etc.) offers itself as a preferred source of identification and reassurance' (ibid.). Rather than providing reassurance, the programme foreshadowed (by a period of six months) Belgium's 'political crisis between 2007 and 2011' (Hooghe 2012).[4] In this case, the docudrama articulates and represents a potential 'hot nationalism' (Billig 1995) in Belgium, where issues of political independence and sovereignty for Flanders rise explicitly to the surface, to a point when they lead, in the programme's terms, to the 'implosion-explosion of a country'.

In 2017, francophone Belgian film institutions began to place a greater emphasis on celebrating and valorising francophone Belgian cinema as unique and distinct *within* the nation-state, through two film events. Organised by the Cinémathèque Royale and the Centre du Cinéma et de l'Audiovisuel respectively, they affirm the need to draw lines between the competing 'national' or 'regional' cinemas of Flanders and francophone Belgium (Brussels and Wallonia). Mosley conceives this notion as part of a '"split screen" between French- and Dutch-language cultures [which] largely determines the evolution of Belgian cinema' (Mosley 2001: 2). Firstly, the Cinémathèque Royale, in collaboration with the SCC (Service de Culture Cinématographique), launched an event connected to the emergence of a key publication celebrating '40 years of small studio or production company filmmaking'. The event's abstract neatly summarises the key debates and premises within francophone Belgian cinema, noting

> the importance of *ateliers* [studios] in the Belgian audiovisual landscape [...] and [of] (re-)discovering the little gems that they have created. These films were, at the time of their release, often political, marked by discernible social themes and audacious cinematography. It is possible to identify that the main common element between these small studios is surely the ability to be the home of and to support emerging auteurs. This is irrespective of the filmmakers' form and approach, and this, as a result, produces a rich cinema. (Cinémathèque Royale 2017)

Whilst the event focuses on small studios and emerging and peripheral filmmaking talents in French-speaking Belgium, such as Rachel Lang, Pablo Munoz Gomez, Benoît Dervaux, Olivier Smolders and Danis Tanović, the abstract and the curated film selection indicate an inherent sociopolitical film culture, as well as a vibrant transnational, national and regional film industry in the French-speaking community. The second – and more prominent – event celebrated 'fifty years of Belgian cinema' (1967–2017); what is revealed is an 'auteurist', French-speaking cinema that does little to dispel elitist connotations of francophone Belgian cinema, in contrast to its genre-based and popular cinema sister in Flanders. The films selected for the anniversary do not reveal the initial concerns pertaining to the loss of potential international co-productions. Although the selection is organised by year, key names reverberate throughout, such as André Delvaux, the Dardenne brothers, Jean-Jacques Andrien, Thierry Michel, Marion Hänsel and Chantal Akerman, amongst others. This speaks to some of the historical trends of francophone Belgian film production and necessitates an industrial analysis (as discussed in Chapter One). The anniversary serves as a diachronic reconsideration and re-evaluation of what constitutes francophone Belgian cinema. The schedule celebrates the openness and diversity of cultural representations produced within the linguistic community and/or the regions of Bruxelles-Capitale and Wallonia. In essence, the schedule is inclusive, incorporating classical narratives, pornography, social realism, magical realism, genres such as the road movie and the thriller, and diasporic filmmaking.

As a result, this book represents a timely consideration of francophone Belgian cinema as policy-makers and curators attempt to redefine the 'national' and/or regional cinema at the point of its fiftieth anniversary. The canonical line is peculiarly drawn in 1967, at the installation of a new French language policy, seemingly – or selectively – forgetting the preceding formation of a Flemish–Dutch language cinema and policy three years earlier. The enshrining of the support of cinema in policy, and according to language, was a subject of much debate. As Mosley presciently observes,

> (s)omewhat disingenuously, given the historical construction of 'Belgian' culture in the French language, the francophones felt that the Flemish initiative worked against both the external perception of a developing national cinema in Belgium and the likelihood of international co-production projects. (2001: 104)

This was even though the francophone Ministry for Culture had been supporting film production discreetly since 1964 (ibid.).

This study of francophone Belgian cinema is structured through a series of flashpoints, acknowledging short bursts where filmmakers from the two French-speaking regions of Belgium were recognised and valorised internally and internationally. For instance, the documentaries *Misère au Borinage/ Poverty in the Borinage* (Henri Storck and Joris Ivens, 1933) and *Déjà s'envole la fleur maigre/From the Branches Drops the Withered Blossom* (Paul Meyer, 1960) engage directly with Wallonia's industrial heritage, and, in the latter's case through intentionally embracing international film traditions like Italian Neorealism. The films of André Delvaux, through international co-productions, have addressed the Belgian linguistic divide (primarily through the auteur himself and his self-identity) and Nazi collaboration,[5] Jean-Jacques Andrien's films unroll during the linguistic and territorial conflict of the 1960s–70s and the Dardenne brothers' *Rosetta* (Jean-Pierre and Luc Dardenne, 1999) was the first win for Belgium at the Cannes film festival, inspiring the creation of a new film production model in Wallonia. The year 2001 operates as a clear delineating line, with the creation of new funding bodies such as Wallimage in Wallonia incentivising the increased production of films there. It is from this watershed moment in francophone Belgian cinema that the two main types of filmmakers – (1) the film-school generation of Joachim Lafosse and Olivier Masset-Depasse, and (2) the autodidacts like the Dardenne brothers, Bouli Lanners and Lucas Belvaux – received consistent funding for their productions.

Times are perhaps a-changing for French-language Belgian cinema, as it begins to shift away from the sociopolitical, social realist texts that have achieved critical valorisation at the 'A'-grade international film festival at Cannes to a genre-led tradition, reminiscent of Flemish, Dutch and Scandinavian film and television cultures. This turn has been widely discussed by policy-makers, with a clear tendency for decision-makers to turn towards well-recognised genres. The turn to social realist, sociopolitical texts resonates with a 'topical' – as opposed to 'perennial' – 'theme of the nation' since it captures a specific moment in time and is developed in line with a particular 'historical or cultural formation' according to Hjort's (2000: 106) argument. For Hjort, this inflects on patterns of distribution and exhibition (in terms of mass appeal), since 'topical' themes are 'likely to be of interest to only a small number of people, and for only a limited period of time' (2000: 106). This is representative of the critical and international valorisation of francophone Belgian cinema on the film festival circuit, and its breakthrough in the early 2000s. After watching the thriller, or *polar*, *Tueurs/Killers* (François Troukens and Jean-François Hensgens, 2017), Bourdon polemically asks 'is this the symbol of francophone Belgian cinema of tomorrow, where we can finally marry dramas with *polars*, comedies and other fantastical films?' (Bourdon 2017). It represents a sea change from Mathijs' (2004a) analysis of the cinema of the Low Countries (inclusive of Belgium), which, the scholar posits, 'is never a genre cinema, and is almost always self-reflective, tied to reality while failing to question it' (Mathijs 2004a: 4). The 'diversification' of Belgian cinema occurred through directives organised by decision-makers within Brussels' and

Wallonia's key film institutions, which lamented its stereotyping as a social cinema and intended to support more genre films (Hainaut 2015).

Returning to the notion of Belgian cinema as a 'split screen', Mosley (2001) uses concepts of biculturalism and ethnolingualism as theoretical paradigms to draw borders and boundaries internally and analyse (at least) two Belgian cinemas. In this book, I turn more towards the concept of cinematic transnationalism as a developing conceptual framework to critically analyse trends in modes of filmmaking that seamlessly carry over and beyond national and cultural boundaries. This is in addition to the contrasting, yet complementary substate, the regional and debates in 'cinemas of small nations' (Hjort and Petrie 2007) to highlight the stretch somewhere between the local and the global. Cinematic transnationalism operates as the dominant and lead paradigm for this approach to a cinema that is also fragmented. Song Hwee Lim (2007) offers a breakdown for what the 'trans-' constitutes within cinematic transnationalism. The concept is first a 'spatial marker' as well as translating to notions of 'transformation', 'across', 'beyond', 'becoming' and 'potentiality' (2007: 42–6). It can also serve to 'consolidate', since Lim further posits that 'the prefix "trans," while indexing a crossing of boundaries, can in effect fix the boundaries even more firmly and in an essentialist manner' (2007: 47). Hjort's (2009) typologies of cinematic transnationalism prove instructive for categorising and further nuancing the modes of production, distribution and exhibition in francophone Belgian cinema, as well as its 'marked' and 'unmarked' representational forms. In the case of francophone Belgian cinema, as this book argues, the borders and boundaries begin to be affirmed, and reaffirmed, within a regional and linguistic context as points of orientation for filmmakers and spectators alike. Ezra and Rowden's (2006) seminal introduction to *Transnational Cinema: A Reader* proves useful for outlining approaches to modes of film production, distribution and exhibition, in addition to better understanding the role of auteurs in national cinema contexts and the mobility of both finance and films.

From this premise, let us start by considering the extent to which francophone Belgian cinema operates within models offered in scholarship pertaining to cinematically small nations.

Locating Francophone Belgian Cinema as a 'Small Cinema'

The focus of this monograph on francophone Belgian cinema seeks to analyse the filmmaking traditions of one cross-section of Belgian cinema. Critical and scholarly attention has – in the last ten years at least – sought to form a theoretical approach on 'cinemas of small nations' (Hjort and Petrie 2007) or 'cinema at the periphery' (Iordanova, Martin-Jones and Vidal 2010). Within the context of small cinema studies, Ledo (2017) develops and nuances her analysis through approaches to 'national cinema' as conceived by Elsaesser (2005; 2013), Christie

(2013), Hayward (2000) and Schlesinger (2000). These all provide instructive starting points for a deciphering and analysis of francophone Belgian cinema as a small national cinema and as a potentially regional cinema.

Within the paradigm of 'cinemas at the periphery', the edited collection 'deploy[s] an array of local references and tell[s] very different stories from those of the world's established film industries' (Iordanova, Martin-Jones and Vidal 2010: 5). In so doing, it offers a 'flexible' and 'relational' framework that intersects the transnational and the local, commencing with the local first before reaching out in a textual and contextual way (2010: 17). Hjort and Petrie (2007) set out similar aims and intentions within their theoretical framework, contending that 'the concept of small nation promises to shed light on at least some of the ways in which subnational, national, international, transnational, regional and global forces dovetail and compete in the sphere of cinema' (2007: 2). Elsaesser (2013) offers the 'post-national' in this theoretical mix. In his 'reconceptualising' of 'national cinema' (renewing Crofts' (1998) taxonomical approach), Elsaesser contends that

> national cinema has become a floating designation, neither essentialist not constructivist, but more like something that hovers uncertainly over a film's 'identity'. The national thus joins other categories, such as the opposition posited between mainstream films featuring stars, and art cinema identified by a directorial personality; popular genre films versus documentary style and psychological realism. (2013)

In these cases, the articulation of the local is crucial, since, as Hannerz notes in his analysis of transnational cultures, the local is 'deeper' than the 'surface' of the transnational or global (Hannerz 1996: 28). For Elsaesser (2013), without clear inflections and articulations that pertain to the local, national films 'impersonate' films from different categories or other countries, namely Hollywood or American modes of filmmaking. In so doing, the local operates at the locus of this study of francophone Belgian cinema, since, in the case of each of the films selected for study and critical analysis, the filmmaker positions the film within a decipherable, 'epistemological' (Ezra and Rowden 2006: 4) context for local audiences. The selected films all reach out to the transnational in differing ways, whether it is through the articulation of social issues and concerns, the use of landscapes or intertextual systems carefully constructed through familiar genres.

As Iordanova, Martin-Jones and Vidal further posit, as films are 'brought into contact', 'shared concerns' are produced (2010: 6). It is these 'shared concerns' and local articulations that stretch across Wallonia, the cinema of francophone Belgium, and the north of France in particular, culminating in the concept of a *cinéma nordiste*. Moreover, the concept proposes a dualism to the 'periphery', denoting a subtle difference between cinematically small nations that 'are marginalised in terms of film production' and 'peripheral cultures [...] that are internal to nations' (2010: 7). It is within this dualism that francophone Belgian cinema requires its greatest classification. A question that I am often asked in national and international Film Studies conferences concerns the categorisation of Walloon cinema within francophone Belgian cinema, since they are both articulated in French, as opposed to Walloon cinema (as a regional cinema) finding its identity in the Walloon language. The interpretation of Walloon cinema as viewed by the publication *La revue toudi*, by Rochet (2011), and by Roekens and Tixhon (2011) is a culturally and thematically distinct cinema, representing the local state of crisis, particularly in terms of collective identity, atomisation, social marginalisation and masculinity. Roekens and Tixhon's edited collection is instructive for its chapters on Bouli Lanners and Lucas Belvaux (as well as analysis of Benoît Mariage), and their representation of a Wallonia 'in crisis'. This monograph similarly valorises (with chapters also dedicated to) Lanners' *Ultranova* (Bouli Lanners, 2005) and *Eldorado* (Bouli Lanners, 2008) and Belvaux's *La raison du plus faible* (Lucas Belvaux, 2006), although, in this case there is an emphasis placed on the context of genre filmmaking in Wallonia, that is, the road movie and the *polar*. Mariage's film finds itself a reference point for Olivier Masset-Depasse's debut feature, *Cages* (2006). Walloon cinema's articulation in French places it, rather firmly, as a sub-section of francophone Belgian cinema, which also incorporates filmmaking in Brussels, the 'national' and transnational funding mechanisms, and transnational modes of filmmaking. It is peripheral to French filmmaking and to its 'national' partner in Flanders. The most recent (and a rare) example of filmmaking in the Walloon language arrived as a documentary film in 2015, *Le bout de la langue/Tip of the Tongue* (Xavier Istasse, 2015). In the documentary's trailer, interviewees note that it has been 'forgotten that only two/three/four generations ago, people spoke Walloon' and that it had no class distinctions since it was 'spoken by both the less privileged and public figures'. The use of the Walloon language marginalises Walloon filmmaking from the domestic market and a natural inclination to appeal to the larger French market. Francophone Belgian cinema, in contrast, reaches beyond Belgium's national borders, since it operates in a dominant language in Europe and globally, unlike Flemish Dutch for Flemish cinema in the north of the country.

A further interpretative framework useful to this study of 'community-based' cinema is the increasing critical and academic currency afforded to devolution in a cinematic context or a devolved national cinema. Such an approach similarly marks a stepping away from a national cinema approach. Hjort and Petrie note the importance of devolution in the categorisation of cinematically small nations, since there is a 'struggle for autonomy' within the context of power relations and questions of domination (Hjort and Petrie

2007: 6). Although Belgium contrasts with the generalisation of 'cinemas of small nations' that typically have histories of subjugation (ibid.), the federalisation of the country in the 1990s and the increasing autonomy afforded to its linguistic communities speaks to Hjort and Petrie's concept. For Song Hwee Lim, the 'inherent problems of the national' give rise to an 'imperative to trace how power relations are differently reconfigured in the new paradigms of transnationalism, regionalism and globalism' (Lim 2007: 41). The transnational and the regional, therefore, offer complementary and new ways to analyse trends and traditions produced within hierarchical structures. Mosley interprets Belgian cinema as a small national cinema, prior to the publications of Hjort and Petrie's work (2007), as conceived through a 'low position' in a 'hierarchical power structure', which led to an increase in state intervention in the production sector (Mosley 2001: 4). Moreover, 'external forces' have also confirmed Belgian cinema's 'low position' within a system of domination, with linguistic forces emanating from France, histories of occupation by Germany and Hollywood's domination of Belgium's film exhibition sector (ibid.). It is precisely these transnational interactions that form a key part of the opening reading of francophone Belgian cinema in the context of the modes of film production, distribution and exhibition (Chapter One).

The 'devolution' of film production and the sub-national is split along linguistic lines in Belgium. Similarly, in Canada, the notion of 'two solitudes' operates as 'a standard metaphor for the relations of English and French Canada' (Collins 1990: 190). According to Collins' analysis of television in this context, the 'two solitudes' concept pertains to how citizens and spectators 'respond' to cultural representations differently (ibid.). Language remains the locus of this debate, since, as Collins contends,

> [i]n Quebec (as in English Canada), culture is seen as an arena of struggle in which collective identity is threatened by the pressures of assimilation. [. . .] [L]anguage is a crucial bastion in the struggle for national identity – a bastion that is besieged but, as yet, untaken by the hostile Anglophone forces. (1990: 191)

This notion resonates with the opening reference to the television programme *Bye Bye Belgium*, which centres on the two competing linguistic communities and the 'struggle' of their respective nationalisms. In Belgium, the proximity to France complicates the network of relations between the two linguistic communities further, particularly in the case of Wallonia, with *Bye Bye Belgium* even mooting the potential for cession to France. Spaas notes that Switzerland and Belgium have surface similarities in terms of their linguistic fragmentation and federalisation (2000: 44). Language and linguistic difference underpins Swiss cinema, with Spaas observing a largely Germanic-language cinema until the 1960s, followed by a French-language auteur-driven cinema (2000: 44–5) – a similar dynamic to Belgium and francophone Belgian cinema.

Let us now shift attention to a contextual understanding of questions of nation, nationalism and nationhood alongside the country's political and linguistic 'conflicts', political stasis, and bifurcation along linguistic and cultural lines.

Belgian Nationalism? 'Hot', 'Banal' and 'Silenced'

Since this monograph focuses primarily on the francophone regions of Belgium, it is first necessary to outline the historical, cultural and linguistic reasons for the 'split' (Mosley 2001) in the selected distinct cinemas. This section provides ample opportunity to outline and discuss the reasons for the separation and the focus of this monograph solely on the French-speaking regions of Belgium, Wallonia and Brussels-Capitale. Moreover, the Dardenne brothers, Olivier Masset-Depasse, Joachim Lafosse, Bouli Lanners and Lucas Belvaux all hail from Wallonia, interpellating its culture in their films' cultural representations, articulations and poetics. It may be that, by virtue of the selection of these filmmakers in this study of francophone Belgian cinema, it is canon-forming in its own right, thereby achieving its own 'self-selectivity' (Christie 2013).

Mosley's (2001) considered analysis of Belgian cinema also offers a comprehensive and detailed examination of the country's cultural history, focusing primarily on the notion of Belgium's plural and bifurcated cultural identities up to 1996. In 2002, *Yale French Studies* dedicated a special issue to Belgian culture, identity and memory, with a distinct emphasis on the French-speaking regions of Bruxelles-Capitale and Wallonia. In it, memory, and its Belgian context, is offered as personal, experiential, social, cultural and traumatic. Nevertheless, the issue's construction of memory in a Walloon context appears to be more closely aligned with the region's socialist movements of the 1960s, the withering of industry, and a sense of masculinity and paternalism in crisis. As Adam and Deschouwer observe, Belgium's move to federalisation was primarily due to '[t]he increased salience of the issues of language and territorial reorganisation in the party system' (2016: 1293). However, since 1996, the notion of a Belgian cultural identity has begun to further adapt, particularly in light of the difficulties and complexities in forming a Belgian government between 2007 and 2011. This is evidenced on an ideological level between the two linguistic groups through their voting patterns, which shows that they 'have always voted differently, with a more centre-left south and a more centre-right north' (Deschouwer and Reuchamps 2013: 267). Deschouwer and Reuchamps further posit that, within the 'split' in the political system, '[f]or some of the parties in Flanders the end point is independence' (2013: 265). There has been a greater push from Flanders, and the linguistic community's political representations since at least 2007, for greater autonomy, thereby recalling the political debates of the 1960s and 1970s that led to a progressive and 'gradual federalisation' (Adam and Deschouwer 2016) of the country (formalised in the early to mid 1990s). Edgar Morin observed that the 1960s witnessed 'the re-vitalisation and the counter-offensive for provincial identities (sometimes bestowed with national identity for more effective self-affirmation)' in Europe, with Flanders and Wallonia paradigmatic case studies alongside Catalonia and Scotland (Morin 1987: 151). These identities were aligned somewhere on a scale between 'local culture and national culture' (ibid.).[6] From this premise, Belgium was not the only country facing a period of devolution and regionalism in a post-national context.

In 1992, the filmmaker and ethnographer Luc de Heusch argued that 'I promised my publisher a certain number of pages about Belgium, that country no longer exists. Flanders and Wallonia are living under the terms of a no-fault divorce' (De Heusch 2002: 13). The claim highlights the split and divergence in national and cultural identity that exists along linguistic lines and according to communities. For Pirotte, the (dis)unity of the two linguistic communities has consistently led to the 'perceived fragility' of Belgium even during the period of Romanticism (Pirotte 2002: 26). However, according to Pirotte, Edmond Picard – a 'socialist parliamentarian' – 'discovered the "Belgian soul" born of the amalgamation of two cultures' (ibid.). De Heusch's position chimes with the Walloon politician Jules Destrée's[7] prescient open letter to King Albert I published eighty years previously,

> Sire, [...] allow me to tell you the truth, the enormous and horrifying truth: there are no Belgians [...] You are reigning over two different peoples. In Belgium there are Walloons and there are Flemings: there are no Belgians. (Destrée, cited in Trumpbour 2002: 211)

According to Destrée and De Heusch, the use of the national appellation is becoming increasingly redundant, since cultural identities are essentially formed within the two aforementioned regions and according to ethnic identity. Destrée's letter also seemingly complements a well-versed joke in Belgium that 'there exist only two "Belgians": the King and Manneken Pis' (the famous fountain of a urinating young boy in the centre of Brussels), as symbols of national identity amongst otherwise ethnic, regional and cultural identities (Van den Braembussche 2002: 36). Van De Craen posits that Destrée's famous epithet sparks the start of 'matters of identity' in Belgium in the early twentieth century (Van de Craen 2002: 25). Moreover, the rhetoric is concomitant with the critical currency afforded to the 'Europe of the Regions' slogan as part of the European Union in the 1990s. In fact, Van de Craen posits that Belgium operates as a microcosm of the European Union, and so is 'held up as a model for its ability to reach compromises and for its legal organisation and that this makes Belgium important for future developments in the European Union' (Van de Craen 2002: 26). However, such a positive spin on the bifurcation and federalisation of Belgium overlooks the country's political stasis and failures to form a stable government between 2007 and 2011. Within this period Adam and Deschouwer outline that '[i]n 2010, and again in 2014, [...], N-VA, became the most popular party in Flanders and Belgium as a whole' (2016: 1291), citing the party's policies that started out as 'less migrant friendly' and initially proposed 'stricter rules for citizenship acquisition' (2016: 1297–8). Since the terror attacks in Brussels and Paris (2015–16), the N-VA – the Flemish separatist and right-wing political party – has continued to receive more attention and political importance.[8] Martel instead offers a contemporary interpretation that is more cynical and pessimistic about the future of Europe, noting that Belgium signifies and represents the 'frailties of European culture' (Martel 2010: 399) and the perceived structural weakness of the institution of the EU. These so-called 'frailties' reverberate through interpretations and analyses of Belgian nationalism, national and cultural identity.

Billig proposes the notion of 'banal nationalism' in order to overcome and 'cover the ideological habits which enable the established nations of the West to be reproduced' (Billig 1995: 6). In essence, nationalism is couched in 'everyday life', in constant circulation, 'far from being an intermittent mood in established nations, [it] is the endemic condition' (1995: 6). As Koch and Paasi contend in their reassessment of Billig's 'banal nationalism', the concept has moved away from traditional understandings of nationalism in the context of separatism or even 'social movements of change', as characterised by Ernest Gellner and Benedict Anderson (Koch and Paasi 2016: 1–3). Drawing on Herder and Fichte and their concept that the 'genius' of the nation is inevitably connected to language, Billig contends that

> Belgium, cobbled together out of Flemish speakers and French speakers, not to mention the small community of German speakers, cannot be a 'real' nation. The Flemish separatists, therefore, are seeking to redraw the map of nationhood in a way which accords better with natural human inclinations. (Billig 1995: 14)

The fact that there are two distinct and different languages in operation in the country makes the split and fragmentation seem inevitable, 'natural' and easily comprehensible *outside* the nation (Billig 1995: 13–14). Van den Braembussche draws on the oft-perceived notion that 'Belgium is an *artificial* construction' (Van den Braembussche 2002: 35 – emphasis original). For filmmaker and ethnographer De Heusch, Belgium has experienced a 'strange fate' of continued 'shrinking', and of 'fission, segmentation, and disappearance' (De Heusch 2002:

16). The director of the KVS theatre (Koninklijke Vlaamse Schouwburg), Jan Gossens, notes in an interview with Frédéric Martel that it is the Flemish who see Belgium as an 'artificial nation' as a result of their intention to 'build their nation' (that is, Flanders) (Martel 2010: 400). The 'fate' of Belgium and Belgian nationalism is linked to its ad hoc and devolved symbolism, resulting in a structural weakness 'where lightning has just hammered out a temporary coat-of-arms, giving the lion back to Flanders and granting Wallonia a rooster' (De Heusch 2002: 16). The 'banal' symbolism and cultural representations are not conceived on the level of the 'national', that is Belgium, but within the sub-national/regional communities. According to Van den Braembussche, these 'centrifugal forces are indeed multiple', which leave Belgium as 'a nation in search of itself' (Van den Braembussche 2002: 37) in addition to 'an artificial yoke, a historical conspiracy against the deep aspirations of the Flemish and Walloon communities and their respective self-images, authentic cultures and unique folk-spirits' (2002: 38). In a political sense, there is a lack of the centripetal, created through political, cultural and linguistic continuity. This approach also chimes with Martel's (2010) survey of Belgian culture through the prism of its media as fractured and fragmented along linguistic lines.

Taminiaux contends that the 'bourgeois motivations' of Belgian nationalism extend back to the formation of the nation-state, by positing that '(t)he Belgian revolution of 1830, which led to the constitution of the Modern Belgian nation, was beforehand a bourgeois project motivated by the need for more open and independent commercial trading away from the tutelage of their Dutch neighbours' (Taminiaux 2013: 153). Jack interprets Belgian literature as inherently relational and one that is carefully crafted and mediated in terms of cultural representations. For instance, Jack contends that,

> Belgian writers tend to look beyond their own country both for a literary tradition into which to be grafted and for an audience; or their identity tends to be defined not in terms of their status as Belgians, but rather in their opposition and refusal of French assimilation. In either case, however, most francophone writers publish in Paris as there are few major literary publishing houses in Belgium and a Parisian readership is often more readily accessible than an audience at home. (Jack 1996: 25)

The first tendency coheres with Dirkx's overarching survey on francophone Belgian diasporic literature, which is predicated on the assumption that '[f]rancophone literary production in Belgium has always been characterised by a high level of migration towards France' (Dirkx 2011: 60). The Belgian, or more specifically Walloon, crime writer Georges Simenon operates as an example *par excellence* of the first tendency in Jack's tradition. For instance, with reference to the work of playwright Jean Louvet (a writer and poet valorised in the Walloon publication *La revue toudi*), Dubois conceives of Simenon as nothing more than 'petit-bourgeois' (Dubois 2002: 63).[9] Dirkx draws on Simenon as an example of a francophone Belgian writer 'who make[s] a virtue out of necessity by converting their uncomfortable position into a springboard for creating original forms of writing and niches in the consecration market' (Dirkx 2011: 69). His consolidation as a key member in the French literary market was furthered by the adaptation of the Inspector Maigret series into a quintessential form of French film noir.

Murphy, albeit in parenthesis, argues that 'major Belgian and Swiss authors are simply co-opted into French literature while "minor" writers from these countries are considered mere "regional" authors' (Murphy 2002: 173–4). This can also be attributed to a fate of 'spontaneous indifference, the structural blindness that effectively constitutes a non-differentiating perception, primarily concern[ing] non-French Francophone writers from within Europe' (Dirkx 2011: 63). In essence, from a French perspective, there is little marked difference between French-speaking Europeans, and how that is manifested in their cultural representations. This is further complicated from Dirkx's interpretation of the authors' perspective to 'identify with dominant models', that is, leaning towards the universalism of French first as opposed to French Belgium or Wallonia (Dirkx 2011: 65). In this sense, Belgian literary nationalism speaks to francocentrism in its dominant form, doing little to dispel the cultural and linguistic connections to France in order to generate a unique and unified sense of Belgian nationalism. According to Dirkx's (2011) premise, in terms of Belgian literature written in French, this form of nationalism has inescapable connections and links to France – evincing a turn to the transnational as a conceptual approach – to a point where valorisation and recognition in France is more important than in the 'home' country of Belgium. On the contrary, Jean Louvet operates on the side of the regional author, with clear evocations of Walloon regionalism.[10] François André describes the central themes of social mobilisation and the distinct shift in father–son relations in Louvet's play, *Conversation en Wallonie/Conversations in Wallonia* (1978), as 'one of the fundamental questions of class identity, of a people, of a Nation' (André 2010). Dubois' (2002) analysis of Louvet's theatre work is less explicit in its references to a national articulation. Dubois contends that 'the history of the Walloon proletariat certainly appears as a story of a long frustration, but it is still the story of everyone. And it deserves to be preserved, especially since it is the history of loss and failure' (Dubois 2002: 63). The nation and form of regionalism represented by Louvet pertains to the mass mobilisation in Wallonia in the 1960s, particularly the strikes of 1960–1, as a result of class struggle.

Van de Craen argues that '(b)ecause of their historical ties and shared cultural background, a kind of intercultural togetherness does exist despite political frictions' (Van de Craen 2002: 28). De Heusch ties the national knot in the context of education, postulating that '(i)n school, we had been taught to be Belgians', picking up on national narratives that engendered sentiments of sympathy and empathy for their brethren (De Heusch 2002: 13). In essence, the Flemish and Walloons 'began studying the marvelous common history of Belgium (each in his [sic] own tongue). The history centred on two events of considerable mythic impact' (De Heusch 2002: 18). Schooling, therefore, functions as a key aspect within approaches to nationalism (Gellner 1983; Schlesinger 2000; Smith 2000). As Smith posits on the basis of Ernest Gellner's *Nations and Nationalism*, '(t)he nation is a product of nationalism, which in turn is an expression of modernity's need for "high cultures" – linguistic cultures based on literacy and schooling, and supported by an infrastructure of mass, public, standardised education' (Smith 2000: 46). The notion of 'common history' from this frame of reference that stands out is that, despite linguistic difference, the narratives remain coherent and nation-forming.

Moreover, instances of Belgian nationalism continue to reign with the repeated 'flagging' – to adopt Billig's term – of nationalism on an annual basis, with Belgian national day taking place on 21 July. Paasi notes that national days, as well as celebrations of Independence, provide 'temporary fuel for banal nationalism' (Paasi 2016: 22). Every year, this leads to a shut-down of businesses and daily life in Brussels in order to celebrate, with a carnival through the city's streets, an air display and flags hoisted on national monuments such as the Arc du Cinquantenaire at Parc du Cinquantenaire/Jubelpark, in addition to processions through the large boulevards around the Palais de Justice and the Royal Palais de Bruxelles.

Van den Braembussche (2002) contests Billig's (1995) and Martel's (2010) overlooking of a shared Belgian history and their preoccupation with linguistic difference, by configuring three periods of united nationalism mediated primarily through taboos and a common 'silencing' of key moments in Belgian history or 'dark zones of Belgian memory' (Van den Braembussche 2002: 38). It is what is not said that creates Belgian nationalism, as opposed to what is said. As Paasi posits, '(i)ntellectuals are crucial in shaping both hegemonic national memories and forms of amnesia, and the resulting identity narratives vary considerably' (Paasi 2016: 24–25). To adopt Billig's notion of 'banal nationalism', the daily, 'banal', and deliberate eschewal of discourse on the Congo Holocaust, Nazi collaboration and the so-called 'New Order', and the 'Dutroux affair' – all analysed in detail by Van den Braembussche (2002) – creates a shared form of Belgian nationalism. In essence, for Van den Braembussche, it is the collective 'silence' and collective 'amnesia' of the past that 'cut through the centrifugal forces of the Belgian state' (2002: 40). For Pirotte, Belgian nationalism lies within the symbolic, coming to the fore at times of international sports events and the 'popular worshiping of the monarchy' (Pirotte 2002: 27). The initial interpretation of sport and moments of sporting glory as a means of conceptualising the nation, coheres with Billig's 'banal nationalism' and a natural tendency to think in terms of nations (Koch and Paasi 2016: 2). It neatly packages forms of group identity, overlooking regional, local and transnational similarities and differences. The approach even overlooks the complexities of liminal spaces and the interstices.

Nevertheless, the notion of a Belgian nationalism does have some substance and historical basis, which was still discernible in the 1990s. To some extent the sense of nationalism may be weaker at present due to a shift to a generation born after the linguistic debates of the 1960s and 1970s and even after the period of federalisation in the early 1990s. It was at this point that key debates in '*la belgitude*' arose. In his chapter on Belgian cinema between 1960 and 1975, Mosley outlines how '*la belgitude*' developed as a 'state of mind' in response to a growing disaffection from France and French influence culturally in Belgium and to the increasing recognition afforded to Flemish culture (Mosley 2001: 104). According to Van den Braembussche, the concept pertained to a sense of 'feeling at home in Belgium', 'a unique lifestyle' and 'a kind of conviviality' (Van den Braembussche 2002: 36). It also brought together, in one catchall term, the three French-speaking populations in the country, in Wallonia, in Brussels and the elite in Flanders (Mosley 2001: 104). Taminiaux contends that the neologism served to 'underline their [the intellectual elite and francophone Belgian artists'] cultural alienation' and 'a different identity that still needed to be recognised' (Taminiaux 2013: 150). These interpretations of '*la belgitude*' in the 1960s and 1970s posit a discernible attempt to harmonise and generate the sense of a 'national' culture from a French perspective at a time of socio-economic crisis in the French-speaking regions, namely Wallonia.

For Billig (1995), Mosley (2001), De Heusch (2002), Van de Craen (2002) and Martel (2010), language complicates the notion of a unified and inclusive Belgian nationalism, which for De Heusch arises primarily in the context of written and verbal forms of nationalism (De Heusch 2002: 21). De Heusch posits that in the 1960s, 'the linguistic question became the national question par excellence. The Flemish bourgeoisie suddenly felt close to the lower classes it had ignored thus far. As an indirect consequence, the Walloons became aware of a shared and uncertain cultural identity' (De Heusch 2002: 20). Taminiaux frames the language question as an oft-cited 'community conflict', 'since it [Belgium] implicated two very distinct linguistic communities with different cultural heritages' (Taminiaux 2013: 150). This is further 'enhanced by the fact that in the nineteenth century the linguistic border also became a social border, opposing the industrialised south and the agrarian north' (Van de Craen 2002: 26). The economic developments and the political fracturing in the country have resulted in Wallonia being conceived as 'the deprived daughter of a United Belgium' (Michel Quévit, cited in Thomas 1990: 42). It is precisely at this moment that Walloon nationalism and a strong sense of Walloon regional identity develop to a critical point. Hooghe argues that,

Walloon nationalism was sparked by the Walloon region's economic decline. Uneven development after the Second World War and an increasingly unfavourable demographic balance caused widespread resentment. Walloons feared that in a unitary state their economy would be restructured on Flemish terms. (Hooghe 2004: 60)

It is from this premise that Van de Craen identifies the fourth conflict between ethnic Walloons and Flemings, since '(t)he Flemish have been insisting for a number of years that the richer Flanders "has paid enough for Wallonia" and some Flemish politicians are accordingly demanding that social security become a regional matter' (Van de Craen 2002: 27). Pirotte, however, interprets this from a Walloon perspective at the time of the revised Constitution in 1971 during which 'for the Walloon militants, economic questions had taken priority' (Pirotte 2002: 27). It is at this point that 'the question of identity [in particular Walloon identity] is posed with perspicacity: it is just about mobilising all actors, not only political, but also social, cultural and economic actors around a Walloon project' (2002: 28). The construction of a border, whether that may be linguistic, cultural or social, is salient, since cultural interpretations and representations have tended to align the notion with loaded terminology, such as that of a metaphorical 'wall'.

After the transition to federalisation in 1993, Alain Berliner directed *Le Mur/ The Wall* (Alain Berliner, 1998), which was interpreted as 'a charge against increased regionalism' (Duculot 1998: 5). In 2010, in an interview in a blog post for the French newspaper *Le Monde* that is no longer active, filmmaker Bouli Lanners (of both German-Belgian and Walloon heritage) espoused similar sentiments. Lanners notes that '(o)ur cultures no longer mix at all. It is as if we have constructed a Berlin Wall between the two regions' (Gillet and Barthet 2010). Martel introduces this idiom to an institutional context, positing a 'war of positions' between the two television channels for the linguistic communities, VRT (*Vlaams Radio en Televisieomroeporganisatie*) and RTBF (*Radio et Télévision Belge Francophone*) (Martel 2010: 399). For Martel, although the headquarters lie in the same building, the corridor between the two linguistic 'zones' also resembles the 'Berlin Wall' (ibid.). These interpretations appear to lament the drawing of clear boundaries and borders between the linguistic communities, which is akin to a form of partition within the nation-state.

Mathijs identifies the persistence of the 'uncertainty' and 'anxiety' (to adopt Mosley's (2002) term) around the notion of Belgian national or cultural identity, particularly concerning 'an unwillingness to rally around one cause or an agreed set of cultural symbols, leaving, at best, room for continuous search for identity' (Mathijs 2004b: 87). In the introduction to *The Cinema of the Low Countries*, Mathijs (2004a) asks the same questions as Van de Craen (2002) regarding an 'uncertain' national and cultural identity. Van de Craen deduces that after '(r)eading the nearly 600-page volume [*Belgique toujours grande et belle*] [it] makes one realise that Belgium and Belgians consistent of nearly infinite number of characteristics clustered around the unsolvable question "*what and who am I?*"' (Van de Craen 2002: 24). The lack of assertiveness in the stakes of national and cultural identity arises in the context of cinemas from the so-called transnational grouping of the Low Countries (Belgium, the Netherlands, and Luxembourg), manifesting itself in a 'culture of self-doubt' (Mathijs 2004a: 4). The latent sentiments of 'self-doubt' can also be attributed to Wallonia as a nascent concept. As Pirotte observes,

> [t]hough the word 'wallon' [Walloon] was already in use in the twelfth century [. . .] the term 'Wallonie' [Wallonia], on the other hand, was only forged in 1844 and broadcast only in 1886 with the creation of Albert Mockel's *La Wallonie*, concerning the wave of symbolist poetry. (Pirotte 2002: 28)

The notion of being 'Walloon' and inhabiting 'Wallonia' were relatively new in relation to the birth of Belgium as a nation-state. The notion of 'self-doubt' also arises in the context of an 'inferiority complex' in Belgian critical thought articulated by 'various oppressed majorities [that] coexist' (Pierre Wigny, cited in Van de Craen 2002: 25). The 'inferiority complex' and the power dynamics between France and Belgium were neatly evinced by the Dardenne brothers' acceptance speech at Cannes film festival in 1999, which articulated the Belgian joke of 'de souffrance' [suffering] and 'dessous France' [beneath France] (Benoliel and Toubiana 1999: 53; Mai 2010: 138).

Drawing on the paradigmatic reference points of Bauman and Hall, Mathijs deduces 'the conscious quest for cultural identity as a utopian attempt to produce fixed meanings' (2004a: 3). The consistent threads of 'search' and 'quest' in this line of argument articulate a sense, in the Low Countries and Belgium at least, of non-fixity and fluidity, in defining cultural and national identity. Nationalism through cultural representations is difficult to pin down in this context, due to the Belgian linguistic communities' invariable reluctance to rally around national narratives and national myths. Instead, Mathijs contends, films from the Low Countries 'focus on representations of the real' (2004a: 5). For Smith, a 'national' film – as an articulation of national identity – is inclusive of 'character development, historical reconstruction, pictorial tableaux, accessories, ethnoscape and the "people"' (Smith 2000: 51), which appear to resonate with the heritage film. However, this reluctance in Belgium to engage with such narratives is summed up by Paul Meyer's note on the film *Daens* (Stijn Coninx, 1992), which posits that the film is 'denunciative of the roles of the Flemish bourgeoisie' (Meyer 1998: 12).

Walloon regionalism continues to permeate publications in Wallonia, particularly *La revue toudi*, which appears to be particularly partisan towards films, publications, surveys and critical debate that shine a positive light on the region. The publication has also reproduced white papers and manifestos online that attest to Wallonia's cultural heritage. These manifestos emerged at a time when there was a distinct sense of uncertainty around the notion of Walloon cultural identity. Sojcher, for instance, draws on filmmaker Benoît Lamy's interpretation of Walloon culture in 1978, stating that 'Walloon culture is in decline [. . .] In Wallonia, there is no group consciousness/regionalism; we are under the French model, which takes us back to a culture that is exterior to us' (Benoît Lamy, cited in Sojcher 1999a: 354). The scepticism around francocentrism (latent from the previous period of *'la belgitude'*) remains in this assertion in addition to the aforementioned 'inferiority complex' internally.[11]

However, one key similarity to France that permeated Walloon thought was the spirit of 1968 (a tradition that emerges consistently throughout this monograph in the case of the Dardenne brothers and Bouli Lanners' filmmaking). The strikes of the early 1960s, and the protests of the late 1960s, highlight a move towards mass mobilisation within the region for a given cause. Bajomée notes that 'Belgium like France was interpellated by the extremely virulent Situationist writings concerning the society of abundance which, according to them, would grow into an unstoppable need to consume for the purpose of concealing everyone's true desires' (2010: 13). For Bajomée, Liège – the dominant industrial city in Wallonia – and its university came to represent the 'culture of struggle' (later considered in Chapter Six) that challenged the 'bankruptcy of a system predicated on paternalism, authoritarianism, a bureaucratic government considered out of touch with "real life"' (Bajomée 2010: 19). In so doing, the Walloon 'problem' was articulated and perceived as inherently 'a structural issue' (Bajomée 2010: 18). As a result, drawing on cinema and film as media that appeal to mass audiences, the films *Misère au Borinage* and *Déjà s'envole la fleur maigre* have become major cinematic reference points for contemporary francophone Belgian filmmakers and as articulations of key social issues and concerns in Walloon history. As filmmaker Paul Meyer contends, 'these two films anchored in their respective regions, denounce the exploitative system of men by men' (Meyer 1998: 12). The films are examples and representations of wider thought, actions and movements in society and of nationalisms. As Meyer further posits, there is 'a wider awareness of *identitaire* [forms of identity] and we are falling into a type of hollow nationalism [*en creux*], insipid and without a future' (Meyer 1998: 12). Whilst Meyer does not clearly assert whether the filmmaker is discussing a form of Belgian nationalism or Walloon regionalism as well as the seeming futility of using labels, his negativity with regard to national and regional terms is in contrast to publications, such as *La revue toudi*, that appear to celebrate these films as salient and significant reference points. As Hooghe further contends, a younger generation in Wallonia may produce more 'radical regionalism' as the economy began to recover in small areas of Wallonia prior to the economic crash of 2008 (Hooghe 2004: 84). This postulation does, however, still acknowledge many underprivileged areas in Belgium, as a result of the aforementioned structural and economic issues and concerns, in the region.

As previously noted, Walloon regionalism has a print and online representation in the form of *La revue toudi* – although the analysis of Walloon cinema appears to have ceased in 2011 – which bears out Benedict Anderson's (1991) concept of an 'imagined political community' that is renewed through the medium of print. *La revue toudi* ignores the francophone community in the capital region of Brussels. This is reflected in Hannerz's analysis of culture; the social and transnational anthropologist posits that '(t)o keep culture going, people as actors and networks of actors have to invent culture, reflect on it, experiment with it, remember it (or store it in some other way), debate it, and pass it on' (1997: 5). Film criticism allows for one interpretation of culture that is regularly considered, with cinema and films constituting, along with literature, key forms of cultural articulation and representation.

The position that *La revue toudi* adopts regarding cinema in Belgium coheres more with Elsaesser's (2013) claim that there now exists a 'post-national cinema Europe' in the wake of post-colonialism. From this premise, Elsaesser contends that,

> such nationalism [that is, cinematic nationalism] is highly reflexive, either calculated in order to attract the 'eye of the other', or comparable to the various regional, territorial or ethnic movements, which also claim a distinct cinematic identity in Western Europe. (2013)

In 1998, the theatre writer and one of the key signatories of the *Manifeste pour la culture wallonne* in 1983, Jean Louvet posited that filmmaking in the region was important for 'defending a national and regional cinema' (1998: 6). It could, in Louvet's terms, complement an economy that was 'not doing well' since films could spend money in underprivileged areas (ibid.). The cinema section of *La revue toudi* praises only twenty-four films in individual articles and film criticism from a small cross-section of filmmakers. The majority of the articles constitute the aforementioned names, with the Dardenne brothers (eight) leading the way, followed by Jean-Jacques Andrien (two) and Benoît Mariage (two). An emerging wave of filmmakers from the region are also recognised, including François Pirot, Bénédicte Liénard and Thomas De Thier as well as the anarchic and iconoclastic Jean-Jacques Rousseau. What is most telling about *La revue toudi*'s articles on Walloon cinema is how it reaffirms the status quo and the dominant filmmakers in Wallonia, overlooking the presence of women filmmakers who have achieved recognition in the '*50 ans de cinéma belge*' schedule. The online and print publications are also home to the Walloon cultural manifestos, which all aim to determine and valorise regional cultural specificity (as further considered in Chapter One).

The focus on Walloon cultural identity reached an apotheosis in 1998, with *Le Matin*'s special issue exploring the history and culture of francophone Belgian cinema from 1933 through to the late 1990s, in addition to the edited collection *Oser être wallon!: ouvrage collectif sur l'identité wallone* (Van Cauwenberghe 1998). The latter publication surveyed Walloon culture in architecture, poetry, the media and cinema, with filmmaker and president of Cinéma Wallonie Jean-Jacques Andrien exploring the challenges to come for regional cinema and the questions of cultural identity espoused in his films from the 1980s (Van Cauwenberghe 1998: 125–9).

I have since argued that there are new (or even renewed) and emerging forms of nationalism in Belgium that exist amongst its diasporic communities, which interact with the local and the global at the same time (Steele 2018c). In the same vein as the 'third solitudes' model established in Canadian literature, for instance Jewish Canadian literature (Greenstein 1989) as a comparative example, new forms of the 'national' and of 'nationalism' are emerging in Belgium, such as Moroccan-Belgian filmmakers, Congolese-Belgian enunciating subjects and Jewish Belgian filmmakers, of which Chantal Akerman was the most prominent. Despite a greater critical and academic turn towards the transnational as an interpretative framework, nationalism remains 'the dominant territorial ideology in the contemporary world' (Koch and Paasi 2016: 2). In a cinematic context, this returns us to Ezra and Rowden's 'canny dialogic partners' of the national and the transnational (Ezra and Rowden 2006: 4).[12] To this end, forms of nationalism remain a starting point and site of contestation and analysis, although it is becoming increasingly salient and important to consider how nations, linguistic communities and regions are changing in ways that take into consideration the presence of multiple ethnicities, languages, cultures and traditions that unfold within contemporary countries and nation-states. In the case of Belgium, this concerns the need to apply an inclusive approach to Moroccan-Belgian, Turkish-Belgian and Congolese-Belgian filmmakers, and filmmakers from the former Yugoslavia working within Belgian cinema. It is not quite as simple as considering identities, nationalisms, regionalisms, cultures and traditions within the contexts of the three regions and two linguistic communities of Belgium.

Approaches to Francophone Belgian Cinema

Each of the chapters in this monograph shows the plurality of approaches applicable to filmmaking in francophone Belgian cinema. It offers a reading of the linguistic community's film industry, cinema, traditions and trends before identifying the key auteurs, styles, landscapes and genres that proliferate in francophone Belgian – or more specifically Walloon – culture and cinema in the twenty-first century.

The first chapter, 'The (Francophone) Belgian film ecosystem: trends in production, distribution and exhibition', offers an interpretation of cinematic transnationalism and the 'regional' through an industrial perspective. It offers an analysis of the complexities of the production, distribution and exhibition sectors in a cinematically small nation. The chapter notes that 'transnational' and 'regional' approaches are not mutually exclusive, with the industrial sector operating on a scalar level that shifts between the global and the local (eschewing the dialectical 'glocal'). The analysis of francophone Belgian film production, distribution and exhibition is not neatly contained within borders, as Higson (2000) notes in his reconsideration of 'the concept of national cinema' is 'limiting'. The first section of the chapter outlines the multi-layered and complex funding system that is both heavily reliant on international co-productions, and national and linguistic-based initiatives that fund genre films, auteur films, socio-realist dramas and novice filmmakers. Whilst the Centre du Cinéma et de l'Audiovisuel (CCA) for the Bruxelles-Capitale region and Wallonia and the VAF for Flanders offer a form of production support for the linguistic communities, the tax shelter system pertains to a national mode of funding for a Belgian cinema, irrespective of the film's language. The tax shelter, therefore, continues the presence of a Belgian national cinema, despite the development of regional funding and support structures. The second section of the chapter chimes with Iordanova, Martin-Jones and Vidal's conceptualisation of 'cinemas on the periphery', which outlines that 'the limitations of international distribution [are] caused not only by the fact that small domestic audiences do not provide sufficiently sizeable markets but, first and foremost, also by the limited access to established international distribution channels' (2010: 10). The limitations of the distribution sector, in this context, are nuanced by the contiguous exchanges between France and the francophone community of Belgium. The section primarily draws attention to the importance of 'less acknowledged diffusion channels' (2010: 10), such as film festivals, to achieve recognition and critical valorisation in France and beyond. Moreover, it furthers Bill Marshall's notion of *cinéma-monde*, which argues that Belgium functions as an extension of the French market, like Switzerland (Marshall 2012: 38). In essence, for Marshall, Belgian films operate seamlessly in the French exhibition and 'domestic' markets (ibid.).

Chapters Two through to Six represent a shift from industrial perspectives to representational analysis in the same tradition as Higson's (1989) and Crofts' (1998) approaches to 'national cinema' frameworks. Following Croft's typologies and taxonomy of 'national cinema' and Higson's 'concept of national cinema', it is necessary to consider a film's national-cultural and cultural specificities of film and its industrial model (Higson 1989; Crofts 1998: 386–8). However, as each chapter argues, the analysed films fit somewhere between the local and the global, drawing on cinematic transnationalism as the main theoretical premise, since they serve to represent local, cultural and social articulations as well as wider shared issues and debates.

The second chapter, '"No Future": Social Marginalisation, Social Precariousness and Depictions of Seraing in *Le gamin au vélo* (Jean-Pierre and Luc Dardenne, 2011) and *Deux jours, une nuit* (Jean-Pierre and Luc Dardenne, 2014)', neatly sets the agenda for an analysis that discusses the Dardenne brothers and their films as local and regional articulations of Wallonia and Seraing that are represented in an approach that coheres with traditions in European 'art cinema'. In this chapter, themes of social marginalisation, poverty and social polarisation emerge from a connection to the 'real' situation and 'reality' of a post-industrial Wallonia, but they are articulated through clear spatial dynamics and stylistic filiation that are widely interpretable in different national and cultural contexts. In so doing, it recalls De Heusch's understanding of Belgian art, which 'has always been interregional, international' and that 'Art in Belgium is first of all European [. . .] Issues of paternity are pointless when an aesthetic extends over vast regions, precisely escaping provincialism' (De Heusch 2002: 21–2). Whilst the local is – and remains – salient, it is more about how the works of art, or in this case films, connect and intersect with others produced in similar conditions. The 'inter-regional' appellation, therefore, emerges in the context of the contemporaneous connection and shared concerns with a *cinéma nordiste*.

The third chapter, '"Stills" and Fragmented Families: Contemplating the Private Sphere in Joachim Lafosse's *Wallonia*', moves away from the canonical study of the Dardenne brothers to a detailed examination of young, novice filmmakers emerging in the early 2000s in Belgium. Lafosse (Chapter Three) and Masset-Depasse (Chapter Four) represent the film-school generation in Wallonia and francophone Belgium, whose filmmaking styles bear witness to increasing cinephilia and a move beyond experiential work in the film industry, as is the case with the Dardenne brothers, Bouli Lanners and Lucas Belvaux. For the analysis of Lafosse, Mathijs' (2004b) notion of 'particularism' – in place of national narratives – gains traction in the articulation of small-town spaces and the Walloon countryside. Writing in 1998, the filmmaker Paul Meyer found the so-called 'particularism' of francophone Belgian cinema a new phenomenon, since he posits that '(f)ew "Belgian" films have found their roots in our Walloon landscapes' (Meyer 1998: 12), citing only *Le banquet des fraudeurs/The Smuggler's Banquet* (Henri Storck, 1952), *Déjà s'envole la fleur maigre* (Paul Meyer, 1960), *Le grand paysage d'Alexis Droeven/The Wide Horizons of Alexis Droeven* (Jean-Jacques Andrien, 1981), and *Hiver 60/Winter 60* (Thierry Michel, 1983) (Meyer 1998: 12).[13] This is an aspect that is discernibly absent in the representations of the landscape in Walloon and francophone Belgian filmmaking, which refers to the region's industrial heritage. In Lafosse's films, it is within this heartland that the nation is problematised through the thematic tendency to place the family in a constant state of crisis. Paternalism is configured as the primary threat to the younger generation and the nuclear family unit. This perceived threat arises in two forms: (1) the representation and articulation of fragmented families through linguistic community conflict (that is, between Dutch and French speakers in the family unit); and (2) the Dutroux affair and Dutroux trauma. Van den Braembussche argues that the Dutroux affair and a national sense of 'disbelief' that this took place in Belgium 'then led to a delayed response, a period of latency, during which the suppressed "Dutroux murders" lingered on in the collective unconscious and left behind deep imprints on the collective soul' (2002: 51). This repression of guilt and latent anxiety predicated on the 'Dutroux affair', issues of paedophilia and the mistrust of the authorities that run the nation-state (that is, Belgium) emerges in the representation of abuse from figures of authority and the state apparatus, and the theme of infanticide in Lafosse's films. For Van den Braembussche, the collective silence regarding past traumas and historical facts results in their being 'latent' or hidden within texts – and, for the purpose of this book, film texts – that require deciphering by readers and spectators. Van den Braembussche's article operates as a rallying cry for these traumas to be acknowledged in Belgian society and culture.

In keeping with the analysis of young, emerging and (at the time) novice filmmakers in Belgium, the fourth chapter, 'From Slag Heaps to Cliffs: The "Marked" Regional Landscape in *Cages* (Olivier Masset-Depasse, 2006)', considers Olivier Masset-Depasse's first and breakthrough feature film set in an oblique Nord-Pas-de-Calais/Belgium border region. *Cages* provokes an approach that is predicated on cinematic transnationalism, since the modes of production bring to light 'affinitive' and potentially 'milieu-building' (Hjort 2009) connections between the north of France (Nord-Pas-de-Calais) and Wallonia. The chapter outlines the extent to which particularism and local articulations were removed from the film as text through its transplantation in France, as dictated by issues of production and financial agreements. Citing Masset-Depasse's short films, the issues of paternalism, loss of the metallurgic industries, and sense of disrepair emerge through the representation of the landscape. In this case, the landscape operates as an evocation of 'particularism', which functions as an important theme in francophone Belgian cinema (Mathijs 2004b).

The final two chapters deal more with genre-based filmmaking. In the case of Bouli Lanners, the road-movie genre provides an interpretative framework for his journeys through Wallonia, and the Ardennes in particular, whereas the *polar* and the French film noir, namely the films of Jean-Pierre Melville, offer a point of reference from which *La raison du plus faible* becomes readable and decipherable. Chapter Five, 'The Francophone Belgian Road Movie: *Eldorado* (Bouli Lanners, 2008) and *Ultranova* (Bouli Lanners, 2005)', emphasises the imbrication between two forms of the road movie genre, the European and American genre formats. Drawing on Mazierska and Rascaroli's (2006) scholarly intervention in the field, Lanners' road movies, *Ultranova* (2005) and *Eldorado* (2008), 'semantically' and 'syntactically' (Altman 1984) reference American and auteurist European road movies albeit with stylistic differences. Drawing on Massey's (2005; 2011) theoretical premise (an approach indebted to Henri Bergson), the chapter considers how Lanners' training as a painter informs his contemplative shots of the Walloon countryside.

Chapter Six, the second part on genre in francophone Belgian filmmaking, 'Lucas Belvaux's Return: The Thriller Genre and Heists in Liège', continues the focus on the city of Liège, but develops the analysis into the context of the *polar*, or the French thriller/film noir genre. Lucas Belvaux's only film set and made in Belgium opens up a dialogue with traditions in French cinema, both auteur-based and genre-orientated. A transnational reading is preferred throughout Belvaux's filmmaking career, prior to *La raison du plus faible* (2006), as a filmmaker and actor in France. To this end, Belvaux is considered a transnational director, whose position is associated with the francophone Belgian diaspora living and working in France in other media. For instance – drawing on a model laid out in francophone Belgian literature – Belvaux coheres with 'the "immigrant jet set", [where] intellectuals and especially writers are not defined, nor do they define themselves as *immigrés*, but sometimes refer to their condition as closer to that of metaphorical *exilé*' (Dirkx 2011: 62 – emphasis original). Belvaux's 'metaphorical exile', therefore, places him in dialogue with film references that are inclusive of French genres, such as the *polar* and Jean-Pierre Melville's noirish and 'noir aesthetic' (Hayward 2014: 36) thrillers of the 1960s.

Notes

1. Consult Heyrendt (2012) for the full opening line to *Bye-Bye Belgium* (2006), screened on RTBF.
2. Klinger (1997) presciently outlines 'synchronic' and 'diachronic' approaches to film history, which proves useful for this book in terms of evaluating and assessing the changes in interpretation and perception of francophone Belgian cinema over time.
3. All translations are the author's own, unless otherwise noted in the bibliography.
4. Deschouwer and Reuchamps (2013) also offer a detailed and nuanced analysis of Belgium's political reform in the wake of the political difficulties of 2007 and 2011.
5. See Spaas (2000: 12–22) and Mosley (2001: 21, 106, 116–17) for an overview of Delvaux's films, and the theme of Nazi collaboration explored in his film, *Femme entre chien et loup/ Vrouw tussen hond en wolf/Woman in a Twilight Garden* (1979).
6. Sojcher cites Morin's interpretation of the European project in a positive and

'transnational' context, outlining that it could 'unite our differences' (1996: 11).
7. Jules Destrée's cultural, social and political importance in Wallonia is evidenced by the eponymous research centre, Institut Jules Destrée, based in Namur. See <http://www.institut-destree.org/page.asp?id=1&langue=FR> (last accessed June 2018).
8. In Steele (2018c), I outline the presence of 'competing nationalisms' within Belgium's excluded communities, that is Flanders and Belgium's diasporic communities, in the context of the film *Black* (Adil El Arbi and Bilall Fallah, 2015). In this publication, the 'elitist' and 'bourgeois' foundation of Belgian nationalism is framed in the context of Mosley's (2001: 17) approach to its French-language origins.
9. Dirkx, on the other hand, posits that Georges Simenon and the Inspector Maigret series represent an example of 'low literature' (2011: 69).
10. Van Ginderachter posits that the dominant interpretation of Flemish and Walloon movements concerns Flemish nationalism and Walloon regionalism, despite the fact that scholars are now recognising their 'similarities' (2012: 209).
11. In the following analysis, from the Lamy citation, Sojcher develops the line of argument with claims by José Fontaine – a key Walloon film critic – who notes the 'hollow' and 'mediocre' context of '*la belgitude*' (Sojcher 1999a: 354).
12. Higbee (2007) draws on Higson (2000) and Ezra and Rowden (2006) to offer the possibility of a 'cinema of transvergence' as opposed to being solely 'transnational' in the context of diasporic French cinema.
13. Mosley's (2001) seminal examination of Belgian cinema and the analysis of the country's cinematic bifurcation includes *Le banquet des fraudeurs*' 'Crossroads of Europe' image as its front cover. The image from the film neatly foregrounds the country's linguistic communities, cultural and ethnic differences.

1. THE (FRANCOPHONE) BELGIAN FILM ECOSYSTEM: TRENDS IN PRODUCTION, DISTRIBUTION AND EXHIBITION[1]

Supporting cinema [. . .] is essential to the image of our [linguistic] community in Belgium, for the development of our culture as well as an economic resource [. . .] and for education purposes. (Frédéric Fonteyne and Patrick Quinet, cited in Duplat and Pluijgers 2001)

Francophone Belgian cinema is supporting itself well thanks to its creative talent but it is fragile, and I am well aware of this, it is imperative to consolidate it. (Belgian Minister of Culture, Richard Miller, cited in Duplat 2001)

Belgian cinema does not have a sufficiently large internal/domestic market to amortise its production costs and even less so to make it profitable. The true internal market is France, where in order to exist, there is no other choice than to single itself out through its difference (or its indifference). (Reynaert 2011: personal communication)

The eighth annual 'Small Cinemas' conference (2017) preferred the use of the 'glocal' as a critical category to frame and analyse questions of cultural diversity, language and identity in small national cinema contexts. In this sense, the 'glocal' served to replace the transnational as an apposite means of considering and detailing the in-between spaces of the local and the global – that is in terms of production, distribution and exhibition as well as 'synchronic' and 'diachronic' (Klinger 1997) representational approaches. This is typically the home of cinematic transnationalism. However, Vincendeau highlights the limitations of the composite 'glocal' term, by suggesting that it overlooks the relevance of the 'national' (2011: 339). In the case of Belgium, the idea of 'national cinema', remains under the 'francophone Belgian' label. The national remains as a 'dialogic partner' – to adopt Ezra and Rowden's notion (2006: 4) – to the transnational and the regional. In film scholarship, the national is inescapable as a framework, since, as Elsaesser contends,

> by the mid-1990s the discussion around national cinema had – depending on one's view – hardened into dogma or reached a generally accepted consensus around a particular set of arguments that encouraged the desire to conceptualise the field differently, or at the very least to signal such a need. (Elsaesser 2013)

It is at this point that debates in conceiving Belgian cinema emerged in the form of publications by Thys (1996; 1999), Sojcher (1999) and Mosley (2001). All of these publications implicitly consider the 'split' (to adopt Mosley's term) in Belgian cinema along the lines of the linguistic communities.

As Christie (2013) posits, national cinema still persists in academic work and as a critical category from cinema's classical period through to the present day. It also arises, for Christie, in terms of a process of 'self-confirming selectivity' in which film festivals, events, special screenings and award ceremonies valorise a 'national cinema' (2013: 26). For instance, two film festivals, which both took place outside Belgium, neatly highlight the bifurcated and fragmented nature of Belgian cinema. The Cinémathèque Suisse (2012a: 19–26) organised an exhibition event dedicated to 'le nouveau cinéma belge francophone' (New francophone Belgian cinema). This included the screening of films by the emerging French-speaking Belgian filmmakers Bouli Lanners, Olivier Masset-Depasse, Joachim Lafosse and Fabrice du Welz. The 'Other Belgian Cinema' film festival in Strasbourg (Lemercier 2015) aimed to showcase the oft-neglected production of Flemish-language films that has received higher levels of visibility across Europe since the breakthrough hit of *Rundskop/Bullhead* (Michaël R. Roskam, 2011).[2] The programmes for these two film festivals place a spotlight on increased levels of film production within a country that has seen its film production and funding mechanisms evolve and grow since the creation of Wallimage in 2001.

Mosley (2001) draws on the 'national cinema' models offered by Higson (1989) and Crofts (1998) in order to conceive a Belgian 'national' cinema. Developing through Higson's (1995) approach to British cinema in the 1990s, Mosley posits that the Belgian cinema 'system comprises several cinemas of linguistic and regional difference' (Mosley 2001: 13). This resonates with Higson's 'inward-looking' approach to a 'national cinema' which recognises its cultural differences from within (Higson 1989: 54–60). As a result, francophone Belgian cinema emerges with its own specificity. With reference to Higson's 'concept of national cinema', this section offers an industrial analysis that coheres with the three premises of economic, consumption-based and criticism-based approaches to uncover, to an extent, where the boundaries for the national cinema lie (Higson 1989). What is more, the 'criticism-based approach' chimes with francophone Belgian cinema's modes of distribution and exhibition in terms of representing the 'paradox' of the 'national cinema concept' in which its so-called 'art cinema' is valorised at an international level (Higson 1989: 58–9), such as the Dardenne brothers, Joachim Lafosse and Bouli Lanners' appearances at Cannes film festival. As Rochet observes, the notion of 'New Francophone Belgian cinema' as an 'identitarian' cinema emerged in international publications (2011: 27).

Both Hjort (2009) and Higbee and Lim (2010) identify the notion of 'shared culture' and posit the possibility of a 'regional' paradigm being formed across national boundaries. In Naficy's brief article on a 'theory of regional cinemas', he outlines how the 'regional' concept has not been fully developed, and instead it lies latent in books that have identified 'shared features of films from contiguous geographic regions' (2008: 97). Naficy (2008) draws upon Middle Eastern, Maghreb, Balkan and Central Asian countries – since the dissolution of the Soviet Union – as examples of such an approach to 'regional' cinemas. Caillé (2013), in particular, teases out Naficy's continuities in the form of shared concerns to analyse a contiguous transnational 'regional' cinema in a North African frame of reference. In a European context, the funding of films in Scandinavia highlights such a trend in what Elkington and Nestigen (2005) term 'Transnational Nordic Cinema'. This approach epitomises how the 'transnational' and 'regional' concepts can work together through exchanges in finance, crew and films across the national borders of Denmark, Sweden and Norway. Christie proposes the regional as a category that has begun to 'stand as the national body' since the economic crisis of 2008 (2013: 19). For Christie, this is particularly the case for the Basque country and Catalonia in a cinematic sense (ibid.). It is, incidentally the year when the notion of 'New Francophone Belgian cinema' was first posited in *Positif*. Elsaesser, however, offers a post-national reading of the sub-state, which arises – along with the supra-state, at the point where 'the idea of "nation" and "state" are drifting apart' (2005: 116). This approach echoes Hannerz's social and anthropological understanding of transnationalism, which has come to the fore as the nation 'changes' rather than 'withers away' (1996: 89–90). These notions can be countered, or perhaps nuanced, by the political push for sovereignty on behalf of small nations, such as the Scottish and Catalan referendums for independence in 2015 and 2017 respectively and the increased political representation of the N-VA in Flanders. All of these approaches to cinematic regions retain the idea of a 'national' framework, since they hold a reference to a country as a sovereign entity. The 'national' still has a certain analytical and conceptual value within such a framework, but it remains 'limiting' – in Higson's (2000) words – for a consideration of cinematic blocs or 'regions' that encompass several sovereign countries.

The 'National' as the 'Sub-state' and Linguistic Communities

The perception of francophone Belgian cinema by its decision-makers brings key thinkers and traditional reference points into debate. Bredael and Reyneart (2016) reference the first French Minister of Culture André Malraux and his oft-cited notion that 'cinema is an industry', and Richard Miller, a key member of both the Walloon and Belgian federal parliaments, paraphrases Gilles Deleuze and his view that film history has been 'marked by money' (cited in Duplat 2001). In both cases, film funding and its modes of production appear at the forefront of critical thought for francophone Belgium's main policy-makers, over and above its representational and aesthetic form. In both instances, francophone Belgian cinema is interpreted in economic terms, marked in terms of production, distribution and exhibition. These three aspects operate within a global and local context, where the transnational has gained its critical and theoretical strength.

The Royal Decree of 1952 initially set out the requirements for state funding of Belgian cinema (Mosley 2001: 76), essentially commencing the support of a 'national cinema' through government funding and a 'detaxation system'. In essence, as de Poorter outlines, '[t]he subsidy took the form of the repayment of a percentage of the entertainment tax levied on commercial performances' (1997: 130). However, as Mosley observes, the Royal Decree was implemented primarily to support short films and documentaries, and, was 'of little potential use to feature producers' (2001: 76). Despite state funding for Belgian cinema in the 1950s, the decade, albeit an abstract, limited, and cumbersome means of framing waves in film history, is considered to be 'the poorest in the history of French-language Belgian fiction film [. . .] the only quality Belgian productions of the period were confined to the documentary field' (Thys 1996;1999 401). This can be attributed in part to the Royal Decree of 1952. Belmans' (1974) interpretation of Walloon cinema resonates with this perception, by positing that cinema in Wallonia opened with *Misère au Borinage*. The documentary has since become shorthand and the inescapable reference point for Walloon cinema since the 1930s. However, the Belgian film industry has consistently developed along linguistic and community-based lines since the 1960s. This is concomitant with national cinemas throughout Europe, since Christie observes that 'the cultural impact that film was having in the 1960s [...] is surely key to understanding why so many states launched or revamped schemes to promote native filmmaking, alongside whatever industrial quotas or incentives they had maintained since the prewar period' (2013: 23).

Whilst Thys (1996; 1999: 298) posits that regional cinema in Belgium commenced in the 1940s and was 'off to a bad start' with *Thanasse et Casimir/ Thanasse and Casimir* (René Picolo, 1946), it was in the 1960s and the period of linguistic divergence in cinematic terms that saw the emergence of a 'quality Walloon cinema' with *Le cercle Romain* (Raymond Haine, 1960) (1996; 1999: 397). The so-called 'bad start' to Walloon cinema appears to resonate with Davay's assertion that Belgian cinema at the time was viewed as containing an 'inflexible provincialism' (Davay 1967: 52). As Davay notes,

> The fact is that we still suffer from a [...] serious handicap, namely the division of a small country into two linguistic groups, with the consequence that each side struggles to produce its own regional films at low cost, purely for local consumption, and tries to ensure an adequate reception for them by desperately making every concession to the public. (1967: 52)

An auteur-driven cinema in francophone Belgium emerged around a year after the radical shift in French filmmaking in terms of the continuity of young novice filmmakers and critics turning to an experimental form of filmmaking with the French New Wave, breaking with the codes and conventions of an established, yet deteriorating classical and dominant mode of filmmaking (Thys 1996; 1999: 397). Mosley (2001: 105–6) claims that the Belgian film industry of the mid 1960s and early 1970s conformed to Crofts' notion of a 'cultural mode of production' with 'state legislation overtly supporting production subsidy' alongside no state control of the distribution and exhibition sectors (Crofts 1998: 390–1). Mosley's assertion that there was an absence of state subsidy for the distribution and exhibition of Belgian films further nuances the perceived anxiety around the high volume of films from Hollywood and France in the domestic Belgian market at the time.

In Belgium, the Flemish Community put in place a decree to support cultural production in 1964, and this was followed by a similar decree in 1967 for the French Community of Belgium. The cultural criteria outlined in the 'Arrêté royal du 22 juin 1967 tendant à promouvoir la culture cinématographique' (Fédération Wallonie-Bruxelles, 1967) still remains salient for the CCA selective aid system and its 'cultural project tests'. It is precisely this 1967 decree, which has gained traction in the dominant narrative of 'Belgian cinema', operating as a starting point for a process of self-affirmation and 'self-selectivity' (to adopt Christie's term). The curated series is entitled '*50 ans de cinéma belge/50 ans de découvertes*' (translating to fifty years of Belgian cinema/ fifty years of discovery), commencing in 1967 and continuing through to 2017.³ The premise overlooks the nascent period of Walloon and francophone Belgian cinema for a neat starting point at the inception of a decree and policy document that institutionalised a peculiarly mono-linguistic cinema.⁴ The line-up does little to dispel the perception of francophone Belgian cinema as auteur-driven, since there is limited diversity in the filmmakers occurring across the series. The series' agenda organises the curated selection by year, with little reference to the variety of the films available, such as region (Brussels or Wallonia), location, genre and/or style.⁵ There is evidence of a broad range, with little generic, thematic or stylistic continuity. However, despite the use of the national label with linguistic qualification, the series posits that the linguistic communities operate as if they formed a 'national' cinema in their own right. Thirty-six women filmmakers are included on the list, suggesting gender equality and diversity in the modes of film production for a cinematically small nation. Marion Hänsel (eleven films), Chantal Akerman (nine), Mary Jimenez (four), Hélène Cattet (three), Fiona Gordon (two), Vanja d'Alcantara (two), Géraldine Doignon (two), Ursula Meier (two) feature prominently as key components of the francophone Belgian film industry since 1967. All of the films selected for and analysed in this monograph cohere with the rather effusive and elastic framing of Belgian cinema from a French-language perspective.

The CCA was formed in 1994–5 under the auspices of the controversially named French Community of Belgium or the Wallonia-Brussels Federation (CBWF). This decentralisation of film finance coincided with the federalisation of the country in 1993 (as outlined in the Introduction), which witnessed an increase in political powers and competencies provided to the linguistic communities. As a result, it is possible to suggest that Belgium operates with either two competing 'national' cinemas or two regional/sub-state cinemas.

In Belgium, 'cultural project tests' are tailored towards the communities, since they primarily focus on the audiovisual project's language. As a result, and in the case of francophone Belgian filmmaking, Ingberg (2001) notes that the production of French-language Belgian cinema in the 1990s was primarily predicated on public funds accessed through the CCA, TV companies and Walloon cable and satellite companies.⁶ For example, all francophone Belgian film projects must be articulated in French. These tests demonstrate a level of commitment to cultural objectives and highlight the nation's internal cultural, ethnic and religious diversity. By adhering to this selective aid and 'cultural' criteria, film projects can then qualify for funding from automatic funding systems on a regional level, such as Wallimage and the newly formed – and named – Screen.Brussels. However, it was not until 2001 when (francophone) Belgian cinema truly received adequate levels of funding and support. Sojcher predicted the creation of a tax shelter system and a regional film institution, by positing that the absence of Walloon cinema was linked to the distinct lack of regional film and audiovisual funding (1999b: 152). In *La Libre Belgique*'s dossier on funding in Belgian cinema, Duplat and Pluijgers (2001) noted that in the new millennium, the Minster of Culture for the French Community of Belgium or the Wallonia-Brussels Federation (CFWB), Richard Miller, and the President of the European Bank of Investment, Philippe Maystadt, vowed to 'inject 20 billion Belgian franks into (francophone Belgian) cinema'. It was this investment that led to the creation of regional film funds and support mechanisms and the 'national' tax shelter fund. Bredael and Reynaert, however, outline that these tests and mechanisms were initially conceived during the 1960s, by the Ministry of Culture that later developed along the lines of the linguistic communities (such as the CFWB), without adequately considering the role of the spectator (Bredael and Reynaert 2016: 40). It is as a result of this assertion that it is possible to assume that regional film institutions and mechanisms, such as Wallimage, intend to develop the commercial and the cultural simultaneously.

Prior to the creation of Wallimage in 2001 (see Steele 2018a; Steele 2018b), funding mechanisms were largely based in the Capitale region of Brussels. In the case of Wallimage, the intention was 'to create an equivalent centre to Brussels' (Duplat and Pluijgers 2001). As Bredael and Reynaert contend, there was 'a real infrastructure in Brussels, but not in Wallonia' (2016: 44). The primary funding and film support mechanism at the time was 'Bruxelles Tournage', which closed in 2009, preferring the Wallimage-Bruxellimage funding line. However, it has proven ironic that the creation of Wallimage has largely supplanted the mechanisms and infrastructure in Brussels, offering better support for young, novice filmmakers and emerging film companies. In this sense, the mechanisms in Brussels were primarily outmoded and required revisions in order to compete more effectively. This has occurred only recently with the creation of Screen Brussels as a replacement for Brussels Tournage (defunct since 2009)[7] and the Wallimage-Bruxellimage line.[8] Again, according to Bredael and Reynaert, this is primarily linked to the mixed line 'Wallimage-Bruxellimage' to inherently favour film productions in Wallonia (as opposed to Brussels), which has led to a structural and institutional 'divorce' (2016: 86–7).

In Belgium, the institutional forms of film funding had previously been under-developed, leading to an interpretation of the Belgian – and particularly the Walloon – film industry as 'artisanal' (Mosley 2001; Mosley 2013).[9] This was concomitant with other European cinemas, even dominant European national cinemas, at the time, since Elsaesser posits that 'the current model differs from the "cultural mode of production" as it emerged in the 1970s and 80s, when national governments [...] substantially funded an auteur cinema either by direct subsidies, prizes and grants, or indirectly, via state-controlled television' (Elsaesser 2013). This type of system of state patronage over a national cinema continued in Belgium into the 1990s. The directives from the CCA clearly favoured an auteur-focused system, in lieu of a variegated and nuanced institutional system, with the selection panel opting for projects that were evidently 'marked' and 'personified' by the filmmaker (Ingberg 2001). As Ingberg posits, this was primarily due to a limited annual budget, of approximately 15 million Belgian franks up to 2002 (about 371,000 euros) per project, which had to be distributed wisely and effectively. The decision to 'grow auteurs' was subsequently made to achieve this aim (ibid.). With a lack of institutional structure in Wallonia, a filmmaker's cultural cachet and valorisation as an auteur were previously drawn upon to attract foreign and national investment (from the CCA) for a film project. In the 1960s and 1970s, André Delvaux looked to France, Germany and Italy for film funding (Mosley 2001: 212–13), and whilst discussing their early corpus of feature films post-1996, the Dardenne brothers ludically noted that they would have been unable to create films without co-production funding from France (Cowie and Edelmann 2007: 220). At this point, these filmmakers epitomise Maule's conception of the 'institutional figure of the author' (Maule 2008: 17–18), since they are afforded the opportunity to film in the location and work with producers, technicians and actors of their choice.

In Flanders, the region and the ethnolinguistic community correspond to one another, whereas the French-speaking regions of Wallonia and Brussels do not directly cohere with the overarching linguistic community. Henry Ingberg – the first chairperson of the CCA – neatly emphasised the incongruity of the linguistic community as a 'laboratoire de l'identité' (Sojcher 1999b: 199). This suggests that a francophone Belgian identity is present in a plural form, acknowledging the hyphen placed between the two geographic regions in the Federation. Mosley further outlines the need to decouple Wallonia and Brussels as a result of differences in their respective political aspirations, demographic composition and self-images (2001: 2–3; 207). The cultural and social differences between the two French-speaking regions are profoundly emphasised in the Walloon cultural manifesto (1983), which describes francophone Belgian identity as a 'hybrid and artificial notion that has no firm basis' (*La revue nouvelle* 1983). The manifesto has been revised in three white papers, with the latest version made available in 2009 (*La revue toudi* 2009). This clearly highlights how the two French-speaking regions differ from one another culturally, which in turn foregrounds the relevance of the term 'region' when discussing their respective identities as distinct cinemas. Steele (2018) posits that the regions in Belgium, and Wallimage in particular, have adopted classical film policies that encourage territorialisation, that is audiovisual expenditure in Wallonia, at the same time as supporting co-productions with France, and, in particular, the contiguous region of Nord-Pas-de-Calais.

Funding a 'National' Cinema: The Belgian Film Funding 'Ecosystem' and its Transnational Context

The first port of call in this discussion of a 'larger' or transnational unit (Vincendeau 2011) in the context of francophone Belgian cinema is the use of the 'francophone' label. This is a clear point of distinction between films in Belgium along linguistic lines. Vincendeau considers language as forming a crucial element within the construction of national identity and – by extension – national cinema (2011: 339–42). However, the notion of 'francophone' posits a connection beyond the nation and the state in a relational sense to France and other French-language filmmaking countries, such as Switzerland, Quebec, the former French colonies of North and Sub-Saharan Africa and the French Caribbean. Marshall's definition of 'francophone cinema' emphasises its difference from French cinema and foregrounds 'the role of borders, movement, language and lateral connections' (2012: 41–2). 'Parts' and 'particles' underpin these four key elements, with the flow of filmmakers, personnel, characters and films moving across national borders and into different national cinema markets (ibid.). This, therefore, takes into consideration a de-centred approach to French-language filmmaking that occurs outside France, or 'cinéma-monde', which represents a version of 'world cinema' but from a French perspective (Gott and Schilt 2018). In the case of francophone Belgian cinema, the movement of financial 'particles' between Belgium and France plays an important role in the formation of transnational and regional film production.

In their approach to 'critical transnationalism', Higbee and Lim (2010) outline that the local, regional, national and the transnational are complementary. This approach suggests that filmmaking activities, financial arrangements and cultural policy formed at a local or regional level – in a downsized or devolved sense – have the inherent ability to inform the image of the nation that is distributed beyond its national borders (Higbee and Lim 2010: 18). Higbee and Lim highlight how the concept has been used loosely in relation to co-production agreements, funding mechanisms and cross-border collaboration 'without any real consideration of what the aesthetic, political or economic implications of such collaboration might mean' (2010: 10). This opens up a consideration of why certain countries and film industries co-finance, co-produce and co-venture as opposed to merely recognising certain tendencies as 'transnationalism'. This echoes Hjort's (2009) typologies of cinematic transnationalism in which a film can be 'marked' through its modes of production. These 'marks' are less likely to be apparent – visibly or aurally – within the film text. Overall, it is, therefore, necessary to consider and analyse film policy and institutional frameworks on a local and regional level within this paradigm.

In terms of this case study, these institutions are formed at a community-based or 'regional' level, such as the Centre du Cinéma et de l'Audiovisuel

(CCA) for the francophone community of Belgium, Wallimage for Wallonia, Bruxellimage (renamed Image.Brussels in 2014 and currently operating under the label Screen Brussels) for Brussels, and the Vlaams Audiovisuel Fonds (VAF) and Screen Flanders representing Flanders.[10] The creation of the Screen Brussels mechanism was part of a systematic restructuring at the level of the state ('Réforme de l'État') (Bredael and Reynaert 2016: 85). In the early 2000s, a four-part plan was suggested by Richard Miller to re-energise and stimulate the film sector in Belgium, particularly in light of the Dardenne brothers' critical success in France and at the Cannes film festival in 1999 (Duplat 2001). This plan laid out a new tax shelter-style system, alongside incentives for TV and satellite funding, increased support for short film funding and exhibition, and finally, an advance-on-receipts style system as implemented in France (Duplat 2001). These plans and incentives were primarily focused at a 'national' level or on the level of the linguistic communities, since Wallimage was referenced as an additional and concurrent system that operated in Wallonia.

In Belgium, a study of French-language productions quickly moves beyond the 'national', with notable levels of film funding being acquired through co-production agreements and collaborations between regional film funds. Between 2001 and 2014, co-productions with France accounted for 66.1% of the total of films produced in French. Discounting films funded through only Belgian funding streams, 79% of all co-productions were with France as either the majority or minority partner (CCA 2014: 224). Within this period, the highest number of co-productions occurred with France in 2012 (nineteen) and the fewest in 2002 (nine). The high number of co-productions between France and Belgium nuances the transnational economic cooperation between the devolved francophone regions of Belgium and France. On the basis of these statistics, the co-production relationship with France is important to the development of a Belgian, and in particular francophone Belgian, film production sector. The connection, in this case, is predicated upon a source of 'affinitive transnationalism' (Hjort 2009: 17) in which mutual intelligibility between the languages and the cultures has a role. Moreover, the level of co-production between the two countries is perceived as logical due to the historic patterns of film production. For instance, Sojcher observes that until 1989 (with the creation of EURIMAGES and EU support schemes), France and Belgium had a 'unilateral mini-treaty' in place for the support of francophone Belgian filmmaking (2001: 72). It is therefore logical to contend that this pattern has continued in contemporary modes and exchanges of film production between the two countries, but within the contemporary funding systems.

Under the previous system, in particular during the 1990s, the French system was viewed as 'more generous' than Belgian mechanisms, which allowed for 'only 8 per cent of the film receipts to be kept by the producer' (Duplat and Pluijgers 2001). The directive appears to favour the creation of co-productions, through reciprocal agreements (ibid.). However, according to Bredael and Reynaert (2016: 76), the French predilection for co-productions – with countries such as Belgium – has begun to wane in favour of 'identitarian' films that celebrate notions of French identity and French-ness. For Bredael and Reynaert, this is evinced by Luc Besson's rhetoric, which favoured an insular 'national cinema' and nation-centric approach, 'France for French filmmakers' (2016: 76). From the premise of 'cultural exceptionalism', O'Shaughnessy posits that 'identitarian nationalism' in the French context can be interpreted as 'a high-minded alibi for the defence of narrow self-interest' (2007: 17). As of 2016, the French tax rebate system has been reformed for international co-productions, which has shifted the emphasis for co-productions to be located in France. The TRIP (Tax Rebate for International Productions) system has been extended from 20% of audiovisual expenditure in France to 30% per project (CNC 2016). It is possible to ascertain that this may alter the levels of majority international co-productions that draw on technical providers and technical expertise in Wallonia and in the city of Liège, as surveyed by Steele (2018b). The discourse – which indirectly lends itself to an 'identitarian' understanding of a national cinema – is peculiar for a cinematic powerhouse (in European terms) for France, since Ledo (2017) uses the 'identitarian' approach to typify filmmaking produced in a non-hegemonic and minority linguistic context, such as in the case of Galicia and the Basque country. It is, therefore, a process of self-affirmation and nation-building in a frame of reference for films produced outside the dominant state or without a state.

As a result, according to Bredael and Reynaert, filmmaking and co-producing has become more competitive, with film technicians being cheaper in Belgium than the two neighbouring (and contiguous) countries of the Netherlands and France (2016: 65). This is further compounded by the concentration of film companies and facilities in major cities, particularly in Liège and Mons-Marcinelle in the south-west and south-east of Belgium respectively (Bredael and Reynaert 2016: 66–9; Steele 2018b). Both of the audiovisual hubs border co-production partners in the form of France and Germany. Bredael and Reynaert also see the impetus for francophone Belgian filmmaking to evolve and diversify its funding mechanism as a crucial intervention to nurture novice filmmakers, who had graduated through the Belgian film school system, and prevent a move to France to develop their careers (2016: 41). In fact, as Chapter Six outlines, the creation of more efficient funding mechanisms in Belgium, and Wallonia in particular, has witnessed the return of Lucas Belvaux, after a period of filmmaking and self-imposed 'exile' in France.

As Hjort further outlines, this is primarily the case for cinema systems of small nations with challenges to sustain a 'national' cinema (2009: 18). For instance, Switzerland produced fifteen 'national' films with twenty-six majority and minority co-productions, and the Netherlands funded nineteen 'national' films and thirty co-productions (European Audiovisual Observatory 2013). These statistics highlight the general trends of financial arrangements for film production, but reveal a partial story of the complex set of interactions that are taking place. This interpretation of cinematic transnationalism is primarily concerned with centrifugal forces in the form of state and corporate actors, which includes co-production agreements that have been formalised between countries.

Bergfelder draws on Hannerz's (1996) definition of transnationalism in the context of individuals and businesses forming working relationships beyond borders, since 'it allows us to acknowledge film as a medium whose historical emergence and whose modes of distribution and reception are closely linked to processes of globalisation' (2005: 322). Elsaesser (2005) emphasises the growth of privatisation and flows of private capital/inward investment within the open market for the European Union. As Elsaesser contends

> the sphere of the media, the massive push towards de-regulation, privatisation, centralisation of ownership and global reach, has produced dynamics of dispersal and at the same time new clustering that is very different from the geographically based [...] sub-state nationalisms. These latter, paradoxically, are *sus-tained* and *con-tained* by the European Union. (Elsaesser 2005: 116 – emphasis original)

In the film industry, funding mechanisms are more complex than a reliance on state-funded institutions and partnerships with private investment often required to increase a film's budget. The aspect of private investment is particularly relevant when considering the increase in the number of film productions and co-productions in Belgium. This provides a more nuanced interpretation of the co-production means of funding, since reports by national film bodies and the European Audiovisual Observatory use only national appellations to ascertain the origin of film funding.

The Belgian tax shelter (established in 2004) provides a 150% tax exemption on the amount invested (Taxshelter.be 2015), and it functions as an intermediary between investment groups and the audiovisual industry. The prerequisites are primarily concerned with compliance to the conditions of taxable expenditure in Belgium and the lead producer being resident in the country. The tax shelter has been a rather controversial development in the film funding "ecosystem" in Belgium, as it has not necessarily served its initial purpose – to increase the number of 'national' Belgian films. Instead, as producer of a production company Peter Bouckaert suggests, the rise in funding through the tax shelter has led to an 'explosion in production costs' (Lorfèvre 2013). A 2015 study into the 'cultural diversity' of film production in the francophone Belgian linguistic community foregrounded the tax shelter as a key component to the sector's make-up alongside cultural-economic models such as Wallimage (Blanchart, De Vinck and Ranaivoson 2015). That is to say that the funding derived through the mechanism is not directly and logically increasing the number of Belgian films. The initial ideas for the creation of a tax shelter system were sown in 2000/2001 (around the time that Wallimage was formed) in a four-part plan that was laid out by the Minister of Finance, Didier Reynders, in *La Libre Belgique*'s dossier on francophone Belgian cinema (Duplat 2001). The tax relief and tax shelter system constituted the first point of the plan, although the mechanism took three further years to implement.

Prior to the tax shelter's inception in Belgium, film producers from the country typically drew on almost 'mythical' levels of tax relief and tax write-offs in Luxembourg, which necessitated filming in the Grand Duchy (to the south of Wallonia and Belgium) (Duplat and Pluijgers 2001). For instance, for every '100 Belgian franks invested in a film, 30 could be subsidised by Luxembourg banks' (ibid.). The substantial incentives to co-produce and co-finance with the contiguous 'small nation' has led to a rise in co-production strategies that also draw on European forms of finance and support. This adhered to the criteria set out as part of the MEDIA and EURIMAGES programmes in the 1990s, which favoured co-productions between three countries. Everett suggests that the aforementioned two pan-European programmes have naturally developed in order to 'strengthen' European film industries, particularly their distribution and exhibition sectors, against the backdrop of competition from Hollywood and American film companies (2005: 16–19). In particular, Jäckel notes that the MEDIA II programme was designed to 'develop the potential of countries or regions with low production capacity and restricted geographic or linguistic populations' (BIPE Conseil 1998: 26, cited in Jäckel 2003: 71), for which Belgium operates as one such example. In Belgium, it was also auteur-driven, with the Dardenne brothers opting to co-finance with Luxembourg during their reinvention with *La promesse/The Promise* (Jean-Pierre and Luc Dardenne, 1996). The practice has continued since the inception of Wallimage in 2001, with eighteen co-productions with Luxembourg as the third partner being completed up to 2015, such as *Nue propriété/Private Property* (Joachim Lafosse, 2006), *Mobile Home* (François Pirot, 2012) and *Les géants/The Giants* (Bouli Lanners, 2011). This is particularly substantial when compared with Italy (eight), Canada (seven), Switzerland (six), Spain (three), United Kingdom (two), Argentina (one), the Netherlands (one), Poland (one), Morocco (one), Algeria (one), Denmark (one), Ireland (one) and Sweden (one).[11]

Adopting a diachronic line of thought, Reynaert has been rather critical of the output with Luxembourg, interpreting the films as 'séries C' (in a rather denunciative tone) with an 'American style' and aesthetic and 'limited' artistic and stylistic flair (Bredael and Reynaert 2016: 73). In 1999, the co-productions and co-financing agreements with Luxembourg were particularly prominent with the production of *Une liaison pornographique/An Affair of Love* (Frédéric

Fonteyne, 1999) and *Pourquoi se marier le jour de la fin du monde?/Why Get Married the Day the World Ends?* (Harry Cleven, 2000) This represents an interpretation of a corpus of films that can be elided with the much maligned notion of the 'Europudding'. Instead, Reynaert offers an alternative history of events that led to the creation of the Belgian tax shelter, which sees an uncertainty with the continued viability of the Wallimage regional film fund system, and the Ministry of Culture's desire to create a 'national' form of film funding as a competitive measure (Bredael and Reynaert 2016: 50). As Ingberg (2001) notes, in the 1990s, Belgium lacked an infrastructure that encouraged private inward investment, which was seen as 'almost nothing'. The intention to implement a tax shelter and tax breaks similar to France and Luxembourg was primarily to lessen the dependence for film production on funds solely derived from the public sector (Richard Miller, cited in Duplat 2001).

The 'national' remains salient to this funding mechanism, since it incorporates all of the linguistic communities of Belgium. However, this shows a shift in the film industry in Belgium to the private sector, and towards encouraging inward investment from companies by including tax breaks. In 2013 Belgium had a level of minority co-productions consistent with the largest film-producing countries in Europe – France (59), Germany (37), Spain (38), and Belgium (34) (European Audiovisual Observatory 2013). These minority co-productions are primarily with France, and include award-winning films such as *La vie d'Adèle/Blue is the warmest colour* (Abdellatif Kechiche, 2013) and *De rouille et d'os/Rust and Bone* (Jacques Audiard, 2012) – the latter included the Dardenne brothers as co-producers. This nuances the 'affinitive' nature of the cinematic transnationalism and interactions at play between France and Belgium to one of 'opportunism' – to once again draw upon Hjort's (2009) typologies.

The tax shelter has an intricate infrastructure that incorporates individual producers, intermediary production companies and banking systems (Tesolin and Zylberberg 2009). The complex set of alliances between individuals and intermediary production companies across borders nuances this concept of cinematic transnationalism through a 'regional' lens due to mutual and shared intelligibility between France and Belgium. In 2012, the Dardenne brothers adopted a new business strategy that allows the filmmakers to create their own contacts with investors. This bridges the gap between individual producers and intermediary production companies based in Belgium to attract film productions. To fund the film *Deux jours, une nuit /Two Days, One Night* (Dardenne brothers, 2014) the filmmakers were attached to the operator Cinéfinance through their own production company, Les Films du Fleuve (Carré 2012: 10). By adopting this strategy, filmmakers no longer needed to have an intermediary to fund a project through the tax shelter system, thereby forming a direct link between the investment and the filmmaker. This interpretation privileges producers creating films on a larger budget, relative to the average film budgets in Belgium. From this premise, the working relationships between film production companies and funding mechanisms are functioning within Hannerz's (1996) conception of transnationalism, in essence beyond state patronage of the film industry and production sector.

In terms of the 'national' cinema paradigm, the Belgian film industry is particularly complex due to how the film institutions are organised by linguistic communities and by region. For instance, there is no central film institution – like the CNC (Centre national du cinéma) across the border in France – to coordinate the Belgian film industry, since production funds, distribution and promotion support are provided by either the CCA for the French-speaking regions of Belgium or the VAF for Flanders. In essence, there are two central audiovisual and media services that delineate the country's film output according to linguistic community. Engelen and Vande Winkel state that the 'VAF has three main tasks: to stimulate audio-visual creation, to centralise and organise the (inter)national promotion of Flemish audio-visual creations and to organise and support training for young as well as experienced media professionals in Flanders' (2010: 53–4). To complicate matters further, a fiscal line was established in 2009 between the CCA and the VAF in which a small level of funding from the CCA goes towards projects supported by the VAF. In 2014, this constituted 5% of the CCA's total budget for feature film production (CCA 2014: 26). The most prominent examples of films supported through this line are *Rundskop/Bullhead* (Michaël R. Roskam, 2011) and more recently *Black* (Adil El Arbi and Bilall Fallah, 2015).

The complexities of the film-funding 'ecosystem' (Palmer 2011: 1–13) in Belgium – and primarily the French-speaking linguistic community – highlight how the 'national' remains salient when outlining public funding systems. It also speaks to a centre-margin relationship in which the CCA – located in Brussels – determines the selection criteria for projects that can then receive automatic funding from Wallimage in Wallonia. A 'transnational' and regional approach becomes a profitable way to tease out the continuities that lie within (francophone) Belgian film production. It therefore provides a scalar interpretation of cinematic transnationalism as a more inclusive means of understanding the trends in the francophone Belgian film industry.

Distribution and Exhibition: Cross-cultural Exchanges Between France and Belgium

In terms of forms of film distribution, Pierre Bourdieu posits that 'knowledge of directors is much more closely linked to cultural capital that mere cinemagoing' and foregrounds the role of the critic as a producer of 'legitimate classifications' ([1989] 2010: 19–20). Film festivals – with selection committees – and film criticism are ways in which certain films and filmmakers can reach their markets and public. From Bourdieu's premise, Czach (2004: 82) develops the notion of 'critical capital', which refers to films that gain distinction over and above others through their selection at 'A'-grade film festivals, such as Berlin, Cannes and Venice. Vincendeau further asserts that the 'national' – as a means of categorisation – has not been replaced by the aforementioned approaches in film criticism and at film festivals, as they play a key role in the formation of a 'national' film canon and 'national stereotyping' (2011: 340).

Ingberg (2001) outlines that the Brussels Film Festival in the 1990s and early 2000s 'renews' the sense of francophone Belgian cinema each year, thereby 'confirming its existence'. From this premise, Ingberg posits that 'the Belgian public is [...] an indispensible environment to accompany the development of our [francophone Belgian] cinema' (Ingberg 2001). The former chairperson of the CCA appears to be positing and outlining a system that pertains to 'self-confirming selectivity', which, for Christie, appears to undermine the critical valence of the 'national cinema' paradigm (2013: 26), see, for example the previously mentioned '50 ans de cinéma belge'. L'Écran Total's (Bredael and Reynaert 2016: 107–14) survey of francophone Belgian cinema in fifteen films provides an elastic interpretation of Belgian cinema, ranging from auteur films by emerging Walloon filmmakers like *Ultranova* (Bouli Lanners, 2005) and *Nue propriété/Private Property* (Joachim Lafosse, 2006), to co-produced major box office successes (and comedies) such as *Rien à déclarer/Nothing to Declare* (Dany Boon, 2010) and *Astérix et le Domaine des Dieux/Asterix: Mansion of the Gods* (Louis Clichy and Alexandre Astier, 2014), to international auteur-led co-productions like *Looking for Eric* (Ken Loach, 2009).

However, despite Ingberg's assertions, one of the primary peculiarities of framing a francophone Belgian 'national' canon concerns the categorisation from *outside* as opposed to from *within*. It is primarily the selection and valorisation of francophone Belgian films from international, and primarily French, film festivals that ascertains what defines a French-language Belgian film is. This coheres with Christie's interpretation of the 'A'-grade Cannes film festival and its selection policy, which appears to be turning towards the local and the articulation of localism (2013: 25). Christie further posits that 'these films have portrayed small or hitherto underrepresented countries to a wide audience, fulfilling the ambassadorial role of 1960s art cinema' (ibid.). The valorisation of the Dardenne brothers through this process has led to the international interpretation that the filmmakers serve to epitomise francophone Belgian cinema *par excellence* (as we will see in Chapter Two). The country that Christie occludes from his brief survey is Belgium, and Cannes' celebration of the Dardenne brothers' films on two separate occasions and the 2008 Belgian selection. Moreover, as this section outlines, the Belgian public consume fewer francophone Belgian films than the French public, thereby highlighting the importance of a transnational reading and understanding of Belgian cinema.

In the context of francophone Belgian cinema, the 'national' or 'regional' filmmaking canon is largely established through events and film festivals that take place outside the country. A diverse set of film festivals take place in Brussels and Wallonia – from the Brussels Film Festival dedicated to European cinema, the Brussels International Fantastic Film Festival to the Festival International du Film Francophone in Namur. However, it is the presence of francophone Belgian films at Cannes that has captured the attention of francophone Belgian film critics, and this has increased the level of visibility and international valorisation of a cinema from a 'small nation'.[12] For instance, in 2008 there was an increase in interest in Belgian filmmaking after the Cannes film festival. Five Belgian films were selected for consideration – *Le Silence de Lorna/Lorna's Silence* (Jean-Pierre and Luc Dardenne, 2008), *Eldorado* (Bouli Lanners, 2008), *Élève libre/Private Lessons* (Joachim Lafosse, 2008), *Rumba* (Dominique Abel, Fiona Gordon and Bruno Romy, 2008) and the Flemish film *Aanrijding in Moscou/Moscow, Belgium* (Christophe Van Rompaey, 2008). The French film magazine *Positif* published an eighteen-page dossier of films produced by Belgium since 2001 in February 2009. The magazine's focus was primarily centred on the aforementioned French-language Belgian films screened at Cannes the previous year. This legitimising of francophone Belgian films begins to overlook a more variegated selection of films produced in the country. For Rochet and his approach to an 'identitarian' cinema, the notion of 'new francophone Belgian cinema' has become shorthand for Walloon cinema (2011: 27). The 'national' is further problematised through a survey of film magazines in Belgium. For example, *Cinéma Belge* has produced an annual issue in the build-up to the Cannes film festival since 1987 (*Cinéma Belge* 2002). The May 2002 issue highlighted the shift in focus to – as the title suggests – 'Film productions of the French-speaking Belgian community from Wallonia-Brussels' (Productions de la Communauté française de Belgique Wallonie-Bruxelles 2002). The linguistic and cultural split in film magazines – representing the division in the film industry – occurs in the French-language *Cinergie* (produced since 1985) and the English quarterly *Flanders Image* (produced since 2005), that is a 'regional' or 'community-based' is a more apposite means of categorising Belgian film production.

In terms of film promotion, the Centre du Cinéma et de l'Audiovisuel (CCA) has been actively attempting to reconcile the aforementioned cultural differences on a 'national' level between the two distinct francophone 'regional' cinemas and to create a 'francophone Belgian film identity'. This is borne out through the creation of the Magritte awards in 2010 (first nominees in 2011) and the online portal Cinévox in 2011 ('CCA: Décloisonner et rapprocher' 2014: 1). Both of these strategies were initially designed to provide francophone Belgian filmmakers with a coherent platform for 'national' recognition and valorisation. This consequently begins to disassociate regional and cultural differences evident at a textual level from the distribution, exhibition and reception of francophone Belgian films nationally. Internally, the CCA formed the Magrittes, an award ceremony named after the Walloon surrealist artist René Magritte, which was designed to valorise Belgian cinema from a French perspective. The event is screened live in February on the RTBF channel La Deux (Denis 2018), thereby reaching a primarily French-speaking audience. For Denis (2018), the 2018 award ceremony highlighted the 'limits of the concept', with little competition – 'they were scraping the barrel to line up five films'. The awards have largely reaffirmed francophone Belgian cinema's auteur-led cinema with the familiar names regularly winning the leading awards: Jaco Von Dormael (twice – 2011 and 2016), Bouli Lanners (twice – 2012 and 2017), the Dardenne brothers (2015) and Joachim Lafosse (2013). In essence, it reaffirms the canon outlined in this book. The categories clearly differentiate between French-language and Dutch-language films, with the 'best film' category limited to primarily French-language films, with Dutch films placed in a subsidiary category of 'Best Flemish Film'.[13]

The second strand to this transnational and regional approach, which underpins this monograph and approach to contemporary francophone Belgian filmmaking, pertains to trends in distribution and exhibition, and the extent to which films are able to operate seamlessly in different national contexts. Galt (2006: 6) outlines an internal hierarchy in which European films are defined by their difference from others available on the 'art film' circuit. There is a certain 'economic' and 'cultural capital' assigned to specific national cinemas, particularly from countries with a grand filmmaking heritage (that is, France) (ibid.). Indeed, it is also possible to posit the existence of smaller 'regional' markets with films habitually crossing over into different contiguous and linguistically similar national contexts. For example, Marshall (2012: 38) argues that the Belgian and Swiss film markets can be seen to function as an extension of the French market. In Belgium, French films generally have a share of around 15% of the domestic market, and in Switzerland the share in 2012 was 16.67% (Swiss Films 2013: 17). This contrasts with Christie's assertion that, generally speaking, 'relatively few people get to see them [European films] outside their country of origin' (2013: 20), since more French people will watch a francophone Belgian film than French-speaking citizens of the country of origin (partially by virtue of France operating as a country with the largest French-speaking population). It is also the case that French cinema dominates the francophone Belgian domestic market, leaving 'national' filmmaking at the margins.

The General Secretary for the Fédération Wallonie-Bruxelles, Frédéric Delor, claimed that '[o]ur domestic market is very permeable to films from France. There is no distinction between Belgian films and French films' (Delor, in Biourge 2014).[14] In this sense, there is a conflation between French films and francophone Belgian films in the domestic Belgian market. France produces and distributes a larger number of films per year, which introduces high levels of competition for 'national' Belgian films – in French – in their own domestic market. For example, in 2013 France distributed seventy films to Belgium (21.2% of total films circulated in Belgium), whereas twenty-three 'national' or Belgian films (6.9%) were circulated overall (CCA 2013). The performance of French films in Belgium highlights French cinema's 'economic capital' – as opposed to its 'cultural capital' – since the most-watched films cohere with Bourdieu's ([1989] 2010: 24–6) notion of the 'popular aesthetic'. These films are simply organised, light-hearted and include well-known actors. For instance, since 2008 the top-performing French films distributed in Belgium have been comedies, such as *Bienvenue chez les Ch'tis/Welcome to the Sticks* (Dany Boon, 2008), which had 1,075,497 admissions, and *Intouchables/The Intouchables* (Olivier Nakache and Éric Toledano, 2011), which had 576,071 admissions (European Audiovisual Observatory 2015/2016). Both of these films were circulated in large multiplex and chain cinemas – such as Kinepolis – on release in Belgium, which further suggests that these films are less concerned with 'cultural capital'. Marshall (2012: 45) draws upon *Bienvenue chez les Ch'tis* to further posit a challenge to a nation-centric reading of the film and its exhibition. This recalls the earlier approach to cinematic transnationalism, and more precisely suggests the creation of a contiguous 'regional' film market predicated upon 'shared culture'. Francophone Belgian cinema, therefore, evinces the conundrum offered by Hjort and Petrie (2007) in their approach to 'cinemas of small nations'. As the scholars contend, 'small nations by definition have very limited domestic markets for all locally produced goods and services – including culture – and so have been forced by neo-liberal economic and political pressures of globalisation into a greater dependency on external markets' (Hjort and Petrie 2007: 15). The permeability of the Belgian domestic market presents only a partial view of Belgium's modes of exhibition, since its linguistic bifurcation presents difficulties (and opportunities) for its own film production.

In 2013, the national market share for Belgian films in Belgium was 9.59%, and in Switzerland the share of Swiss films was 5.2% (Marché du Film 2013: 36). When comparing this share to other cinemas of 'small' nations (Hjort and Petrie 2007), the Scandinavian countries and the Netherlands all recorded a more favourable national market share (16.3% in the Netherlands, Denmark 28.7%, Finland 28%, Sweden 24.1% and Norway 17.9%) (Marché du Film 2013: 36–8). These box office statistics therefore foreground some of the complexities in referring to a 'national' film market in countries that are linguistically divided.

Despite the low market share in Belgium for 'national' films or majority Belgian co-productions, the French market presents an opportunity for (francophone) Belgian films to receive higher levels of film admissions. Philippe

Reynaert (2011: personal communication) noted that France is considered the 'true interior market' for Belgian films due to its higher levels of cinema attendance and its greater number of screens in comparison to Belgium. Ingberg further evinces this line of argument, by proposing that 'in the last ten years [from the early 1990s], the release of francophone Belgian films is in some sort of amicable ghetto that has faced up to the international public first, then the national public' (Ingberg 2001). The contemporaneous filmmakers that Ingberg singles out, namely Alain Berliner, Frédéric Fonteyne, and Thierry Michel, are not included in this analysis of francophone Belgian cinema, with their level of film production waning at the turn of the millennium, a slow-down in production and the rise of a new wave of young, novice filmmakers taking their place. This is borne out in the CCA's annual summary, which combines the number of film admissions from the two countries in order to assess the perceived 'success' of French-language films. Tables 1(a) and 1(b) tease out the continuities in this overall summary, and clearly highlight the extent to which the French market contributes more film admissions to 100% 'national' funded Belgian films and majority co-productions. In essence, there is a certain level of reciprocity between exhibition attendances in the two countries. However, there is a limited diversity of francophone Belgian films being consumed in France, since only films by key francophone Belgian filmmakers constitute the largest proportion of film admissions in France from a smaller number of films circulated in the country.

Francophone Belgian films are not 'marked' – in terms of language – with dubbing or subtitling procedures that could initially inhibit their wide distribution in France. Elsaesser posits that

> (a)part from the categories of 'art cinema' and 'festival films', popular films rarely travel across linguistic borders, and where they do – as in the case of imported Hollywood fare – they are usually dubbed (synchronised) [. . . in a way] that make[s] going to the cinema [akin to] attending a ventriloquised pantomime and submitting to aural torture. (2013)

Bergfelder outlines that 'a given audience's understanding of a foreign film is rarely based on its "original" textual meaning [. . .] but [is] negotiated through specific translation and adaptation processes' (2005: 329). Differences engendered at a level of translation and cultural variation can construct a barrier for a given national audience. However, francophone Belgian films are able to easily operate within the French domestic market, which immediately points towards the transnational as a more apposite means of considering the distribution and exhibition practices of francophone Belgian cinema. It is only accents and inflections that 'mark' a francophone Belgian text as different. Instead, it is possible to ascertain that – from these statistics provided for a period of five years – the performance of a francophone Belgian film is more linked to the work of a recognisable filmmaker as opposed to an adherence to generic conventions. For instance, in 2014, the Dardenne brothers' *Deux jours, une nuit* received 511,593 film admissions in France in comparison to 60,488 in Belgium. This constitutes approximately 41.9% of the total admissions to francophone Belgian films in France, whereas the film pertains to only 26.4% in Belgium.

The Dardenne brothers neatly exemplify a challenge to a 'national' interpretation of francophone Belgian exhibition practices, drawing on a means of distribution that requires valorisation in France and a decoding by international film critics. Since 1999, their films have been selected at the Cannes film festival every three years, including *La fille inconnue/The Unknown Girl* (2016). The attention received at the festival is used as a springboard for the release of their films in French and Belgian markets. For instance, the release date of *Deux jours, une nuit* in the two countries corresponded with its opening night at Cannes. This method of release draws upon knowledge of the filmmakers' corpus of work, and appeals to a specific audience both in France and across Europe. However, film critics in Belgium and in France and selection committees at international film festivals have foregrounded a rather limited interpretation of francophone Belgian cinema. Luc Dardenne laments that these selection committees capture Belgian cinema as a 'cinema of [economic] depression and poverty' (2015: 174). These judgements point towards a valorisation of certain filmmakers, such as Lucas Belvaux, Joachim Lafosse and Bouli Lanners, whose films perform best in France and Belgium. A 'national' interpretation and consideration of their works is problematised through the appeal of the films across national borders, which speaks to the existence of cultural imbrications and shared concerns between the two countries.

Drawing on the national market, Verheul posits that Flanders 'witnessed a proliferation of films targeted at its domestic market, while the public's broadening interest in these Flemish productions secured their financial success' (2016: 317). Verheul suggests that the 'domestic market' is drawn linguistically

Table 1(a): Francophone Belgian films circulated in Belgium (2010–14)[15]

Year	Number of films circulated	Film admissions
2010	17	537,072
2011	14	681,246
2012	29	690,398
2013	28	152,853
2014	23	228,737

(Source: compiled from CCA (Centre du Cinéma et de l'Audiovisuel), pers comm, 15 and 16 June 2015.)

Table 1(b): Francophone Belgian films circulated in France (2010–14)

Year	Number of films circulated	Film admissions
2010	13	1,562,502
2011	13	686,031
2012	23	2,444,204
2013	15	1,720,453
2014	18	1,191,373

(Source: compiled from CCA (Centre du Cinéma et de l'Audiovisuel), pers comm, 15 and 16 June 2015.)

in the Belgian case, which coheres with Cucco's (2010) initial approach to a fragmented Swiss 'domestic market' based on language. Verheul (2016) argues that Flemish cinema is distinct from the Netherlands in terms of its articulation of Dutch, that is affirming its subtle difference in vernacular and accent, whilst producing films that are remade. This emphasises 'the social, cultural and linguistic ties between Flanders and the Netherlands, yet simultaneously reveals the increasing erosion of the Dutch language area' (Verheul 2016: 318).

In terms of the distinct cinematic lines between Flemish and francophone Belgian filmmaking, there are discernible differences in the forms of articulation and representation. This is particularly borne out by remakes and the relationship to Hollywood. No contemporary francophone Belgian film has been remade in Hollywood, whereas Flemish-language cinema and filmmaking has followed a Hollywood tradition, with box office successes in Belgium being retold in the USA. As Sojcher presciently notes, Flemish film funds 'privilege cultural-commercial films' that use 'Hollywood cinema as a transnational reference point' (2001: 60). For instance, *Loft* (Erik Van Looy, 2008) was remade into a feature film with the same title and *Bullhead* led to Roskam's production of *The Drop* (Michaël R. Roskam, 2014) in Hollywood. Importantly, both of these Flemish filmmakers have returned to the Flemish Belgian film industry since, with *Le Fidèle/Racer and the Jailbird* (Michaël R. Roskam, 2017) and *De Premier/Prime Minister* (Erik Van Looy, 2016).[16] This further evidences a cultural affinity between Anglo-American film cultures and Flanders, whereas the francophone Belgian film industry has greater reciprocity with France. According to Alain Gerlache, the former president of RTBF

> [o]n one hand, there are the Flemish, who reproach the French-speakers for their pretentious and arrogant culture, like that of the Dardenne brothers; on the other hand, there are the French-speakers who reject the Americanised Flemish cinema and their Nordic Viking pop music. (Martel 2010: 400)

This testimony neatly evidences two different tastes in terms of the two respective cinemas operating within Belgium. Gerlache's interpretation implicitly posits that Flemish cinema 'impersonates' (to adopt Elsaesser's (2013) term) Hollywood and American modes of filmmaking. In the case of francophone Belgian filmmaking, this appears not to be the case in an auteur-driven cinema, since the 'appropriation', arrives in the opposite direction with *The Adventures of Tintin* (Steven Spielberg, 2011) (Martel 2010, speaking of the then-anticipated film: 401). As Higbee and Song Hwee Lim argue in their approach to 'critical transnationalism', transnationality 'has made possible the transplantation not just of films but also of directors' in the East Asian filmmaking tradition (2010: 15). Contextualising this argument to a European context, this 'transplantation' has primarily occurred for Flemish and Dutch-language filmmakers to Hollywood. The translation and adaptation of narratives and stories is not the case for francophone Belgian cinema, but it does occur in Flemish cinema of the 2000s, further evincing the popular 'successes' in box office receipts.

Cumulative box office records and statistics compiled between 1996 and 2010 further evidence this interpretation of the domestic market. Flanders, or more specifically a Dutch-speaking/Flemish audience, constitutes the Belgian domestic market in terms of market share, that is admissions totalling 8.7 million for Flemish-language films produced by Belgium compared to 1.64 million for French-language Belgian films for a francophone Belgian audience. This is all the more striking given that the attendances by region are more or less equal across the three regions and two linguistic communities, approximately 47.97% in Flanders compared to 34.26% in Wallonia and 17.66% in Brussels in 2010 (and remains consistent in this frame across the decade) (Statbel pers comm). As a result, the level of consumption for native Belgian films in Wallonia and Brussels is, therefore, lower than in Flanders, who appear to have a greater predilection for Dutch/Flemish cinema. Comparatively, the francophone Belgian films that perform best at the box office are primarily auteur, social-realist features. This form of performance is predicated on the wave of critical valorisation and 'success' generated at film festivals that filter into box office admissions in Belgium and, more often than not, in France. Importantly, the translatability of the genre films and narratives is absent in francophone Belgian cinema – in distinct contrast to Flemish cinema of the 2000s – since there have been no remakes in France or in the USA. This further attests to the localism and local particularities invested in francophone Belgian filmmaking (as explored throughout this book), which appeals across borders because of their universalism. However, they are not directly translatable and transferable, that is built on easily replicated genres. André captures this difference in the introduction to his review of *Rosetta* (Jean-Pierre and Luc Dardenne, 1999) for *La revue toudi*, claiming that '[t]his is no Hollywood!' (André 1999, emphasis original). It implicitly posits a certain authenticity to Belgian cinema that operates in contrast to 'the organised trips, the safari photos and theme parks of Zolaville, Dickenscity and other Euro-homelessness' (Gauditiaubois and Yernaux 1999). The raw aesthetic, social realist style and topical subject matter distance the film from cinema as a form of entertainment, evincing a turn to social commitment as a form of representation and articulation. For Sojcher, the francophone Belgian films that perform well abroad (and particularly in France) are 'art films', which are 'not in competition' with 'Hollywood super-productions' (2001: 71). As Gauditiaubois and Yernaux argue, '(t)his Belgium wins, by selling a Wallonia that loses (1999). These feature films are not necessarily aimed at the mass and popular cinema market.

Conclusion

The forms of film production, distribution and exhibition in a francophone Belgian context neatly redefine and rearticulate a national cinema. It is linguistically and culturally specific, which draws cultural boundaries and borders internally, that is between the French-speaking and Flemish Dutch-speaking regions. It aligns more closely with the region and the sub-state. To this end, a 'national' cinema remains through the inclusion of the 'Belgian' national label, but it is at once qualified. The 'francophone' component also alludes to a point of identification beyond or outside the nation, forming a relation with its contiguous neighbour France. This recalls Higbee and Lim's (2010) conception of 'critical transnationalism' and the formation of alliances predicated upon the notion of a 'shared culture'. There are pre-formed alliances – in this case between Belgium and France – to supplement funding to films that articulate local settings and local voices. These local and/or nationally and culturally specific films are not 'contained' (to hint at Elsaesser's term (2005)) within a bifurcated and fragmented domestic market, reaching out to France as an extended domestic and national market.

Notes

1. The title of this chapter references Palmer's (2011: 1–13) approach to the 'French film ecosystem'. Sections of this chapter are reprinted, with kind permission, from the author's 2016 article 'Towards a "transnational regional" cinema: the francophone Belgian case study' (Steele 2016).
2. For the film festival's programme list (Lemercier 2015), see <http://cineuropa.org/nw.aspx?t=newsdetail&l=en&did=288287> (last accessed June 2018).
3. The screenings took place on various platforms, that is from live screenings through to video-on-demand, between June 2017 and June 2018 (see <https://www.50cinquante.be/>, last accessed 20 December 2017).
4. It is significant to note, however, that the initiative was supported by (and funded by) the CCA, which comes under the auspices of the CFWB.
5. Christie outlines that the *Stories We Tell Ourselves* event on British cinema

organised its films 'according to a set of "British Values"', which constituted region, location, period, setting and genre (2013: 26).
6. See Roekens (2009) for a detailed and nuanced examination of the television company RTBF and its contribution to Walloon culture and Walloon national identity over four decades, between 1962 and 2000.
7. In 2008, Télébruxelles aired a public debate between key policymakers in Brussels and Wallonia. The programme considered the economic and cultural model required to improve Brussels-based filmmaking in the wake of the creation of Wallimage in 2001. 'Brussels Tournage' was discussed as a largely touristic funding and support mechanism, which offered Brussels as a 'shop window' (Télébruxelles 2008). The system was interpreted as being old-fashioned and in need of a revamp, much like Wallimage for Wallonia.
8. Bredael and Reynaert posit that the change in name from Bruxellimage to Screen Brussels is intended to distance the institution from its francophone origins in search of an international audience (2016: 88). The 'anglicised' name renders the institution more global and transnational in terms of potential partnerships that are more culturally and institutionally diverse.
9. See Steele (2018) and Steele (2018b) for a detailed examination of Wallimage and its relationship with Nord-Pas-de-Calais and for the concentration of filmmaking activities in the city of Liège.
10. In 2009, Wallimage and Bruxellimage established a financial line that connects the two institutions for the funding of feature-length films (Wallimage-Bruxellimage).
11. These figures relate to the author's summary of co-productions funded by Wallimage according to documents supplied by the institution in 2016.
12. For a conceptualisation and detailed interpretation of 'cinemas of small nations', see Hjort and Petrie (2007).
13. See the website for the Magrittes, <http://www.lesmagritteducinema.com/categories.php?lang=fr>, for the full 2018 list and categories.
14. Delor (Biourge 2014) further notes that this is not the case for Flemish films, due to the lack of competition from its linguistic neighbour. In 2013, the Netherlands distributed only ten films to Belgium (3% of the market) (CCA 2013).
15. The statistics included in the two tables pertain to French-language films that have received 100% funding from Belgium or are considered majority Belgian co-productions by the CCA.
16. *La Libre Belgique* surveys the 'Flemish connection' with Hollywood, which is inclusive of Michaël R. Roskam, Matthias Schoenaerts, Felix Van Groeningen, Jakob Verbruggen, Erik Van Looy and Peter Van Hees (H. H. 2015: 39).

2. 'NO FUTURE': SOCIAL MARGINALISATION, SOCIAL PRECARIOUSNESS AND DEPICTIONS OF SERAING IN *LE GAMIN AU VÉLO* (JEAN-PIERRE AND LUC DARDENNE, 2011) AND *DEUX JOURS, UNE NUIT* (JEAN-PIERRE AND LUC DARDENNE, 2014)

In the closing sequence of *Je pense à vous/You're On My Mind* (Jean-Pierre and Luc Dardenne, 1992), Fabrice, a recently redundant worker, searches for his son and his wife amongst the local crowd of the Mardi Gras parade as it passes through the small town of Seraing. The brass-band music, the folk dances and traditional costumes form the backdrop, as the son (dressed as a Walloon Gille in yellow, black and red colours and adorned with bells) passes an orange (the traditional fruit of the event) from son to father to mother (Figure 2.1). Mosley contends that '[t]he sharing of fruit offers a symbol of renewed family life' (2013: 17), bringing the family together within the community. The sequence opens up the question of filiation, and articulates a 'monocultural' 'theme of the nation' in which 'the viewer is bombarded with a large number of monocultural aural and visual elements' (Hjort 2000: 113). This theme is placed more at the surface of the film than Hjort's 'banal aboutness', which pertains to the subtle national nuances that lurk in the background of the frame (2000: 108–9). Within the context of Walloon regionalism, the 'monocultural' is evinced by the literal 'flagging' of Walloon symbols during the carnival. The ending represents a Belgian, or more specifically a Walloon, particularism and articulation of the local, providing a point of orientation and 'local anchoring' (Fontaine 1992). The film questions paternalism and an ailing patriarchal society through father–son relationships, that is, the notion of filiation, and the limited job opportunities enunciated in the region, which can be traced back to *Déjà s'envole la fleur maigre* (Paul Meyer, 1960). As Fontaine (1996) posits, the film offers a 'simple structure' that is predicated on a 'vertical axis' between father and son, as opposed to a 'horizontal axis' between brethren. As the Introduction to this book notes, particularly in relation to the work of Bajomée (2010), the traditional patterns of work between father and son had been drifting apart since the late 1960s in the city of Liège and Wallonia more generally. As O'Shaughnessy points out, *Je pense à vous* reveals the 'raw face of social struggle denied a collective voice, a past and a future and thus condemned to be mute, corporeal and local' (2007: 53). However, it is precisely this 'flagging' and the preoccupation with the local that has been softened in the post-*La promesse* (1996) films. Mélon presciently noted the 'constant worry' to 'shield yourself from the danger of the banality of the imagery' (Mélon 1996/1997: 5) in the context of the Dardenne brothers. The criticism of *Je pense à vous* and its very limited distribution and valorisation has proved a sore subject in Luc Dardenne's published journals (2008; 2015) and series of interviews since. Instead of critical praise, it provides a watershed moment in the Dardenne brothers' filmmaking career, an intention to soften the 'banality' and particularism, leading to a more fruitful analysis through a transnational reading of their films post-*La promesse*.

Figure 2.1 Fabrice and Céline embrace along with their son, dressed as a Gille (a traditional costume) during the local carnival at the conclusion of *Je pense à vous*.

Situating the Dardenne Brothers in a Transnational Context

The concept of cinematic transnationalism nuances and extends the 'monocultural' themes of the nation (Hjort 2000) explored in the Dardenne brothers' films, defining their aesthetics, stylistic and thematic filiation, the exploration of the characters' place within the spatial dynamics of a post-industrial suburb, and, much later, their approach to casting. Shaw proposes the typology of 'transnational viewing practices' to refer to 'the viewing of any film made and/or set in a different national context from that of the audience, and the divergent readings that may arise from the national/regional identities of audiences' (2013: 59). This extends the cinephilic reading beyond the closed borders of the national or regional cinema in favour of citations from different national/regional/global contexts, or, as Ezra and Rowden argue, 'increasingly these frameworks are losing the national and cultural particularity they once had' (2006: 4). The particularist narratives and sequences, captured by the ending of *Je pense à vous*, are no longer desired by cinephiles searching for references, stylistic and thematic filiation and intertextuality. The national remains implicit, beneath the surface, and, as Mosley contends in the context of the Dardenne brothers' *Rosetta*, still readable to local audiences (2013: 92).

Transnational cinema also provides a useful framework for an industrial analysis of the Dardenne brothers' films, particularly in terms of transnational distribution and, more recently, casting. The international circulation of the films and the use of transnational platforms and viewing practices, such as film festivals as noted by Ezra and Rowden, 'unmoor films from their immediate contexts' (Ezra and Rowden 2006: 7). As we saw in Chapter One, the Dardenne brothers' films lead the way in the context of international film distribution, reaching out to French markets through contiguity, mutual intelligibility of language, and 'affinity' (Hjort 2009). The filmmakers have a structured filmmaking pattern in which a film has been produced every three years since the release of *La promesse* in 1996, with the Cannes film festival being used as the primary platform for film release.[1] The awards that the Dardenne brothers have frequently received at Cannes film festival radically contrast with 'national' valorisation of their films, which has been more muted. For instance, since the launch of the Magrittes in 2010, the Dardenne brothers have claimed only one win.

In the context of casting, the Dardenne brothers shifted their traditional approach from non-professional or little-known actors to international stars with *Le gamin au vélo/The Kid With a Bike* (2011), – although their usual method of casting remained with young actor Thomas Doret as Cyril; Doret was discovered after the Dardenne brothers advertised on radio and through the press (Rouyer and Tobin 2011: 11). Shaw offers transnational stars as a typology of cinematic transnationalism, with 'transregional, transcommunity and global stars' (2013: 60). The casting of Belgian actress Cécile de France

(*Le gamin au vélo*), and French stars Marion Cotillard (*Deux jours, une nuit*) and Adèle Haenal (*La fille inconnue/The Unknown Girl* (Jean-Pierre and Luc Dardenne, 2016)) sits between the 'transregional' and global categories of the star typology. With the casting of each star, the Dardenne brothers are stepping away from the national and local context, and from particularism. The decision to cast Marion Cotillard arose from transnational modes of production, as the filmmakers met the star as producers on Jacques Audiard's *De rouille et d'os/Rust and Bone* (Guerand 2014: 136; Rouyer and Tobin 2014: 12). Cotillard and Haenal refer to 'transregional' forms of stardom as established members of the French star system, featuring in mainstream and peripheral films in the context of French national cinema. It is the question of accent that 'marks' the stars as non-Belgian, as opposed to language. As Pluijgers observes, this was a complex knot to untie (that is, language and accent), since 'the month of rehearsals [was intended . . .] to part with the Parisian accent' (2014: 34). In the case of Cotillard, Luc Dardenne described the casting as a 'risk', noting that '[a] star comes with his or her own baggage, of stardom and success. Very quickly, though, we saw that she was no longer Marion Cotillard. She was Sandra' (Gilbey 2014: 14). However, in their view, the French star offered 'a new body and a new face' that placed her (according to Cotillard) 'in the story, in the décor, [and] in the character' (Pluijgers 2014: 32). As a result, Cotillard (as Sandra) fitted in with 'the same family as everyone else' (Gilbey 2014: 14). The casting of Cotillard in a Belgian film is not a complete aberration, given the star's previous role in the Belgian, Brussels-set, comedy *Dikkenek* (Olivier Van Hoofstadt, 2006), alongside the Dardenne regular Jérémie Renier.

Since the Dardenne brothers redefined their filmmaking style with *La promesse*, there has been a critical valency in 'realist' interpretations of their films. Mosley (2013) posits the notion of 'responsible realism' and Mai (2010: 53–63) 'sensuous realism' as a means of incorporating the ethical concerns that lie within their works and the references to forms of 'realism', such as French Poetic Realism, Italian Neorealism and to established contemporary European auteurs.[2] Luc Dardenne explicitly references the Italian Neorealist film *Germania anno zero/Germany Year Zero* (Roberto Rossellini, 1948) as 'our model' (2008: 33). In his two published journals (2008; 2015), Luc Dardenne pinpoints key filmmakers throughout film history who have influenced the formation of their filmmaking style since 1996. These filmmakers – for example Maurice Pialat, Robert Bresson and Roberto Rossellini, to name a few – broadly fit into a 'realist' style of filmmaking in Europe (Mosley 2013: 33–6).[3] O'Shaughnessy notes that Osganian's (2003) approach to *Rosetta* builds on transnational stylistic filiation, and posits that 'Osganian's discussion of a cinema of fragments chimes with Jeancolas's description of a cinema of fragmentary social facts that was in turn inspired by Bazin's account of Italian Neorealism' (O'Shaughnessy 2007: 25). These stylistic references highlight how the Dardenne brothers do not neatly fit into a 'national' paradigm, since they clearly distance themselves from preceding luminary figures in Belgian cinema, such as André Delvaux. Instead, they cohere with key European auteurs, and this consequently encourages a reading of the codified aesthetics within a particularly transnational context.

In certain instances of film scholarship, the Dardenne brothers' films have been collapsed into a framework of French cinema. This is particularly the case in the publications *Contemporary French Cinema* (Austin 2008), *The New Face of Political Cinema* (O'Shaughnessy 2007) and 'Post-1995 French Cinema: Return of the Social, Return of the Political?' (O'Shaughnessy 2003). This point has a certain currency, given that it is a contemporaneous cinema of the francophone Belgian filmmakers.[4] Ince further argues for the universal and 'could be anywhere' approach to the understanding of Seraing in the films, observing that the 'bleak post-industrial landscape stands in for many similar-looking locations across northern Europe' (2008: 12). On an aesthetic level, this results in an 'often urgent, immediate and specific' form of 'enunciation' (O'Shaughnessy 2003: 202). The elision of *Rosetta* with this approach highlights the 'shared concerns' between France's regions and Wallonia. The concept of cinematic transnationalism arises at this point through the analysis of sociopolitical issues in the Dardenne brothers' work alongside films produced in the conterminous region of Nord-Pas-de-Calais, France. Although O'Shaughnessy (2007: 47) recognises that the filmmakers are from Wallonia, the overarching publication and central thesis suggests that their films are not necessarily articulating the south of Belgium.[5]

From this premise, Bénézet (2005) and Mosley (2013: 29) outline the emergence of a *cinéma nordiste*, which concerns the presence of a shared film style, and shared cultural and social concerns between films produced in Wallonia and Nord-Pas-de-Calais. This resonates with Higbee and Lim's (2010) and Hjort's (2009) interpretation of cinematic transnationalism, which encourage a reading of 'shared cultures' beyond a 'national' context. Whilst Bénézet's (2005) interpretation of this 'northern cinema' coheres with the period of *le jeune cinéma* (Prédal 2002), Mosley (2013: 29) extends the period to include filmmakers, such as Lucas Belvaux, Bouli Lanners and Joachim Lafosse, whose films were released post-2005. In this sense, a periodisation of the *cinéma nordiste* concept is more fluid in terms of its time frame than Powrie's (1999) definition of French New Realism.

'Post-Dardenne': A 'National' and 'Regional' Starting Point

In an interview series with a selection of Belgian filmmakers emerging in the early 2000s, Van Hoeij outlines certain phases in the development of contemporary francophone Belgian cinema, in which the final section is entitled 'the post-Dardenne generation' (2010: 15). The complexity of this 'post-Dardenne' appellation relates to the Dardenne brothers' active engagement in filmmaking in Belgium. The Dardenne brothers are viewed as intrinsically 'Belgian' filmmakers. For instance, in Spaas' (2000) survey of francophone cinema, the Dardenne brothers have a prominent section dedicated to their films set in the region of Wallonia in the chapter on Belgian cinema. Moreover, international film critics often refer to the Dardenne brothers as contemporary 'Belgian' filmmakers (Brooks 2006; Dupont 2002; Macnab 2003; Wolfreys 2008) as opposed to other supranational or regional categories such as 'European' or 'Walloon'.

Francophone Belgian cinema and its canonisation tend to coalesce around a group of auteurs, as the discursive reports on the 2018 Magritte awards evince, 'no van Dormael, no Dardenne, no Lafosse, and no Bouli' (Denis 2018). The periodisation concept ('post-Dardenne') – as a purely descriptive and straightforward term in francophone Belgian film criticism – posits that there is a neat timescale that moves between these established filmmakers and young, novice and emerging filmmaking talent from Wallonia. This is, of course, not the case, since francophone Belgian cinema, or even Belgian cinema, cannot be defined simply in relation to a before and after generically, stylistically and thematically in the context of one filmmaker, the Dardenne brothers. Moreover, as this chapter attests, the Dardenne brothers have modified their filmmaking approach over time, slowly evolving away from the 'urgent realism' of the late 1990s and early 2000s, to a more controlled and fluid camerawork that resonates with the increase in the filmmakers' budgets, modes of production and improvement in available technologies (that is, cameras). The Dardenne brothers' 'urgent realism' and intimate handheld camera permeates only Joachim Lafosse's early work (see Chapter Three). Van Hoeij even notes its problematic application, positing that 'for Belgium, a country of contrasts with diverse traditions, it is not peculiar to go in the opposite direction to your predecessors' (2010: 15). In fact, the Belgian critic argues that each of the selected filmmakers offers 'original, unique and singular' approaches to their films (ibid.). This is also the case concerning the following wave of filmmakers to emerge from Belgian film schools as posited inheritors of the Dardenne brothers' filmmaking approach and style, despite their own dense and considered thematic and stylistic patterns. The so-called 'post-Dardenne' filmmakers also arise from two competing contexts, which cumulatively offer a diverse interpretation of francophone Belgian cinema, with the filmmakers falling into the categories of the film school generation, or, like the Dardenne brothers, representing autodidacts. This, similarly, posits a challenge to the 'post-Dardenne' appellation. Thematic continuities, such as the exploration of Wallonia's sociopolitical and socio-economic context, arise synchronically, with a gradual deviation from these shared issues and debates over time, which is the case for Joachim Lafosse and Olivier Masset-Depasse at the early stages of their filmmaking career in the early 2000s.

Women-led narratives also reverberate – as a primary continuity – through the films of the Dardenne brothers, Joachim Lafosse and Olivier Masset-Depasse. This resonates with Hayward's (2000) notion that national narrative and national cinemas are coalescing around women as an articulation of nation. As Hayward presciently notes, '[t]he nation pretends to be gender-neutral (in that it purports to dissolve difference) and yet the woman's body is closely aligned/identified with nationalist discourses' (Hayward 2000: 97). For Hayward, there is a 'symbolic value of the female body within nationalist discourses as a way of discussing the *mise-en-scène* of national culture' (ibid.: 99). In *Rosetta, Deux jours, une nuit,* and, to a lesser extent, in *Le gamin au vélo*, the female body is charged with agency, which heightens and intensifies the withering of patriarchal culture and patriarchal filiation in Wallonia and Walloon filmmaking. Luc Dardenne notes that Seraing offers their films a 'unique backdrop' where the main characters of their films represent the fathers, mothers, sons and daughters of Seraing (2015: 144). The films place an added emphasis on the way women and children are represented in film, and this has a connection to the state of the nation.

The Cinémathèque Suisse's (2012a) film festival offers the notion of a 'new francophone Belgian cinema' that overlooks the Dardenne brothers in favour of 'young' and emerging filmmakers, such as Joachim Lafosse, Bouli Lanners and Olivier Masset-Depasse, who are included in this book, as well as Yolande Moreau, Fabrice du Welz and Micha Wald. The aforementioned 'Fifty years of Belgian cinema' selection (2017–18) is also more inclusive and less invested in catch-all and straightforward appellations that simplify a diverse group of filmmakers. Value judgements and critical interpretations of these filmmakers' works – particularly by film critics and film festival programmers – often cohere with the Dardenne brothers' corpus of work due to either their 'low budget' mode of film financing (Lafosse) or their engagement with social issues and shared thematic concerns (Belvaux, Lanners and Masset-Depasse). This approach to filmmaking arises as a response to the financial constraints that the filmmakers are working under in the context of a 'cinema of small nations' (Hjort and Petrie 2007).

La revue toudi (Centre d'études wallonnes et de République 2013) highlighted the discernible absence of a 'popular cinema' produced in Wallonia. As outlined in Chapter One, the Dardenne brothers' films consistently receive the highest levels of admissions for films made in Wallonia. The online magazine also valorises the work of the Dardenne brothers as part of 'Walloon cinema', commencing with *Je pense à vous* and continuing to *Le gamin au vélo*. Alongside the Dardenne brothers, the short and feature films of contemporaneous filmmakers Benoît Mariage, Bouli Lanners and Thomas De Thier are equally discussed and celebrated by *La revue toudi* as interpellations of a 'regional' cinema in the south of the country.[6] However, it is important to note that the Dardenne brothers did not sign the *Manifeste pour la culture wallonne* in the 1980s, unlike the Walloon filmmakers Jean-Jacques Andrien and Thierry Michel. Instead, the Dardenne brothers have become the reference point for a 'social cinema' and auteur-centred cinema in the (francophone) Belgian context due to their comparatively high levels of Walloon box-office receipts. This 'national' decoding in film criticism overlooks the nuances of the francophone Belgian community's filmmaking output.

Whilst Luc Dardenne (2008: 75) refuses to acknowledge regional, national and supranational appellations as a filmmaker, the regional (Wallonia) and the local remain particularly strong in terms of the location of the films and the themes and issues that are articulated in their works. In his first journal and in interviews, Luc Dardenne indirectly references the relevance of the local and 'national' – or in the case of Belgium the 'regional' – context for film production. In the context of the Polish filmmaker Krzysztof Kieślowski and Norwegian filmmaker Joachim Trier, Luc Dardenne discusses the importance of a 'specificity' linked to a local context:[7]

> [Trier] articulates a place, a language, a way of dressing, specific local customs and food. All of this we see in ourselves, a film is anchored in these specificities – even though we use the same, universal film language. (Dardenne and Fontaine 2013)

In this extract, Luc Dardenne implies the importance of a specific location and local environment to his own films.

Although Mosley contends that there is stylistic and thematic filiation to Kieślowski (Mosley 2013: 36), Jean-Pierre Dardenne posits that Kieślowski's *Dekalog* offered the filmmakers a framework, and an approach to space that resonates with their own personal experience of Seraing (Lowy 2016: 84). Jean-Pierre Dardenne posits that as 'all of the stories [of *Dekalog*] occur in the same apartment building', there is a close proximity and an implicit interaction between the network of stories in the series (Lowy 2016: 84). The *mise-en-scène* of the apartment building offers a recognisable and 'familiar' space that is 'inhabited by millions of Poles' (Mazierska 2004: 26), which resonates with Seraing that could substitute for the post-industrialised and de-industrialised towns across western Europe, particularly the United Kingdom, (northern) France and, of course, Wallonia. Moreover, Kieślowski's articulation of space is 'full of pitiless people, moving in a grey, robotic atmosphere alone, isolated, and lonely' (Santilli 2006: 149). Loneliness and isolation emerge as distinct themes ironically in a space that should be full of possibilities of human interaction. The intentionality – on behalf of the filmmakers – reverberates through

Romney's assessment of *Le gamin au vélo* in which the critic posits that 'the Dardenne brothers have made a bleak industrial town in Belgium a microcosm of all human life' (Romney 2012: 40). As Luc and Jean-Pierre Dardenne discuss in the context of *Deux jours, une nuit,* the apartment block analogy is echoed in their spatial dynamics and sense of place, since they posit that 'Manu and Sandra's house (*Deux jours, une nuit*) is opposite Samantha's salon' (*Le gamin au vélo*), and that the building in which Roger lives in *La promesse* is in close proximity (Lowy 2016: 77).

From this premise, the transnational references are used to, in fact, reaffirm the local. The Dardenne brothers do have a 'regional' and local remit in terms of the filming location of the Liège-Seraing basin throughout their films. The filmmakers have, intentionally, chosen to locate their films within the former industrial area, and this consequently, and indirectly, brings to light certain Walloon social issues, such as sentiments of abandonment, the loss of a 'regional' working-class identity and social marginalisation.

This discussion provides clear references as to how far the Dardenne brothers have come to define (francophone) Belgian cinema from a regional, national and international perspective. This decoding of the filmmakers resonates with Higson's revision of 'the concept of national cinema', in which he reconsiders the assumptions that the 'national' is 'fixed' (2000: 67). The 'national' framework is therefore 'limiting' (Higson 2000), since the Dardenne brothers' stylistic filiation and social themes encourage a 'transnational' interpretation of their filmmaking style in relation to wider European and French cinema and even a 'regional' Walloon cinema. Let us now consider a detailed examination of the spatial dynamics offered throughout the Dardenne brothers' films from *La promesse* in order to better understand how Seraing is depicted and framed through the movement of the characters, and, by proxy, the movement of the camera.

The Spatial Dynamics of the Dardenne Brothers' Seraing

Drawing straightforward continuities from the Dardenne brothers' video documentaries through to the post-*La promesse* films is particularly problematic due to the filmmakers' self-conscious stylistic shift towards character-led characters and an immediate and 'urgent realism' (O'Shaughnessy 2003; Mathijs 2004a; Hessels 2004). The video documentaries (1978–87) and the later *Je pense à vous* (1992) do, however, introduce the semantic building blocks, such as the river, to the representations of a suburban geography. As Luc Dardenne notes, although Seraing exists as a town, it is also an 'imaginary' construct as articulated through film and cinema (Lowy 2016: 64). In the Dardenne brothers' films, the central protagonists are all driven and determined, thereby articulating, nuancing and offering a diversity of spatial dynamics across the post-industrial town of Seraing. The characters' senses of place – their rootlessness and homelessness – rise to the surface through their constant movement and peripatetic work patterns. Nevertheless, an analysis and a deciphering of the Dardenne brothers' spatial dynamics has remained an important topic in film reviews and academic scholarship, particularly in the context of the post-industrial town of Seraing. When considering how the Dardenne brothers articulate space through lines drawn and dynamics created in the movements of the characters, it is important to open with the filmmakers' initial framing of Seraing.

The Dardenne brothers' landscape has proved a site of critical analysis, with space and place underpinning the *Revue Belge*'s (1996/1997) reassessment and celebration of the Dardenne brothers, twenty years after releasing their first video documentary. This covers the reverberations and poetics of the Dardenne brothers' articulation of place, space and landscape up to and including *La promesse*, a clear watermark of their films. Lesuisse proffers three 'stages' of the 'one' industrial-post-industrial landscape (1996/1997: 43–9), which proves instructive for deciphering the filmic representation of Seraing's spatial dynamics. According to Lesuisse, the first stage concerns the 'landscape and architecture of the present [...] that] engages with memory and the act of narrating' (1996/1997: 43), the second concerns the distancing from the landscape on a formal level (such as wide framing and panoramas) capturing the 'industrial vestiges' (1996/1997: 46), and the third stage, inclusive of *La promesse*, offers 'an individual affair, more than place' (1996/1997: 48). This final stage proves most fruitful for interrogating and analysing the Dardenne brothers' feature filmmaking. The stylistic shift is more marked for approaching the spatial dynamics and their evocation in the Dardenne brothers' films, rather than purely location. The articulation of space is tied with the movement and mobility of the character, with a glimpse of the 'industrial vestiges' captured in the background, Seraing and the working-class suburb as milieu. Tomasovic (1996/1997) observes that the journey represents a motif that underpins the Dardenne brothers' films, citing references to forms of transport. These references evidently pertain to movement and mobility. Gabriel (2008) contends that since *La promesse* the filmmakers actively 'hide' (cache) the landscapes through the tight framing and close proximity to the characters – a notion developed from Luc Dardenne's first published journal in which the landscapes are 'covered up' (2008: 170). Since *Le silence de Lorna* (2008), and as analysed in the later section focused on *Le gamin au vélo* and *Deux jours, une nuit,* the Dardenne brothers' aesthetic and style is less preoccupied with so-called 'urgent realism' and immediacy, but it is still character-driven. Since *L'enfant* (2005), the modes of production and the filmmaking approach have gradually developed and become more nuanced, adopting more distance from their enunciating subjects (Mosley 2013: 7).

In the case of *La promesse*, Lesuisse contends that Seraing (or put more simply, the film's location) is conceived as

> a labyrinth that it is necessary to avoid, a spatial value that is necessary to bypass in order to find another possible route, or something that you have to block off by staying confined within yourself, and by signaling the presence of your own walls. (Lesuisse 1996/1997: 48)

Lesuisse (ibid.) notes the fleeting presence of the 'factory platform' and 'the bridge on the way to the station', which configure Seraing, and Wallonia, as a point of departure and one that needs to be escaped. The semantic pieces of the analysed *mise-en-scène* represent places of transit. Rather than ruminating on the significance of 'industrial vestiges', the characters attempt to transcend the town and landscape offered by the filmmakers through motifs pertaining to the act of journeying. In contrast to this interpretation, Fontaine posits that the former industrial suburb evokes a 'concentration camp' through its 'brutal depiction of poverty' and the 'paroxysm of exploitation between men' (Fontaine 1996) in the global, neoliberal capitalist system. It is this pervading sense of exploitation that permeates the subsequent films of *Rosetta*, *L'enfant*, *Le silence de Lorna*, and *Deux jours, une nuit*. Moreover, Fontaine (1996) still draws the line within Walloon cinema and the articulation of space that is concomitant between the established filmmakers of Manu Bonmariage and Thierry Michel. In this case, the spectator continues to be consistently orientated through the framing of the landscape, which, for Fontaine (1996), is still recognisable as local. Fontaine further states that 'these panoramas of the industrial *Liégeois* suburb [. . .] are regularly offered to us throughout Walloon cinema as striking images' (Fontaine 1996). Mosley contends that such imagery gives rise to memory (and more particularly 'anxiety'), positing that '[t]he opening shot of *La promesse*, showing a convoy of transient workers climbing down from an automobile transporter in front of an abandoned factory, powerfully contrasts this post-industrial society with its predecessor' (2002: 164). Developing from Mosley's (2002) approach, Dillet and Puri note that '[t]he only access the audience has to history and time is through the optics of the place' (Dillet and Puri 2013: 368). The industrialism of the suburb speaks from the background, positing and explicating the poverty experienced by the individual characters.

For *Rosetta*, there is a clear delineation between the margins and the centre, which operates thematically as well as spatially and geographically. Lefort contends that the film offers 'a private geography [that] is her personal history, her intimate revenge and last rites' (Lefort 1999). It represents potentially one story of many that unfold, as evinced through the recurrent 'leftover spaces' (Dillet and Puri 2013). In his first published journal, Luc Dardenne proposes the existence of a centre–periphery dynamic for the film that chimes with Bourdieu's (1999a) conception of 'lieux' [sites]. Bourdieu alludes to 'a spatial distance that affirms social distance' (1999a: 126), alongside '[t]he lack of capital [that] chains one to a place' (1999a: 127).[8] The filmmaker describes a society that places the character of Rosetta on the margins: 'and so appears a society for those who find themselves thrown outside; like a fortress that cannot be re-entered' (Dardenne 2008: 66). This certainly highlights the importance of how the town of Seraing is navigated by the character in the film, since it is representative of social relations. In *Rosetta*, the central protagonist lives in a caravan park and she is required to travel through woodland to work first in waffle production and then on a waffle stand. The film offers a centre-periphery model, as Rosetta clearly descends through the woodland to the caravan park, known as Grand Canyon (metonymically referring to a hole), with employment placed at a geographically higher point. The society that Luc Dardenne outlines is one that is characterised as a 'fortress that cannot be re-entered', which suggests that it is an unattainable centre for the characters. Comparing the character of Marie from *La vie rêvée des anges/The Dreamlife of Angels* (Erick Zonca, 1998) and Rosetta from *Rosetta*, O'Shaughnessy contends that '[r]ather than suggesting that the excluded are on the outside because they are insufficiently like insiders, it shows that, faced with structured exclusion, the outsiders can only survive by rejecting the system's "reality principle"' (2003: 198). From this premise, Rosetta can avoid exclusion only through a direct acknowledgement of the frailties, problems and insufficiencies in the neoliberal capitalist system, achieving status as an 'insider' through a rejection of 'competitive individualism', a notion noted by O'Shaughnessy (2003; 2008). This is precisely what underlines Sandra's ambition in *Deux jours, une nuit*. As Sandra walks away proudly from the solar panel factory, she deliberately eschews the neoliberal spirit of competitive individualism, as explored by O'Shaughnessy (2003; 2007), representing a moral victory and one that again, distances her from the so-called impenetrable 'fortress'.

Whereas these previous films explore the interior and exterior of the town of Seraing, creating spatial dynamics through mobility outdoors, *Le fils/The Son* (Jean-Pierre and Luc Dardenne, 2002) is more concerned with interior settings and *mise-en-scène*. Drawing on Luc Dardenne's first journal, O'Shaughnessy (2008: 74–7) describes the construction of space in the film as a 'labyrinth' in which the characters are 'trapped'. The interior *mise-en-scène* is particularly noted by André in his review of *Le fils* in *La revue toudi*, in which the critic observes that 'what distinguishes Walloon cinema or what gives it its own form is its representation of public space and civil society [. . .] The Dardenne brothers do not resort to what could be called "national discourse"' (André 2003). The 'labyrinth', as discussed by Luc Dardenne and O'Shaughnessy, does not engage with André's notion of a Walloon 'public space', but the film still articulates the father-and-son dynamic and a sense of entrapment.

In *L'enfant*, the references to Seraing's industrial heritage lurk in the background, the pipes from the Cockerill steelworks permeate the visual representation of the city, particularly as Bruno and Steve escape on a moped, after snatching the earnings of a second-hand store which are on the way to being banked. The withering industrial blast furnace is glimpsed in the background, particularly as the pair descend through a pedestrian bypass in the heart of the Dardenne brothers' hometown. However, rather than these manufacturing and industrial units being the centre for a productive dialogue (as was the case for the video documentaries) as reference points, in *L'enfant* they are mere glimpses as the camera (and the spectator) focuses primarily on the central protagonist, Bruno. The bus is also used to travel across the post-industrial suburb, positing a certain distance within the space and a dispersed community – a strategy that re-emerges in *Deux jours, une nuit*. Bruno uses the bus on four occasions, three pertaining to the selling and regaining of Jimmy (his son, sold on the black market) in indiscriminate tower blocks and garages on the outskirts of the town, and the fourth when following Sonia and Jimmy back from the hospital to their apartment. On two occasions, the bus runs parallel to the flow of the river (captured in the background), as Bruno is leaving and returning to the centre, their apartment and the shelter. The characters represent mobile 'atoms', without any fixity. The proximity of the camera to the body stretches further back than *Rosetta*. In essence, the 'vestiges', as Lesuisse observes (1996/1997), are captured inadvertently. The Dardenne brothers posit,

> it is necessary to observe him, to see him in the landscape, along the river, and on the bridge amongst the cars. Therefore, it is from this point that we have moved towards another mode of filmmaking, which is prevalent in two moments in the film when he is alone with the baby and when we are with him a little more. We discover things with him, and it is then where we find ourselves a little closer to him [with the camera] and sometimes behind him, like we were behind Rosetta [in *Rosetta*]. (Lowy 2016: 30)

In this case, it is salient to how that the character is situated within the space of the suburb, the references lurking in the background to orientate and locate the spectator, in order to understand how Bruno navigates an alienating and unforgiving place. His place is characterised as isolating, which is evinced by the shelter on the riverbanks, in which Bruno sleeps overnight. François André posits that 'the Meuse [the river] occupies the central role; the final pursuit drives him [Bruno] to climb and descend almost endlessly with the riverbanks sealing his fate when he plunges in it with his accomplice, and Bruno's feelings float literally to the surface: fear, hope, solidarity and also guilt' (André 2006). Following André's line of argument, it is the journey through the small town of Seraing, passing through from one side to the opposite side (that is, through the underpass), culminates in Bruno's decision to eschew theft as the seedy underside of neoliberalism for solidarity with Steve, Sonia and Jimmy. In fact, the river does not constitute a clear 'leftover space', with Dillet and Puri placing more emphasis on the motorway by its side (2013: 375–6). As discussed in the next section, when analysing *Le gamin au vélo* and *Deux jours, une nuit*, the river is more invested with cultural specificity and, consequently, points to particularism.

In terms of *Le silence de Lorna*, Walloon film critic André (2009b) laments the stylistic, filmic (from 16mm to 35mm), and *mise-en-scène* changes in the film that offer a 'demi-rupture' from the films up to *L'enfant*. André observes that the film is marked by a 'temporary goodbye' from the landscapes of Seraing and from the 'nourishing Meuse' river that lurks in the background to 'profit from' the depiction of the centre of the city of Liège. As a result, the film is 'less anchored' and is freed from a 'social texture' (André 2009b), but this enables a consideration in the more 'anonymous' spaces of the woodland that reverberates through the Dardenne brothers' films and marks the conclusion to *Le silence de Lorna* (Dillet and Puri 2013: 373–4). However, in *Le silence de Lorna*, the imagery of Seraing and its industrial heritage speaks from the background. A picture of the Cockerill plant in Seraing is seen one hour and two minutes into the film. The image is situated behind the two characters of Lorna and her partner Sokol as they dance in a bar in the neighbouring city of Liège (Figure 2.2). It is significant to note that the image captures the Cockerill plant in its pomp and during the period of industrialisation in the town and in Wallonia.[9] This further foregrounds the relevance of the loss of employment and collective solidarity in the region that remains beneath the images on a 'topical' (Hjort 2000: 105–7) thematic level.

Overall, the space of Seraing, and the spatial dynamics formed through the camera tracking the character in close proximity, is constructed as a spiral, constantly operating on the margins, and underlining itself in a movement that serves to pull the characters into a vortex. As O'Shaughnessy observes, the Dardenne brothers depict 'a world where values are no longer transmitted between generations, so that the young are left to find their place and to deal with others without symbolic resources or inherited values' (2007: 114). The notion of emptiness permeates the Dardenne brothers' films on a thematic level. Let us now turn to an analysis of how the key socio-economic issues in *Le gamin au vélo* and *Deux jours, une nuit* are represented and articulated in this context.

'NO FUTURE'

Figure 2.2   In *Le silence de Lorna*, Lorna and Sokol dance in a Liégeois bar, with an image of Seraing in its pomp, hidden in the background.

MOBILE BODIES: MARGINAL CHARACTERS AND MARGINAL SPACES IN
LE GAMIN AU VÉLO AND *DEUX JOURS, UNE NUIT*

Le gamin au vélo and *Deux jours, une nuit* were conceived, written and filmed in a different phase of European sociopolitical history to their previous films considered in relation to so-called French New Realism. However, there is a certain imbrication between the economic crisis of 2008 and the subsequent issues of unemployment, social precariousness and social marginality in the case of the Dardenne brothers films from 2011 and 2014, given that Luc Dardenne (2015) extensively notes that *Deux jours, une nuit* was partly inspired by Bourdieu's (1999b) sociological study *Weight of the World* and François Bon's (2004) *Daewoo*.[10] Whereas *Le gamin au vélo* is not necessarily linked to a specific socio-economic context, *Deux jours, une nuit* clearly articulates sociopolitical issues that arose in the late 1990s and have re-emerged after the economic crisis of 2008. In his review of *Le gamin au vélo* for *La revue toudi*, André (2011) outlines the gradual deterioration of the relationship between the father and son across the Dardenne brothers' films post-1996. The question of filiation remains within their work, underpinning the narratives that have gradually turned to more female-orientated stories, as a new articulation of nation. In the case of Cyril, André (2011) contends that there is 'nothing more to transmit' between father and son, and this clearly points to the change in the region's economic base. The 'future' – as initially highlighted by O'Shaughnessy (2007) – has a certain salience to this discussion of *Le gamin au vélo* and *Deux jours, une nuit*, since the two films take place in the same town. They deal with themes pertaining to the change in the forms of employment in the region and competitive individualism.

In the case of *Deux jours, une nuit*, the subject matter clearly bears witness to intertextual and transnational influences, since the film's narrative draws upon events that took place in the USA (the 'reality' show *Someone's Gotta Go*), France (Bourdieu and Bon) and in Belgium. These initial sources of inspiration – from France and Belgium – are particularly suggestive of the 'transnational' and 'regional' interpretations being placed side by side in relation to the Dardenne brothers' films due to their geographically contiguous nature. The Belgian example derives from a news item that Luc Dardenne watched about an individual from Charleroi – an economically deprived town due to the loss of industry in Wallonia – who 'attempted to commit suicide after the CPAS (Centre Public d'Action Sociale) refused to provide the individual with financial support' (Denis 2014b: 5). Bon's novel *Daewoo* charts the closure of three factories in the Lorraine region of eastern France – which borders Wallonia to the south – drawing on official documents and interviews with individuals (Altes 2008: 80–94). Finally, in Bourdieu's *Weight of the World*, Pialoux's (1999: 321–37) section on 'The Shop Steward's World in Disarray' outlines a series of events, from an individual's personal account, that occurred in the new Peugeot plant in Montbéliard, Sochaux (France) – close to the border with both Switzerland and Germany – in the 1990s.[11]

Bourdieu's (1999b) study highlights the breakdown of collective solidarity in the workforce on the assembly line, with a parlous atmosphere being created between the foremen and the workers. As Pialoux (1999: 328–9) recounts, a petition was drawn up to remove the perceived 'weaker' member of the assembly line in order for the rest to receive an extra 50 francs. In this case, the workers are handed a certain responsibility in terms of monitoring their colleagues. In *Le Monde*, the Dardenne brothers assert that 'the new and constant methods of evaluating employees has contributed to the breakdown of the workers' solidarity – with them instead becoming atomised individuals – without being able to oppose the management's logic' (Mandelbaum 2014: 13). In this sense, the vote – set to take place on Monday morning in the film – undermines collective solidarity in the workplace to create an increasingly fragmented working environment on the assembly line. The film consequently highlights the failure of trade unions to support members of their own workforce in small companies, such as the fictional manufacturing firm Solwal in *Deux jours, une nuit*. Beaud's (1999: 282–96) section on 'The Temp's Dream' outlines the struggles of young workers on temporary contracts and their desire for a permanent deal at the Peugeot plant in Montbéliard. In the Dardenne brothers' film, the perceived 'fear' of the foremen – who are able to extend short-term contracts for the temporary and peripatetic workers – casts a shadow over the decisions made in the vote by the workers on short-term contracts. This is articulated through Jean-Marc's manipulation of his employees, as he tries to imbue a sense of fear and mistrust amongst the co-workers regarding their own future at the plant.

The notion of space, and the characters' place within it, becomes a crucial nodal point between *Le gamin au vélo* and *Deux jours, une nuit*. Both films are characterised by movement and the mobility of the characters through space. In his analysis of space in contemporary French cinema, Williams draws on De Certeau to highlight that 'space is always a frequented, "practised" place' (2013: 8). The example that Williams notes via De Certeau is that 'a place is like a street geometrically defined by urban planning, but transformed into a space by walkers' (Williams 2013: 8). From this premise, the Dardenne brothers, through the characters of Sandra and Cyril, take the urban geography of a post-industrial Seraing and modify it through the character and camera's mobility. The spatial dynamics are predicated on movement, and through intertextual references, the suburb is transformed into an evocation of marginality that transcends borders and boundaries. The spaces that the Dardenne brothers include in their narratives are generic, and intensify the characters' marginality. Dillet and Puri's (2013) 'leftover spaces' in the Dardenne brothers' tradition, such as motorways, woodland, and the campsites, arise from Augé's (1995) oft-cited 'non-places' in which 'villages, churches, even factories, disappear from both the landscape and from everyday life, being replaced by hotels, motorways, metros, and shopping centres, which then impose a certain kind of anonymity and homogeneity' (Dillet and Puri 2013: 374). As Williams deduces, these 'non-places' 'discourage organic social life' as opposed to 'places' that 'are historical, relational, concerned with identity, and creative of social life' (Williams 2013: 9). The locations offered in *Le gamin au vélo* and *Deux jours, une nuit* fall somewhere between the two notions, emphasising distance and encouraging mobility through references to fixed points. In part, through the movement of the characters, the Dardenne brothers create spaces and dynamics that hold onto preconceived ideas of constructing 'place'. This results in the river taking on historical and symbolic value, running through the heart of the town and its former industries, in the context of *Le gamin au vélo*. As Hardt and Negri posit,

> What needs to be addressed, instead, is precisely the *production of locality*, that is, the social machines that create and re-create the identities and differences that are understood as local. The differences of locality are neither preexisting nor natural but rather effects of a regime of production [. . .] The Leftist strategy of resistance to globalisation and defense of locality is also damaging because in many cases what appear as local identities are not autonomous or self-determining but actually

feed into and support the development of the capitalist imperial machine. (Hardt and Negri 2000: 45)

The 'leftovers' of the Dardenne brothers' films seemingly represent an industrial mode of production as place, with the nostalgic memory of the working-class location. It also points to the reliance on the question of patriarchal filiation within the context of industrial production, which reverberates through their films. Although, a sense of renewal is offered through the 'maternal body' (Hayward 2000: 99) in *Le gamin au vélo* and *Deux jours, une nuit* as a site of progress and renewal of nation. In *Le gamin au vélo* and *Deux jours, une nuit*, spatial distance is clearly articulated through the banality of the daily routine, the rituals of travel and constant movement, which represent Cyril and Sandra's displacement from the industrial centre.

For *Deux jours, une nuit,* intertextual connections with films outside the Belgian context were limited, with national and international film criticism primarily foregrounding how the film can be read in relation to the Dardenne brothers' previous film *Rosetta* (Bradfer 2014; Lefort and Séguret 2014; Regnier 2014; Stevens 2014). This textual reference within the filmmakers' own films highlights the recurring social themes and issues – such as social exclusion and issues around stable employment – that remain significant in a different socio-economic context, that is in post-2008 Europe. Cohen's (2014) article for *The Observer* entitled 'Two Days, One Night: a film that illuminates the despair of the low paid' uses the film as a starting point to provoke a debate around the difficulty in maintaining a sense of solidarity amongst workers with temporary, short-term and 'bulimic' working contracts in labour markets in the USA and Western Europe. The comparison between the two films is primarily predicated on the inclusion of similar themes, such as issues of (un-)employment and the focus on a central female protagonist who is fighting to retain her job. Luc Dardenne posits a clear difference between the two female characters, Rosetta and Sandra, by suggesting that Rosetta is 'a good little soldier of capitalism' (Stevens 2014: 66). In this sense, Rosetta understands that she is required to compete against her peers for limited opportunities in a neoliberal capitalist economy. She is ruthless in her ambitions to find and create her own place in this 'society'. The Dardenne brothers' concept of 'society' is fragmented with peripatetic contracts for workers. For example, once Rosetta's contract ends, another young worker replaces her on a temporary contract. This focus on female characters at the centre of these employment struggles echoes *La vie rêvée des anges/The Dreamlife of Angels* (Erick Zonca, 1998), which follows Isa and Marie's short-term work in factories across the conterminous border in Lille, Nord-Pas-de-Calais. In *Deux jours, une nuit,* Sandra succumbs to the fear of social exclusion and social insecurity with an attempt to take her own life by overdosing on the antidepressant drug

Xanax. This scene recalls Marie's suicide as she leaps from her apartment window in *La vie rêvée des anges*, and Rosetta's attempt to gas herself and her mother in their caravan in *Rosetta*.

The cartography of a dispersed and fragmented community is emphasised as Sandra travels to the residences of each of her co-workers. As Sandra asks her co-workers to vote for her to retain her employment, she is recalling the social struggle and the collective spirit that O'Shaughnessy (2007; 2008) identifies in the Dardenne brothers' early video documentaries. Sandra provides a muted resistance, since she appeals to her co-workers with a level of understanding for her colleagues' positions. As O'Shaughnessy posits, the continuities on a thematic level have evolved and modified from the video documentaries to the feature films:

> [t]he documentaries recorded the dismantling of the old working class and the failing transmission of collective values. Operating in a space where the collective has been demolished, the fictions pursue the study of a crisis of transmission in the narrower sphere of family. (O'Shaughnessy 2008: 75)

Luc Dardenne suggests a connection back to his earlier video documentaries during the writing of *Deux jours, une nuit*. In the 2015 journal, Luc Dardenne suggests that Sandra (called Samantha at this point in the early screenplay drafts) could visit one of her co-workers in the Fagnes estate, the home to a lady they once interviewed for their documentaries in the 1970s (2015: 133–4). This encourages the filmmaker to consider the changing nature of rivalry and the competitive neoliberal economic environment that has developed since the 1970s in which there is a 'rivalry between individuals and an investment in objects' (2015: 135).

With each of her visits, Sandra is trying to (re-)draw her co-workers back into a sense of community and collective. She is attempting to undermine the competitive environment and rivalry between co-workers that was previously articulated in *Rosetta*. In the impromptu meeting with Julien, he asks Sandra to '*[e]ssaie de te mettre à ma place*' ('try to put yourself in my shoes') (2015: 361). This exchange of '*mettre à ma place*' calls for understanding and mutual respect on behalf of the colleagues, despite Julien's decision not to vote for Sandra. There is a demand to consider the plight and difficulties that all the workers are suffering from in the represented socio-economic situation. This contrasts with Rosetta's need to '*prendre la place*' ('to take the place') of a fellow citizen due to the increased sense of rivalry.

The Dardenne brothers' framing devices articulate Sandra's position as a social 'atom' or 'fragment' (Osganian 2003), as O'Shaughnessy (2007) also draws on with regards to the Dardenne brothers' preceding feature films.

Within each of the meetings, the Dardenne brothers introduce physical borders. Luc Dardenne's journal on re-watching the film's rushes notes that,

> [e]diting [the sequence] into different shots would seem to show an intention to convey meaning when the continuity of our sequence shot attempts to follow only Sandra's body despite the obstacles she comes up against. Obstacles are able to become obstacles between Sandra's body and those that she meets. (2015: 225)

As the meetings unfold, the spectator is offered Sandra's restricted view of each meeting, since the camera only tracks Sandra's body. Nuttens posits that these obstacles are intrinsically physical (2014: 9). For instance, this is represented through the recurrence of the obstacles and barriers in each meeting: with Willy (the frame of an outdoor shelving unit), Nadine (the intercom), Timur (a barrier on the edge of a football pitch), Hicham (a tote box full of carrots), Yvon and Jerôme (two car doors), Anne (the corner of her house's exterior wall), Julien (guttering), Dominique (a doorway) and Alphonse (a laundry basket) (L. Dardenne 2015: 224). The consistent fragmenting of the frame develops an interior/exterior binary that anticipates the vote in which those employed as workers in the solar panel plant hold sway over the possible (social) exclusion of Sandra. To this end, the obstacles operate as 'metonymical (rather than metaphorical) links' (Williams 2013: 8) that point to the characters' place within the conceived space. The spectator sees each worker as an individual, which recalls the atomisation of the regional working class and Walloon sense of identity.

Let us briefly consider the meeting between Sandra and Mireille (Figure 2.3), the third of the nine meetings presented in the film. As the spectator experiences the totality of the interaction – from start to finish in 'real time' – they become aware of the seemingly irrelevant aspects of the *mise-en-scène* (L. Dardenne 2015: 224). Obstacles emerge between Sandra and her colleagues in the frame. This starts with the characters first meeting in doorways, which represents a liminal space between the private and the public spheres. In this sequence, Sandra and Mireille are placed either side of the image, Sandra on the left (the outside) with Mireille on the right (on the inside). The vertical line of the doorway immediately interrupts the image positing Sandra's marginality and exclusion. This is furthered by the introduction of an unknown female individual who walks through the centre of the frame between Sandra and Mireille, with both of the characters taking a step back, reasserting this distance.

Despite the aforementioned transnational influences on *Deux jours, une nuit*'s story, the film is concerned with local and regional issues, particularly the decline of Belgian and Walloon heavy industry. This is engendered by the use of the suburbs of the Liégeois industrial basin, incorporating the areas

Figure 2.3 Sandra meets with Mireille in the reception area of her apartment block in *Deux jours, une nuit*.

of Sclessin, Seraing and Flémalle. These areas all have a rich tradition for communities founded on the steel industries along the river, La Meuse. The clear inclusion of these locations emphasises the shifting economy in the small industrial towns of Wallonia. Seraing has become representative of the plight of Walloon working-class communities in an ever-evolving neoliberal capitalist economy by virtue of its references in the Dardenne brothers' films.

The notion of distance is used twofold in this film, since it highlights the plight of the central character and her struggle to remain in stable employment and income in the factory, as well as the breakdown of the sense of community. Sandra's constant movement is foregrounded through the use of several forms of transport throughout the film, as she travels by bus, car and on foot. The bus emerges as a frequent mode of transport for the Dardenne brothers' characters, since it is used by Rosetta and Cyril as part of their journeys to the 'centre' of the town. Sandra instead uses the bus as a means of locating her colleagues at the solar panel manufacturing firm. During these journeys, the character encounters examples of 'left-over spaces' (Dillet and Puri 2013), such as the motorway that runs through the centre of Seraing next to the river, La Meuse. As Sandra travels on the bus, the spectator glimpses the river in the background (Figure 2.4). As Dillet and Puri note, '[t]he river gave a new spatiality to their film: a desire to enlarge the plan of their film and not to simply produce a closed cinematic experience, not to remain with the handheld camera close to the body' (2013: 375). Luc Dardenne recalls the significance of the river during his childhood as an impulse and energy that

Figure 2.4 In *Deux jours, une nuit,* Sandra takes her Xanax pills as she travels to her next meeting on the bus, with the Meuse glimpsed in the background.

flowed with goods and forms of 'capital' to and from the industrial suburbs of Liège (Centre d'études wallonnes et de République 2013). This 'memory' for Luc Dardenne recalls Seraing in its pomp, placing the river at the centre of the town's industrial prestige. In *Deux jours, une nuit,* the river is part of the milieu for the action to take place, but there is a discernible absence of barges using the waterway, evoking Bruno's bus journeys in *L'enfant*. The glimpse of the river reinforces the changes in the economic background for the town and the region, revealing the reasons for the socio-economic issues that underpin the film.

Luc Dardenne highlights the significance of Sandra's constant movements and the focus on her walking to meet her co-workers, particularly in the context of the end of the film. He writes '[w]alking, it is the movement of those who leave the factory alone, it is the movement of those who look for a job, it is also the movement of those who fight against adversity' (2015: 221). Her body sets the tempo for the movement of the camera, with Denis highlighting how the 'camera has not settled down, it beats to Sandra's rhythm' (Denis 2014b: 4). The distances that Sandra is required to cover to visit each of her colleagues individually implies the difficulty in remaining in this 'centre' of employment and 'society', in the Dardenne brothers' words. It also nuances a reading of the changing composition of the sense of community in the town of Seraing on a local level. Jean-Pierre Dardenne notes how this travelling highlights how the geography of the small former working class town of Seraing has 'disappeared' and dispersed (Benoliel and Toubiana 2014). Sandra does not know where all of her co-workers live, and this highlights the fact that the close-knit, local community, once forged in the period of rapid industrialisation, is no longer apparent in the post-industrial and regional context.

Sandra's residence also highlights the character's position, and serves as a further means of positing her possible social exclusion with the loss of employment. Sandra and Manu live in a modest house on an estate where other working-class inhabitants of Seraing reside (Dardenne 2015: 216). The couple previously lived in an apartment *habitation à loyer modéré* (rent-controlled housing), which is considered by Manu as 'retomber' (2015: 217), or a regression in terms of social status in the Dardenne brothers' conception of society. The vote at the solar panel firm and the potential loss of employment places the family's home – and the location of the household – under threat of displacement.

In international film criticism in the United Kingdom, USA and France, reviewers immediately pointed to *Le gamin au vélo*'s intertextual connections with the Italian Neorealist film *Ladri di biciclette/Bicycle Thieves* (Vittorio De Sica, 1948) (Bradshaw 2012; Debruge 2011: 19; Douin 2011; Fluctuanet.net 2011; Mosley 2013: 129). In the French newspaper *Le Monde*, Douin (2011) discusses the films' comparisons, which are 'aesthetic' (primarily in relation to the Dardenne brothers' filmmaking style) and 'thematic (a context of social marginalisation and poverty, issues around the maintenance of a family unit and a struggle against social injustice)'. The French-language quarterly film magazine *Ciné-bulles* (Hamel 2012: 46–9) – based in Quebec – outlines intertextual references to *Les quatre cents coups/The 400 blows* (François Truffaut, 1959), comparing the young male adolescent character of Antoine Doinel with *Le gamin au vélo*'s Cyril. Mosley (2013: 132) similarly posits that Cyril's opening escape from the youth-care centre is an 'homage' to Doinel's final escape from the youth correctional facility. These 'transnational' interpretations of the film are limited to film criticism and scholarly work outside Belgium, with francophone Belgian magazines – such as *Cinergie* and *La revue toudi* – eschewing such intertextual comparisons.

However, the Dardenne brothers' films *La promesse* and *Le gamin au vélo* have drawn comparisons with the aforementioned *Germany, Year Zero*. Mélon presciently draws the connection between Edmund, in *Germany, Year Zero*, and Igor in the Dardenne brothers' *La promesse* as 'les enfants de Prométhée' (the children of Prometheus) (1996/1997: 4–5). As Mosley contends,

> the teenager Edmund [. . .] resembles the Dardennes' young protagonists in living on the edge of society in difficult circumstances. With a rebellious attitude masking an inner despair, the blond Edmund physically resembles Igor in *The Promise*, Francis in *The Son* and Bruno in *The Child*. (2013: 34)

From this premise, it is not a far stretch to contend that the fair complexion extends to *Le gamin au vélo* and Cyril, who travels by bike around the margins of Seraing. Mai notes '[i]n *La promesse* there were already clear resemblances between the rubble-laden landscape of Rosselini's post-war Berlin in *Germany Year Zero* and post-industrial Seraing' (2010: 71). The documentary on the Dardenne brothers *L'âge de raison, le cinéma des frères Dardenne* (Luc Jabon, 2013) consolidates this intertextual allusion, intercutting between the two films' football sequences. *L'Âge de raison* shows Cyril looking on as a group of youths from the Val-Potet estate play football in a small five-a-side pitch (Figure 2.5), before cutting to Edmund as he briefly participates in the game of street football against the backdrop of Berlin's ruins. Whereas Grist notes that Edmund is 'rebuffed' in this sequence (2009: 20), Cyril looks on mournfully, uncertain as to whether to participate in the match. The barriers of the five-a-side pitch hold Cyril away from the action and the other children on the estate. Cyril is, therefore, positioned as an outsider. However, the documentary notes that Cyril is invited to participate, as the children 'lack a player', opening up the potential for inclusion. The so-called 'rubble' of post-war European cinema, evoked in *Germany, Year Zero*, reverberates through to the rubble of post-industrial and post-2008 Wallonia, and, in this case, the uncertainty of a sense of place in its former working-class suburbs.

In *Le gamin au vélo*, Cyril's struggle against abandonment is framed indirectly through his father's inability to retain reliable employment and to care for his son after the death of Cyril's grandmother. The Dardenne brothers

Figure 2.5 Cyril looks on as a group of children from the Val-Potet estate play a game of five-a-side football.

contend that Cyril's situation is a wider articulation of a breakdown of relations between father and son, and active competition that has led to the withering of social relations in the local community:

> It is true that in our society where relationships between people are rooted in competition and rivalry, where we are more engaged in war than in friendship and in love, the behaviour of this woman (Samantha) seems abnormal. He (Cyril) is accustomed to being lied to – starting with his father – whom he has been waiting for in the youth-care centre for a long time and who has never come to collect him. (Bouras 2011)

The acknowledgement that Samantha's decision to foster Cyril is 'abnormal' highlights the loss of the bonds in the community, compounded by his father's 'lies'. The references to 'war' recall the Dardenne brothers' thematic tendency to follow 'soldiers', as evinced by *Rosetta* and *Deux jours, une nuit*, which, therefore, heightens the individual's struggles in the post-industrial rubble. Moreover, the youth-care centre functions as a temporary 'site' of exclusion for the character of Cyril, in a similar way to how the caravan park is recognised as part of Rosetta's exclusion in *Rosetta*. Both of these 'sites' are geographically located on the fringes of the urban area (in both cases the town of Seraing), and the inhabitants of these spaces are marginal figures due to their lack of permanence, destabilised family units and employment for Cyril's father, Guy. For Cyril and Rosetta, the location of their residences forces the individuals to travel.

For Cyril, mobility is connected to his desire for acceptance into a family and community. Initially, Cyril's search for his bicycle is posited as a journey to find his father, with Jean-Pierre Dardenne suggesting that 'the bike represents both freedom and his father' (Rouyer and Tobin 2011: 12). The bicycle has a certain cultural validity in francophone Belgian cinema as a recurring motif, and this is paralleled by Bazin's interpretation of *Bicycle Thieves* in which 'the bicycle [. . .] is characteristic both of Italian urban life and of a period when mechanical means of transportation were still rare and expensive' (1971: 50). In *Le gamin au vélo*, the bicycle similarly represents a certain capital value for those who live in Seraing, as it is sold once by Cyril's father and stolen once by the estate's gang. In so doing, the film opens an intertextual dialogue with *Bicycle Thieves*: as Cyril searches for his father in the local brasserie, one moment is enough for an opportunistic youth to steal the bike – something that Cyril is forced to fight for. Mosley proposes that *Le gamin au vélo* 'twists' the plot of *Bicycle Thieves*, positing that 'in place of a father and son searching for a stolen bike, a son on his bike searches for his lost father' (Mosley 2013: 129). After escaping the youth-care centre, Cyril finds that his father's apartment is deserted and vacant, and he has sold Cyril's bicycle to pay his bills, echoing

Bruno's decision to rent out Sonia's apartment in *L'enfant* whilst she gives birth. The father figure is perceived as opportunistic and, at times, desperate for money. This opportunism permeates from *Bicycle Thieves*, as Antonio (the father) is drawn into stealing a bicycle, to replace his own. However, whilst Bazin contends that 'he [Antonio] is poor as ever, but now he feels the shame of having sunk to the level of the thief' (1971: 50), Guy does not show the same shame, remorse, or humility for his actions, that is, selling his son's bicycle. For Cyril, the absence of both his father and his bicycle heighten his abandonment.

When Samantha – Cyril's foster mother – returns the bicycle to Cyril, he is able to regain some mobility, but this serves only to further reinforce the dynamic between the margins and the centre. Luc Dardenne (in Dardenne 2011; Bonnaud 2012: 25) asserts that the space was formed in a 'triangular' manner, with the 'petrol station, the forest and the hairdressers' existing as the exterior points between which Cyril is required to travel. Each of these points of reference is non-specific and non-particularist to the local context, resonating with the potential for transnationality in the articulation of space, which is in contrast to the film's conclusion alongside the river. They evoke 'non-places' (Augé 1995), divested of cultural specificity through their anonymity, that is, these sites 'could be anywhere' in western and northern Europe. Whilst working in the restaurant kitchen in the town centre, Cyril's father forms a point of reference in the middle of this constructed triangle (Dardenne 2011). For Guy, money and employment are key factors in the decision to place Cyril in the youth-care centre, since he cannot afford to look after his son due to his limited wages and his long and irregular working hours. With the position of the father figure in the centre of the town (the location of the restaurant), there is a sense of distance created between the male adult and the child. Cyril is situated on the periphery through his repetitious journeys between the three fixed points. This is articulated geographically through the references to the location of Samantha's residence in Val-Potet. This '*cité*' [estate] on the margins of the town of Seraing emphasises Cyril's sense of social exclusion, with the circularity of his journeys being articulated through the repeated locations. With the absence of his mother and the precarity of his father's current employment, the child is placed in a situation in which he is left abandoned and in a fragmented family. These themes of abandoned children and fragmented families recall the so-called French New Realist film *Ça commence aujourd'hui/It all Starts Today* (Bertrand Tavernier, 1999) (see Vincendeau 1999).

Cyril's desired site of inclusion within a stable family environment (with his father) remains at the centre of this constructed 'triangle' (Luc Dardenne in Dardenne 2011; Bonnaud 2012), but this is a possibility that is refused to him by his father's unemotional attachment to his son. The father, Guy, is more concerned with his own individual existence within the competitive environment. Moreover, Guy, is able to obtain employment only in the service industry, which points to issues of filiation that were previously raised in *Je pense à vous* and is consistently referenced throughout the Dardenne brothers' films in terms of the tautological and 'topical' – with reference to Hjort (2000) – theme of loss of working class, male employment in the metal industries of Seraing. In *Le gamin au vélo*, the father has hence become disenfranchised by this shift in the post-industrial economy in Wallonia, since he is no longer able to maintain a relationship with his son. The absence of a father figure is further emphasised when Samantha's partner Gilles leaves her due to Cyril's lack of respect for the couple as foster parents. His foster care is also destabilised, which underlines the solitude and isolation of the individual in post-industrial Wallonia. The characters are unable to maintain consistent relationships, particularly in a family context, and this subsequently highlights the issues of competitive individualism. The 'future' of Wallonia and Seraing does not appear to be male, since it is instead infused with the maternal body in the case of *Le gamin au vélo* and *Deux jours, une nuit*.[12] The maternal also arises at the conclusion of *Le silence de Lorna*, with Lorna's posited pregnancy.

The lack of a father figure for Cyril leads the character to rebuild a sense of collective by siding with the estate drug dealer and petty criminal, Wes. Bauche contends that the theme of crime, and Cyril's descent into petty crime, 'recalls concentric circles' that pull the characters into the darkness (2011: 8) of neoliberal capitalism. Luc Dardenne frames Wes as 'another bad father', as he lures Cyril into the gang and gang culture (Lowy 2016: 60). This leads to Cyril engaging in petty criminal activities, such as stealing money from the local newsagent. The relationship between the elder petty criminal and his young, misguided counterpart chimes with the dynamic between Bruno and Steve in the earlier film *L'enfant* (Jean-Pierre and Luc Dardenne, 2005) (Mosley 2013: 131). In relation to *L'enfant*, the Dardenne brothers outline that

> What we're interested in is what can still happen between a parent and a child. Maybe it comes also from the fact that in the city where we make our films, we have seen families destroyed by economic crisis, drugs, unemployment, truancy, and now kids are earning more than their parents but from illegal means. (Andrew 2006)

This relationship between the parent and the child is suggestive of the economic and social difficulties that are encountered by individuals in the post-industrial town of Seraing and Wallonia. According to the Dardenne brothers, crime is adhering to the aforementioned issues of competitive individualism, with the younger generation turning to crime to earn money in the absence of consistent job opportunities, as explored in their previous film *L'enfant*. In *Le gamin au vélo*, Cyril is persuaded to turn to crime to provide for his surrogate father, Wes, and his biological father, Guy. For Luc Dardenne, both of these fathers are negative for the figure of the child; he posits that they represent 'the father who abandons, and the father who lures him [into petty crime]' (Lowy 2016: 60) In this sense, the character of Cyril conflates money (capital) with stability by offering the stolen money to his biological father, after Wes's rejection, so that they can live together once again. This act further emphasises the socio-economic issues that are present in post-industrial Wallonia, as the child has taken on a more dangerous and precarious role in turning to crime to compensate for their parents' deprived financial situation. Paternalism and patriarchal culture, within the context of Seraing and Wallonia, is clearly denounced through the representations of fathers and father figures in ways that threaten the fabric of community, collective and society. This also reverberates through *L'enfant*, in which Bruno commodifies his son Jimmy by selling him on the black market. As Luc Dardenne notes regarding *Le gamin au vélo*, it is 'the woman who saves the child' (Lowy 2016: 60), resonating with Hayward's (2000: 97) conception of women playing a role in the formation of national culture and national cinema.

The consolidation of the maternal figure at the centre of the family unit, a replacement of paternal filiation for the maternal, coincides with the emergence of the river, La Meuse (Figure 2.6). Bauche contends that it is along the riverbanks that Cyril becomes Samantha's son (2011: 8). It is a transformative space, 'when she [Cécile de France] rides her bike along the river with Cyril along the Meuse, the radiance of this body is transfigured by the river'. There is Cyril's red hair, his determination inscribed into his appearance' (Fagnoulle

Figure 2.6 Cyril and Samantha ride along the banks of the Meuse, with the lateral movement of the camera running by their side.

2011). The elision of son, mother and family, in a metaphorical act akin to birth, places the river, La Meuse, as part of the 'national discourse' (Hayward 2000) that reaches out to a certain particularism. In this sense, it is inscribed with the maternal, as opposed to the previous conceptions and evocations of the paternal. The barges have returned and pass by in the background, which are palpably absent in *L'enfant* and *Deux jours, une nuit*. The camera takes on a degree of distance from the characters and the action, adopting a long shot to frame the river, Cyril, and Samantha in context. The fluidity of the lateral dollying of the camera, from left-to-right, maintains a fluidity that is concomitant with the characters' forward movement. They are inscribed within the *mise-en-scène*. As Tessé observes, the film is 'restrained, humble and framed' (2011: 20). There is no 'urgent realism' to present the *mise-en-scène* as inhospitable for the character and the spectator, the maternal evocations have rendered it more sympathetic. Whereas previous depictions of the river (also captured in the background of *Deux jours, une nuit*) evoke a dirty, green-brown colour palette for the river water, *Le gamin au vélo* contrasts radically with a lighter colour palette. As the filmmakers noted (based on response to spectators' reactions), 'your Meuse is grey, black, and is drowning us' (Euvrard 2011: 274), which was visually and cinematically evident in the case of Steve struggling to stay afloat in the river in *L'enfant* and Rosetta and Riquet's 'drowning' sequences in the murky lakes of *Rosetta*. In *Le gamin au vélo*, the visual representation of the river is no longer purely invested with the industrial and nostalgic evocations through colour. The colouration evokes the tone of the scene, with Jean-Pierre Dardenne positing that '[w]e wanted to film moments of happiness – the River Meuse beneath the sun' (Bonnaud 2012: 25). For André, the local framework still remains, 'anchored in Seraing and Liège, but filmed like it has never been filmed before by the Dardenne brothers, with bucolic scenes on the banks of the Meuse' (André 2011). The 'bucolic' and vibrant colour palette brings the film into a transnational references, citing Jean Renoir (ibid.). Renoir's transnational production *The River* (Jean Renoir, 1951) operates as a point of reference, with the vibrant, saturated Technicolor of the natural environment resonating with the warmer tones of *Le gamin au vélo*'s Meuse. The diegetic soundtrack for *Le gamin au vélo* confirms this through its density of insects and birds, alluding to nature, harmoniously situated alongside the turning wheels of the bike and the frequent barge passing by. There is a sense of a settled natural-industrial environment, consolidated within the maternal family.

Conclusion

The Dardenne brothers can be identified as transnational and European auteurs, whilst acknowledging how their films are located within a specific regional and local context. Their valorisation at the Cannes film festival – which functions as a transnational platform for the filmmakers – has opened up an interpretation, analysis and circulation of their films beyond the 'national' context. As a result, the Dardenne brothers have come to define what (francophone) Belgian cinema is, on a 'regional', 'national' and international level, functioning as a reference point for emerging filmmakers in Belgium and Wallonia since 2001 (that is broadly, and problematically, considered 'post-Dardenne'). The diversity of spatial dynamics evoked in the Dardenne brothers' films offer glimpses of Seraing, as its context and imagery lurk in the background. *Le gamin au vélo* and *Deux jours, une nuit* illustrate the continuities of how marginal and peripheral spaces are constructed in the local and regional setting of Seraing. The socio-economic issues presented in the two films are increasingly relevant to the post-2008 financial crisis, which Luc Dardenne suggested as 'of this moment' (Mandelbaum 2014: 13). The films imbricate a transnational approach through a mediation of influences from post-war cinematic 'realism' to evoke the rubble of the post-2008 crisis and post-industrialisation. In so doing, the 'monocultural' references (Hjort 2000: 107–10) of the local and regional imagery is no longer explicitly on the surface of the film as in *Je pense à vous*, with the key themes, such as post-industrialisation, the fragmentation of the family unit, and paternalism, evoked through spatial dynamics and the characters' places within the representation of the suburb. The theme of filiation remains central, with a shift to the maternal body for the evocation of nation, with the paternal evoking its past and ills. The 'topical' theme of nation (Hjort 2000: 105–7) is shifting programmatically to women-led narratives, as evinced by the Dardenne brothers' recent turns. The focus on women at the centre of the family provides a more hopeful and optimistic consideration of nation, and of region, despite the creation of spatial dynamics that place the character on the margins.

Notes

1. The Dardenne brothers deviated from this filmmaking plan for the first time with the release of *La fille inconnue/The Unknown Girl* in 2016, only two years after *Deux jours, une nuit*. This release coincided with the twenty-year anniversary of *La promesse*.
2. Mosley's (2013) chapters on 'Responsible Realists' and 'Cinematic Reference Points' trace debates within cinematic 'realism' that began in Marxism between key thinkers such as Lukács, Brecht and Benjamin through to Italian Neorealism. This is explored in the context of the Dardenne brothers' feature films from *La promesse* to *Le silence de Lorna* (2008).
3. Jean-Pierre Dardenne noted that he systematically watches a selection of films by Maurice Pialat – such as *Loulou* (1980), *À nos amours* (1983), *Police* (1985) and *Van Gogh* (1991) – before filming commences on their new projects (Bonnaud 2014: 27).
4. The Dardenne brothers have outlined their admiration for Bruno Dumont and

Laurent Cantet, who are both considered part of so-called French New Realism. From this premise, the (francophone) Belgian filmmakers have even noted points of similarity and a shared style between their films and the aforementioned French filmmakers (Dupont 2002).
5. In a discussion session at the ASMCF conference in 2013, O'Shaughnessy – in response to my paper on *Le gamin au vélo* – further suggested that the Dardenne brothers' films 'could be set anywhere' in the contiguous area from the south of Belgium to the north of France.
6. See, for example, *Le signaleur/The signalman* (Benoît Mariage, 1997), *Les convoyeurs attendent/The Carriers Are Waiting* (Benoît Mariage, 1999), *L'autre/The Missing Half* (Benoît Mariage, 2003), *Ultranova* (Bouli Lanners, 2005), *Eldorado* (Bouli Lanners, 2008) and *Des plumes dans la tête/Feathers in My Head* (Thomas De Thier, 2003).
7. In his journal, Luc Dardenne (2008: 75) briefly compares the differences between Kieślowski's filmmaking approach in *Dekalog/The Decalogue* (Krzysztof Kieślowski, 1989) to *Trois couleurs: Bleu/Three colours: Blue* (Krzysztof Kieślowski, 1993). Through this comparison, Luc Dardenne proposes that it is 'difficult' for filmmakers to operate outside their own national context.
8. I would like to place on record my thanks to Professor Guy Austin, who recommended consulting Bourdieu's section at AMSCF in 2013.
9. I'd also like record my thanks to Martin O'Shaughnessy, who provided this observation as feedback to a conference paper presented at ASMCF in September 2013.
10. *Deux jours, une nuit* also received a review in the finance and business-orientated English-based newspaper *The Economist* (2014), which placed an emphasis on how the film articulated the transference of responsibility to co-workers in the wake of the 2008 financial crisis.
11. In the context of 'French Political Cinema', O'Shaughnessy (2007: 8–9) engages with Beaud and Pialoux's *Retour sur la condition ouvière* to outline the increasing peripatetic work pattern for the working-class in France, and the aforementioned factory in Sochaux.
12. Mai (2011) offers an interpretation of the maternal through an ethical and Levinasian perspective in the context of *Le silence de Lorna*.

3. 'STILLS' AND FRAGMENTED FAMILIES: CONTEMPLATING THE PRIVATE SPHERE IN JOACHIM LAFOSSE'S WALLONIA

Since the nascent stages of Joachim Lafosse's career, the filmmaker has received critical valorisation of his work, traced back to his graduation film, *Tribu* (Joachim Lafosse, 2001). The short film was awarded the President of the Jury prize by Wim Wenders at the Munich film festival, and it received a special mention at Locarno (Lorfèvre 2006a: 17). The 2004 Locarno film festival proved a crucial barometer for the valorisation of his films – alongside fellow francophone Belgian filmmaker Olivier Masset-Depasse – in which *Folie privée/Private Madness* (Joachim Lafosse, 2004) was selected for international competition. The short cohered with low-budget filmmaking for which (francophone) Belgian cinema had established its international and national reputation, with the cult film *C'est arrivé près de chez vous/Man Bites Dog* (Rémy Belvaux, André Bonzel and Benoît Poelvoorde, 1992), due to the limited finance and production resources available in the 1990s and early 2000s. As Lorfèvre (2004) notes, the 'autoproduction' label – attached to films financed primarily outside the funding systems – was used as a means of categorising a group of low-budget films produced in Belgium at the time, such as the Dogme 95 film *Strass* (Vincent Lannoo, 2001), *Ordinary Man* (Vincent Lannoo, 2005) and *Last Night on Earth* (Giles Daoust, 2004).

The production context for Lafosse's films has discernibly differentiated as his filmmaking career has progressed. His first two feature-length films *Folie privée* and *Ça rend heureux* (Joachim Lafosse, 2006) were produced through primarily community-based and 'national' funding networks. A shift occurred with *Nue propriété/Private Property* (2006), his third feature film, which drew heavily on funding from France. After producing *Folie privée*, Lafosse was selected and invited to attend the Cinéfondation workshops run by the Cannes film festival to enable novice, emerging filmmakers to meet industry professionals (Schwartz 2007). However, difficulties in obtaining funding for *Nue propriété* led to Lafosse creating *Ça rend heureux*, which served as 'a refusal to wait for the good will of [film] funders' (Lafosse, in Lorfèvre 2005). As noted in Chapter One, these international co-productions, primarily with France, cohere with funding patterns established between francophone Belgian filmmakers and France even prior to the creation of European funding support mechanisms in the early 1990s. However, the funding of *Nue propriété* arrived alongside the inclusion of a French star, Isabelle Huppert, in the role of the mother. As Lafosse openly notes, the casting of stars helps to unlock finance, with the amount of funding doubling from 420,000 Euros after Huppert accepted the role (Lafosse, in Lecomte 2006: 157; Lorfèvre 2006a: 17; Lorfèvre 2007c). The Dardenne brothers noted Lafosse's turn to French film stars to guarantee film funding in 2007 (Cowie and Edelmann 2007: 221), and they have since followed suit by casting Marion Cotillard in *Deux jours, une nuit* and Adèle Haenel in *La fille inconnue*. Since *Nue propriété*, all of Lafosse's feature films have been majority Belgian co-productions with France as the secondary partner.[1]

Film festivals have played a role in foregrounding Lafosse's work and placing it within the framework of recognised auteurs. In the context of the (francophone) Belgian film industry, Lafosse highlights the importance of positive critical valorisation of a film in order to encourage investment in the next project (Bradfer et al. 2009). They have also functioned as a primary form of distributor for the filmmaker's work, generating interest both nationally and, crucially, internationally. For instance, *Folie privée* was screened at Locarno and the first European film festival in Brussels in 2004, *Nue propriété* competed at the Venice film festival, and finally *Élève libre/Private lessons* (Joachim Lafosse, 2008) was included as part of the *Quinzaine des réalisateurs*/Directors' Fortnight at the 2008 Cannes film festival. As a result, the dossier produced by *Positif* dedicated to (francophone) Belgian cinema included a detailed interview with the filmmaker. Since this period of initial recognition, Lafosse's films have regularly appeared at 'A'-grade film festivals – mainly Cannes – with *À perdre la raison/Our Children* (Joachim Lafosse, 2012) being selected in the *Un Certain Régard* focus section and *L'économie du couple/After Love* (Joachim Lafosse, 2016) appearing in the *Quinzaine des réalisateurs* (2016). Whilst these are the noncompetitive strands of the film festival, it has proved to be an important starting point for now recognised auteurs such as Ken Loach, Werner Herzog and the Dardenne brothers (Wong 2011: 24, 92). As Benghozi and Nénert note, the *Quinzaine des réalisateurs* has an established record of being the second most 'advertised' section after the official competition (1995: 70), thereby advocating the levels of international recognition the films of Lafosse have received.

Between 1997 and 2001, Lafosse studied at the film school IAD (Institut des arts de diffusion) located in Louvain-la-Neuve, after having attended the entrance exam at the equally prestigious Brussels-based INSAS (Institut Supérieur des Arts) (Lorfèvre 2006a: 17). It was within this institutional environment that the filmmaker encountered other filmmakers to which he has since been compared, such as Maurice Pialat and John Cassavetes (ibid.).[2] Critics have since considered the filmmaker alongside key figures in European cinema, making particular reference to Belgian filmmakers the Dardenne brothers, French filmmakers Maurice Pialat and Robert Guédiguian, and the German auteur Rainer Werner Fassbinder (Bradfer 2009). The Pialat references arise through the consistency of thematic continuities between Pialat and Lafosse. As Wareheim observes in the context of Pialat's 'family portraits', the French filmmaker engages with 'autobiographical' themes, 'the theme of the breakdown of the family unit', and an 'extraordinary focus on banal moments' (Wareheim 2006: 67–94). Moreover, Lafosse has outlined his own cinephilic education in filmmaking, drawing particular attention to the films of Abbas Kiarostami, Alain Resnais, Ingmar Bergman and Michelangelo Antonioni (Stiers 2007a; Danvers 2013b). In his approach to cinephilia and 'cinematographic fables', Rancière foregrounds the significance of fragments and recollections of shots and sequences from films that have made a profound impact on an individual or cinéphile (Rancière n.d.). This chapter will return to these cinematic reference points, 'moments' and 'fragments' in the following analysis. However, as Mathijs notes, Belgian film criticism is primarily concerned with film form, aesthetic and stylistic filiation as opposed to detailed consideration of a film's relationship and contribution to culture (2004b: 92).

Whereas critics and reviewers both inside and outside Belgium configure Lafosse as an auteur, Joachim Lafosse distances himself from traditional approaches to film authorship and, in particular, Truffaut's initial polemical debate. As François Truffaut notes, auteurs produce films for a close-knit group, as opposed to aiming to appeal to the predilections of a mass audience. Truffaut stated in *Arts* that '(t)he film of tomorrow will resemble the person who made it, and the number of spectators will be proportional to the number of the friends the director has. The film of tomorrow will be an act of love' (Truffaut 1957, cited in de Baecque and Toubiana 1999: 110).[3] Instead, Lafosse posits that he 'objects to making films for a "ghetto" [a select, small audience]. Speaking with my friends is the limit' (Douin 2007: 28). In this context, Lafosse reinforces the collaborative nature of filmmaking, claiming that it is 'a group art [. . .] there is pleasure in working together' (ibid.). For instance, Lafosse frequently works with the editor Sophie Vercruysse, screenwriter-director François Pirot, producer Eric Van Zuylen (Ryva Productions), director of photography Hichame Alaouié, and actor-writer Kris Cuppens (Van Hoeij 2010: 27). As Domenach (2009: 100) observes, *Folie privée* and *Ça rend heureux* were written alongside the central actors, Kris Cuppens and Fabrizio Rongione, thereby evidencing the collective nature of his filmmaking. Lafosse eschews the 'auteur' label by positing that – through this collaboration – the filmmaker is able to 'hide behind the fiction' (Domenach 2009: 100). Lafosse still maintains a high level of input at the screenwriting stage, foregrounding the story and the action over the creative vision of the filmmaker. Moreover, in the early stages of his career – whilst producing his second feature film, *Ça rend heureux* – Lafosse urged caution in terms of the critical valorisation of his films, referencing the initial problems that the Dardenne brothers faced critically and in terms of audience reception in their shift from video documentaries to feature-length filmmaking (Lecomte 2006: 157).

The 'private' trilogy introduces audiences to key themes, issues and concerns that underpin Lafosse's films, including his aforementioned graduation film. To this end, auteurism is assigned with 'duration' (ibid.) across the films. The 'private' connection between the three films arises only in the English translation of the three films, but they articulate coherent personal and social themes and issues. Each film – including his INSAS films *Égoïste Nature/Selfish Nature* (2000) and *Tribu* (2001) – engage with a broken and fragmented family unit, teasing out the difficulties faced by the children and the question of filiation. His first four feature films – *Folie privée*, *Ça rend heureux*, *Nue propriété*, and *Élève Libre* – are highly autobiographical (Colin 2016), ranging from the theme of the 'breakdown of the family unit' to Lafosse's experience as a twin highlighted by the twins of *Nue propriété*, to even Jonas' natural ability for tennis in *Élève libre*. Thabourey considers these connections as 'the exteriorisation of domestic and tribal brutality' (2008: 97). Thematic similarities have persisted beyond these three films, encompassing the later work of *À perdre la raison* and *L'économie du couple*. Moreover, Lafosse scripted *L'autre/The Missing Half* (Benoît Mariage, 2003), a film that also provides an important reference point for questions of the rural context in Wallonia and the questions of family and identity. The magazine *La revue toudi* critically engaged with *L'autre* in the context of Walloon filmmaking, whilst overlooking Lafosse's three contemporaneous 'private' films produced in the same geographic area. Mélon (2012) similarly does not make reference to Lafosse's films of the early 2000s in his survey of Walloon cinema. It is possible to posit that such an eschewal of Lafosse's filmmaking pertains to the fact that his films float between the French-speaking regions of Belgium in terms of setting. *Folie privée*, *Nue propriété* and *Élève libre* are set in Wallonia, whilst *Ça rend heureux* is located in Lafosse's hometown of Brussels. As a result, the French film magazine *Positif* proffered that *Élève libre* 'turned a new spotlight onto Walloon cinema' (Rochet 2011: 27), particularly on an international level.

'IT HAPPENED IN YOUR NEIGHBOURHOOD': SMALL-TOWN SPACES IN *FOLIE PRIVÉE* AND *NUE PROPRIÉTÉ*[4]

Belgian film criticism has, to date, ignored an interpretation of Lafosse's three films in the context of how the films offer a peculiarly 'regional' look of Wallonia and how they chime with their forebears in francophone Belgian cinema. Mathijs contends that Belgian films tend to draw on cinematic realism and 'particularism (culminating with the struggle of the individual to escape his small-town surroundings)' – in addition to magic realism and social solidarity (2004b: 93). In this context, the former two areas of concern resonate with Lafosse's films. Following the exploration of spatial dynamics in the city environment in Wallonia (that is, Seraing in the Dardenne brothers' films), Lafosse's films *Folie privée* and *Nue propriété* engage with a rural setting. An isolated and remote house functions as the backdrop for the action to unroll in the two films.

The choice of a rural, small-town location for *Nue propriété* and *Folie privée* can be viewed as peculiar choices from a filmmaker hailing formatively from Uccle in the city of Brussels. Lafosse configures the articulation of the local or a specific neighbourhood with reference to the Dardenne brothers. As the previous chapter outlined, the Dardenne brothers' films are readable along local, regional and transnational lines, with the tight framing in particular preferring a universal relationship and connection with the individual. The city centre and its key landmarks thus become readable only to local audiences (Mosley 2013: 92). Lafosse notes that '(l)ike them [the Dardenne brothers], I would not say that I am a Belgian filmmaker, but a filmmaker from my neighbourhood [Sainte-Catherine, Brussels]' (Domenach 2009: 102). However, Lafosse spent much of his childhood moving between various locations in Brabant Wallon, such as Grez-Doiceau, Bonlez, Chaumont-Gistoux and Louvain-la-Neuve (Delvaux and Mouton 2012). It is this province that provides the backdrop for the action to unroll in *Nue propriété*. Polet (2002: 23) contends that films of the Walloon region have a proclivity for a specified location as a backdrop. In keeping with this, *Folie privée* provides a keenly pinpointed location in the form of the small village of Grand-Halleux in the hills of the Ardennes. *Nue propriété* unrolls in the small town of Chaumont-Gistoux outside Wavre in the Brabant Walloon province. The Belgian newspaper *La Libre Belgique* pointed to the local-regional articulation in the film, whilst also referencing the earlier cult hit *C'est arrivé près de chez vous* (1992), with a review entitled '[c]'est réalisé près de chez vous' (It was filmed in your neighbourhood) (Lorfèvre 2004). This focus on the local resonates with Bruno Dumont's films of the late 1990s, which are provided with a clear geographical marker in the form of Bailleul in the contiguous region of Nord-Pas-de-Calais.[5]

The representation of the countryside in francophone Belgian cinema can be traced back to one of the key filmmakers of Belgian cinema from the 1930s, Henri Storck and, in particular, his work *Boerensymfonie/Symphonie paysanne/Peasant Symphony*, (Henri Storck, 1942–4).[6] Fowler foregrounds the significance of the rural environment in the context of a Belgian 'national' cinema at the time of the German Occupation, outlining how 'he [Storck] seizes the rural for use in a present moment' (Fowler 2006: 144). For Fowler, the relationship to the countryside is presented in two distinct ways, firstly the private, through the use of close-ups; and secondly the public, in terms of the spectacles (2006: 146). Her understanding of a 'peasant cinema' chimes more with a 'national' reading of Henri Storck's work, in line with interpreting – to an extent – the 'national' as part of folk culture. Aubenas ([1981] 2015) posits that subsequent films, such as *Le grand paysage d'Alexis Droeven/The Wide Horizons of Alexis Droeven* (Jean-Jacques Andrien, 1981), do not neatly cohere with the previous 'peasant cinema' due to the 'poetics of place and space' and the 'restrained camerawork'.[7]

Drawing on *Le grand paysage d'Alexis Droeven*, the film operates as an evocation of the social situation in Wallonia and the discourse around the complexities of Belgium's three linguistic regions in the 1980s (Spaas 2000: 23). As Mosley outlines, the films' evocation of 'socio-economic decline' – evidenced in the film through the use of documentary footage of farmer strikes in 1962 and 1978 – is representative of Wallonia as a whole, thereby avoiding an exploration of issues solely rooted in the Fourons villages (2001: 191). The film is also an immediate point of reference for films produced in the countryside of Wallonia, with Andrien's film being regarded as 'le premier grand film d'un cinéma wallon' (Fontaine 1981; Sojcher 1999a: 184) [the first major film of Walloon cinema]. The film also deals with the complex linguistic and ethnic situation that lies at the heart of Belgian national identity, that is, the conflict between Walloon and Flemish identity (Spaas 2000: 23; Sojcher 1999: 184). These latent issues – which are not dealt with directly in *Le grand paysage d'Alexis Droeven* – also emerge in the family dynamic in *Nue propriété*, as this chapter will later address. Bénézet (2005) draws attention to the rural focus of filmmaking in Northern France and Belgium, concentrating on the work of Bruno Dumont and Benoît Mariage. It is the 'regional anchorage' of these films against a rural backdrop that allows for a detailed analysis of its 'poetics and politics' (2005: 164). However, it is important to note that Mariage's *Les convoyeurs attendent* (1999) is located on the fringes of the former coal-mining town of Charleroi, as opposed to being primarily located in the rural landscapes of Wallonia.

With reference to Lafosse's *Nue propriété*, there have been contrasting interpretations of the rural landscape's significance. Vincendeau (2008: 52) posits that Lafosse's film avoids references to sociopolitical issues in Belgium – and in particular Wallonia – thereby contrasting with the work of the Dardenne brothers and Lucas Belvaux (see, the analysis of *La raison du plus faible* (2006) in Chapter Six). However, Mosley (2013: 30) posits that the focus on the countryside draws on thematic and stylistic references – on a national and regional level – with francophone Belgian filmmakers such as Jean-Jacques Andrien's films of the 1980s and Bouli Lanners' *Ultranova* (2005) and *Eldorado* (2008). Working through this comparative framework, the film, according to Mosley, deals 'indirectly' with significant issues of unemployment in a specific geographical area (2013: 31).[8] The 'indirect' nature of the social comment extrapolated from Lafosse's films coheres with the filmmaker's interpretation of the role of cinema. He states 'the function of cinema must be to make us think about what is going on in our society' (Crousse 2009: 4). In this sense, the films articulate and represent key issues, themes and debates that arise from the contemporary social context in which they are produced. This chimes with Polet's notion of a '"cinema of the region" that deals with the social fabric influenced by Walloon history, as opposed to a "regionalist cinema" that succumbs to the picturesque image of the local environment' (Polet, cited in Rochet 2011: 23). The countryside therefore operates as a symbolic site of marginality and a socio-economic shift in the economic basis from an agrarian to industrial economy in Wallonia.

In both *Folie privée* and *Nue propriété*, the isolated house serves as the central point for the action. It is a unifying point of reference amidst a void and empty rural landscape. The natural, outdoor setting and the on-location shooting cohere with Bazin's conception of cinematic realism, which Williams evokes in the context of Bruno Dumont (2013: 41). The colour palette of *Folie privée* is, in particular, understated, with a green hue draining the images of vibrancy. As Felperin notes, the difference between the negative format (digital) and the printed format (35mm) provides the film with a 'washed-out' feel (2004). This adds to the 'stripped back' and minimalist nature of the film, which also persists in *Nue propriété* with its grainy images of a farm in the countryside of Brabant Wallon.

In *Nue propriété*, the countryside operates as a backdrop for the articulation of the banality of the brothers' daily lives. The spectator is offered only fleeting glimpses of the barren and muddy fields and a murky pond. In short, the images of the countryside bookend the interior sequences in which the family drama plays out. The spectator witnesses François sanding the house's shutters, the brothers weaving their way through a field on their bike, François mowing the lawn and the brothers shooting rats in the pond. The serenity of these situations provides a brief counterpoint for the intense family drama that takes place inside the house. These everyday, and banal, situations further evoke Andrien's images of the countryside in *Le grand paysage d'Alexis Droeven* in which, for example, farmers chase their cattle through the fields of the Fourons.

The final sequence of *Nue propriété* is fundamental to understanding the rural

'STILLS' AND FRAGMENTED FAMILIES

Figure 3.1 The camera retreats backwards, revealing the farmhouse before unrolling through a country lane and a series of fields.

landscape. With a clear evocation of the final sequence of *La gueule ouverte/A Mouth Agape* (Maurice Pialat, 1974) a mobile camera tracks away from a house, weaving its way through the streets of a farmholding and a country lane (Eureka 2011), subsequently revealing the countryside of the Brabant Wallon province (Chaumont-Gistoux) (Figure 3.1). As Warehime (2006: 84) and Edmond (2011: 139) indicate, this mobile shot of *La gueule ouverte* operates in contrast to the preceding action that is elsewhere characterised by static shots. While Pialat noted that his film contained 80 shots (Warehime 2006: 82), Lafosse's film contains the same number of shots (Kaganski 2012: 44), positing a coherence in form and style between the two filmmakers. As Warehime contends,

> Vernet analysed the 'violence' of this shot as it is expressed through its structural tensions: the nostalgia of the image, focused on what remains behind, countering the forward dynamic of the shot; the constant metamorphosis of the image played off against the static frame; the elasticity of the shot versus the sense of being torn away. (Marc Vernet 1991, cited in Warehime 2006: 84)

In Lafosse's film, the rapid travelling shot immediately withdraws the spectator from the narrative as the first non-diegetic soundtrack of Gustav Mahler's Symphony No. 2, 'Resurrection', is played. It is also concomitant with both the opening and concluding shots of *Le grand paysage d'Alexis Droeven*, which

Figure 3.2   The concluding image of *Le grand paysage d'Alexis Droeven* is the sole farmhouse in the Fourons.

consist of long, static shots of a farmhouse and its outbuildings in the Fourons as the non-diegetic soundtrack of Wagner's 'Im Treibhaus' plays (Figure 3.2). The jerky and grainy image attempts to re-frame the family's house, providing an understanding of the scale of the farm. As Jacobowitz notes, it is this shot that reveals the farmhouse is now 'more of an estate' (2007: 41). This is also revealed in the background of the farmhouse's drawing room and entrance hallway, with a large architectural drawing of the former building's floor plan framed and presented on the wall. The red and yellow highlighted sections denote the alterations completed on the buildings. The farmhouse has been renovated in order to provide for the formation of a new and different community in Wallonia's countryside. As the camera pans away from the building to focus on the country lane, ploughed fields and an old farmhouse are revealed with a single bale of hay and used machinery lying next to the road. This resonates with Edmond's interpretation of Pialat's shot from *La gueule ouverte*, in which the mobile shot 'says something about how pertinent this type of shot is to everday experience' (2011: 139). As the narrative denotes, the characters are not engaged with the traditional modes of employment in the region and the local area, which is highlighted by the lack of individuals or characters using the agricultural machinery left by the roadside. Drawing on *Le grand paysage d'Alexis Droeven* and *La gueule ouverte*, there is also a certain nostalgia evoked by the backward-facing camera for the countryside and rural environment that is heightened by the revelatory forward movement of the camera.

However, this is not to say that issues around employment and money are the primary objectives of the film, as the brothers are clearly not in a financially precarious position – unlike the characters in the Dardenne brothers' films – as the narrative more clearly articulates the fragmenting and fracturing of family and the law of the film's title that prevents the mother from selling the house. Darras posits that the friction built up between the brothers and the mother is not due to money, but 'found in the situation' (2007: 35), that is the breakdown of the family and the mother's desire to move on with her life. For Lafosse, the use of non-diegetic music to conclude the film operates as an evocation of 'a type of suffering, I wanted to show that separation is essential' (Bayer and Bouras 2007: 17). This separation and breakdown consequently 'liberates the family from a state of immobility' (Jacobowitz 2007: 42). There is an impetus for the brothers to renew their family life and alter their socio-economic situation, which is heavily dependent on their father, adhering to patriarchal culture and the symbolic law of the father.

As Vincendeau crucially notes, the film's title, *Nue propriété*, references 'a legal category signifying that the house is hers to live in and not to sell, since her ex-husband has passed it on to her sons' (2008: 52). The house therefore functions as a 'symbolic core' (ibid.) as it articulates the breakdown of the nuclear family. It is also at the centre of a key push-and-pull drama between members of the family. In *Nue propriété*, Pascale seeks to sell the house in order to release the equity so that she and her new Flemish boyfriend Jan can open their own hotel across the border in France. However, the complexity around the law – evoked in the title – provides the sons with a degree of power to attempt to maintain the family unit and reinforces the context of patriarchal culture. The need for Pascale to move on is linked to her lack of well-remunerated employment and the paucity of connections to an urban centre. It is the 'particularism' (Mathijs 2004b) that also articulates the unemployment of the two sons, with the countryside and rural environment void of opportunities for a generation. This recalls the socio-economic issues that have emerged and recurred through Andrien's films. In *Folie privée*, the house similarly serves as the predicate for the prevention of the re-creation of a new, nuclear family. Jan refuses to leave the former family home in the Ardennes in order to resolutely maintain a suffocating and pernicious family dynamic for his young son, Thomas.

The countryside is not framed as bucolic, avoiding references to the Ardennes' previous use as a holidaymaking destination for Belgian citizens in the 1970s and 1980s. For instance, *Jambon d'Ardenne/Ham and Chips* (Benoît Lamy, 1977) traces the rivalry between competing businesses in Durbuy in the Ardennes as the seasonal visit of holidaymakers descends on the small, secluded town. Throughout the film, Lamy repeatedly uses a high angle panning shot to clearly locate the site, which emphasises the bucolic Ardennes region for both the visitors and its locals. The shot fetishises the Walloon countryside, showcasing its natural beauty. Instead, in *Folie privée*, the openness of the surroundings and the raw and immediate image serve only to isolate the characters in a more hostile and alienating space.

In Lafosse's film, the camerawork is predicated on tight framing and a close relationship with the characters on screen. The use of lightweight, handheld camerawork chimes with the Dardenne brothers' *Rosetta*, with a certain rawness and immediacy generated through the proximity of the camera to the character. As the Dardenne brothers noted, their early feature films, namely *La promesse* and *Rosetta*, benefited from tight framing, stating that 'il faut être dans les culs des choses' ('it is necessary to be in the arse of things') (Benoliel and Toubiana 1999: 47–53). Lafosse similarly discusses that '(i)n *Folie privée*, I wanted to film everything, and not miss anything' (Domenach 2009: 99). For instance, during the five-minute sequence in which Didier and Pascale's friends from the city arrive at the rural house, the rolling hills and parched yellow fields of the Ardennes are glimpsed only in the background. The 'urgent' camera tracks and focuses unsteadily on Pascale, Didier and Jan (with frequent shots of Thomas looking out of the window). The jerky, handheld camerawork complements the chaotic nature of the exchange between Pascale, Didier, Jan and the visitors. In this context, the rural backdrop operates as an inhospitable milieu for the group escaping the unnamed city for the afternoon.

Folie privée's denouement operates in contrast to the preceding action, shifting from a proximate handheld camera to a more static and distant style of filmmaking. There is a shift from an 'aleatory' filmmaking style – as conceived by O'Rawe (2011: 6–8) – that recalls the camerawork of Dogme 95 films, *C'est arrivée près de chez vous* and the early feature film work of the Dardenne brothers in the 1990s, to a 'figurative frame' (2011: 2–5) that is presented as potentially readable and decipherable.[9] This camerawork creates a sense of proximity to the characters and to the action, whereas the static shots situate the spectator as 'liberated' and freed (Lafosse, in Domenach 2009: 100). In so doing, the denouement generates a sense of affect through the use of the crepuscular sunlight to frame the death of the child, Thomas, at the hands of his father. As the sunlight withers away over the vast emptiness of the Ardennes' rolling hills, the father's struggle to maintain a family unit is articulated through the suffocating of the child (Figure 3.3). At this point, the camera provides a long shot of the fields surrounding the house, with the father and the son located between two trees. There is thus a form of aperture framing as the mother (Pascale) attempts to retrieve her son. The three human figures appear as mere specks in a vast, empty and – at this point – haunting landscape. This is mirrored in three following shots, two of Jan as he flees across a stream into the sun-drained fields, and one of Pascale and Didier as they cradle Thomas' lifeless corpse. These two aspects can be extrapolated from the film's theme,

'STILLS' AND FRAGMENTED FAMILIES

Figure 3.3 Lafosse opts to break free from the focus on the character, adopting a figurative frame as the father (Jan) suffocates his son (Thomas).

'*à nos éloignements possibles*' ('to our possible distances and separations').[10] Within this overarching theme, the film's denouement offers a distancing of the spectator from the immediacy of the characters – as identified through use of the handheld camera – to a point at which the spectator has a relationship with images presented to them in terms of affect. The spectator begins to question the ethics of what is presented on screen and considers the trauma of infanticide committed by a desperate and alienated father.

'Stills': Fragmented Family and Fractured Nation

Photography has also influenced Lafosse's filmmaking style, particularly when analysing the shots in his films as 'stills'. Lafosse outlines how a still photograph represents a loss of time and a 'trace' or vestige, coming from his father's work as a photographer (Bayer and Vlaeminckx 2007: 22). Discussing the influence of photography on his filmmaking style, Lafosse notes '(h)e [Lafosse's father] takes 1 image, me, I take 24. [...] He generates meaning with as few images as possible, without movement and without sound. Photographers are a cut above filmmakers' (Delvaux and Mouton 2012).[11] Lafosse's discernible interest in photography and the highlighting of key differences between the two media invites analysis of the perceived 'stillness' of Lafosse's framing methods in *Nue propriété* and *Élève libre*.

Let us briefly consider some key debates in film and 'stillness', with Bellour, Deleuze and Bergson particularly instructive in deciphering the movement of

93

the image. Firstly, Mulvey (2006: 17–32) and Røssaak (2011: 11–24) have outlined the still and its relationship to technology, with particular emphasis placed on pre-history and early cinema. Recent scholarship, primarily Mulvey's (2006) intervention in the field, is indebted to Bellour. Bellour posits a means of understanding 'film as photography, that is, as grasped through the specter of photography' (1990: 105). In so doing, Bellour draws on Deleuze, Bergson and Barthes in order to draw attention to the freezing of movement both 'the movement *in* the image as well as the movement *of* the image', drawing on key examples such as the freeze-frame ending of Truffaut's *Les quatre cents coups* (1990: 100–2 – emphasis in original). The immediate arresting of movement in the image to create a frozen instant gives rise to the 'pregnant moment' in photography (Ephraim Lessing in Bellour 1990: 107–8).[12] Mulvey, in particular, draws attention to 'privileged moments' from Bellour's premise (2006: 192).

Returning more precisely to Lafosse's filmmaking, these 'stills' draw on the conventions of the long take – a staple of European modernist cinema (Bordwell 1979) and contemporary art cinema (Galt and Schoonover 2010) – to imbue the images and moments with a sense of 'duration'. Song Hwee Lim draws on the work of Campany in order to elucidate his focus on cinematic stillness and cinematic slowness in the context of Tsai Ming-Liang's films and the long take (2014: 77–115). This approach equally applies to the work of Joachim Lafosse. In his comparison of film and photography, Campany proposes that '(t)he film image has duration and thus movement at a mental level' (2008: 24). The pausing and arresting of the image – to convey a degree of stillness in a film – encourages the spectator to contemplate the action unrolling on screen. To an extent, this also resonates with Mulvey's interpretation of Bellour's work that engenders a 'pensive spectator' with the stillness of the image (2006: 181–96). Moreover, Campany highlights the polarities of how the photographic 'still' image is perceived in a cinematic context. He proposes that

> (m)ontage sees the photograph as a partial fragment [. . .] The long take sees the photograph as a unified whole. The shorter a film's shot the more like a photograph it gets, until one ends up with a single frame. The longer the shot the more like a photograph it gets too, the continuous 'stare' of the lens giving us a moving picture. (Campany 2008: 36; Lim 2014: 77)

The two films by Lafosse already referenced in this section operate at the latter end of this scale.

Lafosse first used static *plan séquences* in his eight-minute student film *Égoïste Nature* (2000), immediately recalling the photographic work of his father (Vlaeminckx 2002). The fixed, static camera was also adopted in his first documentary film, *Scarface* (Joachim Lafosse, 2001), in which Raphaël discusses the stories behind his scars with only one subtle movement of the camera when the subject decides to stand up. This filmmaking style is self-consciously adopted, with Lafosse stating 'my role, as a filmmaker, is to operate at the meeting place of form and content. I have fancied taking this risk: confronting the spectator with a story that obliges them to position themselves [in relation to the subject]' (Domenach 2009: 98). This indelible connection between form and content/form and subject is also relevant to Lafosse's earlier form of 'low budget' filmmaking (Bradfer 2007a). As a result, Lafosse draws on different approaches and style, since his camerawork is characterised by fluid movements and 'urgent' camerawork in *Folie privée*, static long takes in *Nue propriété* and *Éleve libre* and a series of time ellipses in *À perdre la raison*.

However, as previously noted, the style is linked to the finance received for the project, with the filmmaker showing a predilection for digital for the low-budget film *Folie privée*, and 35mm for films produced through international co-productions, that is *Nue propriété* and *Élève libre*. As a result, in the filmmaker's later films, the camerawork is less immediate and raw, with the fixed 'stills', in Lafosse's words, 'enclosing' the characters in a limited space (Domenach 2009: 98). The relationship between the spectator and the character takes on greater significance in this context, offering the spectator 'a hollow gap so that he [sic] can imagine' (Lafosse, ibid.). In this sense, these 'hollow gaps' drain away emotion from a given sequence, asking the spectator to interpret and consider the relationships between the characters. It is these moments that are most revealing, the subtle nuances that arise in the 'gaps' and interstices and consequently draw attention to latent and underlying issues. These issues are not overtly discussed and lie beneath the surface, in a 'private' sphere.

In the case of *Nue propriété*, Weissberg foregrounds Lafosse's framing, placing particular emphasis on 'contained' and 'controlled' shots that represent 'a frozen window' (2006a).[13] Vincendeau adopts a similar position, outlining how the film 'unfolds in a series of very long and often handheld takes – several of them depicting mealtimes – punctuated by snapshots of almost still life: Pascale in the bath; the brothers playing video games or table tennis' (2008: 52). These interpretations of the film draw on the lexicon used in analysis of photography and – albeit indirectly – Bellour's interpretation of 'stills' in the medium of film in order to tease out the significance imbued in each shot. In this context, small gestures and subtle nuances in the frame are open to interpretation by the spectator.

In *Nue propriété*, the composition of the characters around the table is repetitious, with seven sequences including the mother and the two sons and two separate sequences with the brothers and Thierry's girlfriend Anne. The 'frozen' and 'still' nature of these instances arises from the use of fixed *plan séquences*. When sitting down to eat their evening meals, Pascale remains at the centre with François situated on the right and Thierry on the left of the frame. This evinces the containment of Pascale in her current inescapable situation, needing to support her two sons into adulthood. It also places the mother in a difficult push-and-pull situation between the sons – the more confrontational Thierry and the more supportive François. Jacobowitz focuses on the table and mealtimes, proposing that the static camera 'serves to further underline the feeling of the mother's isolation and entrapment. People move in and out of the frame but there is a sense of fixity and resistance to the movement which underlines the theme of the film' (2007: 42). The limited camera movement engenders this notion of fixity, thereby capturing a moment that heightens the sense of breakdown within the family. Lafosse notes that he attempts to reduce the number of cuts in his films in order to 'capitalise on the links [between the characters]. To film the characters altogether. [And] to show their symbiotic relationship' (Domenach 2009: 98). The stillness of the image thus focuses the attention on the relationships between the characters in the frame.

These moments are wrapped in profundity when decoding the narrative and 'pregnant' with meaning, since the static camera captures intense instances of the family's drama, which are initially concerned with themes of money and future prospects. The static and frozen nature of these sequences is not only articulated by the lack of movement by the camera, but also the character's limited mobility in the frame. The characters habitually remain seated throughout the heated discussions, particularly concerning the mother's desire to sell the house, and concluding with moments of silence. As Buache observes,

Figure 3.4 Pascale and her two sons François and Thierry sit around the table.

this film highlights 'the difficult to formulate vague hopes dragged behind in contemporary life, which fall into an unexplained and upsetting sense of disarray' (2010: 224). In short, the characters' hopes and desires wither away in the evocation of a contemporary Western and European post-industrial society. As Darras notes, the characters 'find themselves prisoners of the family unit' (2007: 35). The almost still-ness of the camera and the static nature of the framing further serve to enclose the characters and restrict their sense of mobility.

The exploration of the nuclear family represents an intentional evocation of questions of nation and nationhood in the context of Lafosse's three films. When discussing *Nue propriété*, Lafosse has claimed that

> (f)or me, family is the place where the learning process for democracy begins. It is not an accident that I chose the subject of family and – at the same time – I intervened in discussions between the Dutch-speaking community and the French-speaking communities. I think that we will exist peacefully in a multiple Belgium only when living in crisis. (Stiers 2007a: 6)

Whereas Vincendeau (2008) previously posited that Lafosse's film avoided an engagement with politics directly, the filmmaker is clearly articulating a close relationship between his films and wider debates on nationhood in Belgium. In essence, the family functions as a microcosm of the nation, in which a complex and fraught relationship between two linguistically and culturally distinct entities is maintained.

In *Folie privée* and *Nue propriété*, a male, middle-aged character named Jan (played in both films by Kris Cuppens) unsettles the family unit. Both films draw attention to Jan's ethnic and linguistic difference, whether that may be subtly in *Folie privée* through Jan's decision to speak Flemish Dutch to his son or explicitly in *Nue propriété* with the two sons referring to Jan as their 'Flemish neighbour'. In both cases, the Flemish character is uneasily integrated into the family unit – and the narrative – since the French-speaking, and Walloon, characters do not accept him. In *Nue propriété*, the tensions between the sons and the potential stepfather (Jan) are ludic in tone and are primarily predicated on the maintenance of their relatively cosseted lifestyle. Vincendeau observes the exchanges as 'hostile banter' (2008: 52), which is particularly foregrounded in relation to the sons' comment on their mother's 'Flemish hairstyle' and their 'intimation of a Flemish accent during the simulation of their mother's sex life' at the breakfast table (Bégaudeau 2007: 62). Whilst the tensions and exchanges between the linguistically and culturally different characters are hostile, the sentiments are not completely irreconcilable.

Instead, the relationship between the brothers and their father resonates with a line of argument developed by Fontaine (1996) from the Dardenne brothers' video documentaries through to their early feature work. As previously noted, Fontaine (1996) posits that the Dardenne brothers develop a 'vertical axis' from father to son and a 'horizontal axis' between brothers in their video documentaries. This then shifts back to a dispute between the son and the father on a 'vertical axis' in *La promesse* (Fontaine 1996). Applying this notion to Lafosse's film *Nue propriété*, the mother (Pascale) severs the vertical axis between the father, who provides money to his sons in regular personal handouts, and his two sons when she forbids his access to the house. As a result, Thierry clandestinely meets his father in his car before providing his older brother François with a small 20-euro loan. In this case, the vertical axis shifts to a horizontal axis that is subsequently broken by Thierry's vicious attack on his brother.

In *Folie privée*, the presence of the Flemish father unbalances the reconstructed family in the Ardennes house. Pascale returns to the house with her son, Thomas, in order to prepare for her new boyfriend, Didier, to reside with them. Linguistic difference is clearly present between Jan and Didier, with Didier articulating himself only in French throughout the film alongside Pascale and Thomas. In order to communicate with the new nuclear family unit, Jan is required to speak, and argue, in French. Jan's identity as Flemish – and as outsider to the nuclear family unit – is addressed in linguistic terms. As the spectator is first introduced to the father and son, Jan addresses his son in Dutch. Linguistic difference is immediately asserted between the mother, Pascale, and the father, Jan, with Thomas operating in the interstices between the two. Thomas represents a confluence of the French-speaking and Dutch-speaking members of the family, thereby articulating the Belgian nation. There is immediate uncertainty as to whether Thomas fully comprehends his father, with the child speaking only in French (the country's bureaucratic language) throughout the film and Jan's switch from Dutch to French in the initial conversation. As Pascale, Didier and Thomas later visit the pond and discuss the life expectancy of the tadpoles, Jan remains isolated and alone in the house, watching the news in Dutch – a subtle 'banal aboutness' (Hjort 2000). The linguistic shifts between the family conversing in French, and Jan listening to Dutch posits cultural difference, nuancing the breakdown of the family. However, as previously outlined, the death of Thomas is therefore an evocation of the instability and the uneasiness around the linguistic and cultural diversity of which the country is composed. In so doing, it further posits the so-called 'artificiality' of Belgium (as noted in the Introduction), with these linguistic and cultural tensions rising to the surface in a parlous manner (that is, the aforementioned death of a child).

The notion of the fragmented family as an articulation of a divided nation is also a theme of the contemporaneous *Des plumes dans la tête/Feathers in My Head* (Thomas De Thier, 2003). In *La revue toudi*, André (2004) interprets the death of the child as an evocation of 'the decline of heavy and steel industries in Wallonia', 'the difficulty in passing down these regional and local memories', and the 'collective amnesia' of Belgium's colonial past, particularly in the Congo during the reign of King Léopold II. André (2009a) reiterates this interpretation when considering the rural landscape of Lanners' *Eldorado*. Moreover, Lafosse notes the cultural significance of the death of the child to Belgian society, referencing the mass media coverage of Joe Van Holsbeek's murder in Brussels in 2006 and the subsequent absence of *Le fils/ The son* (Jean-Pierre and Luc Dardenne, 2002) from national TV schedules (Mundell 2009). From this premise, the question of filiation arises, which neatly coheres with Lafosse's *Folie privée*, *Nue propriété* and *Élève libre*. De Thier's *Des plumes dans la tête* is set in the small rural town of Genappe in Wallonia, engaging with the region's traditions and the industrial production of sugar beet. The carnival references the importance of the public arena and public spectacles as part of the affirmation of a community identity, papering over the cracks of personal trauma and tragedy as an evocation of the latent socio-economic and sociopolitical issues. It represents something culturally specific (adopting Higson's (1989) terms) and articulates a 'monocultural' theme (Hjort 2000). The fraught father–son relationship is evoked explicitly with the young boy Arthur drowning in the waste of sugar beet production on the fringes of the town. Bénézet (2005: 166) and Mosley (2013: 72) in the context of francophone Belgian filmmaking (Mariage's *Les convoyeurs attendent* and the Dardenne brothers' *Je pense à vous* respectively) posit that the carnival is a 'bonding experience' and a 'celebration' of a sense of belonging to a certain community. For Mosley in particular, the carnival serves as an 'uplifting' event for an 'otherwise depressed and alienated sector of society' (2013: 72). In *Pas son genre/Not My Type* (Lucas Belvaux, 2014), however, Belgian filmmaker Lucas Belvaux uses the carnival in Arras to highlight the cultural and regional differences between the two central characters of Jennifer (from the small French town of Nord-Pas-de-Calais) and Clément (from Paris).

Abuse between Generations: Articulating a Crisis in National Identity

In *Élève libre*, the context of abuse of a minor has led to frequent comparisons to the Dutroux affair of the early 1990s in Belgium. It also draws attention to pertinent and profound questions of national identity, nationalism and sense of community.[14] This is not a case unique to (francophone) Belgian cinema, with discourse and trauma from high-profile cases permeating film production in other European countries. For instance, von Dassanowsky and Speck outline the 'discourse of victimhood' and trauma of cases like Natascha

Kampusch and the crimes committed by Josef Fritzl in the context of New Austrian film (2011: 1–2).

In Belgium, as Mosley identifies, the Dutroux affair resulted in 'a reassessment of national identity' in the 1990s (2001: 24). The case exposed the presence of a 'Belgian disease' (Mathijs 2004b) latent in Belgian society and 'became seen as symptomatic of something rotten in the heart of Belgium' (Dyer 2015: 13).[15] Polet posits that in Wallonia the Dutroux affair entered 'into the collective imaginary [as] the emblem of the fracturing/breakdown of a society that has fallen prey to a general loss of points of reference' (2002: 24). These points of reference constitute the aforementioned loss of the steel industry and issues with unemployment. In this case, the affair clearly had an impact on Belgium, but more particularly on a regional sense of identity in Wallonia that was dealing with a sense of 'anxiety' (Mosley 2002). Both Polet (2002: 25) and Mathijs (2004b: 89) draw on a broad range of short and feature films produced in Flanders, Brussels and Wallonia, such as *Marchienne de Vie* (Richard Olivier, 1993), *Au fond du Dutroux* (Richard Olivier, 1997), *Bal Masqué/The Masked Ball* (Julien Verbos, 1998), *Pure Fiction* (Marian Handwerker, 1998), *Film 1* (Willem Wallyn, 1999) and *Blue Belgium* (Rob Van Eyck, 1999), to highlight the impact of the Dutroux affair on the Belgian population and cinema-going audience.

According to Thabourey, the representation of 'physical brutality [in *Élève libre*] has become more symbolic and more pernicious' (2008: 73). As a consequence, the film articulates the problems of state education and institutions, foregrounding a young and vulnerable individual's fall through the cracks of society. Against this backdrop, Jonas is at an important point in his education, where he is offered a general, technical, artistic or vocational strand to his educational pathway. As a result, Jonas becomes a private/independent candidate, after initially failing his exams, with part-time education being provided outside state structures. This focus on youth resonates with the psychological violence experienced by Cyril in the Dardenne brothers' *Le gamin au vélo*. In *La Régate/The Boat Race* (Bernard Bellefroid, 2009), the filmmaker uses the off-screen space to similarly articulate the physical abuse suffered by the son whilst living with his father. In the first of three represented instances of physical abuse, the camera is positioned outside the room, with the doorway concealing the violence beyond the right of the frame. This operates in contrast with the subsequent action, with the violence dictated by the father not concealed by the frame, such as the attempt to drown his son and the attack that leaves Alex with a broken wrist. The failure of the state structures to support the young male characters is present in these films indirectly. Once again, the young, male characters are residing outside the family unit, living primarily by themselves.

Returning to *Élève libre*, the 'symbolic' can be pinned down further as a comment on the breakdown of the family, with 'the absent mother, the father good at only paying the alimony, [and] his distant brother' (Thabourey 2008: 96). The fragmented family unit, and the absence of parents in particular, play a role in the vulnerability of the minor. In short, the film highlights 'how easily authority, left unchecked, can lead to abuse' (Chang 2008). There is an enforced sense of requiring an adolescent to move into adulthood that navigates the difficult terrain of 'the birth of a young adult or definitively the death of childhood' (Moure 2012: 123). This chimes with the short statement provided at the film's opening 'à nos limites' (to our boundaries). There are boundaries articulated between childhood and adulthood, between tutor and student, and between state structures and individuals. As Lafosse notes, the film 'goes beyond' the nuclear family unit, asking more profound questions of state structures (Bayer and Vlaeminckx 2007: 20). For instance, Lafosse proposes that '(t)he relationship between Jonas and Pierre could also reflect the relationship between a constituent and a politician, or a boss and an employee' (Mundell 2009: 23). For Thabourey, the film explores more than 'one of the last official taboos of our society, paedophilia' in order to analyse 'apprenticeships in our modern society and the forced march towards adulthood' (2008: 97). In this context, Lafosse notes that the film is designed to provoke discussion and debate, as the *L'Écran Témoin* series did for the filmmaker in his formative years (Bayer and Vlaeminckx 2007: 20).[16] In his review, Serpieri asks several questions of the relationship between the tutor and the student, interrogating whether the confusion lies at a point between 'substitute father/son? Teacher/student? Friends? Lovers? Rapist/abused? Perverse manipulator/consenting victim?' (2008: 100). The final question was similarly explored in *Le Soir*'s review of the film (Crousse 2009: 4–5). In a study of Joachim Lafosse's work, the student-run *Cinéma et cetera* programme for Radio Campus Brussels debated the ambiguous nature of the questions posed in the film that the spectator must contemplate and consider afterwards. The discussion primarily focused on the ambiguity of manipulation, and the questioning of authority and of trust, with little consensus between the participants (Cinéma et cetera 2016).

The off-screen space is used to articulate and represent the (sexual) abuse experienced by Jonas.[17] Whereas the aforementioned static long takes at the table accommodate all the characters, Lafosse refuses to frame the sexual abuse and acts committed against Jonas by his private tutor Pierre. In short, the shots serve to 'narrate the abuse without showing it' (Lafosse, in Crousse 2009: 5). The refusal to frame the sexual act and act of abuse, focusing the camera on the victim and their reaction chimes with Wheatley's interpretation of the Austrian filmmaker Michael Haneke's 'cinema of restraint' (2011: 182–4). As Wheatley notes in her analysis of *La Pianiste/The Piano Teacher* (Michael Haneke, 2001), 'the sexual act occurs "on screen" but outside the cinematic frame, thus depicting the act but not the body' (2011: 183). Lafosse does, at times, include parts of the body within the frame, but not the act.

In *Élève libre*, the acts of sex between Jonas and the three adult figures, Pierre, Didier and Nathalie, occur in the *hors-champ*. Williams notes the importance of the *hors-champ* (off-screen space) to the spatial dynamics of French cinema, since the '*hors-champ* [. . .] gestures always towards the world of the imaginary' through its flux, that is characters and objects leaving and entering the frame (2013: 4). The filmmaker refrains from including the sex act within the frame either through tight framing or the placement of certain objects, such as the frame of a living room couch. As Lafosse notes, 'we do not show the fellatio, we hide it' (Domenach 2009: 99). There are three instances in particular, two fellatio scenes and one of penetrative anal intercourse. In the first sequence of fellatio between Pierre and Jonas, the camerawork oscillates between being both fluid and static, including and then excluding the act of fellatio. The shot also moves between a sense of vertical and horizontal planes of action, highlighting the relevance of both planes of action both within and outside the frame. The *plan séquence* – lasting three minutes and thirteen seconds – commences with Jonas sitting upright against his bedroom wall as he studies. As he lies down on the bed, the line of action moves away from a sense of vertical and horizontal planes of action that posit a sense of passiveness on Jonas' behalf. As Pierre enters the room, the shot reaffirms the vertical line, as the camera pans from the right to the left as Pierre unbuckles Jonas' trousers. To this end, the two characters are not included in the same frame due to the proximity of the camera to the action. The static camera is finally focused on a mid-shot of Jonas as he lies clothed on his bed. The interplay of shadows in the background and the subtle diegetic sound of a belt being untied and further muffled sounds posit the act of fellatio. The short, sharp gasps of breath taken by Jonas during the 'still' camerawork posit a sense of unease with the acts taking place just outside the frame. There is a lack of movement within the frame, with Jonas remaining still as if caught in a sense of disempowerment. This is represented through the static positioning of Jonas in the frame, which operates, in Garson's words, as a 'trap' (2009: 48). The film's title is derived from the notion of 'libre arbitre' (free will) with the film articulating the loss of free will and independence (Mundell 2009: 23).

The second act of fellatio followed by penetrative anal sex is also obscured by the frame in a further *plan séquence* (lasting one minute twenty-seven seconds). However, a sense of corporeality and movement is included within the frame with the clothed Pierre located above the further passified Jonas. The authoritarian and adult figure retains his sense of control and power through his positioning in the frame. This stance is furthered by the paucity of dialogue and the brief demands provided by Pierre. The tight framing and static camerawork both includes and excludes the act, concealing and revealing the abuse that is occurring in a domestic and private setting. The boundaries and limits of the frame are concomitant with the issues addressed in the film. As Chang summarises, the film addresses 'the damage that can occur in the absence of boundaries' (2008). Boundaries and perimeters are provided for the spectators through the limits of the frame, thereby highlighting the abuse in the off-screen space. Moreover, the 'absence of boundaries' is derived from the lack of state institutions, namely the state school system and family, which have a certain duty to and responsibility for the young generation.

Conclusion

Lafosse's 'private' trilogy operates as a clear evocation of the fraught and complex social and political issues and crisis that lie within Wallonia. The local and regional focus on these films is considered through a comparative cinematic framework that draws attention to the rural backdrop in which these stories unroll. The three films articulate a certain 'topicality' (Hjort 2000) of issues in the country, and sociopolitical concerns that reverberate across Europe, particularly in terms of employment opportunities for young people and events that serve to epitomise 'national' crisis. In the 'private' trilogy, the nuclear family lies at the heart of this equation, since the breakdown of the family serves as a microcosm of the state of nation and questions of nationhood. The inclusion of Flemish characters – in the role of fathers or potential stepfathers – as both outsiders and as threats to children articulates concerns regarding the coherence and future of Belgium as a bifurcated country. This perceived threat also arises in the form of representatives of the state and institutions through the tutor in the education system, with certain individuals who abuse their authority and power over vulnerable teenagers. This vulnerability arises through Lafosse's framing techniques, which encourage the spectator to contemplate the images.

Notes

1. *Nue propriété* and *À perdre la raison/Our Children* (2012) also included a third partner for film funding – a strategy activity encouraged by Eurimages (currently Creative Europe) – in the form of Luxembourg and Switzerland respectively.
2. Lafosse's second feature film *Ça rend heureux* drew on *Faces* (John Cassavetes, 1968) as a reference (Feuillère and Vlaeminckx 2006).
3. I would like to place on record my thanks to Dr Fiona Handyside, who drew my attention to this quotation from Truffaut on film authorship, whilst discussing the films of Sophia Coppola.
4. This subheading makes reference to Lorfèvre's (2004) newspaper article on Lafosse's film, *Folie privée*.
5. Williams provides a nuanced and detailed close reading of Dumont's films, considering the human presence in the landscape and the focus on the local and regional anchoring of his early films (2013: 41–63).

6. Jules provides a brief survey of both key Flemish and francophone Belgian films from 1934 to 1989 that engage with the Belgian countryside (1990: 105–6). Trinon introduces his analysis of the Belgian countryside by highlighting the similarities as opposed to the differences between Flanders and Wallonia. From this premise, the scholar observes 'One State. Two People. The same farmer.' (1990: 31).
7. In 2015, Les Films de la Drève (Andrien's production company) presented a three-part DVD entitled 'Le grand paysage, une trilogie du monde paysan' (1979–2012)'. This set included the three films: *Le grand paysage d'Alexis Droeven/The Wide Horizons of Alexis Droeven* (1981), *Mémoires/Memoirs* (1984) and *Il a plu sur le Grand Paysage/It Rained on the Great Landscape* (2012).
8. Vincendeau (2008: 52) views the character's 'apathetic' approach to employment as opposed to a clear indication of levels of unemployment for the youth in Belgium.
9. Williams outlines O'Rawe's film poetics (2015: 3) as a means of analysing the camerawork and construction of space in contemporary French cinema, such as the films of Bruno Dumont and Robert Guédiguian.
10. Nuttens identifies the recurring of this theme '*à nos éloignements possibles*' in Lafosse's later film *À perdre la raison* (2012: 16). In this context, Nuttens views the theme as articulating the cultural distance between the Moroccan husband and the (francophone) Belgian wife in Wallonia (ibid).
11. The student-run Cinéma et cetera (2016) draws on Delvaux and Mouton's article to introduce and frame Lafosse's filmmaking style in relation to photography.
12. Blümlinger (2011: 75–84) draws on Bellour's principles pertaining to the interruptions and the pausing of the film in R. W. Fassbinder's work, a filmmaker to whom Lafosse is often compared in terms of his framing.
13. Lafosse acknowledges that the use of long, controlled takes evoke the films of Austrian filmmaker Michael Haneke (Dawson 2013: 60).
14. Lafosse describes the connections raised in the film between the abuse of a minor and the Dutroux affair of the 1990s as a '"simplistic" interpretation of abuse. There are also people who do not report abuse that are subsequently not talked about' (Bayer and Vlaeminckx 2007: 21). Nonetheless, the filmmaker did highlight the personal impact of the affair on his childhood and Belgian national identity, stating that 'I was fourteen years old when Julie and Melissa disappeared. I am Belgian, and it is evident that if I make a film about abuse today, it is because it has made its mark on me' (Crousse 2009: 5).
15. Mathijs (2004b) and Dyer (2015: 12–14) provide detailed accounts of the Dutroux affair and its impact on francophone Belgian cinema of the 1990s.
16. *L'Écran Témoin* consisted of two films screened per year on the francophone Belgian television channel RTBF. It ran for thirty-one years from 1972 to 2003. The films selected were viewed as 'a little more abrasive' (De Bellefroid 2001), and included a post-screening televised debate.
17. Lafosse also crucially uses the *hors-champs* in *Nue propriété*, with the potential death of François occurring outside the perimeters of the frame. His body lies within the confines of the frame, and his potential head injury is just beyond the aperture framing of the door and thus the frame itself.

4. FROM SLAG HEAPS TO CLIFFS: THE 'MARKED' REGIONAL LANDSCAPE IN *CAGES* (OLIVIER MASSET-DEPASSE, 2006)

I make films that I have to make. Not necessarily those that I want to produce. However, what has been most integral is, hopefully, trying to be accessible. I am proud of *Cages*. I did not abandon my own convictions. *My only limits have been financial.*[1] (Masset-Depasse in Bradfer 2006c: 46) (Emphasis added)

The majority of Belgian films need France for financing and to have visibility [...] All Belgian filmmakers want, and hope, to be recognised by France, the country of culture. (Masset-Depasse 2013, pers comm).

Drawing on Hjort's (2009) typologies of cinematic transnationalism, this reading introduces 'marked' and 'unmarked' cinematic transnationalism in relation to the film's setting and how the landscapes of Nord-Pas-de-Calais are framed. Hjort defines a 'marked' form of cinematic transnationalism as being when 'the agents who are collectively its [the film's] author [...] intentionally direct the attention of viewers towards various transnational properties that encourage thinking about transnationality' (2009: 13–14).[2] The film's DVD includes a detailed and informed dialogue between filmmaker Olivier Masset-Depasse and the producer of Versus Productions, Jean-Henri Bronckart, which begins to outline some of the decisions taken at the level of production that have impacted on the film textually. Masset-Depasse acknowledges that the shift in the production of the film represents 'a true co-production that has become artistic' (Masset-Depasse and Bronckart 2006). The quotation that opens this chapter further evinces the film's 'marked' status by pointing to the financial limitations and restrictions. In his original script, Masset-Depasse had written the film with the premise that it was located in his hometown city of Charleroi. In an interview with the filmmaker, Masset-Depasse (2013) discusses at length some of the changes that were made at an artistic level as a result of the relocating of the action across the conterminous border in Nord-Pas-de-Calais.[3] What is more, the filmmaker strictly located his short film *Chambre froide/Cold Storage* (Olivier Masset-Depasse, 2000) in his hometown city, with distinct landmarks being drawn on as local and cultural articulations. In this sense, we are encouraged to interpret the film through the lens of cinematic transnationalism in industrial contexts (production, distribution and exhibition) and in terms of the film's aesthetics. Hjort's (2009) typologies, therefore, operate as instructive categories for interpreting the industrial and representational side to Masset-Depasse's short and feature-length films.

However, this is not to posit that *Cages* adheres to a 'marked' cinematic transnationalism in the same context as the so-called 'Euro-puddings' of the 1980s and 1990s, for example. Elsaesser posits that the key difference between co-productions funded through European initiatives and 'Euro-puddings' is that the former is 'legitim[ised] via the festival circuit and the promotion of the auteur, whereas "Euro-puddings" were banking on stars and literary properties' (2005: 506). *Cages* eschews the casting of stars, and the screenplay was written by Masset-Depasse – over a period of three years (Sépul 2005: 16) – whilst he was producing his series of festival-valorised short films in the early 2000s. Masset-Depasse's commitment and desire to create films pertaining to film authorship have shifted over time, particularly from his nascent period in film school to the production of his early feature-length work. In synchronicity with *Cages*, the filmmaker noted that,

> I am not going to stay within auteur cinema. I know that I need to move towards a "New Hollywood" concept film. If you asked me whether I would prefer a *Palme d'Or* [the ultimate prize at Cannes film festival] or two million film admissions, one year ago I would have said the *Palme d'Or*, [but now] I would say two million admissions. (Bradfer 2006c: 46)

The exigencies of the exhibition market have taken a crucial hold regarding film production and film project selection in a cinematically small nation where screen and film policy is beginning to take a conservative shift towards an economic model (as opposed to being purely and perfunctorily cultural). The filmmaker further evidences this position, by arguing that, unlike other francophone Belgian filmmakers, recognition by France, 'country of culture' as Masset-Depasse states, is of little interest to him, and his focus is on valorisation as a 'Belgian' filmmaker first and foremost (Masset-Depasse 2013). It is for this reason that Masset-Depasse's second feature film, *Illégal/Illegal* (2010), was produced primarily between Belgium and Luxembourg, with a small level of funding originating from incentives from France (ibid.). However, *Illégal* pays lip-service to the economic model and bridged this complex divide by receiving favourable awards at international 'A'-grade film festivals.

Taking a slight detour – which may initially seem specious, but does articulate the shift in filmmaking in Nord-Pas-de-Calais – *Ma Loute/Slack Bay* (Bruno Dumont, 2016) captures the beauty of the northern French coastline, its dramatic cliffs and sumptuous bays. From this premise, Dumont posits that '"European" films are really bad [...] You make a local film, and that might become universal. You can't make a "European film"' (Barnes 2016). Although *Slack Bay* is a French-Belgian-German co-production, it is inherently rooted in local and cultural articulations, primarily through its dialogic references to key towns in the region, such as Calais and Tourcoing, the marked accent of the mussel harvesters, and, most importantly in this context, the dramatic landscape. There are also surface similarities in how the Nord-Pas-de-Calais landscape is framed in *Cages* and *Slack Bay*, particularly in terms of the reverberations in the aerial shots utilised to frame the characters and their location on the regional clifftops. An inter-textual, transnational-local dialogue is generated as a result of these (unintentional, yet artistic and stylistic) similarities. Although the two films were produced approximately eleven years apart, Pictanovo's film and television policy for a 'touristic view' of the region is discernibly evident (Steele 2018). As Reynaert notes, the policy objectives for the Nord-Pas-de-Calais region 'were to clearly change the image of the region', with *Bienvenue chez les Ch'tis* operating as the example of this *par excellence* in 2008 (Bredael and Reynaert 2016: 61). Returning to Dumont's *Slack Bay*, the auteur's film deals with this touristic incentive ludically and playfully, capturing the sheer beauty and virtuosity of the Nord-Pas-de-Calais coastline whilst the locals consume and cannibalise the region's visitors.

Analysis of *Cages* in film criticism has foregrounded the film's universality, particularly in terms of genres and its adherence to melodrama. As a result, the film has been interpreted as 'a love story', despite its focus on the fracturing of a previously stable relationship. This interpretation in film criticism aligns with Hjort's 'perennial themes' – thereby distancing the film from social comment and cultural/local specificity through 'topical' themes – through its use of 'universal or quasi-universal' themes, such as love and the breakdown of a marriage, which is also an 'enduring, lasting concern' (Hjort 2000: 106–7). In essence, *Cages* charts the breakup of a seven-year relationship between Eve and Damien after a tragic accident leaves Eve physically unable to speak. While working through the trauma of the event, Damien has an affair with Léa, who works for the brewery that regularly delivers alcohol to Damien's bar, metonymically named 'Zoo'. The bar's name pertains, in a non-subtle manner, to the annual animal imitation competition that is usually hosted by Damien, shifting the film's tone to one of magical realism and the carnivalesque. The competition and the affair operate as symbolic barriers, a hurdle that Eve is required to overcome.

Identifying *Cages* in a Transnational and Regional Context

Le Monde labelled *Cages* as exclusively 'French' in its synchronic review (Douin 2008a), overlooking the Belgian input at a level of production and creativity. However, the film received little critical consideration or valorisation in France at the time of release. In France, short reviews outlined only the narrative in the leading French newspapers, such as *Le Monde* and *L'Express*. Muted responses and interpretations permeate these reviews, except for *L'Express*, which hinted at a certain artistic merit and individual filmmaking style attached to the auteur's name. The review concluded with the line 'but Masset-Depasse is a *cinéaste*' (E. L. 2008), implicitly pointing to Masset-Depasse's nascent valorisation as a filmmaker of breakthrough short films. This is also posited in film criticism in Belgium, with *Le Vif/L'Express* suggesting that it is impossible to sum up the director's talent – after watching *Cages* – in one article (F. By 2007). Popular press in Belgium, such as the magazine *Elle*, interpreted the film as 'très belge' (very Belgian) (Damiens 2007). More extensive examination was left to francophone Belgian reviewers, alongside interviews with the filmmaker. As a result, the uneven coverage lends more towards a 'national' reading of the film, with small laments concerning its mode of production and limited engagement with the Belgian regions. For instance, in *Le Soir*, Broquet (2005) commences the review with a seemingly pyrrhic victory for Belgian cinema by discussing *Cages*' opening sequence in local terms. He situates the film in the small village of Bossut in the landlocked *Brabant wallon* province south of Brussels yet north of the Walloon capital of Namur (Broquet 2005). This is the only sequence in the film that unrolled in Belgium. In the DVD commentary, Masset-Depasse and Bronckart (2006) similarly locate the sequence as the only truly 'Belgian' sequence in terms of location. The sequence, involving the ambulance crash, initiates the breakdown in Eve and Damien's relationship.

In the Introduction to *Cinema and Landscape*, Harper and Rayner compare the film auteur to an individual mapmaker (2010: 15). This comparison between the mapmaker and the filmmaker is 'particularly prevalent and tempting within national cinema contexts, in which the aura of art is co-opted by motivations of national, ideological and aesthetic value' (2010: 22). It is not restricted to individuals, as waves and valorised films also serve to epitomise the local and cultural articulations expressed and represented through the framing of the landscape, as opposed to a focus on the human body. However, in the case of *Cages*, the film unrolls in an 'undefined French-Belgian north' by virtue of its muted autumnal colour palette (Lorfèvre 2007a). This does not necessarily resonate with the aforementioned aesthetic, stylistic and thematic similarities of the *cinéma nordiste* (Bénézet 2005), since it is instead positing a contiguous region brought together by its use of language (in this case, French). The landscape is not locally specific and the area in which the film is set does not emerge discursively within the film. The landscape shots of the Côte d'Opal are decipherable to a local audience, which, therefore, distinguishes the film from the archetypical particularist approach of francophone Belgian cinema.

Following O'Regan's approach to film criticism in his work on *Australian National Cinema*, denunciation can be 'functional', since it offers an alternative interpretation of a film text, and 'demythologising' as it, in turn, legitimises other films with local concerns and articulations (1996: 340). Reviews of *Cages* have positioned the film as mediocre, receiving between one and three stars in film criticism. What is particularly striking is the inclusion of the phrase 'un film produit en Wallonie!' (a film produced in Wallonia) at the bottom of the film's promotional poster, claiming a certain Walloon and Belgian authority and national/regional reference over the project. Problematising this sub-national and regional appellation, the inclusion of the coastline does not neatly cohere with the linguistic and cultural geography of Belgium. This further emphasises the sense that Belgium is an 'artificial nation'. Hammond and Redmond claim that, 'at the shoreline's edge, the national imaginary can be brought into focus. This is especially true of a national cinema that comes from countries bound by water' (2013: 602). Semantically, the scholars posit that the natural borders and limits of the nation state operate as 'the cage' (ibid.), which provides a neat and incidental connection with the film's title. The inclusion of the coastline in *Cages* draws attention to cultural and linguistic difference in Belgium, with the shoreline being geographically located in the Dutch-speaking region of Flanders in the north of Belgium. The French-speaking community in the film, with a Belgian accent, conflates the geographic borders between France and Flanders. In so doing, the linguistically 'marked' premise of the film, to draw on Hjort's (2009) typologies, proposes a transnational reading of the film and its cinematic landscape – as opposed to merely foregrounding the national, or in this case, sub-national imaginary. The mutual intelligibility of French between Wallonia and Nord-Pas-de-Calais, in this case, occurs alongside interactions between the regions on a historical level, particularly concerning the coal-mining histories of the French region and the conterminous province of Hainaut and the Borinage area in Wallonia.

From Short Films to Feature-length Productions: Masset-Depasse's Stylistic Filiation

Masset-Depasse's two valorised short films, *Chambre froide* (2000) and *Dans l'ombre/In the Dark* (2004), have a more clearly defined geographical location, the filmmaker's hometown of Charleroi. The filmmaker has demonstrated his pride in and loyalty to his hometown, despite relocating to Paris and Brussels, noting that 'we sometimes need to leave the motherland in order to blossom, but we never betray her' (Masset-Depasse in F. By 2007). Reviews and interviews in francophone Belgian film criticism speak to Masset-Depasse as a 'Carolo', pertaining to his upbringing in the formerly industrial and coal-mining Walloon city. The framing of the landscape in the short film *Chambre froide* operates, to an extent, as an augury of a regionally-defined and culturally specific mode of filmmaking. Following the 'demythologising principle' (O'Regan 1996: 340) in relation to *Cages*, *Chambre froide* is perceived as exemplary of a locally articulated Hainaut cinema, named after the province, which funded a wave of approximately forty-five short and documentary films in the early to mid 2000s (Vangoghtoutcourt.be n.d.). However, the analysis of *Cages* is essentially predicated upon a nuanced and informed understanding of the film's poetics, that is how the landscape and bodies are manifested and articulated textually.

Duculot outlines the patterns in the short films to *Cages* at a thematic level, positing that '*Chambre froide* showcased Olivier Masset-Depasse's talent at creating an atmosphere and portraying conflict between two characters. *Dans l'ombre* [...] had a formal virtuosity which precisely conveyed the inner torment of Léone' (2005: 23). Within this analysis, the use of 'virtuosity' – to articulate the filmmaker's thematic and stylistic approach – begins to place Masset-Depasse, on a national level at least, in the cadre of film authorship. *Cages* did not receive the same level of critical valorisation and political comment as the later *Illégal* (2010), which has become the filmmaker's benchmark. *Illégal* received a standing ovation after its screening at Cannes film festival, and led to Masset-Depasse being 'invited to the European Parliament in Strasbourg and in Brussels' (Danvers 2010). This is primarily attributed to the film's polemical subject matter, and, as Masset-Depasse outlines, it is his role as an artist to pose the questions (ibid.). As a result, *Cages* received little academic analysis, with the more in-depth considerations and references reserved for *Illégal* (see Engelen and Van Heuckelom 2013; Gott 2013b; Rosello 2014). *Illégal* was also released in synchronicity with a cross-section of films by white, ethnically Belgian and Walloon filmmakers producing feature films about the plight of economic migrants from Eastern Europe, such as *Le silence de Lorna* and *Problemski Hotel* (Manu Riche, 2015). The film heralded Masset-Depasse's return to Belgium, and to the city of Brussels, Liège airport and the Hermalle-sous-Huy detention centre in Engis (a small former industrial suburb of Liège along the Meuse river). Film critic François Yon, however, considers that the film epitomises the concept of 'transnational cinema', since it resonates with *Welcome* (Philippe Lioret, 2009) filmed across the border in Nord-Pas-de-Calais and 'was not marketed as a Belgian or francophone film' (Van Hoeij 2010: 110). There is also the potential to contend that *Illégal* operates within a similar transnational system as the British film *Last Resort* (Pawel Pawlikowski, 2000), since they both deal with the pernicious and seedy underbelly of Étienne Balibar's 'potential European apartheid' in the context of 'New Europe' and 'New European cinema' (Ezra and Rowden 2006: 9). From this premise, the questioning of the 'national' and/or 'nation' remains at the core of the text.

Masset-Depasse's films lend themselves to critical interpretation and academic consideration, with the filmmaker noting that he intentionally creates films 'with a message' (Stiers 2007b: 6). Similar to the early films of Joachim Lafosse (analysed in Chapter Three), the lack of stylistic consistency in Masset-Depasse's films is framed as his 'uncanny ability to suit form and content' (Duculot 2007: 10). Lorfèvre (2007b) and Sépul (2008), therefore, posit a coherence between the new generation of francophone Belgian filmmakers in the early 2000s, since, according to the two critics, the films of Fabrice du Welz, Joachim Lafosse and Micha Wald are all personal in their thematic and stylistic approach. Masset-Depasse also posits that there is a particular thematic and stylistic coherence with du Welz, evoking an extreme and pictorial approach (Feuillère and Vlaeminckx 2005: 15). The film's thematic preoccupation coheres with the previously discussed form of separation articulated and represented in the early films of Joachim Lafosse (see Chapter Three) (Van Hoeij 2010: 101), with the notion of divorce prevailing in his most recent film, *L'économie du couple/After Love* (2016). It is the complementary notions of 'separation and loss' within the family and relationship that underpin the films as texts, stretching towards a melodramatic genre as conceived by Neale (1986: 19).

As this book considers, there are points of comparison between the filmmakers stylistically that are diverse and uneven, whereas the thematic unity lies in the pervading sense of a Wallonia in economic crisis. It is perhaps best to interpret this auteurist basis as connected to Belgium's film schools, since the aforementioned filmmakers are all graduates of a cinematic system, as opposed to 'autodidacts' such as the Dardenne brothers, Bouli Lanners, Nabil Ben Yadir and Mourad Boucif. Héliot contends that there is a natural and logical 'passage' that novice filmmakers from Belgium adopt after graduating from the aforementioned film schools, honing their skills and film style prior to producing – and gaining funding for – feature-length films (2008: 88). From this premise, Lorfèvre (2006b) acknowledges the tendency to create a 'family through the short films'. Moreover, the continuity that arises from the casting of the same actress, Anne Coesens in the case of Masset-Depasse, chimes with Rachel Lang's repeated inclusion of Salomé Richard from her short films *Pour toi je ferai bataille/For You I Will Fight* (Rachel Lang, 2010) and *Les navets blancs empêchent de dormir la nuit/White Turnips Make it Hard to Sleep* (Rachel Lang, 2011) to the feature *Baden Baden* (Rachel Lang, 2016). Such similarities in approach from graduation films, short films and feature work could be connected to their training as graduates of the Belgian film school IAD (Institut des Arts de Diffusion) in Louvain-la-Neuve.

From this premise, Masset-Depasse's style has been polarising, drawing on contrasting styles from commercial and art cinema. Guiot presciently argues that the styles are heterogeneous, which, therefore, detracts from the film's unity and coherence (2007: 5). Broquet (2005) cites the eclectic mix of Terry Gilliam, John Cassevetes and Ingmar Bergman as reference points. The filmmaker takes the stylistic filiation further, describing the influences through the use of the belgicism 'plic-ploc' (neither here nor there) (Lorfèvre 2006b).[4] This posits a certain inconsistency in the reference points operating in *Cages* that requires a transnational cinephilic framework to decode. In terms of characterisation, German Expressionism, particularly the work of Fritz Lang and F. W. Murnau (ibid.; Jacobs 2007: 11), proves instructive for the exteriorisation of inner struggles. This stylistic filiation emerges through the use of lighting, and the permeating darkness in the close-ups on Eve's face. In an interview with Van Hoeij (2010: 109), Masset-Depasse draws attention to the contrasts of light and darkness, particularly through the use of shadow in a (whilst clearly adopting a neologism) 'neo-neo-expressionist' approach, as the primary form of expression in his films. The highly polished aesthetics are generated through a dialogue with Kar-Wai Wong and David Lynch (ibid.). Interviews with Masset-Depasse point to a transnational cinephilic understanding and intentional dialogue with European and American auteurs, whereas the framing of the landscape – in particular the dramatic coastline and the preoccupation with stones – and the expressionistic tone borrows from Ingmar Bergman, as this chapter will later analyse.

According to Masset-Depasse, *Cages* 'recalls a Hollywood, or at a general level American, cinema style of editing' (Vlaeminckx 2005). The filmmaker even contends that *Cages* fits somewhere between American and European styles of filmmaking, since it has the 'tight causality of an American film' and the 'portrait' or 'look' of a European film (Van Hoeij 2010: 109). In effect, it adheres to the classical cause-effect logic, best known for its use in mainstream American cinema, that Bordwell contrasts with the 'art film' (Bordwell 1979: 57). Despite the limited funds, as the opening quotation to this chapter evinces, Masset-Depasse uses 'close to 500 shots' (Vlaeminckx 2005). However, it is more complex than merely creating a connection with American, and in particular Hollywood forms of filmmaking, at this nascent point. Drawing on the films of the Dardenne brothers as the paradigmatic and dominant mode of filmmaking and authorship in francophone Belgian cinema, the gulf between the number of shots, and thus the form of editing is vast. For instance, *Rosetta* is composed of approximately between 141 and 159 shots, with *Le gamin au vélo* cohering neatly with the former at 141.However, *Cages* falls short of David Lynch by approximately half – with the majority of Lynch's films being closer to 1000 (and often more) shots, with the notable exception of *Eraserhead* (David Lynch, 1977). What is more, the dialogic references to Bergman are further strengthened, cohering with Bergman's masterpieces *Det sjunde inseglet*/*The Seventh Seal* (Ingmar Bergman, 1957) (558 shots) and *Smultronstället*/*Wild Strawberries* (Ingmar Bergman, 1957) (567 shots).[5]

Let us now turn to the posited *mise-en-scène* and setting of the film in the initial screenplay as well as considering Masset-Depasse's breakthrough short films, which achieved critical valorisation and awards at Locarno film festival in the early 2000s. In particular, *Chambre froide* evinces local articulations predicated on Walloon coal-mining histories. Masset-Depasse's short film is laden with an intensity in its references and dialogue with francophone Belgian cinema and its history. It is this heritage and cultural representation that has characterised Walloon cinema since its nascent period, and the major reference point of *Déjà s'envole la fleur maigre* (Paul Meyer, 1960) and before it *Misère au Borinage* (Henri Storck and Joris Ivens, 1933).

Made in Wallonia: The 'Psychological–Physical' Axis and the *Slag Heap*

In his writing on landscape and cinema, Martin Lefebvre proposes an axis of 'exteriority/interiority', where '(a)t one end of the spectrum we find the neutral setting, which relates indifferently to the action or the characters, while, at the other end, lies the formative setting, which seeks to express the character's interior state of mind' (Lefebvre 2011: 64). The second line of this axis is present in the original screenplay for *Cages*, which intended to use the slag heaps of Charleroi as a metaphor for the character's internal psychological struggle. Within Harper and Rayner's typologies of landscape in cinema, the slag heaps operate as a 'metaphoric cinematic landscape', since its primary – and intended – purpose is to 'deepen our understanding of a subject or theme' (Harper and Rayner 2010: 16). Masset-Depasse notes that, when writing the screenplay, he had 'imagined' anchoring the action in Charleroi, which he describes as 'a dilapidated industrial "monster"', using the 'six large slag heaps that encircle the city' that attest to its coal-mining heritage (Masset-Depasse 2013). The eschewal of the location in Wallonia from screenplay to film stretches to a more universal interpretation of the film. Melbye (2010) outlines how the landscape can operate in an 'allegorical' way, highlighting its potential to function as a social and cultural critique. This critique emerges primarily in a prescriptive context, since Melbye posits that a spectator from a given country is able to interpret 'culturally significant' elements that spectators outside the national, regional or local context may not be able to decode (2010: 3–4). Although there are also slag heaps in northern France, and there is evidence of a concomitant history in coal-mining between the two contiguous regions (of Nord-Pas-de-Calais and Wallonia), the slag heap takes on a prescriptive cultural significance for local audiences. From this premise, an extra significance is placed on critical responses and cinephilic interpretations written in a national context, eschewing the importance of a transnational understanding of film.

According to Masset-Depasse, the slag heaps articulate a meeting of the psychological and the physical, by outlining that 'the slag heaps are hills of misery and poverty. Eve on her heap of misery, this is what the slag heap would have represented for the character' (Masset-Depasse 2013) (Figure 4.1). The shot resonates with Meyer's reference point of *Déjà s'envole la fleur maigre*, during which Domenico, a disenfranchised Italian labourer, introduces the young, and newly arrived, Italian boy Luigi to the Borinage atop a slag heap. It is at this point that Domenico points to the suburb, presciently referring to its high levels of unemployment, thereby foregrounding the region's systemic issues for the working class (Figure 4.2). The film's concluding rhyming lines of 'Borinage', 'charbonnage' (coal-mining), and 'chômage' (unemployment)

Figure 4.1 In *Chambre froide*, Rita stands atop a slag heap on the fringes of the city of Charleroi.

Figure 4.2 In *Déjà s'envole la fleur maigre*, Domenico introduces the young Luigi to the Borinage and its issues of unemployment.

further consolidate the theme, with 'hope' only being articulated in Italian. Gabriel outlines the recurrence of the slag heap in Yves Auquier's photography *Pays noir/Black country*, and its presence in films *Les convoyeurs attendent/ The Carriers Are Waiting* (Benoît Mariage, 1999) and *Ultranova* (Bouli Lanners, 2005), to articulate how 'the character is part of the landscape, but also detached from it' (2011: 70). From this premise, Gabriel posits that the slag heap operates beyond the mere setting and *mise-en-scène* for the action to unroll (2011: 70–3). There is a relationship between the character and the landscape, which is then combined with the characters' own personal struggles and histories. Gabriel's analysis – mediated through photography and cinema – highlights that the significance of the slag heap also lies outside the individual filmmaker's work.

In the short film *Chambre froide*, Masset-Depasse includes a series of images of the slag heaps that lie behind the *courée* where the central protagonists (the mother and the daughter) reside. Gabriel (2011: 75) compares the long shot of the slag heap behind the characters' residence, as the mother hangs out her washing in the garden, with a similar photograph captured by Auquier in his *Pays noir* collection, that of the young girl Luise hanging out her washing in the *courée* in *Les convoyeurs attendent*. The recurrence of this image affirms the presence of the slag heap – as well as the *courée* in this case – as regional and local markers for the city of Charleroi and the region of Wallonia (Bénézet 2005). The image also recalls the coal-mining communities of the Borinage, depicted in *Déjà s'envole la fleur maigre*, in which Meyer frames a washing line – laden with work trousers, shirts and tablecloths – in the communal backyards of the Italian workers. The films and the photography enter into a productive dialogue which is evocative of the industrial landscapes and spaces that are captured as part of the *mise-en-scène*. In 2000, the Walloon journalist José Fontaine (2000) identified the paintings (Vincent Van Gogh, Maximilien Luce, Constantin Meunier and Eugène Boch), photographs (William Kessel) and documentaries of the industrial Hainaut region as one of the five aspects of a Walloon culture. For Masset-Depasse, the city produces a distinct and local articulation and aesthetic, contending that 'Charleroi fascinates [...] Its industrial landscapes, noir to start with, reveal a rare aesthetic. It shapes your point of view' (F. By 2007). From this premise, Masset-Depasse's framing of the landscape is produced in relation to the city in question, with a certain intentionality for meaning from the local articulation imbued in each image. Moreover, the consistency of the images of the town and the region has continued from (at least) the 1960s through to the aforementioned films of the late 1990s and early 2000s. This pertains to an indirect engagement with the socio-political and socio-economic situation in the local town, since the photographic and film works draw attention to the deteriorating mining and steel industries in Charleroi. As Masset-Depasse (2013) notes, the slag heaps represent a 'heap of poverty' for the characters and the community who live in their shadows.

The opening of *Chambre froide* lends itself to the ailing paternalism of a coal-based industry, unrolling with a travelling shot from left to right across a graveyard on the margins of the city (Figure 4.3). In the context of the Dardenne brothers' *Rosetta* (1999), Park (2012) contends that the absent father is included in the films as a 'phantom' figure for the young adult. This concept speaks more generally to the Walloon region, known for its de-industrialisation and evocations of absent fathers within a withering patriarchal, industrial system. The opening shot of *Chambre froide* laterally tracks across a graveyard and its seemingly endless cycle of headstones, evoking the heightened and dramatic shift away from paternalism and patriarchal industrial structures that has resulted in the increased absence of father figures from society and its cinematic representations. Masset-Depasse's shot further evinces the notion of a region in poverty, which has gained traction as the 'topical' 'theme of the nation' (Hjort 2000: 105–7). The depth of field captures the blast furnaces in the background, corralling the death of the father and the industry into one shot. The equal focus attributed to the foreground and the background operates as a stylistic signature in Masset-Depasse's early films. Resonating with Lafosse's early filmmaking, the use of low-contrast and low-grade film stock coheres with the social-realist aesthetic oft-used in 1990s francophone Belgian cinema – and the calling card of the Dardenne brothers, particularly in the case of *La promesse*, *Rosetta* and *Le fils*.

Figure 4.3 The opening image of *Chambre froide* reveals Rita and her mother visiting the grave of her deceased father, with the steel plants in the background.

The slag heap also functions as a means of articulating the character's sense of isolation and solitude. In *Chambre froide*, Rita (played by Anne Coesens) decides to briefly scale the slag heap, heightening the individual's alienation, as she gazes down onto the city of Charleroi. The slag heap is evocative, corralling the memory of the region's steel industries within a present, establishing a stylistic dialogue with *Déjà s'envole la fleur maigre*. However, through the use of the extreme long shot in *Chambre froide*, the industrial evocations are situated at a distance, articulated visually through the steel and coalworks as small reference points within the frame. Rita's gaze establishes a connection to the past, but she offers a progressive future, developed through female characters. Similar to the Dardenne brothers' films, Hayward (2000: 97–9) notes that the nation develops according to the representation of women (in relation to its formerly masculine inflection). The ailing paternalism is also held at a distance, and speaks to Mosley's (2002) concept of 'social memory' imbued within the Dardenne brothers' *La promesse* and *Rosetta*.

The significance of the slag heap for contemplation purposes and to heighten the marginality of the character is best exemplified in the contemporaneous *Ultranova*. Bouli Lanners notes that, as Dimitri scales the slag heap, the frame is imbued with the darkness of the coal, which is then viewed in direct contrast to the bright, ethereal white sunlight at the summit (Lanners 2005). According to Gabriel, the 'realist' black-and-white photography of the *Pays noir* and the choice of film stock by the documentarian Benoît Mariage in *Les convoyeurs attendent* are concomitant with the industrial space in which they were produced (Gabriel 2011: 74). Drawing on these salient examples, colour and tone produce local and cultural evocations and articulations, resonating with Harper and Rayner's analysis of cinematic landscapes, colouration and their relation to 'cultural or societal history' (2010: 14). As a result, black-and-white cinematography and colour palette has become synonymous with the representation of coal-mining communities and cinematic landscapes in Wallonia, and this continues to reverberate through Masset-Depasse's pared-down palette in *Chambre froide*.

The composition of these shots resonates with films produced in other European coal-mining communities, particularly *My Childhood* (Bill Douglas, 1972). The autobiographical trilogy has led to Douglas' valorisation as a European auteur, as opposed to a British or Scottish auteur, and the universal aspects of the story also shine through, encouraging an analysis with filmmaking in Scotland. The recent destruction of the film's location of Newcraighall, or gentrification of the area, resonates with the removing of the Walloon slag heaps that surround the Belgian region's former mining towns.[6] Historically, this connection is not particularly specious, given the United Kingdom and Belgium's heritage as the formerly two leading industrial forces in the early to mid twentieth century. The opening sequence witnesses a young child, Jamie, standing atop a slag heap on the fringes of the small Scottish town of Newcraighall. As Murray observes, 'our fleeting access to Jamie's all-encompassing physical perspective stems directly from his glaring emotional lack: he crouches, exposed and alone, high above his fellow children because they have parents and he does not' (Murray 2015: 206). Jamie's physical location above the group of children who remain on the same level as their parents further highlights the character's sense of exclusion and isolation. It also articulates the issue of filiation. The use of low-cost, low-contrast film stock further enhances the gritty, raw and black-and-white aesthetic (Atkinson 2008) that is concomitant with the surrounding coal-mining society.

Let us now turn back to *Cages* in terms of a nationally orientated reading of the film. Stiers posits that the only 'Belgian' part of the final film is the final sequence in which the characters perform as beasts on stage in Eve and Damien's bar, since it is an inheritor of 'fantastique à la belge' (Belgian weird fiction), inspired by Belgian authors such as Jean Ray, Thomas Owen and Françoise Mallet-Joris (2007b: 7) or even a connection to Belgian filmmaking traditions such as magical realism (Ruëll 2007: 4–5). The notion of a 'fantastic realism' is posited as 'another notable characteristic of French and Dutch language literatures in Belgium' (Dirkx 2011: 70). André Delvaux, oft-cited as the 'father of Belgian cinema', is typically perceived as the purveyor of cinematic magic realism in a Belgian context. At this point, it is salient to stress the 'Belgian' appellation, with no clarification against regional or linguistic communities, since Delvaux remains one of the few filmmakers to bridge the divide. It is from this premise that Eve's line proves epiphanic, noting that 'on est unique' (we are unique/individual).

Masset-Depasse contends that the sequence is inspired by his childhood and the region; 'my Belgian reptilian brain recalled an animal market somewhere in the Walloon countryside. As a child I saw a competition there for imitators of animal sounds' (Masset-Depasse in Ruëll 2007: 5). A similar thematic approach and understanding of Masset-Depasse's filmmaking also emerges in his discussion of Charleroi, contending that 'I have definitely been marked by its [Charleroi's] violence, its animality' (Masset-Depasse in Broquet 2005).[7] The sequence's cathartic function arises when the animal sounds enable Eve to express and articulate herself once again. In fact, the sequence coheres with the *deus ex machina* endings of the melodrama genre (Neale 1986: 6). It provides little substance, detail or reasoning as to why and how Eve suddenly overcomes her disability and psychological handicap, and thus draws the narrative to a clear-cut solution.

The film's denouement frames the confrontation through the town's annual ritual, in which the locals compete to imitate an animal in a public arena. Douin (2008b) draws attention to this final act's painterly filiation, positing a reference to artwork of Belgian painter James Ensor. Masset-Depasse self-consciously addresses this painterly filiation, positing artistic influences from Ensor, Hieronymus Bosch and Francis Bacon in his films (Guiot 2007: 5; Jacobs 2007: 11; Lorfèvre 2007a; Ruëll 2007: 5). Masset-Depasse emphasises the natural filiation with painting, describing film as 'a painting in sound and movement', which is, as a result not hermetically sealed (*La Tribune de Bruxelles* 2007). In Smith's assessment of nationalism in cinema, the scholar argues that 'artists help to create a reproduce the very fabric of national communities to which they belong, and thereby disseminate and perpetuate the idea of the nation itself, its history, development and destiny' (2000: 57). The filiation with Hieronymus Bosch evinces this 'national articulation' in Smith's term. As Van den Braembussche argues, '[o]n a cultural level there undeniably exists a Belgian imaginary, characterised by a unique blend of realism and magic. This characteristic can be found not only in Flemish painting [...such as] Hieronymus Bosch, a Dutch painter influenced by the Flemish primitives' (2002: 36). Through these artistic references, there is something primordial in *Cages*' depiction of the animalistic half-human forms, performing their automatic and instinctive impulses on stage.

The stylistic references to Ensor, in particular, articulate a form of the national that could bridge the 'hollow' gap between Flemish and francophone Belgian culture, with De Heusch presciently asking 'Did James Ensor of Ostend, who wrote in French, paint in Flemish?' (2002: 22). Following this line of argument, to what extent is Masset-Depasse's film, written and articulated in French, capturing a Flemish style landscape? According to De Heusch, the coastline and the beaches contained aspects of the 'national' and represented Belgium, by positing that '(s)hells were our national currency' (2002: 13). The shoreline and the coast appear not to solely represent and articulate incongruity in Belgian culture, instead they appear to evoke a national nostalgia and mutual intelligibility between French-speaking and Flemish Belgian citizens. Let us now turn to the representation and the articulation of the coastline and the cliff tops of *Cages*.

The Cliffs of Nord-Pas-de-Calais: The Shift in Regional Landscape

The use of the majestic cliff-edges of Nord-Pas-de-Calais has come to identify as *Cages*' 'narrative image' (Ellis 1992: 30), cutting across the film's promotional material. The Nord-Pas-de-Calais cliffs open and close the film, appearing beneath the first mention of the film's title (Figure 4.4), as well as being included at the centre-point. The imagery of the cliffs, stones, coastline and the human body points to a film that firmly fits into the context of art cinema, with its evocations of the Swedish auteur, Ingmar Bergman. In the same way that the hilltop death dance has come to represent the 'narrative image' of Bergman's *Det sjunde inseglet/The Seventh Seal* (1957) and an emblem of the auteur's 'regional aesthetic' (Hedling 2010: 319), the image of Eve pulling a wheelchair-bound Damien across the Nord-Pas-de-Calais cliff-tops reverberates through *Cages*' promotional material. The depth of field also draws attention to the 'beauty' of the coastline, capturing the white cliffs, the turbulent sea and the beach stretching into the distance. The focus

Figure 4.4 *Cages*' title sequence unrolls on the majestic cliffs of Nord-Pas-de-Calais.

on the landscape, in a similar way to Bouli Lanners (see Chapter 5), evokes Flemish landscape painting.[8]

Whereas the previous section and the analysis of the Walloon landscape in Masset-Depasse's valorised shorts pertains to symbols of decline, collective bonds and collective/community memory – or as Mosley (2002) interprets 'social memory' with particular emphasis on the 1990s works of the Dardenne brothers in Wallonia – the cliff-top landscapes further precipitate connotations of death, which is concomitant with the evocations of Bergman's films. Death as a thematic motif permeates films 'at the shoreline', since '(d)eath at the edge of the water can also be a type of new beginning, involving purification and contemplative transformation as the final moment arrives' for troubled adults (Hammond and Redmond 2013: 601). Death arises through the references to Bergman's work, and also operates symbolically, suffused within the image of the coastline. In the film's opening sequences on the cliff-edges, the space initially reinforces Eve and Damien's relationship, since the personal memories of their relationship – also articulated in the promotional material and the titular sequence through the act of sex – are literally inscribed in a stone, situated at the top of the cliff. The space and the stone, in particular, neatly function as 'conduits to memories' (Harper and Rayner 2010: 13), without cultural, local or regional significance. For Harper and Rayner, the elision between cinematic landscapes and memory is generated by Henri Bergson's analysis of 'referential characteristics' within the 'instantaneous section' of film (ibid.). At the denouement, Eve throws the rock, inscribed with their names, into the sea, reinforcing the representation of the sea as cleansing and purifying as well as articulating the death of the seven-year relationship and marriage. The stone and the act of discarding it into the sea is, therefore, metaphorical and evidently liberating for Eve. Adopting Hammond and Redmond's notion, the cliff-edge and shoreline operate as 'the point of no return for doomed lovers' (2013: 601). Hammond and Redmond further posit that 'the relations between sea and land can create liminal, often transgressive possibilities for representational and phenomenological encounters between people who "find themselves" at the water's edge' (ibid.). The articulation of the conflicting notions of solidarity and alienation is discernibly present, with the two bodies intertwined on the cliff edge representing both the raw and corporeal intimacy of the central protagonists' relationship, in addition to their distance from a sense of community and collective (Figure 4.4).

Developing on from the initial analysis that offers a 'psychological–physical' axis in Masset-Depasse's Walloon-based shorts, the Bergman cinematic point of reference becomes salient *a fortiori*. As Hedling posits, 'Bergman creatively employed geography to metaphorically depict mental landscapes, at first with influences both from Italian Neorealism and from American film noir' (2010: 308), as neatly evinced by images of Bergman's personal screening room, which includes *The Asphalt Jungle* (John Huston, 1950), for instance, in his extensive VHS collection. Although the connection between Bergman's regional images of Skåne and the northern regions of France could be considered perfunctory initially, an understanding of their economic histories proves revelatory. Hedling (2010) describes Skåne's regional history as predicated on an industrial and agricultural history and economy, particularly since the end of the Second World War. This echoes the economic histories of both the Nord-Pas-de-Calais and Wallonia regions/provinces.

The use of the coastline is evidently symbolic, functioning as an outward projection of the character's inner torment and struggles. As Anne Coesens (Eve) notes,

> We saw the cliffs [of the French coastline] and we understood the significance of them as a counterpoint. Filming on a slag heap would have continued the tone of the narrative with its preoccupation with sequestration. The sunshine and the open environment gave the film a fresh energy set against the sense of constriction in the other spaces. (Bayer 2008)

There is hence a transition from the man-made slag heap to the natural cliff tops, which have subsequently changed the tone and the potential meanings articulated in the *mise-en-scène*. Masset-Depasse (2013) similarly asserts that the coastline offered the film a different artistic perspective and edge, attesting to the 'romanticism of the côte d'Opale' with the cliffs, therefore, lending themselves effectively to 'the story of *désamour* [no longer being in love]'. Returning to Harper and Rayner, the scholars neatly posit that there is a degree of 'interpretational license [that] becomes the offer of such representational flexibility that any cultural aspect of the national environment is negated by the economic potential of offshore production' (2010: 23). *Cages* provides the example *par excellence* of such a 'marked' interpretation of the cinematic landscape.

The deserted shoreline has the binary effect of representing solitude, articulating a simultaneous opening up and closing down for the central protagonist. As Masset-Depasse crucially observes, 'if one places the character on a clifftop, facing the ocean, it also has the appearance of isolation in the same way that one films in a small room' (Stiers 2007b: 7). Solitude is conceived through the discernible distance from a sense of community, but a personal and human connection is suggested through Eve and Damien's relationship in the film's opening sequence on the coastline. However, a sense of solitude and sequestration is not imbued in the same way as the aforementioned slag heaps of the Hainaut province in photographic and film representations.

Instead, the tight framing of the individual's body in this interior sequence heightens Eve's disaffection from the small-town, provincial and particularlist community. Coesens neatly describes the tight framing as 'une caméra intrusive' (an intrusive camera) (Stiers 2007b: 7). The film's title further evidences the sense of claustrophobia and proximity between camera and body. Lorfèvre (2006b) posits that there is no point of comparison in Belgian cinema in terms of how the body is framed sensorily by Masset-Depasse. This is primarily because, although the film uses travelling shots and a handheld camera, it is 'far from a documentary approach' (Feuillère and Vlaeminckx 2005: 15). However, Weissberg (2006b) is more critical of this filmmaking approach, observing it as 'nervous handheld camerawork [that] calls attention to itself rather than providing insights into the characters' inner lives'. Whereas the setting and framing of the landscape of *Chambre froide* evokes Mariage's *Les convoyeurs attendent* and Meyer's *Déjà s'envole la fleur maigre*, the semantic use of the camera's 'nervousness' resonates with the Dardenne brothers' 'social-realist' films between *La promesse* and *L'enfant*. The camerawork is consistently jerky, uneven and restless throughout the film, articulating Eve's fraught mindset. The liminal space of the cliff face offers a point of renegotiation between her and her partner and the potential for a sense of assimilation into a community. This slowly unrolls through the frequent visits to this setting.

The long shots frame expansive views of the coastline behind the characters placed firmly in the foreground. These shots operate in contrast to the close-up, tight framing of the interior sequences that lend themselves to a sense of claustrophobia. Within this preoccupation with closeness and proximity, particularly in relation to the human body, there is a primary focus on Eve's eyes (Masset-Depasse and Bronckart 2006). The intentionality of the proximity to the body and the face is discernible, foregrounding the 'centrality of emotion' and a move 'towards the sensorial' (Sépul 2010: 10). Feuillère and Vlaeminckx (2005: 14) emphasise the salience of the eyes and the face in *Cages* and further evince an intertextual line with Bergman by using a quotation from the Swedish auteur to introduce their interview and analysis.

Masset-Depasse highlights the significance of these 'transitions' between the interior and exterior spaces, by stating 'I leave on these interior images [before a subsequent shot of the coastline] in order to develop them as much as possible and move towards the most profound interiority of the character' (ibid.). The intensity of the sequences is broken up through the rhythm of the film's poetics, which move between different beats, that is, the extreme close-ups on the entwined bodies, the long shots of the vertiginous cliff-edges and the images of the sky, populated by soaring seagulls (Masset-Depasse and Bronkart 2006). The images of the sky and the seagulls posit an omniscience on behalf of the spectator, withdrawing them systematically from the unfolding action. Nevertheless, this contrasts with the filmmaker's intention to produce films that are predicated purely upon 'psychological action' (Stiers

2007b: 7). Whereas Masset-Depasse's short films articulate loss through the *mise-en-scène* and setting, the transformations leading to darkness and the close interior shots of *Cages* operate with similar significance – but without the cultural particularities and reference points. As the following section evinces, the use of the close-up references Ingmar Bergman's use of the camera, with very much less sophistication, but with an intentionality that seeks an affective response from the spectator and evokes a certain carnality. Masset-Depasse's approach to the interior *mise-en-scène*, therefore, textualises the film's key themes. Eve's psychological condition is textualised through a pervading verticality and sense of imprisonment. The vertiginous cliff-edges attest to the character's sequestration and alienation in the same manner as the projection of the bed's headboard onto Eve's face (as Damien is forcibly tied to the bed), the strobes of light that fragment Eve's face as she opens the curtains and hosts the animal imitation competition and the glass window panes of Léa's office at the brewery. On each of these occasions, the framing captures Eve's face within a fragmentation of vertical lines, textualising the couple's impending break-up. The lighting effects across Eve's face make reference to the expressive and patterned lighting effects produced by Hollywood film noirs in the 1940s – as Keating proposes (2009: 244–64) – that extended the ambiguity and meaning of the films beyond classicism (see Figure 4.5).

Figure 4.5 Before Eve walks on stage to confront her inability to speak, Masset-Depasse focuses on Eve's eyes through a noirish vertical pattern of lighting.

Corporeality and Fluids

The key thematic signifier that joins the dots between the exterior and interior *mise-en-scène* articulations of Eve's psychological condition and inner turmoil is the reverberation of fluids in the film. Adopting a discursive strategy, discourse leans towards the 'carnal', 'emotional' and 'sensorial', thereby encouraging an affective and phenomenological approach to the film. According to Masset-Depasse, the film's 'carnal charge' emanates from the lead female protagonist's 'combat', battle and struggle (Sépul 2010: 10).[9] In the context of Bergman's filmmaking, Wen (2014) foregrounds the haptic, tactile, carnal and sensory experience – posited as 'tactile encounters' – created through the use of close-ups on the human body, and particularly the face. Van Hoeij contends that the actor's face and body are essential elements to Masset-Depasse's films (2010: 100). In so doing, Olivier Masset-Depasse's use of the camera, as an evocation of Bergman, resonates with Wen's first typology, which critically considers 'proximity vs. distance' (Wen 2014: 21–2). From this premise, Masset-Depasse uses two love-making scenes that contrast in tone and approach. The film's title sequence neatly evidences such an analysis, with highly polished and stylised camerawork alternating between extreme close-ups on the hands (drawing attention to the characters' wedding rings and tattoos) and faces of the two characters as they have sex, before revealing a sense of distance through the extreme long-shot with immense depth of field. The extreme-close ups and extreme long shots form the poetics for Masset-Depasse's sex sequences. It is at this point that the 'nervousness' and frantic movement of the camera is less pronounced. For Lorfèvre, the body is filmed 'with sensuality, marking a finely crafted love-making scene with a modest eroticism' (Lorfèvre 2007b). The stability of the camera and its objectivity, eschewing the characters' perspectives, articulates the momentary stability in the relationship. The revelatory use of the extreme-long shot and the shoreline articulates the impending drama and shift in their relationship, as they have reconciled within a liminal space – on a cliff face, just above the stretch of beach, known for its inevitable shifting, fluidity and flux according to the elements (wind and water). It is vertiginous for both the spectators and the characters, further enhancing the emotional decline for Eve and Damien. The presence of the sea, captured by the deep-focus cinematography, maintains the inclusion of water as a thematic motif within Eve and Damien's relationship.

The second sex sequence, which takes place in the domestic environment (the couple's bedroom), shifts in tone to evoke a certain carnality. The natural lighting of the coastline, evoking a light blue colour palette between the sea and the sky, is replaced by black and orange hues developed from the neo-noir style of lighting. This coalesces with the themes unrolling on screen and explores the sinister act of borderline enforced and non-consensual sex on behalf of the male protagonist. In this instance, it is within the interior settings that the characters' sinister desires emerged, as 'modulated' (Keating 2009: 249) by the dark lighting techniques. The extreme-close-ups place less emphasis on the conjoining of hands, and instead focus on the characters' breasts and shoulders. In so doing, the sequence takes the act of sex into a raw and carnal form. The extreme-long shots and the deep-focus cinematography is no longer required, with the long shots pinpointing the entwined bodies in the centre of the frame as the room fills with darkness. The film noir and neo-noir themes emerge not only through the choice of lighting (and the 'modulated' (Keating 2009: 249) lighting in particular), but also by virtue of the male character being prisoner to Eve, as the representative of a femme fatale. The long shots reaffirm Damien's position, tied down to the bed, and restricted in his movements, emasculating him through the lack of control. The high-angle, oblique angles of the cinematography follow this line of argument that disempowers the male character in the act of sex in this sequence, whereas the opening sequence atop Nord-Pas-de-Calais cliffs represents a mutuality in their relationship.

The generic term 'fluid' is most productive at this point, as opposed to water, although each manifestation is a derivative of the fluid. The depth of the shots of the Nord-Pas-de-Calais cliffs is inclusive of the shifting and flowing patterns of the sea and the waves that crash against the cliffs. The denouement – in which Eve casts a stone, inscribed with their initials, into the sea – operates as a symbol and metaphor for the cleansing and refreshing at the end of her relationship with Damien. There is a certain curative function for the lead protagonist. In Lanners' *Eldorado*, Yvan and Elie wash themselves in a river that flows through the Ardennes, functioning as a textual representation of Elie breaking away from his destructive relationship with his father and from his heroin addiction. At the same time, Masset-Depasse incorporates more subtle nuances of fluids and fluidity within the film. The intimacy generated through the consistent use of close-ups throughout the film emphasise the human fluids of sweat, saliva and semen in the acts of sex and kissing, tears at the moment of break-up, rain as an evocation of Damien's affair with Léa, and abject spit from Léa on the animalistic Damien at Eve's moment of overcoming her disability.

Camera operator Tommaso Fiorilli – who worked with Masset-Depasse in the nascent part of his career – foregrounds the rain-soaked sequence in which Eve discovers Damien's affair as the film's strongest scene, filled with emotional charge (Cinergie.be 2008) (see Figure 4.6). The coalescing of tears and rain during Eve's discovery of the affair between Damien and Léa pertains to its associations with the melodrama. *Cages* also articulates the binary opposition of lightness and darkness as part of the intertextual references pertaining to Bergman. Bradfer's review of *Cages* touches on this opposition and how it is generated; 'the melodrama is dark, the characters are savage,

Figure 4.6 Eve confronts Damien, after realising that he is having an affair with Léa. Rainwater operates as a key motif in the sequence.

extreme and impassioned, but the wildness of their feelings and emotions are not dampened by sunny and well-lit landscapes. There is something romantic in this approach' (Bradfer 2007b). Bradfer's use of the notion of melodrama in the context of a certain *noir*-ish quality chimes with the early reviews of film noir classics, which were synchronically considered as melodramas.

Neale (1986) explores the complexities of the act of crying and the representation of tears in the melodrama. The primary line of argument, which chimes with this sequence and the uncovering of the affair, concerns 'the narrative structure of many melodramas that mutual recognition, union through love, the attainment of the object of desire are impossible – because it is always too late. Tears come in part as a consequence' (Neale 1986: 22). The rain and the tears evoke the emotional split in the relationship and the inevitable parting of the couple; this is the point of no return in their relationship and marks their turn to 'doomed lovers'. The sequence also recalls the short film *Dans l'ombre* in terms of its reliance on symbolism. To this end, the film is rich in symbols – an aspect that has been readily identified in film criticism in both positive and denunciative terms.[10] *Cages*, therefore, is not laced with ambiguity. The film's reliance on subtext and nuance cohere with the expectations of the melodrama genre.

Conclusion

Masset-Depasse's *Cages* highlights the complexity of filmmaking within the context of a small 'national' cinema, with the medium's mode of production inflecting the film as text. The denunciative tone and oblique analysis of the film's landscape stretch to a contiguous region that is inclusive of an area known for its references to the *cinéma nordiste*. What is most telling is how the feature film deviates from the celebrated short filmmaking of the early 2000s, which foregrounded – in the case of *Chambre froide* – the former industrial areas of Wallonia and Charleroi. Rather than focusing on ailing paternalism, a 'topical' theme (Hjort 2000: 105–7) the beauty of the landscape in *Cages* places the film in dialogue with the later work of Bruno Dumont, and the often magical realist representation of the coastline as well as Ingmar Bergman's thematically death-laden cliff-edges. It is the interior sequences that offer a reading of internal psychological struggles and a breakdown in the nuclear family unit through an intertextual system that pertains to the melodrama and film noir styles.

Notes

1. 'Je fais les films que je dois faire. Pas nécessairement ceux que j'ai envie de faire. Mais j'espère avoir été le plus intègre en essayant d'être accessible. Je suis fier de *Cages*. Je ne me suis en aucun cas renié. *Mes seules limites ont été financières.*' (Masset-Depasse, in Bradfer 2007: 46)
2. Hogdin draws on this definition of 'marked' transnationalism by Hjort as a means of approaching the films of Joris Ivens, who worked in Belgium in the 1930s (2016: 42).
3. See Steele (2018a) for a further discussion of *Cages* in the context of 'affinitive' policy-making in Wallonia and Nord-Pas-de-Calais.
4. The phrase 'plic-ploc' is viewed as a 'true belgicism' and 'unique to the use of French in Belgium' (Mercier 2008). It is used widely and often in three different contexts (ibid.).
5. See the Cinemetrics.lv database (http://www.cinemetrics.lv/database.php) for a comprehensive list of the number of shots in the films of the Dardenne brothers, David Lynch and Ingmar Bergman.
6. In the DVD commentary for *Ultranova*, Lanners (2005) notes that the slag heap on which the film's poignant sequence unrolls no longer exists outside the world of the film.
7. During the DVD commentary, Masset-Depasse (2006) observes that the intention of the competition was to maintain a sense of intimacy between the characters even in a state of madness, although the filmmaker acknowledges that the final version of the sequence in the film was not entirely successful in conveying the intended meaning. He further posits that the idea of the competition can be traced to animal sounds made in hunting circles (Masset-Depasse and Bronckart 2006).
8. In an interview with Van Hoeij, Masset-Depasse describes cinema as 'like Flemish landscape painting; there is the impression that it is painted by one person, but the fact is, it requires a team of twenty-five people' (2010: 105).
9. Masset-Depasse discusses both of his feature films, signposting *Cages* and

Illégal, in his interpretation of the lead female protagonists (Sépul 2010: 8–10).
10. The *Zone02* (2007: 26) review laments the film's rich symbolism, positing that it is 'tiring' and easily perceptible at a surface level. The headline contends that the film operates as an example of 'pseudo-psychology' (ibid.), thereby chiming with Alfred Hitchcock's *Spellbound* (1945).

5. THE FRANCOPHONE BELGIAN ROAD MOVIE: *ELDORADO* (BOULI LANNERS, 2008) AND *ULTRANOVA* (BOULI LANNERS, 2005)

In February 2016, the Cinémathèque Royale in Brussels dedicated a two-month 'Belgorama' programme to the films of Bouli Lanners in the lead-in to the Berlinale release of *Les premiers, les derniers/The First, the Last* (Bouli Lanners, 2016). The 'Belgorama' strand provides a space for a celebration and valorisation of Belgian films and filmmakers, both French-speaking and Flemish, throughout Belgium's film history. For instance, in recent years, Emile-Georges de Meyst, Manu Bonmariage, Lydia Chagoll and producer Pierre Drouot amongst others have been included. The Lanners programme, however, is particularly salient to an analysis and interpretation of his corpus of work due to the incorporation of films that operate as intertexts in terms of stylistic filiation as well as attesting to Lanners' presence as a veritable Belgian film and television star. The transnational context of Lanners' stylistic filiation is neatly evidenced by the selection of *Dersu Uzala* (Akira Kurosawa, 1975) and *Deliverance* (John Boorman, 1972) to open the 'Belgorama' programme. As this chapter will later outline, Lanners' cinephilic knowledge and ciné-literacy of the post-war European 'art cinema' canon and films by key auteurs in a global context adds a certain depth to the filmmakers' use of static, long takes and road movie references.

Lanners' pre-cinema and television background is also crucial to take into consideration at this point, since the filmmaker initially trained as a painter at the prestigious Acadèmie des Beaux-Arts in Liège. The painterly filiation is evident in his filmmaking style, as Lanners notes, 'painting is always present when I film.

Every time I create a frame that is aesthetically pleasing, it represents a tableau that I had always wanted to complete' (Vlaeminckx and Feuillère 2008). As an 'autodidact', Lanners observes that his approach to filmmaking does not cohere with convention, stating that 'by not having a film school background, I have not learnt to respect the standard rules of filmmaking' (Lanners, in Vlaeminckx 2004: 17). His editing technique also appears as ad hoc and experimental, with Lanners noting that he analyses other filmmakers' editing, and changes the technique 'if it does not work' (Lanners, in ibid.: 16). Lanners' visual style is, therefore, created in relation to his cinephilic knowledge and his background working in front of the camera as an actor. The filmmaker has also shown his support for filmmaking outside the dominant mode of production, starting his filmmaking career producing short films, such as *Non, Wallonie, ta culture n'est pas morte/No Wallonia, Your Culture is Not Dead* (1996), *Travellinkx* (1999) and *Muno* (2001), made by independent and local film companies such as Versus Productions in the mid-1990s and early 2000s.[1] Moreover, Lanners started the alternative film festival *Festival de Kann* (a homophonic reference to the 'A'-grade festival Cannes in France) to support 'marginal cinema' (Rouchy 2008). This posits a certain predilection for the local and the regional modes of film production in a cinematically small nation.

Crucially, it is Lanners' choice of genre that facilitates such an interpretation along the lines of intertextuality and allusive 'semantic' and 'syntactic' content, as Altman (1984) notes in the context of genre. As Sargeant and Watson posit, '(t)he road movie's status as an intertextual and generic hybrid allows it to be read through a variety of theoretical approaches which highlight different areas of film production' (1999: 6). To this end, the road movie provides a neat interpretative framework for Lanners' early feature-length filmmaking, particularly as part of a transnational dialogue with the road movies of Aki Kaurismäki and Wim Wenders.

From this background, the connection between painting and Lanners' visual style is particularly strong and salient. This is primarily the case for the representation of the countryside, which Lanners similarly observes in his own painting (Cinémathèque Suisse 2012b). Moreover, in his review of Lanners' first feature film *Ultranova*, Lovat crucially notes how the opening shots of Dimitri next to his upturned car (an image that also reverberates through the film's publicity material on DVD covers and film posters) shows an 'affinity to the paintings of Edward Hopper' (2006: 82). This image is also evocative of Fernand Flausch's *La Mort de l'Automobile* artwork on the Sart Tilman campus at the University of Liège. Moreover, Lovat contends that '(m)any of the shots and sequences are worthy of gallery exhibition', which is crucial to Lanners 'developing a distinctive aesthetic of his own' (ibid.). This filiation speaks to the sheer virtuosity of Lanners' camerawork and cinematography that transcends film as a medium.

Writing about *Eldorado*, Mosley states that Lanners 'eschews the brothers' [the Dardennes'] unadorned realism in favour of a hyper/magic realist style [...] showing ordinary people and places in an extraordinary, painterly light' (Mosley 2013: 30). In film criticism, Roy (2008) further observes the 'symbolic farce' of Thierry Zéno's filmmaking and magic realist synchronicity with Dominique Abel, Bruno Romy and Fiona Gordon's road films *L'iceberg* (2005) and *Rumba* (2008) in a Belgian context.[2] The drawing of a synchronic citation between *Rumba* and *Eldorado* emerges through the two films' valorisation at the aforementioned Cannes film festival in 2008. In *Eldorado*, the farcical nature of the comedy, including the small vignettes of a nude Alain Delon and a classic car collector with a certain predilection for cars that have led to the deaths of pedestrians, chimes with national and regional tastes. For instance, in *France-Soir*'s review of *Eldorado*, Loison (2008) describes Lanners' film as 'an episode of *Strip-Tease*, in its "art-house" version'. The cult television show *Strip-Tease* was characterised by its absurd form of comedy, and it proved to be the testing ground for novice filmmakers in the 1980s and 1990s such as Benoît Mariage. Upon its release, critics for the (francophone) Belgian film magazine *Cinergie* saw *Ultranova* as the inheritor to a series of internationally valorised and recognised French-language Belgian films from the 1990s, including *Toto le héros/Toto the Hero* (Jaco Van Dormael, 1991), *C'est arrivé près de chez vous*, *Rosetta* and *Les convoyeurs attendent* (Verhaeghe 2005). Similarly to Jaco Van Dormael's *Toto le héros*, Lanners' filmmaking alludes to Hollywood and American film culture. Moreover, the latter two films have been frequently cited throughout this book as key 'national cinema' reference points.

Lanners' narratives are difficult to pin down and succinctly summarise due to their lack of character motivations in a classical form. The film eschews causality and a classical tightness of storytelling. Bordwell's (1979) notion of 'ambiguity' in the 'art cinema' context is, therefore, a more apposite point of reference for the narrative construction. According to Lanners, and this is particularly the case for *Ultranova*,

> the films are composed like puzzles, made of dozens of pieces, each one reproducing little stories that were either told to him, that happened to him or that he stole as the attentive listener from the counters of commercial cafés. But these pieces are put together in such a way that they constitute a delicate tableau that can affect us. (Verhaeghe 2005)

The narratives are, in this case, like mini-stories and fragments within a larger patchwork of sometimes banal or even extraordinary activities and events that occur on a daily basis.

As Mandelbaum (2008) argues, the spirit of May 1968 and themes of solidarity are inescapable in Lanners' films. The inculcation of socio-political topics and a focus on themes such as social marginalisation and precarity chime with Archer's (2013: 43) post-1968 generation of French filmmakers. Following this line of argument, Lanners belongs to the same group of filmmakers in France 'born after the 1950s, who entered adulthood after the post-war boom years of economic prosperity' (ibid.). However, unlike the Dardenne brothers, born in the early 1950s,[3] it is not possible to argue that May 1968 (and the strikes that took place in and around the city of Liège in particular) profoundly affected Lanners in his early life, since he was born in the German-speaking region of Belgium much later, in 1965. Filmmakers like Lanners, and to an extent Masset-Depasse and Lafosse, do not have the same filmmaking background as the Dardennes, which commenced with a 'militant' and committed style of filmmaking in the 1970s (Mélon 2010; Mai 2010; Mosley 2013). As documentarians, the Dardennes were 'politically minded filmmakers in the post-1968 context [. . .] exploring the crossroads of history, politics and personal identity' (Mai 2010: xi). Lanners, instead, remains on the cusp of the group of filmmakers that emerged in the mid to late 1990s in France (so-called French New Realism), such as Erick Zonca and Bruno Dumont, through their depiction of 'localised struggles' (O'Shaughnessy 2003) and indirect social concerns.

'Lonesome Zonings': Liège and the City's Post-industrialism

The notion of a 'zoning' is particularly instructive for considering the films of Bouli Lanners as being in-between the city and the countryside. It resonates with the Walloon 'self-image' that Mosley explores in his seminal work on Belgian cinema, which the scholar characterises as 'standard urban-rural' (Mosley 2001: 2). Mosley's description of space in Lanners' *Eldorado*, however, coheres more with the filmmaker's first feature film *Ultranova*, which considers 'underclass characters each facing a life crisis and struggling against the odds laid by urban and rural decay' (Mosley 2013: 30). It is precisely this 'vision' of the underclasses that highlights 'a need for [. . .] change' (H. H. 2005). The deleterious margins of the city represent francophone Belgian cinema's dominant image, or as film critic Rouchy (2008) neatly posits, 'the honey of Belgian cinema'.

However, *La Libre Belgique* contends that Lanners offers something more nuanced in the context of francophone Belgian cinema, by positing that 'Lanners rejects the codes of the social film, refusing the hostility and the rage, [instead] preferring naivety and emotions' (H. H. 2005). Lanners' films move away from the social films and social cinema of Marianne Theunissen and Richard Olivier in Wallonia in the 1990s. Theunissen and Olivier's films 'explor[ed] shadowy zones in Wallonia across often disturbing films, but films that have a great richness [...] of doubts, of investigations, but also a human warmth and rage contained against all forms of inequality' (Duculot 1998: 5). Lanners offers a new poetics of the formerly industrial landscape, which reverberates through *Ultranova* through book-ending shots that punctuate sequences. O'Shaughnessy's (2003) argument contends that the disparate films in France and Belgium in the late 1990s (which stretches into the early 2000s) 'draw on what is at hand to resist the utopian and totalising drive of neoliberalism' (O'Shaughnessy 2003: 202). As a result, Lanners' poetics are no longer 'urgent' in their enunciation of social and political issues and concerns in the local setting. They are instead mournful and enriched by lament with their emphasis on the landscape, its emptiness, and the turn to tactile objects as mediated memories. The emptiness of the shots and the Walloon spaces points to a displacement of a collective, thereby evoking a sense of loss. As Massey argues,

> [t]he dislocation of place that globalisation implied, the pressures of long-distance migration, the flows of cultural influences and power; all were frequently argued to be leading to a sense of displacement, and all continually and in a host of ways fed into and, we would argue, fed counter-arguments about belonging. (Massey 2011)

The inclusion of abandoned houses, warehouses and factories resonates with Jacques Charlier's photographic work showing the rapidly de-industrialising suburb of Seraing, on the outskirts of Liège, therein heightening this sense of emptiness and loss.

This section's 'Lonesome Zonings' appellation arises from the pre-production title for *Ultranova* and the first article on the film in *Cinergie*. Lanners describes the 'zoning' as a negative shift in the urban environment, leading to social polarisation that is part of wider government policy changes in Belgium. The filmmaker notes that they are 'constructed in order to better serve cars; the town centres are deserted [...] this unravels the social fabric [...] There is no longer a social life, no more shops or cafes. There is no coherent urban policy in Belgium' (Heyrendt 2005a). The fabric and tissue of a society is shattered, necessitating the characters to fetishise and substitute human interactions. *La Libre Belgique* further contends that *Ultranova* focuses on 'the industrial "zonings" without any soul and pre-fabricated houses that uniform the horizon' (H. H. 2005). The notion of 'uniformity' and processes of standardisation, articulated through Lanners' cinematography, is considered later in this section, since it alludes to neoliberal, capitalist and global forces.

The absence of 'soul' (an idea that repeatedly permeates francophone Belgian film criticism on the film) is articulated by Lanners through fetish and tactile encounters. The characters' fetishisation of objects serves to reinforce a

Figure 5.1 Dimitri caresses a pair of tights, as he sits alone on the periphery of the city of Liège.

society formed on a surface that lacks its former depth and nuance, replacing it through moments of touch. These optics coalesce around personal, local and regional memories. This is particularly the case for the three central characters of Dimitri, Cathy and Jeanne, who substitute the emptiness around them with objects that engender nostalgia and memory through touch. It contrasts quite radically with Spaas' interpretation of the Dardenne brothers' *Rosetta*, in which 'the caravan is laid bare with nothing in it to remind Rosetta of her past and throughout the film no memories are evoked' (Spaas 2000: 42). The tactile encounters are addressed in *Ultranova* in four ways, (1) tights, (2) grass, (3) hands and (4) a purse (see Figure 5.1).

The first example of such a tactile encounter occurs as Dimitri sits alone in a cold, bleak, overcast and grey industrial suburb, replete with small slag heaps lining the road. His isolation and loneliness is quelled by his slow and careful stroking of a pair of women's tights, slowly unrolling the nylon material along his arm. The tights are a clear fetish for Dimitri, replacing something lost and forgotten amongst the industrial ruins. The pleasure – that Dimitri gains – is one of comfort and consolation, connecting the sensations from touch to a nodal point of memory. The tights are symbolic of a former process of manufacture, a traditional form of employment and work pattern in Wallonia (for instance, Andrien's *Australia* (1989) addresses the decline of the wool industry in the region, and the outsourcing of material and labour to the New World). The garment also has a female inflection and evocation, further articulating, on a quasi-Oedipal level, the loss of his mother and the nuclear family and a partner that represents stable human interactions. Within the neoliberal capitalist society, objects and materiality are fetishised as substitutes for filiation, family and, more generally, human relationships. As Lanners notes, 'we are not in the process of forming revolutionary regiments in Belgium [...] the fabric of the family is unravelling' (Bradfer 2005b: 4). Attachments are not sustained, they are fleeting – much like Cathy and Jeanne's friendship and Dimitri and Cathy's relationship – culminating in a brutal and vicious cycle of abandonment and social anxiety that is released briefly through materialism.

Prior to the initial 'contemplation shot' (Gabriel 2011: 86) in *Ultranova*, Dimitri slowly caresses the grass beside him, as he gazes out across the city of Liège with its industrial reference points (the bridge and the train) in the foreground (Lanners 2005). The grass provides Dimitri with a degree of comfort in his surroundings, despite his apparent isolation and alienation on the geographical fringes, gazing towards the centre. The blades of grass operate as a tactile encounter that engenders memory as well as addressing the former rural and pastoral connotations of the city's margins (prior to suburbanisation). The long, soft blades of grass evoke the caressing of silky hair (Lanners 2005), articulating and highlighting the absence of a nuclear family unit and the absence of a partner for Dimitri (epitomised through his disappointment with Cathy's reference to their relationship as siblings). The grass substitutes and fetishises his need for comfort and stability through stable human interactions, thereby referencing his alienation and marginal position. The society that Lanners presents is shattered, where there is a failure of individuals to communicate – a parable for Belgium as a nation-state. Cathy's purse represents a similar tactile function, in terms of human interactions and social bonds, as Dimitri, sat along the Meuse, caresses his face with its fabric.

Hands become significant through the film, particularly between Cathy and Jeanne, as symbols of touch, social bonding, and – on a philosophical level – the 'life line' on the palms. In so doing, the hands symbolise the working-class and blue-collar stratifications for the two characters, as traditional manual labourers in a furniture factory. On a thematic level, the peripatetic nature of the women's employment recalls Zonca's *La vie rêvée des anges* (1998) and the Dardenne brothers' *Rosetta* (1999). Jeanne's readings of the hands posit the futility of their future and their consolidation within rigid work patterns that are beginning to wither away. The closure of an adjacent factory and the discarding of their plants evokes the short-term nature of employment in Wallonia and their perennial existence close to expiration. Although Jeanne mutilates herself to change her path, Cathy embraces her hands as tools of the trade, completing work in the furniture store and the cutting/styling of her mother's hair.

Gabriel (2011) draws a key stylistic filiation between the films of Benoît Mariage and Bouli Lanners in terms of their representations of the urban and industrial landscape. For Gabriel, Lanners and Mariage's industrial landscapes operate as a key aspect of the *mise-en-scène*, in direct contrast to the character-focused work of the Dardenne brothers (Gabriel 2011: 67). In so doing,

Lanners stretches away from the 'purview' of the characters,[4] encouraging a contemplation of the film's poetics constructed through the road movie genre and the framing of the landscape. The notion of a peripheral zone neatly highlights the characters' sense of isolation. Lanners' films place little emphasis on the city centre, with fleeting glimpses of Place Cockerill in the heart of Liège in *Eldorado* when Elie falls back into his heroine habit. The name of the square clearly evokes the city's former industrial development under British industrialist John Cockerill, which has since withered away. Mosley contends that the inclusion of the industrial areas of Liège in *Eldorado* is an 'homage' to the Dardenne brothers (Mosley 2013: 30). Whilst the choice of location does place these films in immediate dialogue, particularly when using post-industrialism, questions of identity and the crisis of masculinity as an interpretative frame, the articulation and representation of space is more variegated in Lanners' films. *Ultranova* and *Eldorado* consider the peripheral zones of Liège, and it is within these zones that the issues of social marginalisation and social polarisation are viewed as most acute.

Both *Ultranova* and *Eldorado* are concerned with 'localised struggles' (O'Shaughnessy 2003) – resonating with the transnational, contiguous 'shared concerns' of so-called French New Realism (Powrie 1999) – since, as Lanners notes, 'I am very sensitive to my roots. Wallonia has sublime landscapes, linked to its history, but it is submerged in a horrific urbanism, and exists an example of total misconduct' (Bradfer 2005b: 4). The new-build, pre-fabricated houses built in the countryside, and the formerly industrial suburbs of Liège, are conceived as 'a metaphor of dehumanisation in modern society' in which 'Lanners uses the camera like a painting, composing mournful and sombre landscapes' (Heyrendt 2005b). For Verhaeghe (2005), Lanners achieves a poetic representation of daily life that is laced within these 'vast landscapes of empty spaces'. It is precisely this emptiness that evokes isolation and alienation for the individual. The poetic and lyrical framing of the Walloon countryside, therefore, resonates with O'Shaughnessy's analysis of so-called French New Realism in which, purely in terms of location and the representation of the local, *Ultranova*'s suburbs of the former steel city of Liège is perceived as 'a distinctly unpastoral rural' (O'Shaughnessy 2003: 195). On a thematic level, the film is inclusive of the gentrification of abandoned former working-class towns, such as Flémalle, but its emptiness and its representation as devoid of workers highlights its systematic failure.

Emptiness permeates the representations of the landscapes and the uniform, standardised manufacturing units. Lanners adopts the modernist technique of the 'seriality shot', borrowed from past masters (Keating 2011), to further 'dehumanise' the industrial settings and comment on the surface standardisation of western society and its materialism. As Jeanne and Cathy discuss their fatalism, the camera slowly unrolls through towers of crates that seemingly

Figure 5.2 In *Ultranova*, the camera dollies forward through the mundane warehouse, full of boxes, but with a limited number of workers.

'reproduce themselves' (Keating 2011) in a constant, forward-moving cycle of mass production. However, the 'seriality shot' 'dialectically' – to adopt Keating's terms (ibid.) – articulates an absence amongst the sea of crates, which appear to constantly and consistently regenerate without workers (Figure 5.2). It is precisely through these shots and the slow, constant dollying of the camera that constructs 'a Wallonia void of workers, but in a poetic way' (Heyrendt 2004). The poetics of Lanners' depiction of the manufacturing units eschews the Dardenne brothers' urgent realism for – as Keating contends – 'motifs of modernity' that evoke silent cinema and the movement of the camera (Keating 2011). In so doing, Lanners posits that the film 'is based [. . .] more on the atmosphere' (Heyrendt 2004). A symbolic and evocative atmosphere of mass reproduction that distances the traditional working classes from forms of manual labour, thereby enhancing the changing working patterns in post-industrial Wallonia as well as lamenting the deterioration of industrial practices.[5] The lateral 'seriality shot', *Ultranova*'s second, continues to develop these 'topical' themes (Hjort 2000: 105–7) of absence and economic crisis imbued within the empty spaces. The travelling shot dollies horizontally, from right to left, across the frame, consistently revealing an ongoing process of empty lorries, lined up with no certain destination. Combined with the lack of goods and materials being loaded onto the vehicles, a cycle of mass production and 'mass repetition' – again referring to Keating's (2011) terms alluding to masters of modernity – reinforces the absence of depth to the images in a system that is failing the individuals and workers of Wallonia. These factors tie the loose knot of the film's narrative with the themes of abandonment evoked through the fragmented and absent nuclear families (Cathy and Dimitri are both orphans). Moreover, the working environment is conceived as sterile and bland, evoking the 'surface' culture of globalisation in a transnational context (Hannerz 1996: 28) through the whiteness and minimalism of the office environment and the multiple billboards advertising the new-build, pre-fabricated housing estates.

In these two Lanners films, a centre-periphery model is partly engendered through recognisable and readable particularities to local audiences that have created historical and traditional associations with the city centre and Liège's rapid growth during the period of industrialisation. Lanners claims that the film's 'ambient urbanism [...] also has a dramatic value even if it is in the background' (Vlaeminckx 2004: 17). As geographers, Loopmans et al. argue,

> Liège has retained part of its bourgeois population in the city centre, early suburbanisation being hampered by the steep slopes of the River Meuse, which significantly reduced accessibility to the city centre. Suburbanisation has colonised the southern periphery of the city only in more recent times. (Christian Kestelout et al. 2001, cited in Loopmans et al. 2007: 87)

This distinct topography that delineates two stratifications of society historically is neatly evinced by the 'contemplation shot' in *Ultranova* (Gabriel 2011: 86). Dimitri is positioned in the foreground of the shot in front of the river. The river offers a distinctive geographical marker and barrier that emphasises Dimitri's position as an outsider within the suburban reaches of the city. In *Ultranova*'s DVD commentary, Lanners (2005) notes the intentionality of this fusion with the city's economy, with the small aspects of the train and the bridge evoking Liège's industrial heritage. A 2005 *Hep Taxi!* episode recreates this shot, with Lanners positing in diegetic voiceover, 'wait here a minute ... to contemplate' (Colin and Lanners 2005), before the soundtrack foregrounds the diegetic ambient sounds of a passing train as it travels slowly over the bridge. The reverberation of this shot from interview to film creates a productive dialogue between filmmaker-text-spectator, in which the spectator is invited to decode the images for the duration of ten seconds. This visual vocabulary also resonates with the analysis of the spatial dynamics of the Dardenne brothers' films in Chapter Two.

Gabriel posits that these two 'contemplation shots' are invested with meaning, since they do not clearly cohere with the rhythm of the narration (2011: 86–88). In these images, 'the landscape becomes the common target of crossed views', exemplified by the 'ironic' representations of the landscape in Lanners' short films and the 'silent contemplation' of his feature-length work (ibid.). The lingering of the camera – in this case for ten seconds – on the industrial images of the city is nostalgic, imbued with the memory of an industrial past. The 'contemplation shot' is inclusive of the semantic building blocks of Walloon visual culture – the bridge, the river, the tower blocks and *courée*

– evoking the tautology of its industrial background. The 2015 'Landscapes of Belgium' curation at the Musée d'Ixelles attested to the prominent role of industrial images in Belgian art and visual culture, crucially observing that after the period of de-industrialisation, artwork in Belgium tended to focus on the 'vestiges' in a poetic way. The 'coldness' of the colour palette (Sotinel 2005) – primarily grey and undersaturated – is mournful in a manner that appears as though Dimitri and the spectator are gazing at the dying embers. In essence, the 'contemplation shot' laments the emptiness and hollowed-out manufacturing units and the gentrification of now-abandoned villages and houses poised for demolition. Dimitri 'contemplates' as one of the last remaining survivors of a withering economic institution, with exclusion offered only through the lack of replacement opportunities to come. The lead character Dimitri has employment, as a salesman of new-build properties, but, as Sotinel (2005) posits, he holds himself at a distance from forming social bonds with Jeanne due to his orphaned background.

Returning to the image of the upturned car that opens and closes *Ultranova*, there is a further connection, beyond the aforementioned artistic filiation, in terms of poetic reverberations of filmmaking in Wallonia (Figure 5.3). Bénézet reads the long shot of a crashed car in an empty and deserted field in *Les convoyeurs attendent* in relation to Deleuze's notion that characters and landscapes are 'part of the compound of sensations' (2005: 168). For Bénézet it therefore represents the breakdown in communication between father and son (2005: 169). Rather than the direct father–son relationship that is fractured and fragmented, *Ultranova* pertains more generally to the lack of parent–child relationships, as evinced by Cathy and Dimitri both being orphans. The two characters bond over their mutual understanding and position as outsiders,

Figure 5.3 The opening sequence of *Ultranova* ends with an image of Dimitri standing alone next to his upturned car.

articulating an increasingly atomised society. Bradfer (2005a) interprets the opening image as a metaphorical birth of the character, Dimitri. The character's perceived 'birth' at this moment articulates his position as an orphan and as an atom, without a biological mother and father. The relationship to post-industrial and postmodern society is perceived in relation to the car, born in a society of surplus and predicated on neoliberal capitalism, Dimitri is introduced as devoid of a nuclear family, a relationship to a sense of belonging, and, on a wider scale, to a nation constructed through working relationships between men. In *Ultranova*, the six characters are all provided with employment, either as workers in a furniture depot or as estate agents selling new and purpose-built properties. However, their sense of social marginalisation is primarily articulated through their lack of parent–child relationships, which configures their status as outsiders. In the documentary *On the Road Again – Le cinéma de Bouli Lanners/On the Road Again – The Cinema of Bouli Lanners* (2011), Lanners keenly outlines what he terms as 'parental resignation' in contemporary society, which leads to a 'lost' generation. After Dimitri's 'metaphorical birth' (Bradfer 2005a) from the upturned automobile in his mid-twenties, the spectator is introduced to his 'birth' into a nuclear family at the age of twelve after the death of his biological parents.

Open Fields, Open-ended Images: The Poetics of Lanners' Walloon Countryside

Yvan and Elie's 'buddy' journey is punctuated by a series of chance encounters, comedic and tragic interludes, and moments that encourage the spectator to contemplate and decipher the image. As previously noted in this chapter, Lanners consciously offers moments of introspection and contemplation. The film does not have a neat and tightly bound causality, as the long takes and travelling shots offer an interpretative approach. The representation of the rural landscape is crucial in this framework, with static, long takes invoking a still image that resonates with the previously analysed work of Joachim Lafosse in Chapter Three and travelling shots, concomitant with the semantics of the road movie, that pass through open fields. In the 1990s, Duculot posited that 'Walloon landscapes were rarely present on cinema screens, even in documentaries' (Duculot 1998: 4). Lanners' films mark a break with this tradition, moving away from a focus on corporeality and the urban centres to depict the Walloon countryside and the natural beauty of the Ardennes. Whereas Lafosse's films are predicated on corporeal presence, Lanners' images reveal a landscape often absent of humans and characters.

As noted by the Cinémathèque Suisse (2012b), the landscape, in particular the natural world, seamlessly operates as a character in its own right. The programme notes that the first Brussels Urban Landscape Exhibition at Bozar in October 2016 was based on the theme 'the same provincial road', incorporating the Flemish filmmaker Michaël R. Roskam's short film *Carlo* (2004) and Lanners' *Eldorado* (Boie 2016). It implicitly posits a connection between photography and Lanners' filmmaking, 'capturing the landscape's temporal dimension in one image' (ibid.). This temporality had been equally presented in the (albeit primarily urban) photography of Georges Charlier (1980), Jan Kempenaers (2004) and Michiel De Cleene (2014), which 'visualised the changes of the landscape' (ibid.).

In the tradition of landscape painting and photography, Martin Lefebvre posits that 'the landscape has come to signify the depiction of a natural space freed from any emphasis on the representation of human figures and eventhood' (Lefebvre 2011: 63). Lefebvre earlier notes 'the emancipation of the landscape from its supporting role as background or setting to events and characters; as a result, it establishes the condition of its emergence as a completely distinct aesthetic object' (2006: 23). The spatial thinker Doreen Massey developed an approach to the long take in the context of the landscape in which they operate 'in the midst of the rush and flow of globalisation, a certain stillness. But they are not stills, they are about duration' (Massey 2011). This interpretation bears witness to Henri Bergson's notion of *durée* (Massey 2005: 57–8; Massey 2011). In his analysis of space and place in French cinema, Williams draws on Massey's (2005) open and non-fixed approach that 'liberate[s] space from chains of meaning which embed it with closure and stasis (as opposed to time as change) in order to place it within other more productive chains alongside openness and heterogeneity' (Williams 2013: 11). From this premise, Massey proposes that 'space must itself be imbued with temporality. Space as a simultaneity indeed, but a cut through on-going histories. Not a surface but a simultaneity of stories-so-far' (Massey 2011).[6] Imbued within the image, there are corrals of stories, of history, of memory, unrolling in the non-static and mobile time (mobility *within* the image) offered through the long take. Through 'simultaneity', the past rises to the surface of the present, evoked through the long-take focused on the landscape. This proves to be the theoretical and interpretative basis for Massey's (2011) analysis of space and the so-called 'stories-so-far', which are layered as a 'palimpsest' in the context of the films of Patrick Keiller and his framing of the British rural landscape. Questions of space and place are brought to the fore and immediately addressed.

Let us also turn to Deleuze's interpretation of Yasujirō Ozu, in which he discusses landscapes in nature – without immediate movement and characters (Deleuze [1989] 2013: 16). For Deleuze, 'they [empty spaces] reach the absolute, as instances of pure contemplation, and immediately bring about the identity of the mental and the physical, the real and the imaginary, the subject and the object, the world and the I' (Deleuze 2013: 16). Lanners' long takes of the landscape posit an optic of memory, highlighting the enduring agricultural fields that are emptied of human beings. As Lafosse notes, Lanners' filmmaking resonates with the Flemish 'pictorial tradition' (Domenach 2009: 102). The filiation with painting coheres with cinemas of the Low Countries, particularly in the context of local painterly traditions (Mathijs 2004a: 8).

In *Eldorado*, the length of the shot – twenty-two seconds to be precise – encourages a contemplation of the agricultural fields as the grey clouds close in overhead with the 'absent presence', in Massey's (2011) terms, of human activity (that is, the agricultural use of the fields). Lanners offers brief pauses, short 'still' interludes, in *Ultranova* and *Eldorado* that capture and frame the urban and rural landscapes of Liège's working-class suburbs and industrial units (*Ultranova*) and the Walloon countryside (*Eldorado*). Like paintings, the long takes encourage momentary reflection and contemplation from the spectator, deciphering their relationship to the narrative, to heritage and to memory. The length of the take encourages the spectator to 'parse the world so as to bring out its significance' (Andrew 2010: 34), as Andrew notes in the context of Henri Bergson's 'matter and memory' (ibid.). This brings out the small semantic pieces of Wallonia's rural heritage from the spectator's memory. As Massey argues, the 'long takes are not about stasis either. Stuff is happening' (Massey 2011).

Lanners draws on 'duration' of a painterly still image that is engendered by the use of CinemaScope, widescreen framing to depict a nostalgic view of the Walloon agricultural landscape (Figure 5.4). The booming non-diegetic music replicates the mid-west American blues, exoticising the depiction of the Walloon agricultural fields. The dark-grey clouds (a motif established in *Ultranova*) slowly move from left to right across the frame in a diagonal direction from the fore to the background of the image. The wheatgrass flickers in

Figure 5.4   In *Eldorado*, Lanners fixes the camera on the agricultural fields of Wallonia for twenty-three seconds, leaving the spectator to notice the slight movement of the clouds and the flickering of the wheatgrass in the wind.

the wind, showing action that gives the image movement. Unlike a painting, the subtle movements in the frame, that are generated at an elemental level, highlight that the film is concerned with movement and mobility, as opposed to stasis. Gendron, in his review of *Eldorado* in *Ciné-Bulles*, posits that the vast Walloon landscapes 'counteract the doom and gloom that rise to the surface' and 'immediately leaves references (*salutations*) to [its] past use' (Gendron 2008). The use of 'salutations' in this case posits that Lanners' framing of the landscape is almost an ode to the region's former past as an agrarian economy. The story, in Massey's terms, 'spirals out of the landscape' (Massey 2011). Agriculture represents a key and salient strand to a Walloon and even Belgian sense of identity, emerging in relation to Andrien's films. This 'still' of the empty Walloon agricultural landscape resonates with Andrien's long shots of the deteriorating and ailing rural Fourons. Dubois (2002) identifies the salience of memory to Andrien's films, particularly concerning a crucial crossroads in the region's history at the end of the period of industrialisation. For Dubois,

> memory is initially filtered through the melancholy that suffuses the landscapes. Each time the sustained quality of the gaze and the photography enable Andrien to pay homage to rural or urban settings, which become the most tangible witnesses of a past and a lost grandeur. (Dubois 2002: 65)

As a result, Andrien's capturing of the rural landscape is almost 'nostalgic', in Dubois' (2002) terms, in *Le grand paysage d'Alexis Droeven* (Jean-Jacques Andrien, 1981) and *Australia* (Jean-Jacques Andrien, 1989). As Mosley similarly asserts in the context of Walloon filmmaking (and Andrien) in the 1970s, 'Walloon directors explore the processes of memory as part of a cinematic expression of personal and communal identities' (Mosley 2001: 190). This memory and sense of loss, consequently, is corralled into Lanners' 'stills' of the rural Walloon landscape. In so doing, the articulation of memory in cinema in Wallonia continues to reverberate through to contemporary forms of filmmaking in the region. The intertextual allusions imbue the long takes and seemingly single images with greater cultural significance, creating a crucial and informed link to local history and key linguistic and regional debates in Wallonia.[7]

The caravan park in which Elie and Yvan seek refuge further evinces the filmmaker's nostalgic worldview in addition to articulating the themes of abandonment and loss. With this disrepair of the caravan park, there is a sense of loss and a changing relationship with the landscape. As represented in *Rosetta*, the caravan park is configured as a semi-permanent dwelling for Rosetta and her mother on the fringes of the town of Seraing, and, as Mosley posits, operates as the last point of refuge before homelessness (2013: 86). However, in

Eldorado, the caravan site amongst the rolling hills of the Ardennes is intended as a temporary holiday space that is clearly now in decline. This is neatly evidenced by the absence of people in the space and the lack of activity.

As Kaplan contends, '(t)ravel is very much a modern concept, signifying both commercial and leisure movement in an era of expanding Western capitalism' (Kaplan 1996: 3). The caravans evoke and represent a sense of mobility – central to Massey's (2011) argument on politics, landscape and memory – since they imply constant movement to and from the park, and the Ardennes as a site of holiday-making, of leisure, as opposed to an articulation of nature. In this sense, it becomes invested in capital and part of the neoliberal flows. Crousse posits that the 'former holiday village of Dolimarts' (the location where this sequence unfolds) operates as a 'cruel metaphor of a beautiful but poor Wallonia' (2007) The caravans, therefore, represent vestiges of a bygone era in which the Ardennes proved a popular holiday destination for Belgian citizens, who now, because foreign travel has become more accessible to the general population, choose to holiday in foreign locations. The notion of holiday-making in the Ardennes is most notably addressed in Benoît Lamy's *Jambon d'Ardenne*, a film that considers the rivalry between restaurants during the region's competitive holiday season. In *Eldorado*, the caravans therefore bear witness to its holiday-making and leisure time past, which is no longer apparent. Instead, the location becomes a brief overnight stopping point for two travellers whose identity and sense of home is in a state of flux and instability. Elie particularly represents this absence of fixity, and it is suggested in the narrative that he is homeless (in a perilous and uncertain situation) in the city of Liège. Within this frame, the Ardennes as a now empty location evokes a mysterious and almost sinister articulation in francophone Belgian filmmaking and television production, as evinced by the Belgian 'noir' series *La Trêve/The Break* (2016–) and Fabrice du Welz's horror genre Ardennes trilogy.

Journeying through the Ardennes: Exploring Questions of Home and Regional Identity

The motifs of travel and journeying operate as key motifs in Lanners' *Eldorado*, and, to a lesser extent, *Ultranova*. It could also be extended to *Les géants/The Giants* (Bouli Lanners, 2011), which, whilst not evoking the codes, conventions and iconography of the road movie genre, illustrates a group of teenagers' 'coming of age' within the surroundings of a verdant Ardennes. Drawing on a diachronic approach and understanding of *Ultranova*, Danvers (2013a) observes that the film's sensibility and originality is developed across *Eldorado* and *Les géants*. The imagery of *Eldorado* and *Les géants* is equally concomitant with the representation of the Ardennes as an American frontier, citing films from post-classical Hollywood cinema, particularly the work of John

Boorman. Tonally *Eldorado*, and latterly *Les géants*, contrast radically with the drained and 'washed out' colour palette of contemporary francophone Belgian filmmaking, distancing themselves from the raw, immediate cinematography of the 1990s and early 2000s (as Chapter Three outlined in relation to *Folie privée*) and the black-and-white tones concomitant with filmmaking in coal-mining societies (analysed in Chapter Four). To this end, the colour palette portrays a more vibrant and 'warmer' tone than the 'clichéd' *Ultranova* (Les Inrockuptibles 2008; M. M. 2008).

Scholarship on the European road movie operates as an important interpretative framework for better understanding and deciphering Lanners' films, particularly *Eldorado*. To this end, the scholarly work of Laderman (2002), Everett (2004), Mazierska and Rascaroli (2006), Archer (2013), and Gott (2016) provide a critical backdrop and framework for understanding the road movie in a European and, more recently, francophone context. The road movie in a European context has gained increased critical and academic currency as a means of analysing the fluidity and the ever-shifting notions of identity, society and community. Laderman ascertains the salient identifying differences between the European road movie and the American road movie as the following:

> Characters on the road out of necessity rather than choice, seeking work, family, or a home; less valorisation of the individual Road Man or the outlaw couple, more emphasis on travelling groups; less fetishism of the automobile; less emphasis on driving as high-speed action spectacle. (Laderman 2002: 248)

Lanners' second feature film falls within the interstices of the European road movie and the American road movie in terms of how it draws on the genre's 'semantic' and 'syntactic' features, to adopt Altman's (1984) approach to genre. In *Eldorado*, Yvan and Elie are not necessarily on the road out of necessity, since it is articulated as a choice for Elie to return to his parent's home. In so doing, the film journeys towards a sense of home, remaining within Wallonia in screen time.

The notion of the francophone road movie represents a newly culturally and linguistically specific approach to the European road movie, incorporating France, Belgium and Switzerland into one analytical frame (Gott and Schilt 2015; Gott 2016). Gott further explores the French-language Belgian iteration of the genre in its own national context due to the level of road movie films produced in the country and due to the notion of a so-called 'Belgian particularity' (including Lanners' *Eldorado*) (2013a; 2016: 9-10). Mathijs, however, contends that 'Low Countries cinema is never genre cinema [due to uncertainty and a "culture of self-doubt"], and is almost always self-reflective, tied to reality whilst failing to question it' (Mathijs 2004a: 4). However, as outlined in Chapter One, the creation of regional film funding mechanisms and the greater investment in film production in Belgium since 2001–2004 (with the Belgian tax shelter), a greater number of films adhering to genres have been funded and produced. The road movie operates as one primary evolution, including at least the films of Bouli Lanners, *Quand la mer monte/When the Sea Rises* (Yolande Moreau and Gilles Porte, 2004), *Cow-boy* (Benoît Mariage, 2005), *L'iceberg, Rumba, Dikkenek* (Olivier Van Hoofstadt, 2006), *Mobile Home* (François Pirot, 2012), and *La tendresse/Tenderness* (Marion Hänsel, 2013),[8] but – more importantly – it also represents an increased investment in questioning and searching for cultural identity, as outlined in the Introduction.

For Everett, the road movie represents 'a fluid and open-ended genre which uses the narrative trajectory of the road as an extended metaphor of quest and discovery through which to approach fundamental concepts of identity' (2004: 18–19). Mazierska and Rascaroli adopt a similar position regarding the European road movie and its connection to the articulation of identity, drawing primarily on Baumann's notion of the postmodern 'problem of identity' (Mazierska and Rascaroli 2006: 1). Everett further extends the analysis of identity into the contexts of 'memory, language and culture' (2004: 20).

According to Mazierska and Rascaroli (2006: 2), borders, therefore, play a fundamental role in affirming and contesting these articulations. In his analysis of the French road movie, Archer draws on Mazierska and Rascaroli (Mazierska and Rascaroli 2006) to identify a shift in the European road movie genre from one of 'containment' to an opening-out with the greater fluidity of borders in New Europe (Archer 2013: 6). This chimes with Higson's (2000: 67) reinterpretation of 'the concept of national cinema' as inherently 'limiting', since it implies that borders are 'effective'. Within the genre of the European road movie, this is not necessarily the case. Drawing on these two examples from Lanners, borders are not crossed, which, consequently, aligns with the aforementioned notion of 'containment' and proffering a sense of European 'smallness' in Archer's words (2013: 6).

As André (2009a) notes in his review of Lanners' film, as a result of *Eldorado*'s adherence to the road and the journey, the film's narrative structure is not as complex as the previously explored *Ultranova*. Instead, Wallonia 'is crossed from top to bottom and from side to side' (ibid.). In so doing, the region's borders are affirmed, particularly in relation to France. As the characters of Elie and Yvan travel towards Elie's hometown on the conterminous border with France, it provides the end point to their lateral trajectory. It is a circulatory place in which the central protagonists loop back on themselves. This is also the case in *Ultranova*, in which Lanners' film 'takes us full circle, suggesting lives on a loop, endlessly repeating, going nowhere' (Boyle 2005). The narrative is therefore marked by a certain tautology. Gott (2013a) contends that this circularity is a tradition of francophone Belgian road movies, since it articulates both 'stasis' and a complex 'mapping' of identities in Belgium. As the characters return to Liège from the unnamed border town (Elie's *bercail* according to Gendron (2008)), Yvan and Elie continue from the positions that they had previously left. The static nature of the social roles and positions – within which the characters are trapped – is similarly evoked in the Walloon road movie *Mobile Home*. In this instance, the ironic immobility of the caravan stops the male characters' journey in a bucolic *Liégeois* location.

The cartography of a region is, therefore, imagined for the spectators as fixed and, to draw on Higson's (2000) term, 'effective' in geographic terms. Gott challenges the importance of the geographic and sovereign border in the context of *Eldorado*, by drawing on the film's on-location shooting in France (2016: 9). *Les Inrockuptibles* (2008) similarly posit that the Belgian landscape is 'dilatory', as well as stretchable in order to encompass 'an infinite European dream'. Adopting this line of argument, the use of Walloon and Belgian landscapes come to represent a nondescript and anonymous European space that is not indelibly local, but transnational and fluid. However, whilst the border between France and Belgium is not enforced on a pragmatic level for shooting (and considering the film is a French–Belgian co-production and received funding from the regions of Wallonia and Nord-Pas-de-Calais), the national border is imagined because of its dialogic references within the film as text. In essence, drawing on Hjort (2009), the representation of Wallonia, the Ardennes and the countryside is not 'marked'. From this point, the salience of natural and symbolic borders, and the role of the river, is increased, with Yvan and Elie travelling between the city and the countryside, wilderness and small towns.

In *Eldorado*, Lanners draws on a semantic peculiarity that arises primarily in the context of the European road movie, that is the fork in the road and the divergent pathways 'off-road' (Everett 2009: 169) (see Figure 5.5). Whereas the open highway characterises the American road movie (Sargeant and Watson 1999: 12), the twists in the European roads highlight the complexity and lack of linearity in the journeys experienced by individuals. This is self-consciously noted when Yvan deliberately avoids the highway to the unnamed border town. After his unsuccessful break-in, Elie is initially left by Yvan at the fork in the road between the city and its outskirts, 'the hills' that Yvan dialogically notes in the film. For Elie, it is, therefore, an interstitial location in which the character is uncertain as to which pathway to take. In so doing, the notion of 'home' and 'home-coming' is problematised for Elie.

Lanners' films also imbibe cinematic influences from European transnational auteurs Wim Wenders and the dark humour of Aki Kaurismäki. Both of these filmmakers are referenced in Mazierska and Rascaroli's (2006) approach to the European road movie, whilst Everett notes that these filmmakers, amongst

Figure 5.5 Yvan finds Elie still standing at the crossroads on the outskirts of the city of Liège.

other European directors, 'have so widely adopted this genre while ruthlessly subverting it from within so as to provide a telling commentary on the complex and multiple identities of European cinema' (2004: 19). It is this knowing subversion 'from within' that keenly highlights the transnational dialogue taking place between the codes and conventions of the American template and a European setting, which Laderman suggests as 'crucial to the genre' (2002: 247). Within the analysis of a certain 'transatlantic ambivalence' of road movies in the USA, Meikle (2010) observes Kaurismäki's 'dry sense of humour' and 'bleakness'. This infusion of comedic respites from dour and depressing undertones also resurface in *Eldorado*, with the introduction of the nude 'Alain Delon' to help polish the Chevrolet and Yvon's decision to tape his hair to the roof of the car in order to stay awake at the wheel. The comparison between Lanners and Kaurismäki's road movies moves beyond the films' poetics into a cinematic epistemology. Mazierska and Rascaroli observe the 'crisis of masculinity' articulated in Kaurismäki's Finnish/Eastern-European filmmaking that is predicated on 'the disappearance of traditionally masculine industries and conversely, of female labour gaining in importance' (Mazierska and Rascaroli 2006: 20). Whilst female labour in Lanners' films is represented relatively fleetingly in *Ultranova*, a synchronic reading of francophone Belgian cinema reveals the increasing presence of women in the workplace, particularly in the Dardenne brothers' films since *Rosetta, Une part du ciel/A Piece of Sky* (Bénédicte Liénard, 2002), and Belvaux's *La raison du plus faible/The Right of the Weakest* (2006). This is also where Mosley's (2013) frequent comparisons to Kaurismäki's films gains greater salience in this context, with the scholar using *Tulitikkutehtaan tyttö/The Match Factory Girl* (Aki Kaurismäki, 1990) as a reference point to the Dardenne brothers' filmmaking and to Lucas Belvaux.

Returning to Mazierska and Rascaroli, the scholars identify an 'inferiority complex towards their larger and more powerful neighbours' that lies beneath the lack of personal attachment to the Finnish imaginary space and Finnish homeland (Mazierska and Rascaroli 2006: 22). These 'epistemological' (2006: 26) concerns equally arise in the francophone Belgian context, with a potential 'inferiority complex' emerging in relation to its linguistic neighbour, France. As Mathijs writes regarding the cinemas of the Low Countries, the films, created in a local context, articulate a 'culture of self-doubt' (2004a: 4). Mathijs identifies a questioning of cultural identity rather than affirmative action (ibid.). In *Eldorado*, the character of Elie evidences this turn, whose lack of connection to his parents and the lack of a relationship with his father, articulate a breakdown with a sense of home and belonging. The narrative's circularity shows how Elie returns to Liège without rebuilding the relationship with his parents and a return to a marginal way of life in a drugs den.[9] In *Ultranova*, a similar interpretation arises in the postulation of Dimitri as an orphan, and the ambiguity in the relationship between him and his fleetingly seen foster parents. The notion of a fracture in the family is equally posited in *Le gamin au vélo*, which similarly concerns questions of fostering and kinship.

The circulatory narrative also points to a certain pessimism and fatalism for Elie's role and status in society. As Mosley outlines, there is a certain similarity with Claudy in *Le silence de Lorna* (Jean-Pierre and Luc Dardenne, 2009) in terms of the characters both being 'junkies', unable to escape their heroin addiction (2013: 30). The synchronic release of the two films concerning drug abuse, particularly heroin, in the post-industrial, former working-class suburbs of Liège highlights the region's social issues. Lanners extends this fatalism into the realm of metaphor and the symbolic. For instance, the film reaches a critical apotheosis when a dog, legs bound in duct tape, unexpectedly lands on top of Yvan's Chevrolet. The quivering dog articulates wider notions of abandonment, loss and impending fatalism for a lost generation. The injured dog becomes further symbolic of Elie's plight at *Eldorado*'s denouement, in which Yvan buries the body on the outskirts, overlooking the former industrial city. In this sense, instead of purchasing heroin to alleviate the dog's pain and suffering, Elie disappears in a move that seemingly highlights his need for the substance in his socio-economic situation. Reading the injured dog as symbolic of Elie's plight demonstrates the difficulties for a generation to cope in a fraught, post-industrial space where opportunities for the younger generation appear limited. In the documentary on Bouli Lanners' films *On the Road Again – Le Cinéma de Bouli Lanners*, the filmmaker was particularly struck and 'depressed' by the evenings that he followed 'social workers and squats'. It was on the basis of this experiential knowledge of the drug dens and of the social workers (whom he describes as the real heroes) in Liège that the film could not have a 'happy end'. For Lanners, it needed to be stark and harsh, and this permeates the open ending in which Elie cannot and does not return to change his life. The futility of the younger generation in Wallonia and the city of Liège is placed at the forefront, articulating a lack of future and hope that is compounded by the sequence unrolling in Place Cockerill. In contrast, Yvan represents the embers of manual labour in Wallonia, working as a mechanic that restores high-end American cars for competitions.

Wenders and Kaurismäki are further considered as examples of crossover auteurs who have adopted the 'American format' (Mazierska and Rascaroli 2006: 3). This highlights the film's complexity as a nodal point for local, regional and transnational filiation, placing their films somewhere between a European and an American road movie. Drawing on the Kaurismäki example, the scholars note that the filmmaker has a tendency, in the magical realist tradition, to 'defamiliarise [. . .] American landscapes' (2006: 31) In so doing, Lanners' transnational stylistic filiation also defamiliarises – 'incongruently' according to Denis (2008: 4) – the Walloon landscape, framing it as both exotic and bucolic. French critics and reviewers drew on *Western* (Manuel Poirier, 1997) as a reference point (D. F. 2008), thereby forming a connection between the regional northern French landscape of Brittany with the south of Belgium, and the 'wide American spaces' concomitant with Montana (Crousse 2008), Colorado (Borde 2008; D. F. 2008; M. M. 2008) or even the Canadian wilderness (I. R. 2008). Denis contends that *Eldorado* is evocative of Wenders' films of the late 1970s and early 1980s in terms of a European filmmaker's interpretation and vision of the American landscape (2008: 4). This results in the 'reconstruction of an imaginary Wallonia', generated through the framing of 'rectangular highways', 'hostile places', and 'wide open deserted spaces' (Denis 2008: 4). The transatlantic references pertain to the American road movies' inheritance from the Western genre in which 'the *mise-en-scène* emphasises the vastness of the terrain, not only locating the individual protagonist's journey within the greater zone of the wilderness, but also allowing the audience the visual pleasure of the spectacle of the landscape' (Sargeant and Watson 1999: 13). Transnational stylistic and aesthetic filiation provides an articulation of Wallonia through the road movie genre that does not neatly cohere with previous drained images of the Walloon countryside. As a result, this representation of the Walloon landscape becomes a source of spectacle for the audience. The long shots of the countryside fetishise Wallonia as exotic through intertextual allusions that seek to Other the landscape.

The introduction to the small-border town (Elie's *bercail*) on the conterminous border with France recalls Jarmusch's opening sequence of *Down by Law* (Jim Jarmusch, 1986). As Jarmusch's film adopts a series of travelling shots to represent and capture the variegated margins of the American city (New Orleans, in this case), Lanners similarly defamiliarises the Belgian small-town that is no longer a 'home' to Elie, passing by houses in contrasting directions.

The thematic reference further posits that the characters exist and operate as outsiders, who come together and form a bond through mere circumstance. Whilst Yvan is not searching for a place in the dominant society, Elie clearly represents a disenfranchised stratification of society that requires a sense of inclusion. The two characters recall Powrie's notion that 'a very traditional road movie [focuses] on a pair of male losers' (1997: 142). Archer further notes in the context of the aforementioned *Western* that, '"Home", as an essentially static construct and thereby resistant to the impulses of cinematic movement, fails to provide a secure basis for the masculine wanderer' (2013: 105). The defamiliarised hometown is, therefore, not a site in which Elie '*feels*' welcome due to his father's 'phantom-like' absence and the fact that the town remains unnamed and unspecified. His presence is disembodied through the penetrating voice that emerges from the *hors-champ*/off-screen space. A haunting paternalism emerges, reminscient of the absent fathers of *le jeune cinéma*, *Rosetta* (as outlined by Park (2012)), and the literal 'death of the father' in Masset-Depasse's *Chambre froide* (2000).

The fracture and instability of Wallonia is best exemplified through the limits of patriarchal society. The absence of the father is, therefore, discernible, which Park (2011; 2012) details in the context of so-called French New Realism and francophone Belgian cinema of the late 1990s (that is, *Rosetta*). The link between patriarchy and nation is formalised in *Eldorado*, and evinced by Elie's ability to recite the words to the national anthem, *La Brabançonne*. Elie notes that his father, a former soldier in the Belgian army, strongly encouraged him – as a child – to learn the national anthem. The sequence represents an instance of implicit 'banal aboutness', since it offers a brief 'flagging' to Wallonia (Hjort 2000: 108–9). The singing makes the film loosely 'about' (Hjort 2000: 108) Wallonia and the complexities that belie national or regional solidarity, rather than a generalised French-language film that merely articulates, on a general or topical level, social exclusion, social marginalisation and shattered families. However, the imagined bond, at this point, is undermined by virtue of Elie's false persona. Yvan later discovers his name is in fact Didier, thereby highlighting the gradual deterioration and mistrust formed between the country's citizens and between the two generations. This breakdown between generations, highlighting the gradual withering with patriarchal society and authority, is further compounded by the lack of a father–son relationship. Whilst the national anthem initially posits a sense of allegiance and recognition between generations, Elie's father is presented as a disembodied 'phantom', and, to adopt Park's term in this context, the 'absent father' (Park 2012).

Finally, with regard to the film as adhering to the road movie as a format, the car operates as a key semantic element of the road movie genre, particularly in the American context, with Everett noting that 'it represents a clear sense of male identity for the protagonist through its status as an object that combines technology and modernity' (2004: 24). This is particularly the case for Lanners' fetishisation of the American car, a Chevrolet '79 in *Eldorado*, as the primary means of transport for the variation on the 'buddy movie'. The restoration of automobiles represents employment and social function for Yvan, thereby underpinning his sense of 'male identity'. The car also places the film in dialogue with Kaurismäki's representations of Finnish post-industrial society. In *Ariel* (Aki Kaurismäki, 1988), as Taisto loses his job in the closing coal mine – an example of Ezra and Rowden's individuals 'caught in the cracks of globalisation' (2006: 7) – he continues to drive, and at times even reside in, his convertible Cadillac Series 62. Like Taisto's Cadillac, the Chevrolet '79 in *Eldorado* does not appear to be concomitant with the sociopolitical concerns and articulations witnessed by the spectator. Elie also mistakes Yvan's Chevrolet '79 for a Cadillac, creating a fleeting cinematic utterance to Kaurismäki. This is primarily because, as Mazierska and Rascaroli observe, 'the car favoured by Kaurismäki's characters is the Cadillac, irrespective of the country in which the film is set' (2006: 18). In essence, it seems out of place, drawing further attention to the comments on global neoliberal consumerism. The choice of the automobile's brand is salient, since it contrasts with the standardised, 'mass-produced' and 'ubiquitous' cars that 'no longer affor[d] the kind of display-value with which it might previously have been associated' (Archer 2013: 16). From this premise, the car represents a constraint, since it is a financial burden in terms of the costs involved with automobile ownership. It is evidently not a freedom affordable to all, which is further underlined by Elie's marginal position.

Conclusion

As an autodidactic filmmaker, Bouli Lanners' films arise from his cinephilic and experiential knowledge of genres. The primary continuity that reverberates through his films is the fetishisation of the car and the open road, that is the semantic blocks of the road movie genre. Referring to Lanners' short films, the filmmaker's engagement with the landscapes, both industrial and rural, and Walloon culture is uncovered. In the documentary *On the Road Again*, Lanners, in conversation with fellow filmmaker Stefan Liberski, states that he seeks to eschew a continuity in spaces represented in his films, which is evidenced by the industrial 'peri-urban' zones of *Ultranova*, the city and the countryside of *Eldorado* and the verdant forests of the Ardennes in *Les géants*. *Ultranova* reveals a transition away from industrial society, the building block of Walloon nationalism and culture after the creation of the Belgian nation-state, in the 'peri-urban' (as outlined in *On the Road Again*) and suburbs of the primary industrial city of Liège. The post-industrial society has left a certain emptiness and void for the younger generation situated in a society of fragmented families and disenfranchisement (culminating in moments of introspection and suicide). *Eldorado* harks back to questions of region in terms of the pre-industrial agrarian society and nation through holiday-making through its representation of the countryside. The nostalgic references emphasise that the nation has shifted into a transnational era of tourists and transcending national boundaries, seeking temporary relief from the nation and state.

Notes

1. Whilst starring for the Belgian television show *Les Snuls*, Bouli Lanners initially met the producer of Versus Productions Jacques-Henri Brockart, who was working as the show's lead camera operator (Rouchy 2008).
2. The infusion of magic realism and a syntactic understanding of the American road movie are also evident in emerging film talent and film school productions from Belgium. For instance, the graduate short film *Conte sur moi/The Unexpected Taste of Apple* (Jonas Bloquet, 2015) elides the syntactical 'outlaw couple' of the American road movie and the violent shoot-out denouement of *Bonnie and Clyde* (Arthur Penn, 1967) with the dreamy and hyper-real landscapes of an ambiguously located woodland and symbolic emphasis on the apple. The short film creates a moral underpinning to the film and the exploration of abuse, such as the scars on the back of the lead female character and the offering of candied apples as part of a system of abuse – an element that resonates with Lafosse's *Élève libre* in which filmmaker Bloquet plays the lead role (see Chapter Three).
3. Jean-Pierre Dardenne was born in 1951 and Luc Dardenne in 1954.
4. Park (2011) notes that the spectator interprets Seraing and Rosetta's marginal position in the Dardenne brothers' *Rosetta* through her 'purview'.
5. In her work on landscapes in the Dardenne brothers' video documentaries and fictional work up to *La promesse*, Lesuisse posits that the 'empty landscapes' are symbolic, since they include the lack of speech and voices within the industrial structures 'like an echo of a disappearing body' (Lesuisse 1996/1997: 45).
6. Dr Paul Newland's conference paper, presented as part of the Regions and Representation Symposium in 2012, drew my attention to Massey's article as potentially salient to regional filmmaking.
7. Mosley (2001) and Thomas (1995) outline in detail the debates surrounding the Fourons and the context of *Le grand paysage d'Alexis Droeven*. Mosley posits that '[c]ompilation footage of the 1962 and the 1978 demonstrations marks earlier stages in the protests of farmers against changing patterns of land use and agribusiness following a process of controversial political decision making' (Mosley 2001: 191). Such an interpretation nuances Thomas' posing of ontological questions pertaining to remaining a farmer or not in a 'mutating region' (Thomas 1995: 207).
8. *Les Inrockuptibles* (2008) considers Lanners' *Eldorado* within the context of an established Belgian road movie tradition. For instance, the magazine highlights how the film resonates with *Le Far West/Far West* (Jacques Brel, 1973), *Quand la mer monte* (Yolande Moreau and Gilles Porte, 2004), *Dikkenek* (Olivier Van Hoofstadt, 2006) and *Aaltra* (Benoît Delépine and Gustave Kervern, 2004). Gott (2013a) offers a similar listing of francophone Belgian road movies up to 2012.
9. In Mazierska and Rascaroli's (2006) chapters on Aki Kaurismäki and Patrick Keiller, the notion of circular narratives and journeys permeates as a key feature of their road movies.

6. LUCAS BELVAUX'S RETURN: THE THRILLER GENRE AND HEISTS IN LIÈGE

This chapter considers a second filmmaker, in the shape of Lucas Belvaux, who draws significantly on pre-established codes and conventions developed in distinct genres. The filmmaker has floated between different genres throughout his career. This is most notably the case for the France-based trilogy – *Après la vie/After Life* (Lucas Belvaux, 2002), *Cavale/On the Run* (Lucas Belvaux, 2002) and *Un couple épatant/An Amazing Couple* (Lucas Belvaux, 2002) – in which each film corresponded to a different genre. As a result, the attempt to weave three interlinked and interlocking narratives with the same characters imbricates both genre and film authorship. The trilogy's English-language publicity material evinces the turn to auteurism, describing the films as examples of 'staggering virtuosity' (EXE BD 63400 2017). Such a discursive interpretation of the trilogy articulates a potential for Belvaux's adherence to Sarris' oft-discussed third concentric circle of the ambiguous and maligned 'interior meaning' that identifies an auteur (Sarris 1962: 453). The trilogy may not be quite as 'unparalleled' as the publicity material immediately posits, since the film experiment recalls the work of Krzysztof Kieślowski (the *Dekalog* (1989) series for Polish television) and Alain Resnais (Poirson-Dechonne 2011: 22) or even 'network narratives' (Bordwell 2006) by contemporaneous filmmakers such as Alejandro González Iñárritu.

On the basis of his own experiential engagement with French film production, Belvaux contends that genre films, with a strong history and identity (such as comedies and *polars*) are more likely to be successfully funded in France

(Ghennam and Hélié 2010: 149). For instance, Belvaux discusses his second film *Pour rire!* (Lucas Belvaux, 1996) as an example that draws '*a priori*' on the codes and conventions of the comedy genre (ibid.). This intentionality is clearly evidenced by the film's title. It is also predicated on pragmatic decisions made by the filmmaker to guarantee funding and gain the confidence of film producers after the commercial failure of his first film, *Parfois trop d'amour* ('Sometimes there's too much love'; Lucas Belvaux, 1992) (Duculot 1997: 33).[1] Excluding Belvaux's four made-for-television movies, political and crime thrillers populate his films most, with *38 témoins/One Night* (2012), *Rapt* (2009), *La raison du plus faible/The Right of the Weakest* (2006), and *Cavale* (2002) being the most prominent. This is closely followed by romantic comedies in the form of *Pas son genre/Not My Type* (2014), *Un couple épatant* and *Parfois trop d'amour* and pure comedy with *Pour rire!*. The third outing in *La trilogie*, *Après la Vie*, is referred to in the aforementioned publicity material as a melodrama. As a result, Belvaux has created a corpus of work that places the filmmaker in the cadre of genre filmmaking, indebted to both French and American cinematic traditions. Such a filmmaking style and approach coheres with Shaw's typology of 'transnational modes of narration' in an art cinema context (2013: 54). To this end, Shaw draws on filmmakers that 'use an internationally recognised film language' (ibid.). In this frame of reference, commercial films draw on well-established genres in a bid to appeal significantly to international film audiences (Hjort 2009; Higbee and Lim 2010; Shaw 2013).

Hayward (2005), Prédal (2002: 155) and Williams (2013: 23) similarly identify both the comedy genre and the *polar* as two popular forms of French film production, consolidating their place in the 1990s French 'cultural and political imaginary'. Hayward contends that the proclivity of audiences to view these two genres throughout French cinematic history proves that France 'does have a national cinema – precisely because of its diversity' (2005: 331). However, what is of greater interest in this case is how the genres operate in between national contexts, spilling across the conterminous border. As a result, this position proposes that the *polar* functions as an example of mainstream filmmaking in France.

In the context of *le jeune cinéma*, Prédal surveys the occasional turn of young, emerging filmmakers to the *polar* and thriller genres, particularly Mathieu Kassovitz and Cédric Kahn (2002: 151–5). The 1990s marked a period of decline for the *polar* genre, with these successes indicative of an infusion with American traditions of the thriller and martial arts of East Asian Cinema (Hayward 2005: 298). Hayward posits that the *polar* operates as an example of 'universal genres that become specified, amplified, even subverted, within a particular culture' (2005: 10). To this end, the *polar* shifted in the 1950s to 'refer to' – in Hayward's terms – the American cop/thriller genre (ibid.).

The 'universality' of the *polar* is particularly instructive when considering how, in the case of *La raison du plus faible*, the genre has become culturally and regionally specific in terms of location and news stories from Wallonia that informed the film's storyline. The historic popularity of the genre in France (since at least 1945) is further borne out by *La raison du plus faible*'s performance in France (receiving 186,920 admissions in the year of its release) with a significantly lower number of admissions in Belgium (15,048) in the same period (EAO 2016). It is important to note that, in this case, this number of film admissions represents a small proportion of the French and Belgian cinemagoers with an exhibition pattern that is consistent across francophone Belgian cinema (see Chapter One). Moreover, discourse around the release of *La raison du plus faible* – primarily film criticism in film journals, magazines and newspapers – concentrates on the film's 'noir aesthetic'. The re-emergence of the *polar* and crime thrillers in France by young, novice filmmakers in the mid to late 1990s evidently precedes Belvaux's turn to the genre across the border in Belgium, thereby highlighting how the francophone Belgian film industry imbibes cinematic traditions from France at a contemporaneous period. To this end, it is particularly revealing that two of the first three films funded by Wallimage, the regional film fund based in Wallonia, were the *polar* genre films *Gangsters* (Olivier Marchal, 2002) and *Un honnête commerçant/ Step by Step* (Philippe Blasband, 2002).

Similarly to Joachim Lafosse, Lucas Belvaux's films have avoided critical attention in Walloon-centred magazines such as *La revue toudi*. Instead, Lucas Belvaux's films are positioned more widely as part of a 'culture produced by Walloons, occasionally in Wallonia' that operates primarily as a form of export (Govaert 2001). The use of the regional appellation coheres with a purview that seeks to distinguish clearly between Walloon and francophone films. The Belvaux family name does, however, have resonance in the context of Walloon cinema with Rémy Belvaux – brother of Lucas – co-directing the cult hit *C'est arrivé près de chez vous*, which is partially set in their birthplace of Namur. Belvaux grew up in the small regional area of Philippeville in the Ardennes, close to the French border, before moving to Paris at the age of sixteen (Denis 2006). It is this move to Paris as an actor that has characterised his work as that of a Belgian 'exile', following a well-trodden path of (francophone) Belgians to Paris.

Transnational Director, Regional Images: Belvaux's 'Exile' and Small-town Film Settings

Mélon (2004) proposes that (francophone) Belgian cinema operates as a 'land of exile' and as a point of intersection of flows of migration to and from the region's film industry. The flows out of the (francophone) Belgian film industry is directed towards France, and particularly Paris, in the case of Jacques Feyder,

Charles Spaak, Eve Francis, Chantal Akerman, Lucas Belvaux and Marie Gillian (Mélon 2004: 342). The draining of film production talent away from Belgium has been a tendency since at least the introduction of sound in the 1930s, with the creation of talkies 'amplifying the exodus' to France (Thomas 1995: 43). These flows of personnel can be traced to 'affinitive' (Hjort 2009) connections between the two film industries. For these filmmakers, writers and actors, Mélon (2004) draws on the verb *'s'exiler'* in order to characterise a unidirectional pattern of filmmaking emigration to its linguistic neighbour, France. To this end, the auteur can no longer be interpreted through a national lens as a mere 'bearer of national and/or ethnic identity' (Ezra and Rowden 2006: 3). In fact, Higson contends that the transnational movement of filmmakers is one example of the 'limiting' and 'inappropriate' nature of the national cinema concept in the current film industry (2000: 73). Filmmakers working outside their 'national' framework in other film industries constitute one example of Higson's 'subtle' (2000: 64) turn to cinematic transnationalism. As Higbee and Lim identify, this approach is primarily predicated on modes of film production, alongside distribution and exhibition (2010: 9). The flow of filmmakers across national borders is nothing new to the film industry, and is perhaps an element taken for granted. Drawing on Ezra and Rowden (2006), the filmmaker – or auteur – constitutes a degree of 'capital' that is used to help circulate the film domestically and abroad, as well as attract funding from numerous international sources. Returning to the case of Mélon (2004), the use of the reflexive verb, in this case, encourages a reading that pertains directly to a self-imposed 'exile' in cinematic terms.

The notion of 'exile' is particularly elastic within a cinematic context, given its wide application and use. In Shaw's taxonomy of cinematic transnationalism, the scholar draws on Naficy (2001) and outlines two approaches to 'exile' in the film industry, firstly taking into account filmmakers who left South America during a time of dictatorship and secondly filmmakers of 'economic exile' with the prospect of big budgets encouraging directors to leave their home nation for the USA in particular (Shaw 2013: 56). Working through this theoretical framework, the notion of 'exile', as touched on in film scholarship in Belgium, pertains more to cinematic transnationalism. To this end, the flows and movement of people chime with the concept of transnationalism, as conceived by social anthropology scholar Hannerz (1996) and in a cinematic context by Ezra and Rowden (2006).

Shaw's form of 'economic exile' is generally applicable to Belvaux, who made the decision in his teenage years to work in a larger national film industry in France. However, to complicate matters further, Belvaux did not commence his career in his native Belgium before leaving for France. In fact, the filmmaker 'returned' to a national/regional/linguistic community-based film industry that he had never participated in the first instance. As of 2018, *La raison du plus faible* is Belvaux's only Belgian film, produced in Belgium and Wallonia. In a separate, yet interlinked, taxonomy, Shaw conceives the notion of 'transnational director', which considers funding connections between national film industries, distribution of films beyond the national context and a 'fluency' in 'transnational modes of narration' (2013: 60–1). As this chapter will later outline, Belvaux has a detailed understanding of French genres and auteurs, particular the *polars* and Jean-Pierre Melville, that, in turn, enables his films to appeal to French and ciné-literate audiences. As a result, Belvaux's films articulate a 'fluency' in national and cultural specific genres that then underpin his films.

Buache (2005) positioned Belvaux within his work dedicated to 'Twenty-five Years of French Cinema' and film magazine *L'Avant-Scène Cinéma* (Alion et al. 2014) included the filmmaker in their 'Generation 2000' edition that considered 'Fifty French Filmmakers of the Twenty-first Century'. More crucial is Belvaux's omission from critical work that looks at the other side of the conterminous border, with *Positif* avoiding reference to Belvaux in their 2008 edition on contemporary francophone Belgian cinema and Van Hoeij's (2010) only references to the filmmaker are included in an appendix. However, in 2005, the film magazine show on French-language Belgian television channel RTBF, *L'Envers de l'Écran,* interviewed Lucas Belvaux as part of a series that also included Bouli Lanners, Jaco Van Dormael and Frédéric Fonteyne, drawing attention to critical reception of *La trilogie*, his early acting career and his upbringing in Belgium. As his inclusion immediately preceded the release of his first Belgian film, *La raison du plus faible,* the incorporation of Belvaux alongside these key figures of (francophone) Belgian cinema at the time operates as a gradual reclaiming of the filmmaker as Belgian. In Denis (2006), Belvaux notes that he does not cohere with the so-called 'Belgian school' of filmmakers, which draws attention to both the country's most celebrated and valorised filmmakers, such as the Dardenne brothers and the 'Liège film school' of the 1970s and 1980s (Mélon 2010), and Belgium's highly regarded film school system that has recently produced filmmakers like Olivier Masset-Depasse, Joachim Lafosse and Rachel Lang amongst others. As Belvaux has outlined, his interest in film and cinema is eclectic and wide-ranging, avoiding a fundamental *ciné-club* and exclusive 'art cinema' form of film consumption (Belvaux, in *L'Envers de L'Écran* 2005).

Belvaux's concern with regional areas outside the main city centres of France resonates with Marshall's (2012) notion of 'cinéma-monde' which is inclusive of non-metropolitan French filmmaking, such as *Bienvenue chez les Ch'tis/ Welcome to the Sticks* (Dany Boon, 2008) and the films of André Téchiné. From this premise, the concept of 'cinéma-monde' is particularly instructive in terms of interpreting a de-centred French-language cinema, that is, a form of filmmaking that eschews Paris (the 'centre' of French film production). The films, therefore, articulate a regional and local focus that clearly differentiates them from mainstream, bourgeois and middlebrow French filmmaking.[2] In the context of 1990s French cinema, Prédal (2002: 119) notes that the proclivity for films to be produced in the countryside and regional locations outside Paris was partly due to the increased film funding in the regions. Moreover, Prédal places particular emphasis in this context on the north of France (2002: 117–19), which has proved the primary location for Belvaux's films over the course of his filmmaking career.

Belvaux posits that he is a 'geographic filmmaker', travelling between different cities in France and Belgium for his films, such as Grenoble, Le Havre, Arras and Liège (Denis 2014a: 5). There is an indelible sense of 'anchoring' of his characters in a specific region in which Belvaux films 'very precise locations' (Alion 2006: 152). The aforementioned *Trilogie* is set in the southern French town of Grenoble, and supported by the Rhône Alps regional film fund. It is a project, however, that was reliant on funding from Belgium and the production company Entre Chien et Loup, as funding through the CCA – which Belvaux describes as an equivalent of the *avance-sur-recettes* system in France – resurrected the trilogy (Belvaux, in Binh et al. 2010: 113). At this nascent funding stage, Belvaux had even considered locating the trilogy in Namur, the capital of Wallonia, as part of his desire to produce a 'Belgian' film (Duculot 2006). This desire would not occur until 2005 with *La raison du plus faible* and a fleeting sequence in *Rapt* (2009) that unrolls on the beaches of the Flemish town of Ostend. The *noir*-ish thriller *38 témoins* takes place precisely in the city of Le Havre on the northern French coast. Belvaux uses the port as a recurrent point of orientation for the narrative, with the frequent long shots of the distinct area and the foghorn in the soundscape demarcating the regional location. In an interview with *Libération*, Belvaux emphasised the film's regional setting and locality, referring to the 'Normandy dock workers' that populate Le Havre (Lefort 2012: iii). Martinez (2012: 33) further places Belvaux's film in the context of a contemporaneous set of films that pay homage to the port city. Tonally, Martinez observes the blue colour palette of *La Fée/The Fairy* by Belgium-based filmmakers Dominique Abel, Fiona Gordon and Bruno Romy (2011), the blue-grey tones of *Le Havre* (Aki Kaurismäki, 2011) and the greyness of *38 témoins* (2012: 33). Moreover, as Martinez argues, the greyness of the colouration and the fog that rolls in across the port is evocative of the poetic realist masterpiece *Le Quai des Brumes/Port of Shadows* (Michel Carné, 1938) (ibid.). However, Belvaux notes the intentionality of 'more metallic colours' in the film (Bell 2012). The shots of the port in action at night evoke the colour palette of Melville's crime thrillers, with a certain emphasis placed on the dark, almost indigo, blues that this chapter will return to with *La raison du plus faible*.

As the filmmaker further notes, each town is selected on its own 'sociological' merits, pinpointing Arras' – for the film *Pas son genre* – geographic proximity to Paris at the same time as highlighting its provincial cultural life (Denis 2014a: 5). Belvaux's *Pas son genre* recalls Boon's aforementioned *Bienvenue chez les Ch'tis* significantly. In the film, the young philosopher Clément is relocated from his Parisian school to an equivalent in Arras against his will, only to eventually fall in love with a local hairdresser, Jennifer (an *'Arrasienne'* in her words) and the provincial city. The frequent shots of Clément in his sparse hotel room in Arras juxtaposed with his book-laden apartment in Paris point to the interstitial nature of the relationship, employment and interactions that are all left ambiguously open-ended by the concluding shot of Jennifer's empty apartment. As opposed to articulating a veritable northern or *nordiste* identity, Belvaux's films instead foreground their distance from the notion of a 'centre', namely Paris, thereby representing a 'regional' or non-metropolitan setting. Let us now turn to and consider more closely the only Belgian, and even more specifically Walloon, film within Belvaux's filmmaking corpus.

The 'Social' Thriller: Unemployment, Social Precariousness and Heists

A subheading of Denis' (2006) newspaper article on Lucas Belvaux at the time of the release of *La raison du plus faible* neatly sums up the poetics and the politics of the film – 'a thriller able to hide/conceal a portrait of Wallonia'. The film thus operates on two imbricating levels, first the use of genre codes and conventions to appeal to the predilections of a mass audience, and second revealing the latent sociopolitical issues that underpin cinema made in Wallonia. This is not distinct from Belvaux's previous films, with Buache drawing attention to Belvaux's preoccupation with contradictory representations of politics, the economy and social values (2005: 208). As Buache further notes, Belvaux's films 'demonstrate a desire to express his worries, because he is part of the rare spirit that is still present in the last generation of the twentieth century, still marked by the already distant May 1968' (ibid.). The spirit of May '68 and Left-leaning ideologies is an aspect that remains latent in *La raison du plus faible*, concealed in the film's poetics.

Writing in relation to *La raison du plus faible*, Fevry (2011: 106) posits that the film requires the spectator to be a 'receptive partner to the visual experience proposed to him/her' whilst also foregrounding the film's focus on economic crisis. This resonates with Andrew's interpretation of Bazin in which the spectator 'fills in' as part of the film's 'project' (2010: 92).[3] In *La raison du plus faible*, the notion that the spectator and the audience read the images presented to them is particularly significant. Interpretations of the film focus on the images of sociopolitical decline and 'semantic' and 'syntactic' elements of genres (Altman 1984) realised through the film's poetics. As Thabourey neatly contends, 'the

Figure 6.1 Patrick's family, alongside Marc, Robert and Jean-Pierre, sing 'La p'tite gayole'.

images are often encumbered with meaning' (2006: 31). The images as representations and articulations are intended to be readable. *La raison du plus faible* represents a curious aberration from Belvaux's previous films, which is in turn evinced by the film being his only selection at the 'A'-grade Cannes film festival. It also marked the first occasion that a film 'financially supported by Wallimage had been selected for the official competition at Cannes' (Bredael and Reynaert 2016: 109). For Reynaert, this served as a particular moment of national pride, with the film offering a paean to Wallonia in the form of '*La p'tite gayole*' (Wallonia's anthem) (ibid.) (Figure 6.1). Fevry interprets this sequence as a moment that localises the film (2011: 92), which can, in turn, be extended to Hjort's (2000) theme of 'banal aboutness'.

Belvaux notes that

> *La raison du plus faible* [. . .] is, on paper, my closest film to a defined genre, with a knowledge of the *policier* and film noir. But it is not a *polar* for me – or else it is a *polar* without cops and pretty much without any crime. (Ghennam and Hélié 2010: 148)

However, it is possible to contest this position by focusing on the narrative, characters and film directly. The police are included periodically as Marc is required to log his positions after work each day following his release from prison. Moreover, undercover police trail Marc from his apartment to the tower blocks of Droixhe following the heist. The heist clearly represents a turn to crime by the otherwise disenfranchised former proletariats. Despite Belvaux's eschewal of the references to the *polar* genre, *La raison du plus faible* can be interpreted as partly a return to the 1970s *polars* that 'articulate socio-political concerns' – from a Left-leaning political position – by virtue of their subject matter (Powrie 1997: 75). As Mandelbaum (2006) in *Le Monde* points out, Belvaux's film draws on 'the suspense of the *polar*' for a narrative that is located at a site of 'an unprecedented social and political disaster'. In this review, it is the 'terrain' that is imbued with social and political significance, since the film represents 'an industrial wasteland, mass redundancies and delocalisation, the foundering of trade unions, resulting impoverishment, the sidelining of the poorest in society and the breakdown of collective solidarity' (ibid.). The representation of these socio-political concerns cohere with the Dardenne brothers' and Benoît Mariage's contemporaneous films in Wallonia, thereby highlighting that Belvaux's film deals with themes left over from the so-called French New Realism (Powrie 1999) of the 1990s that struck a chord with critics at film festivals.

Despite this anchoring of the social issues in a particular and clearly delineated space, *La raison du plus faible*'s poetics articulate a complex patchwork of stylistic filiation to American, French and Belgian filmmaking. In film criticism, Alion (2006: 151) and Vincendeau (2007: 89) draw a connection between the male-centred crime narratives and the suburban locations of *Le cercle rouge* (Jean-Pierre Melville, 1970) as a crucial point of reference,[4] and Mello (2007: 61) describes the film as articulating the 'rhythm of a "realist *polar*"'. Thabourey (2006) teases out the semantics of the film noir and crime genres in relation to Belvaux's film, drawing attention not only to Melville, but also to Julien Duvivier and the contemporaneous films *Ma petite entreprise/My Little Business* (Pierre Jolivet, 1999) and *Le couperet/The Axe* (Costa-Gavras, 2005).[5] Belvaux even contends that it coheres with 'film noir' in the same vein as John Huston and Jean-Pierre Melville, since it 'allows the background to be shown through ordinary people' (Frois 2006). The patchwork of intertextual references to the *polar* genre and the film's 'noir aesthetic' (Hayward 2014) are not entirely incongruous since both pertain to an interweaving of similar literary and cinematic traditions. For instance, Powrie's analysis of the *polar* ties together 'French and American literary strands', such as the hard-boiled detective narratives of Chandler and Hammett as well as 'Hollywood gangster films of the 1930s' (1997: 76). Bordwell, Staiger and Thompson (1988: 77–80) – as well as Walker (1992) – tease out similar points of reference for classical film noirs between 1941 and 1958. Powrie further proposes a link between the two that is predicated on a 'crisis of masculinity' in the post-war period, particularly in the USA (1997: 11).

What is most revealing about the intertextual comparisons to Melville's *Le Doulos/The Finger Man* (Jean-Pierre Melville, 1963) and *Le cercle rouge* is where these films fit into Hayward's cycles of French film noirs: 'in this postindustrial age, technology replaced masculine labour and economic crises compounded unemployment, which brought in its wake renewed weakened, submissive, emasculated identity' (2014: 38–9). Whilst Hayward is analysing a period that spanned 1963–79 in French cinema, the overarching themes and contexts reverberate through Belvaux's post-industrial Wallonia in the early 2000s. Turim (2014) also offers a 'hermeneutics of noir' that stretches from Melville's 1960s films (conceived as French neo-noir in this case) through to the gangster crime thriller *Un prophète/A Prophet* (Jacques Audiard, 2009). This is inclusive of the heist film subgenre – to which Belvaux's film equally corresponds.

Beyond the use of genres as an interpretative filter, Belvaux positions the film as part of a '*cinéma de contrebande*' – on the surface the film appears to cohere with generic codes and conventions, but beneath these poetics are indirect politics and a 'social aspect' (Reynaert 2006). The film articulates significant and prominent issues of social precariousness, marginality and unemployment – themes that we previously encountered in this book in the context of the Dardenne brothers and Bouli Lanners in particular. Thabourey (2006: 130) views the region of Wallonia as a 'fertile terrain for social cinema', citing the inescapable example of Henri Storck and *Misère au Borinage*. As Spaas notes, early filmmakers in the Belgian tradition emphasised 'strong social awareness and used film as a means to reveal and address social problems' (2000: 9). *La raison du plus faible* continues in this (francophone) Belgian thematic tradition whilst referring to genres at the same time. This is particularly evidenced by the film's title that clearly connotes the break between generations, between the loss of father–son relations in an industrial context, and increased levels of social marginality and precariousness linked directly – in this case – to (primarily male) unemployment in the region.

The film's title subtly evokes Bernard Lahire's sociological study carried out in the early 1990s in France, entitled *La Raison des plus faibles: Rapport au travail, écritures domestiques et lectures domestiques et les lectures en milieu populaires* (1994).[6] The study considers 'the connections between spaces of professional and domestic socialisation, between work [. . .] and printed forms of [cultural] appropriation, and between work and school' for the working classes (Lahire 1994: 5). In this sense, the cultural positioning and appropriation of the '*plus faible*' (that is, the weakest) in terms of class stratifications is with the working classes and the proletariat. Belvaux film further recalls – and inverts – Patric Jean's *La Raison du plus fort/The Right of the Strongest* (2003), a documentary that considers the closing of the factories and the subsequent issues concerning delocalisation in cities across France and Belgium, namely Brussels, Marseilles, Amiens and Lyons. As Jean notes, the film is intentionally political in terms of its approach to the subject matter, with his previous film, *Les enfants du Borinage, lettre à Henri Storck/The Children of Borinage, A Letter to Henri Stork* concentrating more on social determinism, generational decline, and poverty (Vlaeminckx 2003). The documentary is crucially characterised by the high-rise blocks of apartments that dominate the skyline of Paris' and Lyons' *banlieues*, resonating with the images captured on the fringes of Liège in Belvaux's film. From this premise, despite *La raison du plus faible*'s regional setting in Liège, the framing of the city could easily represent and articulate narratives from cities across France and Belgium, adding a contiguous transnational dimension. This is neatly evidenced in *L'Humanité dimanche*, since it argues that, in Belvaux's film, 'Liège symbolises Lorraine, the North and all the regions hit hard by deindustrialisation' (M. M. 2006).

Let us briefly consider the sociopolitical context from which these latent themes and issues arise in the city of Liège. Historically, this extends back to at least the 1960s. Bajomée outlines the Walloon economic crisis, with particular emphasis on Liège, where during the 1960s there was a loss of 15,000 jobs while Brussels and Flanders noted a gain of around 25,000 posts (2010: 14). There was a perception that Wallonia was in a period of underdevelopment with key structural problems – including a call for increased autonomy – that gave rise to a 'culture of struggle' (2010: 19). The post-1968 period in Liège also witnessed a generational shift, with 'the opening of faculties to young people who were not "their fathers' sons"' (2010: 13), that is an increase in young men seeking education over following in their fathers' footsteps to the steel industry. As Mello contends, Patrick in *La raison du plus faible* belongs to a different generation and social class – having obtained a university education – but he remains without employment and thus part of the collective struggle (2007: 62).

Mello further posits that the film represents 'a portrait of men in crisis, reflected by Liège, the prosperous and effervescent industrial activity of the nineteenth century that is today confronted by an elevated level of unemployment and deserted factories' (2007: 62). As Vincendeau (2007: 89) crucially notes, the themes of unemployment and its consequences are primarily configured from a male-centric position, fitting into preconceived notions of the role of men in industrial society. The film, therefore, represents 'a personal engagement' (Fevry 2011: 90), with issues around employment and the aforementioned shifting economic landscape in Wallonia as the steel industry atrophies in the region. Belvaux notes that his maternal grandfather and his brothers worked in a foundry in the Charleroi region – a form of employment that is delocalising away from the Sambre-Meuse axis (Alion 2006: 154; Bradfer 2006b: 2–3). From this premise, Belvaux laments the short termism of employment and its peripatetic contracts – as evinced by films like the Dardenne brothers' *Rosetta* – which has resulted in the 'decomposition of social relations' in the context of a community's 'struggle' (ibid.).

The impact of deindustrialisation is viewed from the loss of employment directly on men, followed by their wives and family indirectly. However, the representation of women and their working role rises to the surface in *La raison du plus faible*, with the only prominent female character, Carole, being able to maintain her job in an industrial laundry facility (Thabourey 2006:

130).⁷ Carole's regular journeys to work on the bus are tightly framed, and they are concomitant with Claudine's tram journeys in *Une part du ciel/A Piece of Sky* (Bénédicte Liénard, 2002) and *Deux jours, une nuit* (Jean-Pierre and Luc Dardenne, 2014) in which Sandra travels between the houses of her co-workers. The casting of Natacha Régnier in the role of Carole creates a further transnational dialogue with the shifting relationship between women and the world of work in the northern regions of France and Belgium, since Régnier formerly played the struggling unemployed Marie in *La vie rêvée des anges* (Erick Zonca, 1998). As Mosley notes in the context of *Rosetta* and *L'enfant*, the Dardennes use 'local buses as an exemplary realist tactic' (2013: 130). In *La raison du plus faible,* through Carole's employment, the film exposes a particularly parochial interpretation of a distinctly patriarchal society. It demonstrates a tendency to analyse and read these films from a male-centric position, overlooking the role of women in contemporary society. The 'weak presence' of women in the film also coheres with trends in the *polar* genre in which women are 'little represented', 'play stereotyped roles' and are even 'relegated to secondary roles' (Poirson-Dechonne 2011: 20). Powrie recalls the 'crisis of masculinity' through a psychoanalytic lens – an approach that is heavily used in the context of classic film noir – in addition to its potential as an 'unresolved' 'social phenomenon' (1997: 8–12). This is an area that is little addressed in contemporary francophone Belgian filmmaking, but which has, as Poirson-Dechonne (2011: 20–1) observes, shifted in French cinema since at least 2001. However, in the case of *La raison du plus faible*, Carole's employment functions to further highlight Patrick's sense of emasculation, taking the female character out of the domestic arena into the world of work (and manual labour) operates as a means of supplanting traditional roles afforded to men, quite reductively.

A 'Crisis of Masculinity' in a Walloon Context: *L'homme Fragile et Fatigué*

Whilst reviewing Bouli Lanners' films *Ultranova* and *Eldorado*, André (2009a) identifies the increasing presence of the 'devalorisation of man' in francophone Belgian filmmaking, particularly in the context of the steel industry. This strand continues to gain critical currency in *La raison du plus faible*. The emasculation of the central characters chimes with the filiation from Melville's French film noirs, and is manifested in plural forms. Although Fevry's (2011) chapter on the film is entitled 'bodies in crisis', the representation of this corporeal crisis is primarily articulated through its relationship with the city space and the film's poetics. However, in this section, the notion of a particular 'crisis in masculinity' is considered through character relations, performance and corporeality. In *La raison du plus faible*, we can identify three forms of

Figure 6.2 Carole's broken-down mobylette is walked back by Patrick.

emasculation: (1) Carole's aforementioned ability to sustain work in a competitive arena; (2) humiliation; and (3) the crippled or fragile male body. Bullot contends that the film places the 'used body by work and alcohol consumption' in the *mise-en-scène* (2014: 316).

The notion of humiliation arises in the interstices of the relationships in the family unit between father and son, husband and wife and son and father-in-law. When Carole's *mobylette* (a type of moped) breaks down on her return to work, her ability to maintain her post becomes difficult due to her reliance on public transport, namely the bus (Fevry 2011: 97) (Figure 6.2). With Patrick unemployed and Carole's low-paid work, the young couple are unable to purchase a new or second-hand scooter, as Fevry notes. In a similar vein to the Italian Neorealist film *Ladri di biciclette/Bicycle Thieves* (Vittorio De Sica, 1948), social status is attached to the bicycle, since the physical mobility it enables permits social mobility and the possibility of retaining employment. Belvaux notes the metaphorical connotations associated with the moped in traditions of French and Italian cinema, highlighting its revelatory significance to 'witness the fragility' of the adult characters (Denis 2006: 4). The father-in-law (Carole's father) purchases a scooter for his daughter, leading to Patrick's physical attack on him in front of his young son. Patrick interprets the father-in-law's move as an indirect attack on his status in the family unit – a symbolic emasculation that leads to his attempt to reclaim his status through the subsequent heist.

The film is punctuated by a series of visits to the former steel plant, with the young children from the small suburb of Liège learning about their local history. A school trip visits the factory as it is being dismantled, in which a former worker outlines the processes of working in the plant and its perilous nature, which led to the crippling of men due to limited safety procedures. This sequence evokes Fabrice and his son's visit to the 'hollowed shell' of a steel plant (as O'Shaughnessy (2007: 49) observes in the case of *Pour que la guerre s'achève, les murs devaient s'écrouler/For the War to End, the Walls Should Have Crumbled* (Jean-Pierre and Luc Dardenne, 1980)), in Seraing in the Dardenne brothers' *Je pense à vous*, thereby highlighting the reverberations of these social issues – in the intervening thirteen years – in a de-industrialised and post-industrial Wallonia. Moreover, the guide's accent connotes a potentially Italian heritage, which presciently cites *Déjà s'envole la fleur maigre* (Paul Meyer, 1960). Meyer's film primarily focuses on first and second generation immigrant Italian workers in the post-World War II coal industry in the Borinage (the Hainaut region of Belgium), foregrounding the systemic inequalities experienced by the migrant workers as outsiders in Belgian society and the rise in unemployment (resulting in the threat of deportation). In *La raison du plus faible*, Carole informs her son that his grandfather worked in this factory, and this therefore allows the father to have enough savings to pass down this gift to his daughter. Carole highlights the importance of the work to her son, evidenced by a recurring line which states that the workers were referred to as 'the aristocrats of the working class'. Patrick represents the 'lost' generation, the sons who were unable to follow in their fathers' footsteps.

Whereas the children's visit to the steel plant enhances the film's sociological depth, Robert and Marc's heated discussion in the plant's grounds operates as a means to present character interiority (Figure 6.3). The scene opens with a long shot of the blast furnace under the cover of darkness. The furnace is merely represented by blurred lights that cut across the frame with a blue hue that evokes the metallic coloration of Melville's post-industrial cities. The blast furnace, which lies at the centre of the conversation, is perceptually located

Figure 6.3 Marc and Robert have a heated discussion against the backdrop of the abstract lights that evoke the recycling and breaking-down of the former steel plant.

in the background. The motivation for the hold-up is laid out clearly. The subsequent shot then develops the relationship between the two men: Robert, the former worker, and Marc, the former criminal. The shot is focused on Robert as he recites the former daily routine when the plant was operative for the locals. Their gaze is fixed ahead, beyond the frame, as the ambient sounds of the dismantling continue. The post-industrial context remains salient on the diegetic soundtrack. In this sense, it functions as a revelatory sequence for both male characters. As with the French neo-noirs of the 1970s, a sense of betrayal permeates the film. Robert laments,

> (t)hey exploit us for five generations and just when we manage to make a decent wage, [. . .] they move it all away. To exploit folk even poorer, even more fragile than us. [. . .] Look at what you see here. It's a fortune. [. . .] If they sell my life off, the money's mine too.

Within this exchange, there is a limited level of ambiguity to the character's motivation. The sequence compresses the relevant local history and context, before justifying the actions as 'reclaiming' the lifeblood that pulsed through the region. As Fevry observes, Robert 'talks of delocalisation' and sees the region's 'new capital' (2011: 98). However, this radically contrasts with the contemporaneous work of the Dardenne brothers, particularly *La promesse* through to *L'enfant*, in which – as Mosley neatly outlines in the context of *Rosetta* – there is a 'lack of an explanatory context [which] allows the Dardennes to avoid any explicit social commentary' (2013: 90). In the case of *La raison du plus faible*, a certain profundity emerges from these revelatory conversations that highlights the collective struggles of the former proletariat in a local context.

An imbrication between the humiliation of the central male protagonists and the ailing, crippled and emasculated male body occurs when Robert carries his fellow tower block tenant Jean-Pierre, a paraplegic, ungraciously down several flights of stairs to meet their group of friends in a local café. The reasons for Jean-Pierre's disability are explicitly addressed in the film, through Robert and Marc's aforementioned conversation and the horror stories of the precariousness of working in the steel industries recited to the children of the region. The central characters, namely Robert and Patrick, refer to their own bodies as shattered, fragile, tired and broken. As a result, Robert is an alcoholic, regularly consuming the well-known Belgian beer Jupiler (or Jup as it is referred to in the film). Robert, in this sense, functions as an example of Bullot's 'used body' (2014: 316), and when Patrick is shot in his lower abdomen, Jean-Pierre carries his near-lifeless body down the tower block in the lift to the awaiting paramedics. This represents a clear echo of the earlier scene, foregrounding the continued emasculation of the male characters. There is a sense of reciprocity and cyclical forms of the ailing male body that is in need of being physically supported by others. As Fevry notes, the 'crisis' of the male body is further exacerbated by the freedom of movement afforded to Marc Pirmet, an outsider who has just been freed from prison for armed robbery (2011: 96). Marc operates as a potential surrogate for the filmmaker, with parallels being developed between the filmmaker and the character. For instance, Lucas Belvaux plays the role of Marc, with reverberations in the character's history generated from the filmmaker's previous acting roles. In *Cavale*, Bruno (played by Belvaux) is an escaped convict, who has been jailed for his revolutionary Left-wing activities in a post-68 era. This is neatly evinced by the ambiguity of the film's ending, with Marc fleeing across the snow-covered landscape of Grenoble. As Olsen contends in his review of *Cavale*, 'there is a poignancy in watching this man [Bruno] discover that the life he thought he was returning to is no longer there [...] no one seems concerned about the fate of the proletariat masses anymore' (2003). In *La raison du plus faible*, the former armed robber, Marc (also played by Belvaux), has a limited back story and history, but his outsider status arises through the stories of the steel plant that are recited to him by Robert.

From this premise, the sense of a collective is re-forged from an increasingly disenfranchised community. This is furthered through Marc's rhythmic movements across the city. Fevry (2011: 96–7) initially posits that Marc is afforded a 'greater freedom of movement' due to his 'mechanical' daily routine that encompasses his trips to work and to the police station. However, Marc's role is more nuanced, since he visits each of the characters face-to-face in a manner that is concomitant with Sandra in the later *Deux jours, une nuit* (2014). As Marc travels to each of their houses, he begins to uncover details of their family life, their idiosyncrasies and their disenfranchisement. Through developing relationships in the private sphere, Marc is able to develop a new social bond between the former male workers, bridging a generational divide in the case of Robert, Jean-Pierre and Patrick, to enable them to try and take back responsibility for their own social position – but this time through the heist. For Belvaux (Dervaux 2006), it represents a 'film of the community' that has a strong bond 'on the margins of the margins'. By virtue of the male characters' proletarian history (Robert and Jean-Pierre), lineage (Patrick) or current situation (in the case of Marc), the group has forged a cohesive identity. The sense of a collective forged between the men is an evocation of the bonds and lasting friendships that date back to the factories (Belvaux, cited in Alion 2006: 153). The card games in the local café recall the impromptu 'pretexts' for strikers in the documenatary *Misère au Borinage* against rising unemployment in the province. The creation of an all-male group chimes with Melville's crime and gangster films of the 1960s and 1970s, which, as Vincendeau contends, 'featured "families" or groups of men among whom loyalty and betrayal emphasised interdependence' (2003: 179). This is neatly evidenced through the evening meal that they collectively produce at Patrick's house whilst they await Carole's return from her day shift, and the hold-up that includes only the three local men, Jean-Pierre, Robert and Patrick. Marc refrains from taking part in the heist at the former steel plant, remaining in his apartment overnight. Belvaux posits that his male characters and the core group

> no longer believe in politics, in trade unions, and in collective struggle. Because of globalization, the repeating [economic] crises have fragmented the working class. They are outside the system and their class [. . .] It is a form of struggle that worked during the last century, but it does not work any more. (Denis 2006: 4)

La raison du plus faible therefore 'gives a voice to a forgotten group of people' not only in the francophone regions of Belgium but also across Western Europe (Bradfer 2006a: 33). Such a 'critical view of contemporary society' chimes with Beugnet's interpretation of *le jeune cinéma* that arose across the conterminous border in the French language in the mid to late 1990s (2004: 285). In this sense, neo-liberal policies in the industry sector have changed the patterns of employment in countries and regions that developed alongside the steel and mining industries. Vincendeau (2007) and Pascal Merigeau (2006) place Belvaux's film in the same frame as British social realist films of the early to mid 1990s, such as *Raining Stones* (Ken Loach, 1993) and *The Full Monty* (Peter Cattaneo, 1997). Let us now turn to the film's poetics in order to further understand the significance of *La raison du plus faible*'s *mise-en-scène* and location.

The Poetic Representation of the Post-industrial Liégeois Suburbs

The film's poetics emphasise the importance of the space and location in which the film unrolls. From this premise, the opening sequence is particularly significant, given that it clearly articulates the themes of exclusion, employment and loss. Belvaux introduces bilateral horizontal movement in opposite directions across the frame, first from left to right followed by movement from right to left across the field of the frame. This is furthered by a pan that tracks from right to left back across the frame, focusing on the glum faces of disenfranchised former workers peering through the newly erected steel fence. The opening shot is static, whilst producing the perceptual illusion of movement in a horizontal direction. This is evidenced by the deep-focus cinematography, which keeps the blast furnace in the centre of the frame. An electronically controlled gate severs the image, disorientating the spectator. This is further compounded by the immediate entrance of an empty train carriage arriving to carry away the tons of steel across the second plane of action from the opposite direction. In so doing, the spectator is perceptually and immediately aligned with the excluded former workers. Fevry posits that,

> Belvaux, therefore, poses a correlation between obstructed view and *impuissance motrice*. The *perspective bouchée* [the reverse shot] corresponds to the characters' forced immobility. The object of their point of view [the plant] is inaccessible, they can no longer return to their place of work. (2011: 96)

For Fevry, this double movement of the camera pertains to the characters' 'double alienation' – a restriction in mobility and of point of view (ibid.). The elastic movement across the frame and multiple planes of action in this opening sequence present a future–past dialectic – the illusion of a forward movement of the camera presents an exclusionary future of an atrophying steel industry that is then followed by a pan of those left behind, that is, a 'lost' generation. The exclusionary gesture is further heightened by the perception of movement in the frame. Neyrat (2006: 50) further contends that the opening *champs-contrechamps* foregrounds the central protagonists' sense of exclusion. The glimpses of the faces that the spectator is afforded occur through the fence panels, which evoke the bars of a prison cell. The use of barred fence panels and gates reverberates through Belvaux's films as a stylistic signature, since the filmmaker uses a similar technique in the opening sequence of the aforementioned *38 témoins*.

Nessolson draws attention to the use of long shots and widescreen that stretch the frame to include Liège's river, factories, public housing and workers' cottages with gardens (2006: 40). The region's industrial architecture is placed at the forefront of the film's *mise-en-scène*. Echoing Lanners' use of CinemaScope for the painterly vistas of the Ardennes, Belvaux adopts the use of CinemaScope cinematography for a 'romantic' and 'unexpected' representation of the Droixhe district of Liège (Reynaert 2006). In distinct contrast, Fevry describes the shots as 'folkloric vignettes that confirm a stereotyped representation of a Walloon region in crisis' (2011: 92). For instance, Marc sits on the outskirts of the city, gazing in a contemplative manner at the steel plant, and in particular the almost-hallowed blast furnaces, which are positioned in the centre of the frame. The adoption of this technology imbibes a certain aesthetic and style by virtue of deep focus cinematography and widescreen. Bordwell (1985) draws heavily on Bazin's work on ontology, realism and ambiguity to develop an approach to CinemaScope and widescreen aesthetics. As a result, CinemaScope has a revelatory and participatory function. The shot shows a 'simultaneous presence of character and object, figure and landscape' that 'allows the viewer to notice the nuances of character interaction by virtue of the director's gradation of emphasis' (1985: 20). The 'folkloric' (Fevry 2011) nature of these shots resonates with the contemplative CinemaScope shots of Dimitri on the outskirts of Liège in *Ultranova*, Yvan in the same city in *Eldorado* and, most strikingly, the clear intertextual reference to *Les convoyeurs attendent* in which the struggling photographer Roger sits upon a *terril*, gazing down at the coal-mining plant in Charleroi – as included on the front cover of Roekens and Tixhon's (2011) survey of 'a Walloon cinema in economic crisis'. Belvaux, therefore, generates a productive dialogue with contemporary Belgian – and more specifically Walloon – filmmaking that clearly locates and situates the action. The use of CinemaScope, widescreen and deep-focus cinematography, in this instance, forges an immediate relationship between the dismantled steel plant and the disenfranchised male characters, with the viewer drawing the line between the individual and the blast furnace. However, Belvaux avoids the use of the long take alongside CinemaScope technology dialectically, introducing a gradual dissolve twelve seconds into the shot that moves the unrolling of time from dusk to night and the removal of the character. The break in the conventions of the widescreen aesthetic – as outlined by Bordwell (1985) – epitomises the two sides of the film. One side highlights the immediate relationship between character and landscape through deep-focus cinematography (proffering a social reading) at dusk, with the second side emphasising the *noir*-ish *mise-en-scène* that portends the hold-up.

Fevry's (2011) denouncement of how the industrial landscape is framed resonates with the earlier criticism of the Dardenne brothers' *Je pense à vous*. However, the films *Le gamin au vélo* and *Deux jours, une nuit* (explored here in Chapter Two) cohere more with Belvaux's framing, which is characterised by long shots and pans that view the characters as they navigate the suburban spaces of the Liège industrial basin. Moreover, this framing and revelatory use of *mise-en-scène* valorises the industrial landscape and the architecture that is dotted across the region and the city. In 2015, the Musée d'Ixelle's exhibition of 'Landscapes of Belgium' provided representations of Wallonia that were primarily concentrated in the sphere of industrial landscapes. The exhibition drew particular attention to the region's metallurgic industries and slag heaps, making prominent reference to the photography and video work of Jacques Charlier. Belvaux's so-called 'romantic' shots of the landscape chime with Charlier's photographic work *Paysages professionnels du STP 1964–1971*, which concentrated on the withering steel plants and blast furnaces in Seraing – home to the Dardenne brothers and a town part of the *Liégeois* industrial basin.

La raison du plus faible is punctuated by frequent long shots that frame the industrial landscape as it is slowly being dismantled at night, thereby imbibing the 'noir aesthetic' (Hayward 2014). In terms of Hayward's fourth cycle of French film noir, she posits that the colour palette of these films, including *Le cercle rouge*, is 'metallic blue, steely grey [. . .] – usually bleak tones for these type of film emulsions' (2014: 55). The equipment being used to deconstruct the former steel plant cuts through the dark-blue hues of the night sky by generating flashes of light. Tonally, Neyrat outlines the grey and green colour palette for the area that covers the representation of Liège (2006: 51). To this end, the palette evokes Parisian painter Maximilien Luce's *Terril de Charbonnage* (1896) of the Walloon Hainaut region, in which the emerging industrial landscape is primarily characterised by grey, green and blue hues. In *La raison du plus faible*, the nighttime cinematography produces an image of industrial Wallonia that does not neatly cohere with the coloration of the region in visual culture. Seret proposes a dominant reddish hue to Walloon metallurgic representations, drawing on the Walloon artists Léonard Defrance and Constantin Meunier through to filmmakers like the oft-cited Dardenne brothers and Manu Bonmariage (Fontaine 2007). The latter filmmakers, nevertheless, emerged during a period of socially and politically engaged video making in the 1970s and 1980s in Liège and, more generally, in Wallonia.[8]

As Vincendeau (2007: 89) notes, although Belvaux's film is set in a similar location to the Dardenne brothers' corpus of work (that is, the suburbs of the city of Liège), the tone and style of the film is differentiated through inferences and references to the thriller genre. The film's style draws on the semantics of film noir, with Vincendeau foregrounding the 'moody shots of the city at night, its lights glittering from a distance, or the extraordinary views of the high-rise blocks, stretched like medieval towers across the wide screen' (2007: 89). The cinematography of the final sequence and its emphasis on verticality is more concomitant with the classic American film noir. Murat (2006) notes its filiation to John Huston's 'American noir thrillers'. *La raison du plus faible*'s concluding shot presents an aerial view of the tower blocks and the *Liégeois* suburb that chimes with the opening sequence of the film noir *The Naked City* (Jules Dassin, 1948), in which the unsteady, floating camerawork and whirring noises of an aeroplane captures New York 'as it is' according to the authoritarian, documentary-like voiceover. Belvaux keenly pinpoints these tower blocks – in the Walloon cinematic tradition following Polet's (2002) line of argument – in a dialogic manner, with the character Jean-Pierre uttering the location of Droixhe. As previously discussed in the interpretations of the representation of the dilapidated steel plant and references to the tower blocks, Belvaux's film encourages a sociological reading. This contrasts with Vincendeau's analysis of Melville's *Le Doulos*, which is 'stripped of its sociological depth' through its eschewal of a precise location (Vincendeau 2003: 153). The Droixhe tower blocks were modernist buildings and social housing built during the 1950s and completed two decades later in the 1970s on the left bank of the Meuse (Frankignoulle 2011: 227–9). However, it was not until the 1980s that the area was considered a 'difficult estate' (ibid.). This aspect of the location is overlooked in Belvaux's film, but it does arise in the documentary *Un été à Droixhe/A Summer in Droixhe* (Richard Olivier, 1996).

The doomed protagonist permeates *La raison du plus faible* in the case of the character of Marc, which resonates with Vincendeau's (1992) seminal work on the French film noir and the films of Jean-Pierre Melville. *La raison du plus faible*'s denouement was received negatively in film criticism, denounced for its 'Hollywood-style' ending, in which Marc is surrounded by police in helicopters on a rooftop high above the city.[9] However, Vincendeau draws on classicism and the instilling of a moral framework in her interpretation of the denouement of Jean-Pierre Melville's two film noir films *Le Doulos* and *Le Deuxième Souffle/Second Wind* (Jean-Pierre Melville, 1966) (2003: 153). Palmer (2002) and Vincendeau (2003) place a particular emphasis on Melville's fascination with Hollywood cinema and his predilection for American stylistic filiation. The classical narrative structure is underpinned by 'the heist, as usual, mark[ing] both the apotheosis of the gangsters' skills and solidarity and the beginning of their demise' (Vincendeau 2003: 161). Whilst Belvaux's protagonists are presented as amateurs and out of their depth as gangsters, the hold-up operates as a similarly initiating force that propels the heroes to their inevitable doom. Critical reviews of *La raison du plus faible* have, therefore, lamented the film's adherence to classicism, removing the ambiguity from the characters' motivations (as previously discussed in this chapter) and an ending in which the former male workers turned criminals are inevitably punished for their actions either by death, severe injury or a potential prison sentence. From this premise, the characters have been viewed, rather ludically, as 'stooges caught in a tricky situation' (Heymann 2006; Tinazzi 2006).

The denouement is, nevertheless, reportedly inspired by events that transpired in the same tower blocks in 1989, when gangster Philippe Delaire jettisoned his loot from the windows of the building to a crowd below (Einstein 2006).[10] The integration of a *fait divers* (news story) chimes with the 'hermeneutics of film noir' (Turim 2014), with Belvaux further positing its allusion to the prolific and influential Belgian crime writer Georges Simenon (Bradfer 2006b: 3).[11] As a result, the literary influences on the development of French film noir from Hugo, Balzac and Simenon shine a light on 'the dark universe of crime, failure and melodrama, almost always ending in death' (Vincendeau 2016: 45). Mosley (2013: 30) and Kaganski (2006) read this gesture by Marc as a redistribution of wealth from the newly wealthy to the 'poor and needy', that is a Robin Hood-style narrative. The gesture portends a mythological status for the anti-hero, chiming with the *fait divers*. It is also concomitant with Jean Gabin's protagonists of French Poetic Realism who 'attain a mythological dimension, but that myth is connected to their "ordinariness" as characters as to their class identity' (Vincendeau 1992: 57). Marc's Left-wing political sensibilities and proletariat nature – he works full-time in the local Jupiler beer factory on the assembly line – imbibes the spirit of Gabin's 'ordinariness', connecting the character with the local withering working-class community. The gesture suggests that the crime committed by the small group is not entirely for personal gain, but it is representative of a latent desire of the community to rise up in a time of punishing and severe austerity. Adopting Hayward's interpretation of the 'protagonist's trajectory [as] one long suicidal death wish', the death is 'chosen by *himself*' in the Poetic Realist tradition (Hayward 2014: 39). This form of characterisation coheres with Hayward's 'purist take on noir' in a French context (ibid.). Returning to *La raison du plus faible*, Marc imbibes this tradition in his own death. He is in control of his last fight against the police and the institutional symbol of control and order. Despite his limited involvement in the hold-up, he takes the stolen money from Robert, Jean-Pierre and Patrick and leads the police to a final shoot-out on the rooftop. In this sense, Marc chooses to bear the burden of 'responsibility' for the actions of the disillusioned and disenfranchised – an honorable death. The location of the central male protagonist in *La raison du plus faible* as the doomed anti-hero isolated at the top of a building recalls the Poetic Realist tradition of French cinema in the 1930s – a postulated antecedent of the film noir style – of Jean Gabin's François in *Le jour se lève/Daybreak* (Marcel Carné, 1939).

Conclusion

Lucas Belvaux's films navigate a complex patchwork of genres and stylistic and thematic filiation with key filmmakers in French cinema, namely Jean-Pierre Melville. The portrait of Wallonia is closely tied up with (and to an extent sublimated within) the *polar*, noir and French gangster films. On a thematic level, *La raison du plus faible* evokes a 'noir aesthetic' (Hayward 2014) and conforms to the French 'hermeneutics of noir' (Turim 2014), particularly through its representation of emasculation and the cityscape. *La raison du plus faible* does not neatly cohere with films produced in Wallonia in terms of their narrative set-up and clear articulation of character motivations through character interiority, explanatory and revelatory sequences and the *mise-en-scène*. The poetic representation of Liège generates intertextual comparisons with photographic and artistic rendering of the city and its industrial heritage. However, film criticism and scholarly work in relation to the film and its local articulations remain lukewarm and 'stereotypical' in the words of Fevry (2011: 92). In so doing, the issues and concerns of social marginalisation and social precariousness are offset by the film's adherence to classic genres and well-established film styles from French film history.

Notes

1. Belvaux's first film, *Parfois trop d'amour*, was co-produced by Brussels-based film production centre Les Films de la Drève, with Walloon filmmaker Jean-Jacques Andrien serving as the Belgian producer. (The company is now based in the province of Liège in Wallonia.)
2. Hayward's (2016) conception of middlebrow in a French cinematic context is

particularly instructive in terms of aligning the middlebrow with Truffaut's 'tradition de qualité' (tradition of quality) and 'cinéma du papa' (Daddy's cinema) in which literary works were adapted in order to appeal to a mass audience irrespective of class.
3. Mai (2011: 447) draws on the 'iron filings' analogy from Andrew (2010), and his interpretation of Bazin, to better understand the Dardenne brothers' *Le silence de Lorna*.
4. In the context of *La trilogie* (Lucas Belvaux, 2001–2), Belvaux addresses the influences that derive from the works of Jean-Pierre Melville, by positing that he 'does not seek to hide [his] admiration for Melville' (Alion 2002: 96). This cinematic reference point is particularly instructive when considering Stratton's typographical pun in his review of *La trilogie*, in which he refers to the filmmaker as 'Lucas Belville' (Stratton 2002).
5. In the context of his film *Cavale/On the Run* (2002), Belvaux outlines a particularly nuanced understanding of Melville's filmmaking when discussing the film's minimalist *mise-en-scène* (Alion 2002: 96).
6. Lahire's sociological study draws on *'faibles'* in plural form as a more inclusive and all-encompassing term, whereas Belvaux's title clearly pertains to the singular *'faible'*, thereby suggesting the limited focus of the film on the notion of 'crisis' articulated in the white, working-class males of the post-industrial setting.
7. The launderette as a place of work also emerges as Lorna's first job in the Dardenne brothers' *Le silence de Lorna/Lorna's Silence* (2008) – a position she wishes to escape in order to open her own café, that is it is on her journey for increased social mobility.
8. For a more in-depth and nuanced analysis of video-making in the city of Liège, see Mélon (2010).
9. The denouement also recalls the classical/post-classical Hollywood action film *Die Hard* (John McTiernan, 1988), when the FBI attempt to storm the towering Nakatomi building in helicopters in Los Angeles with the stricken protagonist John McClane attempting to save the remaining hostages on the rooftop. The money distributed from the Droixhe tower blocks is concomitant with the thousands of blank papers (possibly the bonds that Hans Gruber wishes to steal in the elaborate heist) that snow down on the crowd at *Die Hard*'s climax.
10. Belvaux states that he was initially directed to this news story whilst presenting a film masterclass at the Cinéma Le Parc in Liège (Duculot 2006).
11. As Vincendeau argues, two Belgian crime writers, Georges Simenon and Stanislas-André Steeman had a profound impact on French film noir due to their 'predilection for the teeming *faubourgs* of Paris and low dives in the port towns of Le Havre or Marseille' (2016: 42).

CONCLUSION

On a conceptual level, this book considers francophone Belgian cinema, and the notion of a devolved Walloon cinema, through the lens of two complementary notions of cinematic transnationalism and regional cinema. By adopting a scalar approach to global and local understandings of films, and eschewing the dialectical form of the 'glocal' (which has also been offered as an alternative conceptual model within debates in the context of small national cinemas), this book highlights the complexities, issues and concerns with 'the concept of national cinema' (Higson 1989), that is, the national alone is not entirely sufficient for better understanding the varieties of francophone Belgian cinema. As Ledo contends, it is possible to ascertain that the nation operates as merely 'a starting point for analysis' for a cinematically small nation (2017). However, for Elsaesser, the sub-state and the supra-national are complementary and competing notions that avoid the national, as well as foregrounding the need to consider distinct films and cinemas in a regional context (Elsaesser 2005: 116–19). The knot between the sub-state and the supra-state is tied within the context of the European Union, which actively encourages the development of the local and the regional within a post-national European context (2005: 116–17). Belgium sits within these interstices with notions of 'allegiance' (2005: 120) extant within the linguistic communities, as analysed in the Introduction, the engagement with the forms of Belgian nationalism, and the TV drama *Bye Bye Belgium*. The transnational, and the supra-national, remain salient through the industrial analysis of francophone Belgian filmmaking.

CONCLUSION

Prior to 2017, francophone Belgian cinema had not been canonised in a formal and holistic manner. A push by the CCA on the fiftieth anniversary of the Royal Decree of 1967 has provided a neat and coherent starting point for a process of 'self-selectivity' (offered by Christie (2013)). However, it obfuscates filmmaking that preceded this time within the regions of Wallonia, Bruxelles-Capitale and Flanders that pertain to each of their cultural specificities and ethnolinguistic nationalisms. It also overlooks films that have become enmeshed in an intertextual dialogue among contemporary filmmakers, such as *Misère au Borinage* and *Déjà s'envole la fleur maigre*'s stylistic filiation with the films of Bouli Lanners, Olivier Masset-Depasse, the Dardenne brothers and, as Gabriel (2011) posits, Benoît Mariage. The tendency to periodise within this context has also emerged with the so-called 'post-Dardenne generation', which requires problematising due to its process of positing a starting point and end point for a mode of filmmaking that has been in a constant state of renewal (as Chapter Two analyses). The Dardenne brothers serve to represent a simplistic idiom of francophone Belgian cinema that deals with social marginalisation, social polarisation and the region's industrial heritage thematically. It is precisely this idiom that permeates the approach to the diversity of filmmakers offered in this book.

An industrial analysis of francophone Belgian cinema opens this book, since it maintains a firm place within analyses of cinematic small nations, particularly evinced within the edited collection of 'cinema at the periphery' (Iordanova, Martin-Jones and Vidal 2010). The industrial model offered in Chapter One serves to highlight the clear 'split screen' (Mosley 2001) between Flemish and francophone cinemas, which, therefore, proposes the use of national and regional cinema concepts alongside the two major linguistic communities present in the country (the small German-speaking community falls into the political and institutional sphere of French-speaking Wallonia). The inherent fragmentation of the nation-state (as outlined in the Introduction) has filtered down into cultural and economic institutions, particularly cinema, television and print media, to produce two competing 'national' (or regional) cinemas from *within*. However, given that cinema – as a medium – is not restricted by national and regional borders, transnational interactions in an industrial context proliferate. The transnationality of the modes of production, distribution and exhibition has produced the perception of an imbalanced relationship with one of Belgium's two linguistic neighbours, France. The power dynamics and the contiguity of transnational agreements create a hierarchy that places Belgium as a cinematically small nation. This historical relationship – which can be traced back to the French filmmaker and Pathé employee Alfred Machin's work in Belgium in the silent era – has continued in the contemporary context of open borders in the European Union and its derivative programmes. As I have outlined elsewhere, the creation of Wallimage and the institutional shift in filmmaking in Wallonia has further facilitated the turn to contiguous and reciprocal agreements between Wallonia and Nord-Pas-de-Calais in the early 2000s within classical policy documents (Steele 2018).

The question of distribution and exhibition is also salient within the industrial model, since it continues to reaffirm the hierarchical power relations between France and Belgium cinematically. Key policy-makers and decision-makers note the fluidity of Belgium's domestic market that can be extended across national borders to France. Or, drawing on Marshall (2012: 38), Belgium can be considered an 'extension' of the French domestic market, along with the French-speaking cantons of Switzerland. Both of these positions highlight the significance of cinematic transnationalism as a means to decipher these trends in which francophone Belgian films generally perform better in France. It is a form of cinematic transnationalism that is predicated on 'affinity' (Hjort 2009), mutual intelligibility of language and historical patterns of distribution and exhibition prior to the dominance of Hollywood and films produced in the United States of America from 1968.[1] This is combined with critical valorisation at international film festivals, and the general perception that the Cannes film festival is the critical point of entry to France and the French film industry.

The 'topical' themes (Hjort 2000) are not only established within the nation or region, since they not contained within the national borders between the north of France and the south of Belgium. Each cinematic representation opens up a dialogue with shared concerns and articulations that transcend borders, particularly with northern France and *le jeune cinéma* (Prédal 2002). The industrial context, therefore, conjoins the representational, with the two institutions adhering to 'affinitive' and 'milieu-building' forms of cinematic transnationality (Hjort 2009) to support a cinematically small nation and a regional cinema that moved away from Paris by offering local images. Iordanova, Martin-Jones and Vidal interpret this move as a 'type of synergising, which aims to highlight mutual interrelatedness' (2010: 8). To this end, cinematic transnationalism offers us a platform and 'interface' (Marsha Kinder, cited in Higbee and Lim 2010: 8) to interpret contiguous regional images. As Hannerz presciently outlines,

> (i)n the late twentieth-century phase of globalisation, many people have increasingly experiential access to flows of cultural form which used to be localised elsewhere, as well as to that which we think of as belonging to our own locality. And some currents of culture are perhaps hardly identifiable as belonging to any particular place at all. (Hannerz 1997: 8)

The 1998 survey and critical analysis of francophone Belgian cinema by the newspaper *Le Matin* evidences the contiguity and shared concerns between French and Belgian cinema in this period. The survey includes an article concerning French cinema produced in Nord-Pas-de-Calais, hinting at the particularism of the films, '[the region's] urban décor, mythology of the mining and textile-based working-classes, producing a current taste for social realism' (Pliskin 1998). The note to particularism arises from Pliskin's decision to include the locations for a cross-section of the selected films in this social realist and northern context, such as Lille for *La vie rêvée des anges*, Bailleul for *La vie de Jésus/The Life of Jesus* (Bruno Dumont, 1997), Calais and Aire-sur-la-Lys for *Nord/North* (Xavier Beauvois, 1991) and Dunkirk for *Parfait Amour/Perfect Love* (Catherine Breillat, 1996) (ibid.). In francophone Belgian cinema, as this book has outlined, the films of its auteurs, with the exception of the 'marked' (Hjort 2009) film *Cages* (Masset-Depasse, 2006), unroll in the region's major cities, namely Liège, and the industrial suburbs. In the case of francophone Belgian cinema, the films do not exist within a hermetically sealed national and cultural framework, that is solely within Walloon, *Bruxellois*, or, more broadly, francophone Belgian context.

Within this frame, the films – as cultural representations – are at once locally rooted and potentially 'culturally specific' (to adopt Higson's (2000) term) as well as transnational by virtue of their recognisable and easily readable *mise-en-scène* and intertextual references for global audiences (as Ezra and Rowden (2006: 4) argue). Walloon cinema and francophone Belgian cinema do not speak their own language cinematically, which contrasts with the 'alternative cinemas' that sit 'at the periphery' by articulating their own language, such as Basque cinema and Scottish Gaelic cinema as two examples (Iordanova, Martin-Jones and Vidal 2010: 5–7).

The films selected for this study generally deal with Wallonia's industrial heritage, the region's de-industrialised and post-industrial struggles as it attempts to find its feet in a new context. They all resonate with Hjort's (2000: 105–7) 'topical' approach to the 'theme of nation' for Wallonia. These themes and stories neatly map onto the cultural specificity of francophone Belgian cinema as a regional and sub-national cinema, thereby reaffirming a form of national narrative. In the context of 'cinemas of small nations', Hjort and Petrie assess Willeman's view that even though there is a tendency to analyse films through a transnational lens, 'the engagement with national or cultural specificity remains [...] both legitimate and necessary' (Willeman, cited in Hjort and Petrie 2007: 12). Adhering to this line of argument, the films consistently deal with absent paternalism and the suffering of patriarchal structures, leading to a renewed emphasis and focus on women characters with agency (Sandra in *Deux jours, une nuit* and Eve in *Cages*) as well as ailing and struggling male leads (*Ultranova*, *Eldorado* and *La raison du plus faible*) and fragmented nuclear families (*Le gamin au vélo*, *Folie privé*, *Nue propriété*, *Élève Libre* and *Ultranova*). This facilitates the potential contiguity and inclusion within a wider French cinema, and complements a transnational approach that places these films within a wider European 'art cinema' (Bordwell 1979). That is to posit that the films 'could be set anywhere', the potential 'impersonation' (Elsaesser 2013) in a post-national context with France, and become readable to local audiences (as Mosley argues in the case of the Dardenne brothers' films post-*La promesse* (Mosley 2013: 92)).

Whilst thematically the selected films for this book are concomitant with the primary representations and articulations of a particularist francophone Belgian cinema, they dovetail in their avoidance of a local and regional 'flagging' (to draw on Billig's (1995) notion of 'banal nationalism') that epitomises and espouses a 'banal aboutness' (Hjort 2000: 107–10). The 'monocultural' (Hjort 2000) references to forms of Walloon nationalism have infrequently unrolled in the critically unsuccessful films which have been briefly discussed in this book, such as *Je pense à vous*/*You're On My Mind* (Jean-Pierre and Luc Dardenne, 1992) and *Des plumes dans ma tête*/*Feathers in My Head* (Thomas de Thier, 2003). Both of these films include carnival scenes which locate and anchor the representations culturally, economically and locally in Wallonia. The performance of these films led the filmmakers down different pathways: the Dardenne brothers towards their focus on a character-driven and character-focused plot (Park 2012; Mai 2010; Mosley 2013); and Thomas de Thier towards limiting his filmmaking output. There has also been no diachronic change regarding *Je pense à vous*, since the film was overlooked as part of the canon in the 'Fifty years of Belgian cinema' event. It is salient to note that *Je pense à vous* and *Des plumes dans ma tête* were valorised in the regionalist and local publication, *La revue toudi*. As a result, the 'post-Dardenne' generation includes subtle nuances and implicit references to particularism, decipherable through further research. This is with the exception of two sequences that reverberate through *Eldorado* and *La raison du plus faible* in which, whilst sat around a table, the group of characters burst into national anthems. These sequences signal a 'banal aboutness' (Hjort 2000: 107–10) in francophone Belgian cinema that places the films in Wallonia.

The three selected films from Joachim Lafosse's corpus of films, forming the informal 'private' trilogy, evidence an engagement with questions of regional identity and nation, through the fragmented family unit (Chapter Three). The films *Folie privé* and *Nue propriété*, therefore, present a rather bleak and harsh image of Belgium's linguistic communities, the Belgian family, that is fragmented at its core and doomed to failure. The countryside and Belgium's rural landscape offer particularism and a return to the local, resonating with key reference points such as the films of Maurice Pialat (as one example), to present an uncertain future for individuals residing outside the region's major cities. The absence of a future is articulated by the death or the systematic abuse of children, which at once articulate the socio-economic realities of Wallonia in which prospects in the regional economy are fleeting, and a distinct mistrust in figures of authority and in positions of power. The analysis of Masset-Depasse's *Cages* radically contrasts with the particularism and the localism of Lafosse's 'private' corpus, by extemporising 'marked' transnationality (Hjort 2009). Instead, *Cages* draws from a wide cinematic framework, particularly using techniques and motifs developed within the context of the melodrama (as a genre) to represent and articulate the inner psychological trauma experienced by Eve. The coastline is used as a nodal point for the gradual breakdown and fragmentation of a marriage.

The final two chapters of this book on Bouli Lanners and Lucas Belvaux begin to point to a changing vision of francophone Belgian cinema as its policy-makers and decision-makers step towards genre-based filmmaking. As the Minister of Culture for the Fédération Wallonie-Bruxelles, Joëlle Milquet, implies that the previous modes of filmmaking (hinting towards the industrial/post-industrial context) present 'this clichéd image' that is perceived as 'social and boring' (Hainaut 2015: 24). It stresses the fleeting nature of 'topical' 'themes of nation' (Hjort 2000: 105–7) that has subsequently led to an increasing focus – at a level of film policy and selection – to address 'perennial' themes (ibid.) in their place. The 'topical' theme lies at the heart of Roekens and Tixhon's (2011) edited collection about a Wallonia in a state of 'economic' and social 'crisis'. Lanners' films, their articulation of spatial dynamics, and composition of the frames evidence this, since they are concomitant with the contemporaneous *Les convoyeurs attendent* (Gabriel 2011). Fevry (2011) further aligns the representation of regional crisis through the depiction of the male body – 'a body in crisis'. Sojcher's (1999) seminal work on Belgian cinema historicises the 'topical' theme as emergent in the 1960s and 1970s. Jeanne Brunfaut, the current head of the CCA, further contends that '[w]e need stronger themes, so that's something we are very vigilant about, in terms of selection' (Wise 2016). This turn has, therefore, become more formalised over time, slowly since 2001 and the creation of Wallimage, moving from an 'artisanal' (Mosley 2001) and auteur-driven cinema to start with, developing to greater institutional support for film school graduates (particularly from the Centre du Cinéma et de l'Audiovisuel), through to genre-based films. The structure of this book represents this gradual and logical development. However, it is still salient to note that the films selected for this book are couched in particularism and the articulation of the local. The reverberations of film poetics or 'impersonations' – to adopt Elsaesser's (2013) terms – lie in stylistic and thematic filiation.

What is most telling for the films analysed in this book is how they operate seamlessly in global and local contexts. As Hjort and Petrie note, films created in a small national cinema context 'are orientated towards a global as well as local audience, whether that of the ubiquitous multiplex, the cosmopolitan art house or the specialised festival' (Hjort and Petrie 2007: 18). This approach to distribution and exhibition resonates with the question of 'visibility' and 'participation', which are key themes of Hjort and Petrie's study of small national cinemas (2007: 7). In the context of international film festivals, francophone Belgian cinema has not disappointed, receiving recognition, selection and awards, particularly in the case of the Dardenne brothers in France (as noted in Chapter Two). This is also the case for younger, novice and emerging filmmakers and their short films, since the festival in the Swiss city of Locarno has proven to be an effective barometer for talent, as evidenced by Joachim Lafosse (Chapter Three) and Olivier Masset-Depasse (Chapter Four). Film festival events dedicated to Belgian cinema, with a particular emphasis on a francophone inflection, in international contexts, such as in the Netherlands (Utrecht, 2016), France (Angoulême, 2015), Peru (Lima, 2016) and Switzerland (Cinémathèque Suisse in Lausanne, 2012). In March–June 2018, the online film festival platform *Festival Scope* launched a free global celebration and festival dedicated to 'French-speaking Belgian cinema'. This, of course, complements regular series of events that occur in the WBI (Wallonie-Bruxelles International) base in Paris. Internally, strategies have been adopted to increase 'visibility', since 'the CCA devised a promotional strategy [. . .] that includes both high-end tastemaker screenings and advance previews in remote areas, to create strong word of mouth' (Wise 2016). Moreover, since March 2017, twelve local TV channels in Wallonia have increased the number of films produced in Wallonia broadcast to their audiences, including an introduction by Philippe Reynaert (Wallimage.be 2017). The level of 'participation' has also led to a significant development in the opportunities available to emerging novice filmmakers since the late 1990s in short filmmaking (Steele 2018b) that has filtered through into feature-length films studied in this book.

The dissemination of Belgian culture, and more precisely Belgian film culture, has increased and developed in international contexts, increasing ciné-literacy and understanding of Belgian visual culture beyond the case of the *Tintin* comic books and, to a lesser extent, *Les Schtroumpfs/The Smurfs* (an aspect that has been canonised by tourist shops, graffiti artwork and statues placed around the city of Brussels). For instance, the website and programme *becultural.co.uk* is inclusive of sections dedicated to raising awareness and visibility of Belgian cinema produced in a francophone context and Belgian filmmakers. At the time of writing, the agenda reaffirms the continued importance and salience of the filmmakers addressed in this book, screening films by the Dardenne brothers, Joachim Lafosse, Lucas Belvaux and starring Bouli Lanners. This is in addition to the latest releases of Fiona Gordon, Dominique Abel and Bruno Romy and the film *Innen Leben/Insyriated* (Philippe Van Leeuw, 2017) – the Magritte 'best film' winner of 2018. The visibility and distribution of (francophone) Belgian film and visual culture potentially reaches out to Belgian diasporas living across Europe, in both French-speaking and English-speaking contexts.

In essence, this book proposes a way of better understanding the regional-national-transnational dynamic of contemporary (francophone) Belgian cinema, as well as nuancing broader issues and debates in Film Studies concerning questions of the national/transnational, 'cinema at the periphery' (Iordanova, Martin-Jones and Vidal 2010) and 'cinemas of small nations' (Hjort and Petrie 2007). Through the structure of this study, the analysis contends that the parameters of the national and national cinema are not entirely sufficient to discuss and engage with industrial practices and cultural representations offered within (francophone) Belgian cinema. The combined analysis, opening with the industrial reading, highlights that issues of production are closely entwined with issues of cultural and cinematic representation in a given (trans-)national cinema.

Note

1. As Jaumain and Vandenbulcke include in their exhibition tables of the Belgian domestic market, 1968 was the last year when French films dominated the Belgian exhibition sector (51.3%) (Jaumain and Vandenbulcke 1986: 65).

WORKS CITED

50cinquante.be (2017), <https://www.50cinquante.be> (last accessed 20 December 2017).
Adam, Ilke and Deschouwer, Kris (2016), 'Nationalist parties and immigration in Flanders: from Volksunie to Spirit and N-VA', *Journal of Ethnic and Migration Studies*, 42:8, pp. 1290–1303.
Alion, Yves (2002), '*Un couple épatant, Après la vie, Cavale*: Rencontre avec Lucas Belvaux', *L'Avant-Scène Cinéma* 518, pp. 95–9.
Alion, Yves (2006), 'À propos de *La Raison du plus faible*: Entretien avec Lucas Belvaux', *L'Avant-Scène Cinéma* 553–4, pp. 151–5.
Alion, Yves, Laurie Deson, René Marx and S. A. (2014), 'Génération 2000: Cinquante cinéastes français du XXIème siècle', *L'Avant-Scène Cinéma* 613, May, pp. 45–53.
Altes, Liesbeth Korthals (2008), 'Traces: Writing the Visual in "Daewoo" by François Bon', *Yale French Studies* 144, pp. 80–94.
Altman, Rick (1984), 'A Semantic/Syntactic Approach to Film Genre', in Leo Braudy and Marshall Cohen (eds.), *Film Theory & Criticism*, seventh edition, Oxford: Oxford University Press, pp. 552–63.
Anderson, Benedict (1991), *Imagined Communities: Reflections on the Origins and the Spread of Nationalism*, London and New York: Verso.
André, François (1999), 'Rosetta de Jean-Pierre et Luc Dardenne: un film de résistance', *La revue toudi* 23, November–December, <http://www.larevuetoudi.org/fr/story/rosetta-de-jean-pierre-et-luc-dardenne-un-film-de-r%C3%A9sistance> (last accessed 29 January 2018).
André, François (2002), 'Cinéma wallon et réalité particulière', *La revue toudi*, September–October, <http://www.larevuetoudi.org/fr/story/cinéma-wallon-et-réalité-particulière> (last accessed 19 August 2012).
André, François (2003), 'L'étrange "vengeance" du dernier film des Dardenne', *La*

revue toudi 52–3, February–March, <http://www.larevuetoudi.org/en/node/449> (last accessed 7 February 2018).

André, François (2004), 'De Thier: un cinéma quasi "biologique"', *La revue toudi* 65, September–October, <http://larevuetoudi.org/de/node/734> (last accessed 8 June 2016).

André, François (2006), 'L'enfant', *La revue toudi*, January–February–March, <http://www.larevuetoudi.org/en/node/237> (last accessed 22 January 2018).

André, François (2009a), 'Non, Wallonie ta culture n'est pas morte', *La revue toudi*, 19 February, <http://www.larevuetoudi.org/fr/story/non-wallonie-ta-culture-n'est-pas-morte> (last accessed 22 August 2016).

André, François (2009b), 'Le silence de Lorna, un chapitre s'est achevé', *La revue toudi*, 4 March, <http://www.larevuetoudi.org/fr/story/le-silence-de-lorna-un-chapitres%E2%80%99est-achev%C3%A9> (last accessed 13 February 2018).

André, François (2010), 'Conversation en Wallonie (Jean Louvet)', *La revue toudi*, 29 January, <http://www.larevuetoudi.org/fr/story/conversation-en-wallonie-jean-louvet> (last accessed 22 December 2017).

André, François (2011), '"Le gamin au vélo" ou le choix de la famille élective des frères Dardenne', *La revue toudi*, 23 September, <http://www.larevuetoudi.org/fr/story/le-gamin-au-vélo-ou-le-choix-de-la-famille-élective-des-frères-dardenne> (last accessed 24 October 2015).

Andrew, Dudley (2010), *What Cinema is! Bazin's Quest and its Charge*, Oxford: Wiley-Blackwell.

Andrew, Geoff (2006), 'Luc and Jean-Pierre Dardenne', *The Guardian,* 11 February, <http://www.theguardian.com/film/2006/feb/11/features> (last accessed 21 December 2013).

Archer, Neil (2013), *The French Road Movie: Space, Mobility, Identity*, New York: Berghahn Books.

Atkinson, Michael (2008), 'Mr. Vengeance', *Museum of the Moving Image*, 22 September, <http://www.movingimagesource.us/articles/mr-vengeance-20080922> (last accessed 30 July 2018).

Aubenas, Jacqueline ([1981] 2015), '*Une caméra pudique*', *La Revue Nouvelle*, reprint, Paris: Shellac.

Augé, Marc (1995), *Non-Places: Introduction to an Anthropology of Supermodernity*, London: Verso.

Austin, Guy (2008), *Contemporary French Cinema: An Introduction*, Manchester: Manchester University Press.

Bajomée, Danielle (2010), 'Fragments d'une époque: Le mai 68 liégeois', in Nancy Delhalle, Jacques Dubois and Jean-Marie Klinkenberg (eds), *Le tournant des années 1970: Liège en effervescence*, Brussels: Les Impressions Nouvelles, pp. 13–20.

Barnes, Henry (2016), 'Ma Loute director Bruno Dumont: "You can't make a 'European Film'"', *The Guardian*, <https://www.theguardian.com/film/2016/may/13/bruno-dumont-european-film-ma-loute> (last accessed 11 August 2017).

Bauche, Nicolas (2011), 'Le Gamin au Vélo: La coiffeuse et l'enfant', *Positif* 604, June, pp. 7–8.

Bayer, Katia (2008), 'Cages d'Olivier Masset-Depasse', *Cinergie*, 1 January, <http://www.cinergie.be/webzine/cages_d_olivier_masset_depasse_2008_01_01> (last accessed 15 August 2017).

Bayer, Katia and Dimitra Bouras (2007), 'Rencontre avec Joachim Lafosse à propos de "Nue Propriété"', *Le Moniteur du film en Belgique* 258, January, pp. 15–17.

Bayer, Katia and Jean-Marc Vlaeminckx (2007), 'Entretien avec Joachim Lafosse à propos d'Elève libre', *Le Moniteur du Film en Belgique* 267, November, pp. 20–2.

Bazin, André (1971), *What is Cinema? Volume II*, trans. Hugh Gray, Berkeley, Los Angeles and London: University of California Press.

Beaud, Stéphane (1999), 'The Temp's Dream', in Pierre Bourdieu (ed.), *Weight of the World: Social Suffering in Contemporary Society*, trans. Priscilla Parkhurst, Cambridge: Polity Press, pp. 282–96.

Bégaudeau, François (2007), 'Nue propriété', *Cahiers du Cinéma* 620, February, pp. 61–2.

Bell, Anne-Laure (2012), 'Lucas Belvaux: réalisateur', *Le film français* 3467, 2 March, p. 19.

Belmans, Jacques (1974), *Cinéma de Wallonie*, Namur: Centre d'action culturelle de la Communauté d'expression française (CACEF).

Bellour, Raymond (1990), 'The film stilled', *Camera Obscura* 8 (3:24), pp. 98–124. DOI: 10.1215/02705346-8-3_24-98.

Bénézet, Delphine (2005), 'Contrasting visions in le jeune cinéma: poetics, politics and the rural', *Studies in French Cinema* 5:3, pp. 163–74.

Benghozi, Pierre-Jean and Claire Nénert (1995) 'Création de valeur artistique ou économique: du Festival International du film de Cannes au marché du film', *Recherche et Applications en Marketing*, 10:4, pp. 65–76.

Benoliel, Bernard and Serge Toubiana (1999), 'Il faut être dans le cul des choses: Entretien avec Luc et Jean-Pierre Dardenne', *Cahiers du Cinéma* 539, October, pp. 47–53.

Benoliel, Bernard and Serge Toubiana (2014), 'Les frères Dardenne par eux-mêmes: Une leçon de cinéma', 28 May, <http://www.cinematheque.fr/video/433.html> (last accessed 4 November 2014).

Bergfelder, Tim (2005), 'National, transnational or supranational cinema? Rethinking European film studies', *Media, Culture & Society*, 27:3, pp. 315–30.

Beugnet, Martine (2004), 'French Cinema of the Margins', in Elizabeth Ezra (ed.), *European Cinema*, Oxford: Oxford University Press, pp. 283–98.

Billig, Michael (1995), *Banal Nationalism*, London: Sage Publications.

Binh, N. T., François Margolin and Frédéric Sojcher (2010), 'Lucas Belvaux et Patrick Sobelman', *Cinéaste et Producteur: un duo infernal?*, Paris: Klincksieck, pp. 109–36.

Biourge, C. (2014), 'Le Belge francophone boude-t-il son cinéma?', *RTBF.be*, 17 January, <http://www.rtbf.be/info/medias/detail_le-belge-francophone-boude-t-il-son-cinema?id=8178379> (last accessed 12 May 2014).

Blanchart, Jean-Louis, Sophie De Vinck and Heritiana Ranaivoson (2015), 'La diversité culturelle dans la production cinématographique belge francophone entre 1995 et 2011', Observatoire des politiques culturelles de la Fédération Wallonie-Bruxelles, *Repères* 7, June, <http://www.laconcertation-asbl.org/IMG/pdf/opc_repe_res_n7.pdf> (last accessed July 2018).

Blümlinger, Christa (2011), 'The figure of visual standstill in R. W. Fassbinder's films', in Eivind Røssaak (ed.), *Between Stillness and Motion: Film, Photography Algorithms*, Amsterdam: Amsterdam University Press, pp. 75–84.

Boie, Gideon (2016), 'Ecopolitique à Bruxelles: Bas Smets et la biennale du paysage urban de Bruxelles', 10 October, <http://a-plus.be/fr/recensie/eco-politiek-in-brussel-bas-smets-en-de-brussels-urban-landscape-biennal-2/#.WzohvdJKicw> (last accessed 11 April 2017).

Bon, François (2004), *Daewoo*. Paris: Librarie Arthème Fayard.

Bonnaud, Frédéric (2012), 'The Kid with a Bike', *Film Comment*, March–April, 48:2, pp. 22–5.

Bonnaud, Frédéric (2014), 'Après la catastrophe', *La Cinémathèque Française Programme Juin–Juillet '14*, pp. 26–31.

Borde, Dominique (2008), 'Eldorado', *Le Figaroscope*, 18 June.

Bordwell, David (1979), 'Art Cinema as a Mode of Film Practice', *Film Criticism* 4:1, pp. 56–64.
Bordwell, David (1985), 'Widescreen Aesthetics and Mise en Scene Criticism', *The Velvet Light Trap* 21, Summer, pp. 18–25, <http://davidbordwell.net/articles/Bordwell_Velvet%20Light%20Trap_no21_summer1985_118.pdf> (last accessed July 2018).
Bordwell, David and Kristin Thompson (2006), 'Lessons from Babel', *Observations on Film Art*, 27 November <http://www.davidbordwell.net/blog/2006/11/27/lessons-from-babel/> (last accessed 1 October 2016).
Bordwell, David, Janet Staiger and Kristin Thompson (1988), *The Classical Hollywood Cinema: Film Style and Mode of Production to 1960*, London: Routledge.
Bouras, Dimitra (2011), 'Les frères Dardenne: *Le Gamin au vélo* par Les frères Dardenne et Cécile de France', *Cinergie*, 17 May, <http://www.cinergie.be/webzine/les_freres_dardenne_le_gamin_au_velo> (last accessed 22nd October 2015).
Bourdieu, Pierre ([1989] 2010). *Distinction: A Social Critique of the Judgement of Taste*, trans. Richard Nice, London: Routledge.
Bourdieu, Pierre (1999a), 'Site Effects', in Pierre Bourdieu (ed.), *Weight of the World: Social Suffering in Contemporary Society*, trans. Priscilla Parkhurst, Cambridge: Polity Press, pp. 123–9.
Bourdieu, Pierre (1999b), *Weight of the World: Social Suffering in Contemporary Society*, trans. Priscilla Parkhurst, Cambridge: Polity Press.
Bourdon, Christophe (2017), '*Tueurs*: un impressionnant polar . . . et peut-être même plus', *RTBF.be*, <https://www.rtbf.be/culture/dossier/christophe-bourdon/detail_tueurs-un-impressionnant-polar-et-peut-etre-meme-plus?id=9779954> (last accessed 12 January 2018).
Boyle, John (2005), 'Ultranova, UGC De Brouckère', *The Bulletin*, 28 April 2005.
Bradfer, Fabienne (2005a), 'Bouli Lanners, la naissance d'un auteur', *Le Soir*, 10 February.
Bradfer, Fabienne (2005b), 'Bouli Lanners s'est réveillé, et son premier long nous réveille', *Le Soir*, 27 April, p. 4.
Bradfer, Fabienne (2006a), 'Lucas Belvaux a raison', *Le Soir*, 26 May, p. 33.
Bradfer, Fabienne (2006b), 'Lucas Belvaux, cinéaste de contrebande', *Le Soir*, 13 September, pp. 1–3.
Bradfer, Fabienne (2006c), '"Cages" a captivé les jeunes et le public', *Le Soir*, 7 October, p. 46.
Bradfer, Fabienne (2007), 'Cages', review, *Le Soir*, 9 May.
Bradfer, Fabienne (2009), 'Joachim Lafosse et nos éloignements possibles', *Le Soir*, 13 October.
Bradfer, Fabienne (2014), 'Sans les autres, on n'est rien', *Le Soir*, 21 May, p. 3.
Bradfer, Fabienne, William Bourton, Nicolas Crousse and Philippe Manche (2009), 'Il n'y a pas de liberté sans limites', *Le Soir*, 31 January.
Bradshaw, Peter (2012), 'The Kid with a Bike – review', *The Guardian*, 22 March, <http://www.theguardian.com/film/2012/mar/22/the-kid-with-a-bike-review> (last accessed 24 October 2015).
Bredael, Jacques and Philippe Reynaert (2016), *Par ailleurs, le cinéma est une industrie*, Marcinelle: Les Editions du CEP.
Brooks, Xan (2006), 'We're the same: one person, four eyes', *The Guardian*, 9 February, <http://www.theguardian.com/film/2006/feb/09/features.xanbrooks> (last accessed 14 June 2010).
Broquet, Julien (2005), 'Deuil pour deuil', *Le Soir*, 19 December.
Buache, Freddy (2005), *Vingt-cinq ans de cinéma français, parcours croisés 1979–2003*, Lausanne: Éditions l'Âge d'Homme.

Buache, Freddy (2010), *Sous tout de paupières: Bergman avant la mondialisation des écrans*, Lausanne: Éditions L'Âge d'Homme.
Bullot, Fabienne (2014), 'L'usine vide comme imaginaire cinématographique', *Contemporary French and Francophone Studies*, 18:3, pp. 314–22.
Caillé, Patrice (2013), 'Cinemas of the Maghreb: Reflections on the transnational and polycentric dimensions of regional cinema', *Studies in French Cinema* 13:3, pp. 241–56.
Campany, David (2008), *Cinema and Photography*, London: Reaktion Books.
Carré, Patrick (2012), 'Un nouvel opérateur pour le tax shelter', *Le film français* 3511, 28 December, p. 10.
CCA (2013), 'Le bulletin du cinéma: L'année 2013 en bref', *Centre du cinéma et de l'audiovisuel*, <http://www.audiovisuel.cfwb.be/index.php?id=5735> (last accessed 21 June 2015).
CCA (2014), 'Le Bilan: production, promotion et diffusion cinématographiques et audiovisuelles', <http://www.audiovisuel.cfwb.be/index.php?eID=tx_nawsecuredl&u=0&g=0&hash=d86aca3f96bb97915864f9da2649c8ec7b0f5479&file=fileadmin/sites/avm/upload/avm_super_editor/avm_editor/Publications/Telechargement_pdf/Bilan_CCA/bilan_14/Bilan_2014_CCA_version_DEF_5_mars_2015.pdf> (last accessed July 2018).
Centre d'études wallonnes et de République (2013), 'Chapitre XI: Un cinéma wallon populaire en Wallonie? (suite de l'interview de Luc Dardenne)', *Le revue toudi*, 22 December, <http://www.larevuetoudi.org/fr/story/chapitre-xi-un-cinéma-wallon-populaire-en-wallonie-suite-de-linterview-de-luc-dardenne> (last accessed 22 October 2015).
Cinéma Belge (2014), 'CCA: Décloisonner et rapprocher' 15, May, p. 1.
Cinéma et cetera (2016), '2 films de Joachim Lafosse', *Radio Campus Brussels 92.1*, 10 May, <https://www.mixcloud.com/radiocampusbruxelles/cinéma-et-cetera-2-films-de-joachim-lafosse-10-mai-2016/> (last accessed 28 July 2016).
Cinémathèque Royale (2017), '40 ans de Cinéma en Atelier', 25 March–23 May <https://www.evernote.com/shard/s294/sh/87c9c87e-afbd-4425-bc7e-e5ef2cb497a8/92db05ce1b73d0850cb04bae06f79586> (last accessed July 2018).
Cinémathèque Suisse (2012a), 'Le nouveau cinéma belge francophone', *En janvier et février à la Cinémathèque Suisse* 265, pp. 19–26, <http://www.cinematheque.ch/fileadmin/user_upload/Projections/bulletin/bulletins/bulletin_265.pdf> (last accessed July 2018).
Cinémathèque Suisse (2012b), 'Discussion Avec Bouli Lanners – 19.01.2012', *Videokhoj*, <https://videokhoj.co/video/acskuaAaLxoM8c8/discussion-avec-bouli-lanners-19-01-2012> (last accessed 10 January 2018).
Cinergie.be (2008), 'Tommaso Fiorilli, chef opérateur et cadreur de Cages d'Olivier Masset-Depasse', video interview, *Cinergie.be*, February, <https://www.cinergie.be/actualites/tommaso-fiorilli-chef-operateur-et-cadreur-de-cages-d-olivier-masset-depasse> (last accessed 27 September 2017).
Chang, Justin (2008) 'Private Lessons', *Variety*, 9–15 June, p. 32.
Christie, Ian (2013), 'Where is National Cinema Today (and Do We Still Need It)?', *Film History* 25:1–2, pp. 19–30.
Cinéma Belge (2002), 'Productions de la Communauté française de Belgique Wallonie-Bruxelles', 103, May.
CNC (2016), 'The Tax Rebate for International Productions (TRIP)', <http://www.cnc.fr/web/en/tax-rebate> (last accessed 6 February 2016).
Cohen, Nick (2014), 'Two Days, One Night: a film that illuminates the despair of the low paid', *The Observer*, 30 August, <http://www.theguardian.com/commentisfree/2014/aug/30/minimum-wage-poverty-low-pay-reform> (last accessed 14 April 2015).

WORKS CITED

Colin, Jérôme and Bouli Lanners (2005), 'Bouli Lanners, un regard nostalgique', *Sonuma.be*, 19 April 2005.
Colin, Jérôme (2016) 'Joachim Lafosse dans le taxi de Jérôme Colin: L'interview intégrale', *RTBF.be*, <http://ds.static.rtbf.be/article/pdf/lafosse-1452692634.pdf> (accessed 1 August 2016).
Collard, Christophe (2014), '*Bye-Bye Belgium*: remediating Flemish nationalism in prime time', *Rethinking History*, 18:4, pp. 543–55.
Collins, Richard (1990), *The Case of Canadian Television*, Toronto: University of Toronto Press.
Cowie, Phil and Pascale Edelman (2007), 'An Opportunity to Resist: An Interview with Jean-Pierre and Luc Dardenne', in Phil Cowie and Pascale Edelmann (eds), *Projections 15*, London: Faber and Faber, pp. 218–24.
Crofts, Stephen (1998), 'Concepts of National Cinema', in Pamela Church-Gibson and John Hill (eds), *The Oxford Guide to Film Studies*, Oxford: Oxford University Press, pp. 385–94.
Crousse, Nicolas (2007), 'Dis, Bouli, wallons-nous?', *Le Soir*, 24 July.
Crousse, Nicolas (2008), 'Eldorado, le pays où l'on n'arrive jamais', *Le Soir*, 4 June, p. 4.
Crousse, Nicolas (2009), 'L' "Élève libre" est-il une victim consentente?', *Le Soir*, 21 January, pp. 4–5.
Cucco, Marco (2010), 'The borders of the domestic market and their importance for the economy of the film industry: The Swiss case study', *European Journal of Communication* 25:2, pp. 153–67.
Czach, Liz (2004), 'Film festivals, programming, and the building of a national cinema', *The Moving Image* 4:1, Spring, pp. 76–88. DOI: 10.1353/mov.2004.0004.
Damiens, Manuella (2007), 'Cinéma: *Cages* extremement romantique', *Elle Belgique*, May.
Danvers, Louis (2010), 'Entretien avec Olivier Masset-Depasse: Cinéaste révolté', *Le Vif/L'Express*, 31 December.
Danvers, Louis (2013a), 'Ultranova', *Le Vif/L'Express – Focus Vif*, 29 November.
Danvers, Louis (2013b), 'Profession Visionnaire/Close Up Cinéma Michelangelo Antonioni', *Focus Vif*, 14 June, pp. 12–15.
Dardenne, Luc (2008), *Au dos de nos images*, Paris: Editions du Seuil.
Dardenne, Luc (2015), *Au dos de nos images II 2005–2014*, Paris: Editions du Seuil.
Dardenne, Luc and Jean-Pierre Dardenne (2011), 'Featurette: Return to Seraing with Jean-Pierre and Luc Dardenne', *Le gamin au vélo* (DVD), London: Artificial Eye.
Dardenne, Luc and José Fontaine (2013), 'Chapitre X: Peut-on penser l'inconsolable sans consolation ? (Interview de Luc Dardenne) Conversation avec Luc Dardenne à propos de son livre "Sur l'affaire humaine"', *La revue toudi*, 2 December, <http://www.larevuetoudi.org/fr/story/chapitre-x-peut-penser-linconsolable-sans-consolation-interview-de-luc-dardenne> (last accessed 22 October 2015).
Darras, Matthieu (2007), '*Nue propriété*: La faute à personne', *Positif* 552, February, pp. 34–5.
Davay, Paul (1967), 'Belgium', in Alan Lovell (ed.), *Art of the Cinema in Ten European Countries*, Strasbourg: Council for Cultural Co-Operation.
Dawson, Thomas (2013), 'Fear eats the soul', *Sight and Sound*, June, pp. 58–60.
De Baecque, Antoine and Serge Toubiana (1999), *Truffaut: A Biography*, trans. Catherine Temerson, New York: Knopf.
De Bellefroid, Éric (2001), 'Trente ans d'Écran Témoin', *La Libre Belgique*, 2 September, <http://www.lalibre.be/culture/medias-tele/trente-ans-d-ecran-temoin-51b87475e4b0de6db9a62a02> (accessed 25 July 2016).
De Heusch, Luc (2002), 'Ceci n'est pas la Belgique', trans. Barbara Harshav, *Yale French Studies: Belgian Memories* 102, pp. 11–23.

Debruge, Peter (2011), '*Le gamin au vélo/The kid with a bike*', *Variety* 423:2, p. 19.
Deleuze, Gilles (1992), *Cinema 1: The Movement-Image*, trans. Hugh Tomlinson and Barbara Habberjam, London: Athlone.
Deleuze, Gilles ([1989] 2013), *Cinema II: The Time-Image*, trans. Hugh Tomlinson and Robert Galeta, New York and London: Bloomsbury Academic.
Delvaux, Béatrice and Mouton, Olivier (2012), 'Joachim Lafosse: "Un fils ne peut pas être père de son père"', *Le Soir*, 11 August, <http://plus.lesoir.be/49128/article/2016-07-06/joachim-lafosse-un-fils-ne-peut-pas-etre-le-pere-de-son-pere#49126> (last accessed August 2018).
Denis, Fernand (2006), 'Les raisons de Lucas Belvaux', *La Libre Belgique*, 13 September, p. 4.
Denis, Fernand (2008), 'Sur la route, un break', *La Libre Belgique*, 4 June, p. 4.
Denis, Fernand (2014a), 'Lucas Belvaux, un cinéaste géographique', *La Libre Culture*, 7 May, p. 5
Denis, Fernand (2014b), 'On achève bien les panneaux solaires', *La Libre Culture*, 21 May, pp. 4–5.
Denis, Fernand (2018), 'Les Magritte, un concept qui montre un peu ses limites', *La Libre Belgique*, 3 February, <http://www.lalibre.be/culture/cinema/les-magritte-un-concept-qui-montre-un-peu-ses-limites-5a74b26fcd70f924c7cdd325> (last accessed 3 February 2018).
De Poorter, Wim (1997), 'From *Y Mañana?* To *Manneken Pis*: Thirty Years of Flemish Filmmaking', trans. Julian Ross, in *The Low Countries: Arts and Society in Flanders and the Netherlands 5*, pp. 130–41. <https://www.dbnl.org/tekst/_low001199701_01/_low001199701_01_0017.php> (last accessed July 2018).
Dervaux, Benoît (2006), 'Making of', *La raison du plus faible* (DVD), Brussels: Cinéart.
Deschouwer, Kris and Reuchamps, Min (2013), 'The Belgian Federation at a Crossroad', *Regional and Federal Studies*, 23:3, pp. 261–70.
D. F. (2008), 'Eldorado', *Le canard enchaîné*, 18 June.
Dillet, Benoît and Puri, Tara (2013), 'Left-over spaces: The Cinema of the Dardenne brothers', *Film Philosophy*, 17:1, pp. 367–882. <ISSN 1466–4615>.
Dirkx, Paul (2011), 'Antinomy and Forms of Literary Migration: The Case of the Belgian Francophone Diaspora', *Australian Journal of French Studies*, 48:1, pp. 60–73.
Domenach, Élise (2009), 'Entretien avec Joachim Lafosse: Du creux s'est immiscé dans mon cinéma', *Positif* 577, March, pp. 98–101.
Douin, Jean-Luc (2007), 'La caméra se chatouille le nombril: Entrien Luc Moullet et Joachim Lafosse, cinéastes', *Le Monde*, 20 June, p. 28.
Douin, Jean-Luc (2008a), 'Cages' (review), *Le Monde*, 26 November.
Douin, Jean-Luc (2008b), '"Cages": les handicaps d'un couple aphone', *Le Monde*, 25 November, <http://www.lemonde.fr/cinema/article/2008/11/25/cages-les-handicaps-d-un-couple-aphone_1122634_3476.html> (last accessed 23 April 2016).
Douin, Jean-Luc (2011), '"Le gamin au vélo": la course effrénée à vélo d'un enfant insoumis', *Le Monde*, 14 April, <http://www.lemonde.fr/festival-de-cannes/article/2011/04/14/le-gamin-au-velo-de-jean-pierre-et-luc-dardenne_1507912_766360.html> (last accessed 22 October 2015).
Dubois, Jacques (2002), 'Wallonia: The Will to Remember', trans. Barbara Harshav, *Yale French Studies: Belgian Memories* 102, pp. 53–67.
Duculot, Pierre (1997), 'Lucas Belvaux: Les chemins de l'exil', *Cinéma Belge* 96/97, pp. 32–3.
Duculot, Pierre (1998), 'Tentative (téméraire) d'esquisse d'une cinématographie wallonne', *Le Matin*, September, pp. 4–5.
Duculot, Pierre (2005), 'Cages by Olivier Masset-Depasse: Two people close to suffocation', *Belgian Cinema* 106, May, p. 23.

Duculot, Pierre (2006), 'La raison du plus faible de Lucas Belvaux', *Cinéma Belge* 107, May, p. 9.
Duculot, Pierre (2007), 'Cages by Olivier Masset-Depasse: A Silent Cry', *Belgian Cinema* 108, May, p. 10.
Duplat, Guy and Jean-François Pluijgers (2001), 'Ma vie en rose (et noir)', *La Libre Belgique*, 12 January, <https://web.archive.org/web/20020323171416/http://www.lalibre.be/article.phtml?id=5&subid=105&art_id=5018&folder_id=25> (last accessed 1 February 2016).
Duplat, Guy (2001), 'Le projet cinéma de Speedy Miller', *La Libre Belgique*, 12 January, <https://web.archive.org/web/20020323171847/http://www.lalibre.be:80/article.phtml?art_id=5040&folder_id=25&id=5&subid=105> (last accessed 1 February 2016).
Dupont, Joan (2002), 'Belgian brothers' working class heroes', *New York Times*, 29 October, <http://www.nytimes.com/2002/10/29/style/29iht-dard_ed3_.html> (last accessed 14 July 2010).
Dyer, Richard (2015), *Lethal Repetition: Serial Killing in European Cinema*, London: Palgrave.
Economist, The (2014), 'Two days, one night, no fuss', 23 August.
Edmond, John (2011), 'Moving landscapes: film, vehicles and the travelling shot', *Studies in Australasian Cinema* 5:2, pp. 131–43. DOI: 10.1386/sac.5.2.131_1.
Einstein, Frank (2006), 'Au tour de Droixhe', *La Libre Belgique*, 13 September, <http://www.lalibre.be/culture/cinema/au-tour-de-droixhe-51b88ff4e4b0de6db9ae858d> (last accessed 22 September 2016).
E. L. (2008), 'Cages' (review), *L'Express*, 27 November.
Elkington, Trevor and Andrew Nestingen (2005), *Transnational Cinema in a Global North: Nordic Cinema in transition*, Detroit: Wayne State University Press.
Ellis, John (1992), *Visible Fictions: Cinema, Television, Video*, London and New York: Routledge.
Elsaesser, Thomas (2005), *European Cinema: Face to Face with Hollywood*, Amsterdam: Amsterdam University Press.
Elsaesser, Thomas (2013), 'ImpersoNations: National Cinema, Historical Imaginaries and New Cinema Europe', *Mise au Point*, 1 April, <http://journals.openedition.org/map/1480> (last accessed 18 December 2017). DOI: 10.4000/map.1480.
Engelen, Leen and Kris Van Heuckelom (2013), 'Introduction: From the East to the West and Back: Screening Mobility in Post-1989 European Cinema', in Leen Engelen and Kris Van Heuckelom (eds), *European Cinema after the Wall: Screening East–West Mobility*, Lanham: Rowman and Littlefield, pp. vii–xxii.
Engelen, Leen, and Roel Vande Winkel (2010), 'Made in Flanders (Redux): Film Production, Government Funding and Television Participation in Flanders, Belgium', *Film International* 8:6, pp. 50–9.
Eureka (2011), 'Nue propriété – Joachim Lafosse – 2007', 15 February, <http://silencio.unblog.fr/2011/02/15/nue-propriete-joachim-lafosse-20071420/> (last accessed 30 July 2018).
European Audiovisual Observatory (2013), *Yearbook: Television, Cinema, Video and On-demand Audiovisual Services – the Pan-European Picture*, Strasbourg: European Audiovisual Observatory.
European Audiovisual Observatory (2015/2016), *Lumière Database*, December, <http://lumiere.obs.coe.int> (last accessed 12 December 2016).
Euvrard, Michel (2011), 'Le Gamin au Vélo: Cyril et Samantha', *Séquences: la revue du cinéma* 247, pp. 42–3.
Everett, Wendy (2004), 'Leaving Home: Exile and Displacement in Contemporary

European Cinema', in Wendy Everett and Peter Wagstaff (eds), *Cultures of Exile: Images of Displacement*, New York: Berghahn Books, pp. 17–31.

Everett, Wendy (2005), 'Re-framing the fingerprints: a short survey of European film', in Wendy Everett (ed.), *European Identity in Cinema*, 2nd edition, Bristol: Intellect, pp. 15–34.

Everett, Wendy (2009), 'Lost in Transition? The European Road Movie, A genre "adrift in the cosmos"', *Literature/Film Quarterly*, 37 (3), pp. 165–75.

EXE BD 63400 (2017), publicity leaflet in Bill Douglas Cinema Museum. http://www.bdcmuseum.org.uk/explore/item/63400/ (last accessed July 2018).

Ezra, Elizabeth and Terry Rowden (2006), 'What is Transnational Cinema?', in Elizabeth Ezra and Terry Rowden (eds), *Transnational Cinema: The Film Reader*, London: Routledge, pp. 1–12.

F. By (2007), 'Olivier Masset-Depasse: Camera obscura', *Le Vif/L'Express*, 22 June.

Fagnoulle, Christine (2011), 'Critique: "Le gamin au vélo" des Dardenne', *La revue toudi*, 23 May, <http://www.larevuetoudi.org/fr/node/3216> (last accessed 11 February 2018).

Fédération Wallonie-Bruxelles (1967), 'Arrêté royal du 22 juin 1967 tendant à promouvoir la culture cinématographique', <http://www.audiovisuel.cfwb.be/index.php?eID=tx_nawsecuredl&u=0&file=fileadmin/sites/avm/upload/avm_super_editor/avm_editor/reglementation/Cinema/Aides_publiques/CF_ar19670622_coord.pdf&hash=27cd8ac7709d077f4a15dca70f1c42f2c753d8c5> (last accessed 16 May 2011).

Felperin, Leslie (2004), 'Private Madness', *Variety*, 17 August <https://variety.com/2004/film/reviews/private-madness-1200531628/> (last accessed 19 July 2018).

Feuillère, Anne and Jean-Michel Vlaeminckx (2005), 'Cages: Oser la couleur et les extrêmes', *Le Moniteur du Film en Belgique* 246, December, pp. 14–16.

Feuillère Anne and Vlaeminckx, Jean Michel (2006), 'Ca rend heureux, entretien avec Joaquim Lafosse et Samuel Tilman', *Cinergie.be*, 8 September, <https://www.cinergie.be/actualites/a-rend-heureux-entretien-avec-joaquim-lafosse-et-samuel-tilman> (last accessed 30 July 2018).

Fevry, Sébastien (2011), 'Des corps en crise. À propos de *la Raison du plus faible* de Lucas Belvaux', in Anne Roekens and Axel Tixhon (eds), *Cinéma et crise[s] économique[s]: Esquisses d'une cinématographie wallonne*, Namur: Presses universitaires/Éditions Yellow Now, pp. 89–106.

Fluctuanet.net (2011), 'Le gamin au vélo: les Dardenne réalisent le film de trop', <https://web.archive.org/web/20150920090545/http://fluctuat.premiere.fr/Cinema/News-Videos/Le-Gamin-au-velo-les-Dardenne-realisent-le-film-de-trop-3242272> (last accessed July 2018).

Fontaine, José (1981) 'Le premier grand film d'un cinéma wallon', *Le Monde*, 26 March, <http://www.larevuetoudi.org/fr/story/le-premier-grand-film-dun-cinéma-wallon-le-grand-paysage-dalexis-droeven-1981> (last accessed 20 July 2016).

Fontaine, José (1992), '"Je pense à vous": le premier grand film d'amour du cinéma wallon', *La revue toudi*, October, <http://www.larevuetoudi.org/fr/story/je-pense-à-vous-le-premier-grand-film-damour-du-cinéma-wallon> (last accessed 5 November 2015).

Fontaine, José (1996), 'L'argent porno', *La revue toudi*, November, <http://www.larevuetoudi.org/en/node/958> (last accessed 22 January 2018).

Fontaine, José (2000), 'Cinq aspects de la culture wallonne, an 2000', *La revue toudi*, December, <http://www.larevuetoudi.org/fr/story/cinq-aspects-de-la-culture-wallonne-2000> (last accessed 20 September 2017).

Fontaine, José (2007), 'L'exposition de Charleroi de 1911', *La revue toudi* 74, February–March–April, <http://www.larevuetoudi.org/fr/story/lexposition-de-charleroi-de-1911> (last accessed 4 January 2017).

Fowler, Catherine (2006), '*Symphonie paysanne:* An Embodied and Embedded Picturing of the Land', in Catherine Fowler and Gillian Helfield (eds), *Representing the Rural: Space, Place, and Identity in Films about the Land*, Detroit: Wayne State University Press, pp. 135–49.

Frankignoulle, Pierre (2010), 'Urbanism: Une politique de la ville', in Nancy Delhalle, Jacques Dubois and Jean-Marie Klinkenberg, *Le Tournant des années 1970: Liège en effervescence*, Brussels: Les Impressions Nouvelles, pp. 219–31.

Frois, Emmanuèle (2006), 'Lucas Belvaux, un cri', *Le Figaro*, 24 May.

Gabriel, Jean-Benoît (2008), 'Ils cachent plus qu'ils ne montrent: autour du cinéma des frères Dardenne', *French Forum* 33:1–2, Winter/Spring, pp. 227–43.

Gabriel, Jean-Benoît (2011), 'La Wallonie révélée: Esthétique du paysage industriel chez Benoît Mariage and Bouli Lanners', in Anne Roekens and Axel Tixhon (eds), *Cinéma et Crise[s] Économique[s]: Esquisses d'une cinématographique wallonne*, Namur: Press Universitaires de Namur/Yellow Now, pp. 67–88.

Galt, Rosalind (2006), *Redrawing the Map: The New European Cinema*, New York: Columbia University Press.

Galt, Rosalind and Schoonover, Karl (2010), *Global Art Cinema: New Theories and Histories*, New York and Oxford: Oxford University Press.

Garson, Charlotte (2009), 'Élève libre de Joachim Lafosse', *Cahiers du Cinéma* 642, 2 February, pp. 47–8.

Gauditiaubois, André and Paul Yernaux (1999), 'En route vers l'Oscar?', *La revue toudi* 20, June–July, <http://www.larevuetoudi.org/fr/story/en-route-vers-loscar> (last accessed 29 January 2018).

Gellner, Ernest (1983), *Nations and Nationalism*, Ithaca: Cornell University Press.

Gendron, Nicolas (2008), 'Ovni belge à identifier/Eldorado de Bouli Lanners', *Ciné-bulles* 26:4, p. 59.

Gilbey, Ryan (2014), 'For a Few Euros More', *The Guardian*, 8 August, pp. 14–15.

Gillet, Caroline and Elise Barthet (2010), 'La belgitude des choses vue par deux cinéastes', *Le Monde*, 1 August, <http://belgique.blog.lemonde.fr/2010/08/01/la-belgitude-des-choses-vue-par-deux-cineastes/> (last accessed July 2018).

Ghennam, Michel and Roland Hélié (2010), 'En contrebande: Entretien avec Lucas Belvaux', in Nicolas Marcadé (ed.), *Chronique d'une mutation: Conversations sur le cinéma (2000–2010)*, Paris: Éditions Les Fiches du Cinéma, pp. 148–51.

Gott, Michael (2013a), 'Cowboys, Icebergs, and "Outlaws": The Paradoxes and Possibilities of the Francophone Belgian Road Movie', *Transfers* 8, pp. 47–69. DOI: 10.3167/TRANS.2013.030204. *Academic OneFile*, http://link.galegroup.com/apps/doc/A397007457/AONE?u=bsuc&sid=AONE&xid=a938261e (last accessed August 2018).

Gott, Michael (2013b), 'West/East Crossings', in Leen Engelen and Kris Van Heuckelom (eds), *European Cinema after the Wall: Screening East–West Mobility*, Lanham: Rowman and Littlefield, pp. 1–18.

Gott, Michael (2016), *French Language Road Cinema*, Edinburgh: Edinburgh University Press.

Gott, Michael and Thibaut Schilt (2015), 'Crossing borders and queering identities in French-language European road movies', *Studies in European Cinema* 12:3, pp. 275–91. DOI: 10.1080/17411548.2015.1094259.

Gott, Michael and Thibaut Schilt (2018), *Cinéma-monde: De-centred Perspectives on Global Filmmaking in French*, Edinburgh: Edinburgh University Press.

Govaert, Serge (2001), 'Culture wallonne ou culture francophone', *La revue toudi* 35, January–February 2001, <http://www.larevuetoudi.org/fr/story/la-controverse-sur-la-culture-wallonne-dans-le-monde-diplomatique> (last accessed 19 September 2016).

Greenstein, Michael (1989), *Third Solitudes: Tradition and Discontinuity in Jewish-Canadian Literature*, Montréal: McGill-Queen's University Press.
Grist, Leighton (2009), 'Whither Realism? Bazin re-considered', in Lúcia Nagib and Cécilia Mello (eds), *Realism and the Audiovisual Media*, Basingstoke: Palgrave Macmillan, pp. 20–30.
Guerand, Jean-Philippe (2014), 'La Bourse ou La Vie', *Avant Scène Cinema* 613, May, pp. 134–7.
Guiot, Nicolas (2007), 'Cages' (review), *Les Ciné-fiches de Grand Angle* 318, p. 5.
H. H. (2005), 'La vie avant l'étincelle', *La Libre Belgique*, 27 April.
H. H. (2015), 'Repères: La Flemish Connection', *La Libre Belgique*, 4 November, p. 39.
Hainaut, David (2015), 'Mais où est donc passé le public belge?', *Cinéma Belge* 116, May, pp. 22–9.
Hamel, Jean-François (2012), '"Autour d'une imagerie humaniste" Ouvrage recensé: *Le gamin au vélo*, Jean-Pierre and Luc Dardenne, Belgique, 2011, 87 min', *Ciné-bulles* 30:3, pp. 46–9.
Hammond, Brady and Sean Redmond (2013), 'Introduction: This is the Sea: Cinema at the Shoreline', *Continuum: Journal of Media & Cultural Studies* 27:5, pp. 601–2.
Hannerz, Ulf (1996), *Transnational Connections: Culture, People, Places*, London: Routledge.
Hannerz, Ulf (1997), 'Flows, Boundaries and Hybrids: Keywords in Transnational Anthropology', *Mana (Rio de Janeiro)* 3:1, pp. 7–39.
Hardt, Michael and Antonio Negri (2000), *Empire*, Cambridge, MA and London: Harvard University Press.
Harper, Graeme and Jonathan Rayner (2010), *Cinema and Landscape*, Bristol: Intellect Books.
Hayward, Susan (2000), 'Framing National Cinemas', in Mette Hjort and Scott Mackenzie (eds), *Cinema and Nation*, New York and London: Routledge, pp. 88–102.
Hayward, Susan (2005), *French National Cinema*, 2nd edition, London and New York: Routledge.
Hayward, Susan (2014), 'French Noir 1947–79: From Grunge-Noir to Noir-hilism', in Homer B. Petty and Robert Barton Palmer (eds), *International Noir*, Edinburgh: Edinburgh University Press, pp. 36–60.
Hayward, Susan (2016), 'Middlebrow Taste: Towards a new middle class – a certain tendency of 1950s French cinema', in Sally Faulkner (ed.), *Middlebrow Cinema*, Abingdon and New York: Routledge, pp. 33–50.
Hedling, Erik (2010), '"On the Rocks": The Scanian Connection in Ingmar Bergman's Early Films', in Erik Hedling, Olof Helding and Mats Jönsson (eds), *Regional Aesthetics: Locating Swedish Media*, Stockholm: National Library of Sweden, pp. 307–22.
Héliot, Louis (2008), 'L'effervescence du cinéma belge francophone', *Festival international du film de la Rochelle*, pp. 88–107, http://archives.festival-larochelle.org/festival-2008/l-effervescence-du-cinema-belge-francophone (last accessed August 2018).
Hessels, Walter (2004), 'Rosetta', in Ernst Mathijs (ed.), *The Cinema of the Low Countries*, London: Wallflower Press, pp. 239–47.
Heymann, Danièle (2006), 'La Raison du Plus Faible de Lucas Belvaux: les pieds nickelés de la mouise', *Marianne*, 15 July.
Heyrendt, Hubert (2004), 'Il y a une vie après les Snuls', *La Libre Belgique*, 14 April, p. 4.

Heyrendt, Hubert (2005a), 'Bouli Lanners, peintre de la tristesse', *La Libre Belgique*, 26 April, <http://www.lalibre.be/culture/cinema/bouli-lanners-peintre-de-la-tristesse-51b88999e4b0de6db9abfae7> (last accessed 7 June 2017).
Heyrendt, Hubert (2005b), 'L'Attente d'une étincelle', *La Libre Belgique*, 17 February.
Heyrendt, Hubert (2012), 'Les leçons de "Bye Bye Belgium"', *La Libre Belgique*, 20 January, <http://www.lalibre.be/culture/medias-tele/les-lecons-de-bye-bye-belgium-51b8e4dae4b0de6db9c54dd3> (last accessed 10 January 2018).
Higbee, William (2007), 'Beyond the (trans)national: towards a cinema of transvergence in postcolonial and diasporic francophone cinema(s)', *Studies in French Cinema*, 7:2, pp. 79–91.
Higbee, William and Song Hwee Lim (2010), 'Concepts of transnational cinema: towards a critical transnationalism in film studies', *Transnational Cinemas* 1:1, pp. 7–21.
Higson, Andrew (1989) 'The concept of national cinema', *Screen* 30:4, Autumn, pp. 36–46.
Higson, Andrew (1995), *Waving the Flag: Constructing a National Cinema in Britain*, Oxford: Clarendon.
Higson, Andrew (2000), 'The limiting imagination of national cinema', in Mette Hjort and Scott Mackenzie (eds), *Cinema and Nation*, London: Routledge, pp. 63–74.
Hjort, Mette, and Scott Mackenzie (eds) (2000), *Cinema and Nation*, London and New York: Routledge.
Hjort, Mette (2000), 'Themes of Nation', in Mette Hjort and Scott Mackenzie (eds), *Cinema and Nation*, London and New York: Routledge, pp. 103–17.
Hjort, Mette (2009), 'On the plurality of cinematic transnationalism', in Nataša Ďurovičová and Kathleen Newman (eds), *World Cinemas, Transnational Perspectives*, New York: Routledge, pp. 12–33.
Hjort, Mette and Duncan Petrie (2007), 'Introduction', in Mette Hjort and Duncan Petrie (eds), *The Cinema of Small Nations*, Edinburgh: Edinburgh University Press, pp. 1–22.
Hodgin, Nick (2016), 'The cosmopolitan Communist Joris Ivens, transnational filmmaker before transnationalism?', *Transnational Cinemas* 7:1, pp. 34–49.
Hooghe, Liesbet (2004), 'Belgium: Hollowing the Center', in Ugo Amoretti and Nancy Bermeo (eds), *Federalism and Territorial Cleavages*, Baltimore and London: John Hopkins University Press, pp. 55–92.
Hooghe, Marc (2012), 'The Political Crisis in Belgium (2007–2011): A Federal System without Federal Loyalty', *Journal of Representative Democracy*, 48:1, pp. 131–8.
I. R. (2008), 'Le film de Bouli Lanners, imprégné d'humour pince sans rire et délirant, est un petit bijou', *Le Monde*, 18 June.
La revue toudi (2009), 'Culture et citoyenneté en Wallonie', 12 May, <http://www.larevuetoudi.org/fr/story/1-culture-et-citoyenneté-en-wallonie> (last accessed 29 May 2015).
Iordanova, Dina, David Martin-Jones and Belen Vidal (2010), *Cinema at the periphery*, Detroit: Wayne State University Press.
Ince, Kate (ed.) (2008), *Five Directors: Auteurism from Assayas to Ozon*, Manchester: Manchester University Press.
Ingberg, Henry (2001), 'Le cinéma belge, aveuglé par son succès', *La Libre Belgique*, 12 January, <http://www.lalibre.be:80/article.phtml?id=11&subid=118&art_id=5022&folder_id=25> (last accessed 30 October 2017).
Jack, Belinda Elizabeth (1996), *Francophone Literatures: An Introductory Survey*, Oxford: Oxford University Press.
Jäckel, Anne (2003), *European Film Industries*, London: British Film Institute.

Jacobs, Pierre (2007), '"Cages" ou les troubles de langage', *Metro*, 9 May, p. 11.
Jacobowitz, Florence (2007), '*Nue propriété* with Isabelle Huppert', *CineAction* 71, pp. 40–2.
Jameson, Fredric (1991), *Postmodernism, or, The Cultural Logic of Late Capitalism*, Durham, NC: Duke University Press.
Jaumain, Michel and Guy Vandenbulcke (1986), *L'Exploitation Cinématographique en Belgique: Audience et Mutation de l'Offre*, Brussels: Centre de recherche et d'information socio-politiques.
Jeancolas, Jean-Pierre (1997), 'Une Bobine d'Avance: Du Cinéma de la Politique en Février 1997', *Positif* 434, pp. 56–8.
Jules, Dominique (1990), 'Filmographie', in Guy Hennebelle and Marcel Oms (eds), *Champs-Contrechamps (Le Cinéma Rural en Europe)*, Paris: Éditions du Centre Pompidou, pp. 102–28.
Kaganski, Serge (2006), 'La Raison du Plus Faible de Lucas Belvaux', *Les Inrockuptibles*, 18 July.
Kaganski, Serge (2012), 'Joachim Lafosse: "La vérité, on s'en fout"', *Les Inrockuptibles*, 15 August, pp. 42–8.
Kaplan, Catherine (1996), *Questions of Travel: Postmodern Discourses of Displacement*, Durham, NC and London: Duke University Press.
Klinger, Barbara (1997), 'Film History as terminable and interminable: recovering the past in reception studies', *Screen* 38:2, pp. 107–28.
Koch, Natalie and Anssi Paasi (2016), '*Banal Nationalism* twenty years on: re-thinking, re-formulating and re-contextualising the concept', *Political Geography* 54, pp. 1–6.
Keating, Patrick (2009), *Hollywood Lighting from the Silent Era to Film Noir*, New York: Columbia University Press.
Keating, Patrick (2011), 'Motifs of Movement and Modernity', *Movie: A Journal of Film Criticism* 7, p. 98.
L'Envers de l'Écran (2005) 'Lucas Belvaux, cinéaste expérimental et populaire', *Sonuma.be*, online: 11 December 2012, <http://www.sonuma.be/archive/lucas-belvaux-cinéaste-expérimental-et-populaire> (last accessed 18 January 2017).
Laderman, David (2002), *Driving Visions: Exploring the Road Movie*, Austin: University of Texas Press.
Lahire, Bernard (1994), *La Raison des plus faibles: Rapport au travail, écritures domestiques et lectures domestiques et les lectures en milieu populaires*, Paris: Presses Universitaires de Lille.
Lanners, Bouli (2005), 'Commentaren Van Bouli Lanners (Regisseur)', *Ultranova* (DVD), Ghent: Lumière.
La revue nouvelle (1983), 'Manifeste pour la culture wallonne', <http://www.larevuetoudi.org/fr/story/manifeste-pour-la-culture-wallonne-1983> (last accessed 2 January 2018).
La Tribune de Bruxelles, Revue Belge du Cinéma (2007), 'Rencontre avec l'Auderghemois O. Masset-Depasse', 3–9 May, p. 10, <http://dynamedia.be/storage/tribune//tbx_20070503_tbx_full.pdf> (last accessed July 2018).
Lecomte, Olivier (2006), 'Le cinéma belge montre les dents', *Télé moustique*, 4 October, pp. 156–7.
Ledo, Margarita (2017), 'Rethinking diversity: cinema in non-hegemonic languages as a symptom', *8th Annual Small Cinemas Conference: Diversity in Glocal Cinemas: Language, Culture, Identity*, 20 September, Conference paper.
Lefebvre, Martin (2006), *Landscape and Film*, London: Routledge.
Lefebvre, Martin (2011), 'On landscape in narrative cinema', *Canadian Journal of Film Studies* 20:1, Spring, pp. 61–79.

Lefort, Gérard (1999), 'Rosetta d'urgence', *Libération*, 24 May, <http://www.larevue toudi.org/en/node/1296> (last accessed 22 January 2018).
Lefort, Gérard (2012), 'Cinéma: Belvaux, Capitaine à Docks', *Libération*, 14 March, pp. i–iii.
Lefort, Gérard and Olivier Séguret (2014), '"Deux jours, une nuit", l'enjeu des 1000 euros', *Libération*, 21 May.
Lemercier, Fabien (2015), '"The Other Belgian Cinema" on show in Strasbourg', *Cineuropa*, 24 March, <http://cineuropa.org/nw.aspx?t=newsdetail&l=en&did=288287> (last accessed 23 June 2015).
Les Inrockuptibles (2008), 'Eldorado', 17 June 2008.
Lesuisse, Anne-Françoise (1996/1997), 'Trois étapes: Un paysage', *Revue Belge du Cinéma* 41, Winter, pp. 43–9.
Lim, Song Hwee (2007), 'Is the trans- in transnational the trans- in transgender?', *New Cinemas: Journal in Contemporary Film* 5:1, April, pp. 39–52.
Lim, Song Hwee (2014), *Tsai Ming-Liang and a Cinema of Slowness*, Honolulu: University of Hawaii Press.
Loison, Guillaume (2008), 'Bouli and Clide, une bonne histoire belge', *France-Soir*, 19 June.
Loopmans, Maarten, Sarah Luyten and Christian Kesteloot (2007), 'Urban policies in Belgium: A puff-pastry with a bittersweet aftertaste', in Leo van den Berg, Erik Braun and Jan van der Meer (eds), *National Policy Responses to Urban Challenges in Europe,* Aldershot: Ashgate, pp. 79–102.
Lorfèvre, Alain (2004), 'C'est réalisé près de chez vous', *La Libre Belgique*, 28 April.
Lorfèvre, Alain (2005), 'Atelier pour films en chantier', *La Libre Belgique*, 11 May, <http://www.lalibre.be/culture/cinema/atelier-pour-films-en-chantier-51b889c3e4b0de6db9ac0acb> (last accessed June 2018).
Lorfèvre, Alain (2006a), 'Le jeune homme à la caméra', *La Libre 2*, 28 July, p.17.
Lorfèvre, Alain (2006b), 'Un cinéma belge "transgenres"', *La Libre Belgique*, 17 October.
Lorfèvre, Alain (2007a), 'Olivier Masset-Depasse va "là où il a peur"', *La Libre Belgique*, 9 May, <http://www.lalibre.be/culture/cinema/olivier-masset-depasse-va-la-ou-il-a-peur-51b89305e4b0de6db9afaaf4> (last accessed 20 April 2016).
Lorfèvre, Alain (2007b), 'Ne me quitte pas', *La Libre Belgique*, 9 May.
Lorfévre, Alain (2007c), 'La soif de tourner de Joachim Lafosse', *La Libre Belgique*, 13 October, <http://www.lalibre.be/culture/cinema/la-soif-de-tourner-de-joachim-lafosse-51b88654e4b0de6db9aafeb5> (last accessed June 2018).
Lorfèvre, Alain (2013), 'Même absents, les Belges font parler d'eux à Cannes', *La Libre Belgique*, 24 May, <http://www.lalibre.be/culture/cinema/meme-absents-les-belges-font-parler-d-eux-a-cannes-51b73594e4b0de6db975b647> (last accessed 1 February 2018).
Loughlin, John (1996), '"Europe of the Regions" and the Federalisation of Europe', *Publius: The Journal of Federalism* 26 (4), pp. 141–62.
Louvet, Jean (1998), 'La petite histoire', *Le Matin*, p. 6.
Lovat, Simon (2006), 'Ultranova', *Sight and Sound*, 1 January, p. 82.
Lowy, Vincent (2016), *Dardenne par Dardenne: Entretiens avec Michel Ciment*, Brussels: Collection La Muette.
Macnab, Geoffrey (2003), 'Timber!', *The Guardian*, 27 February, <http://www.theguardian.com/film/2003/feb/27/artsfeatures> (last accessed 14 June 2010).
Mai, Joseph (2010), *Jean-Pierre and Luc Dardenne*, Urbana, Chicago and Springfield: University of Illinois Press.
Mai, Joseph (2011), 'Lorna's silence and Levinas's ethical alternative: form and viewer

in the Dardenne brothers', *New Review of Film and Television*, 9:4, December, pp. 435–53.

Mandelbaum, Jacques (2006), '*La Raison du plus faible*: un polar social, lyrique, révolté', *Le Monde*, 25 May, <http://www.lemonde.fr/culture/article/2006/05/25/la-raison-du-plus-faible-un-polar-social-lyrique-revolte_775953_3246.html> (last accessed 29 December 2016).

Mandelbaum, Jacques (2008), 'Deux cinéastes belges, deux visions de l'héritage de Mai 68', *Le Monde*, 22 May.

Mandelbaum, Jacques (2014), 'Les frères Dardenne: "Des digues ont sauté"', *Le Monde*, 22 May, p. 13.

Marché du Film (2013), *World Cinema Trends: Tendances du Marché Mondial du Film*, Paris: Marché du Film.

Marshall, Bill (2012), 'Cinéma-monde? Towards a concept of francophone cinema', *Francosphères*, 1:1, pp. 35–51.

Martel, Frédéric (2010), *Mainstream: Enquête sur la guerre globale de la culture et des médias*, Paris: Éditions Flammarion.

Martinez, Dominique (2012), '38 témoins: Elle criait et je n'ai rien fait', *Positif* 613, pp. 32–3.

Masset-Depasse, Olivier and Jacques-Henri Bronckart (2006), 'Director's Commentary', *Cages*, DVD, Brussels: Cinéart.

Masset-Depasse, Olivier (2013), 'Cages – Doctorat des études cinématographiques' (pers comm), 30 September.

Massey, Doreen (2005), *For Space*, London: Sage.

Massey, Doreen (2011), 'Landscape/space/politics: an essay', <https://thefutureoflandscape.wordpress.com/landscapespacepolitics-an-essay/> (last accessed 29 January 2018).

Mathijs, Ernest (2004a), 'Introduction: Cinema in the Low Countries and the Question of Cultural Identity', in Ernest Mathijs (ed.), *The Cinema of the Low Countries*, London: Wallflower Press, pp. 1–13.

Mathijs, Ernest (2004b), '"Nobody is innocent": cinema and sexuality in contemporary Belgian culture', *Social Semiotics* 14:1, pp. 85–101.

Maule, Rosanna (2008), *Beyond Auteurism: New Directions in Authorial Film Practices in France, Italy and Spain Since the 1980s*, Bristol: Intellect.

Mazierska, Ewa (2004), 'Domesticating Madness, Revisiting Polishness: The Cinema of Marek Koterski', *Journal of Film and Video*, 56:3, pp. 20–34.

Mazierska, Ewa, and Laura Rascaroli (2006), *Crossing New Europe: Postmodern Travel and the European Road Movie*, London: Wallflower Press.

Melbye, David (2010), *Landscape Allegory in Cinema: From Wilderness to Wasteland*, Basingstoke: Palgrave Macmillan.

Meikle, Jeffery L. (2010), 'Transatlantic Refractions: Ambivalence and Cultural Hybridity in the Euro-American Road Movie', *European Journal of American Studies* 5:4, <https://ejas.revues.org/8806> (last accessed 16 March 2017).

Mello, Marie-Hélène (2007), 'La raison du plus faible: Il nous restera l'ardoise', *Ciné-bulles* 25:3, pp. 61–2.

Mélon, Marc-Emmanuel (1996/1997), 'Les enfants de Prométhée', *Revue Belge du Cinéma* 41, pp. 4–5.

Mélon, Marc-Emmanuel (2004), 'Le non-lieu de l'exil dans le cinéma francophone de Belgique', Actes du Colloque d'El Jadida (El Jadida Conference Proceedings): *Trajectoires interculturelles. Exils imaginaires et exils réels dans le domaine francophone: théorie, histoire, figure, pratiques* (Morocco 10–12 December 2002), El Jadida, Publication de la Faculté des Lettres et des Sciences humaines de l'Université d'El Jadida, pp. 341–53.

Mélon, Marc-Emmanuel (2010), 'Cinéma et video: Utopie et réalité', in Nancy Delhalle, Jacques Dubois and Jean-Marie Klinkenberg (eds), *Les tournant des années 1970: Liège en effervescence*, Brussels: Les Impressions Nouvelles, pp. 117–38.
Mélon, Marc-Emmanuel (2012), 'Le cinéma et les arts audiovisuels [en Wallonie]', in Bruno Demoulin (ed.), *Histoire Culturelle de la Wallonie*, Brussels: Fonds Mercator, pp. 314–26.
Mercier, Jacques (2008), 'Plic-ploc', *La Libre Belgique*, 8 February, <http://www.lalibre.be/culture/medias-tele/plic-ploc-51b89854e4b0de6db9b184fc> (last accessed 16 August 2017).
Merigeau, Pascal (2006), 'Frères humains …', *Le Nouvel Observateur*, 20 July.
Meyer, Paul (1998), 'De bric et de broc', *Le Matin*, p. 12.
M. M. (2006), 'Quand les chômeurs tentent leur malchance au braquage', *L'Humanité dimanche*, 20 July.
M. M. (2008), 'Eldorado. La Belgique, c'est l'Amérique!', *L'Humanité dimanche*, 19 June.
Morin, Edgar (1987), *Penser l'Europe*, Paris: Gallimard.
Mosley, Philip (2001), *Split Screen: Belgian Cinema and Cultural Identity*, Albany: State University of New York Press.
Mosley, Philip (2002), 'Anxiety, memory, and place in Belgian cinema', *Yale French Studies* 102, pp. 160–75.
Mosley, Philip (2013), *The Cinema of the Dardenne Brothers: Responsible Realism*, New York: Wallflower Press.
Moure, José (2012), *Le plaisir du cinéma analyses et critiques des films*, Paris: Klincksieck.
Mulvey, Laura (2006), *Death 24x a Second: Stillness and the Moving Image*, London: Reaktion Books.
Mundell, Ian (2009), 'You can look but you can't touch', *The Bulletin.be*, 22 January, p. 23.
Murat, Pierre (2006), 'La Raison du plus faible', *Télérama*, 19 July.
Murphy, David (2002), 'De-centring French Studies: Towards a Postcolonial Theory of Francophone Cultures', *French Cultural Studies* 13:165, pp. 165–85.
Murray, Jonathan (2015), 'The Bill Douglas Trilogy', in Bob Nowlan and Zach Finch (eds), *Directory of World Cinema: Scotland*, Bristol: Intellect, pp. 204–8.
Naficy, Hamid (2001), *An Accented Cinema: Diasporic and Exilic Filmmaking*, Princeton: Princeton University Press.
Naficy, Hamid (2008), 'For a theory of regional cinemas: Middle Eastern, North African and Central Asian cinemas', *Early Popular Visual Culture* 6:2, July, pp. 97–102. DOI:10.1080/17460665080215036.
Neale, Steve (1986), 'Melodrama and Tears', *Screen*, 27:6, pp. 6–23.
Nessolson, Lisa (2006), 'The Right of the Weakest/La Raison du plus faible', *Variety* 403:2, 29 May–4 Jun, p. 40.
Neyrat, Cyril (2006), '*La Raison du plus faible* de Lucas Belvaux: Debout jusqu'au bout', *Cahiers du Cinéma*, July–August, pp. 50–1.
Nuttens, Jean-Dominique (2012), 'À perdre la raison: Possession', *Positif* 619, September, pp. 15–16.
Nuttens, Jean-Dominique (2014), 'L'affaire humaine', *Positif* 639, May, pp. 8–15.
Olsen, Mark (2003), 'The Trilogy', *Film Comment*, September–October, 39:5, p. 75.
O'Rawe, Des (2011), 'Towards a poetics of the cinematographic frame', *Journal of Aesthetics & Culture*, Vol. 3. DOI: 10.3402/jac.v3i0.5378.
O'Regan, Tom (1996), *Australian National Cinema*, London and New York: Routledge.
Osganian, Patricia (2003), 'D'amerika rapports de classe à *Rosetta*: Sortie du naturalisme et subjectivation du réel', *Mouvements* 26–7, pp. 51–7.

O'Shaughnessy, Martin (2003), 'Post-1995 French Cinema: Return of the Social, Return of the Political?', *Modern and Contemporary France* 11:2, pp. 189–203.
O'Shaughnessy, Martin (2007), *The New Face of Political Cinema: Commitment in French Film since 1995*, New York: Berghahn Books.
O'Shaughnessy, Martin (2008), 'Ethics in the ruin of politics: the Dardenne brothers', in Kate Ince (ed.), *Five directors – Auteurism from Assayas to Ozon*, Manchester: Manchester University Press, pp. 59–83.
Palmer, Tim (2002), 'Jean-Pierre Melville and 1970s French film style', *Studies in French Cinema* 2:3, pp. 135–45.
Palmer, Tim (2011), *Brutal Intimacy: Analysing Contemporary French Cinema*, Middletown, CT: Wesleyan University Press.
Park, Eun-Jee (2011), *From Paternal Hegemony to the Ethics of Fraternity: The Place of Absent Fathers in Le Jeune Cinéma Français*, unpublished PhD thesis, Newcastle: Newcastle University.
Park, Eun-Jee (2012), 'The politics of friendship and paternity: The Dardenne brothers', *Rosetta*', *Studies in French Cinema*, 12:2, pp. 137–49.
Paasi, Anssi (2016), 'Dancing on the Graves: Independence, Hot/Banal Nationalism and the Mobilisation of Memory', *Political Geography* 54, pp. 21–31.
Petrie, Duncan (2000a), 'The New Scottish Cinema', in *Cinema and Nation*, ed. Mette Hjort and Scott Mackenzie, London: Routledge, pp. 143–58.
Petrie, Duncan (2000b), *Screening Scotland*, London: British Film Institute.
Pialoux, Michel (1999), 'The Shop Steward's World in Disarray', in Pierre Bourdieu (ed.), *Weight of the World: Social Suffering in Contemporary Society*, trans. Priscilla Parkhurst, Cambridge: Polity Press, pp. 321–37.
Pirotte, Jean (2002), 'Une image floue', *Louvain* 133, November, pp. 26–8.
Pliskin, Fabrice (1998), 'Nord: une mine de cinéma', *Le Matin*, p. 29.
Pluijgers, Jean-François (2014), 'Héroïne de la vie réelle', *Focus Vif*, 9 May, pp. 32–4.
Poirson-Dechonne, Marion (2011), 'Polar français au cinéma (1961–2011): Une esthétique au service d'un engagement politique', *Mouvements* 67, March, pp. 19–27. DOI: 10.3917/mouv.067.0019.
Polet, Jacques (2002), 'Un enracinement porteur d'universalité', *Louvain* 133, November, pp. 23–5.
Powrie, Phil (1997), *French Cinema in the 1980s: Nostalgia and the Crisis of Masculinity*, Oxford: Clarendon Press.
Powrie, Phil (1999), 'Heritage, History and "New Realism": French Cinema in the 1990s', in Phil Powrie (ed.), *French Cinema in the 1990s: Continuity and Difference*, Oxford: Oxford University Press, pp. 1–21.
Prédal, René (2002), *Le jeune cinéma français,* Paris: Nathan.
Rancière, Jacques (n.d.), 'The gaps of cinema', *NECSUS*, <http://www.necsus-ejms.org/the-gaps-of-cinema-by-jacques-ranciere/> (last accessed 9 February 2016).
Regnier, Isabelle (2014), 'Face au capitalisme le plus cynique, le parcours d'une combattante', *Le Monde*, 22 May, p. 13.
Reynaert, Matthieu (2006), 'La raison du plus faible de Lucas Belvaux', *Cinergie.be*, 8 September, <http://www.cinergie.be/webzine/la_raison_du_plus_faible_de_lucas_belvaux_2006_09_08> (last accessed 7 January 2017).
Reynaert, Philippe (2011), *FW: Interview*, pers comm, 22 June.
Rochet, Bénédicte (2011), 'Esquisse d'une cinématographie wallonne: un cinéma identitaire', in Anne Roekens and Axel Tixhon (eds), *Cinéma et Crise[s] économiques: Esquisses d'une cinématographie wallonne*, Namur: Presses Universitaires de Namur, pp. 15–28.
Roekens, Anne (2009), *Mon bel écran, dis-moi qui est encore belge . . . La RTB(F) face au débat identitaire wallon (1962–2000)*, Namur: Presses Universitaires de Namur.

Roekens, Anne and Axel Tixhon (eds) (2011), *Cinéma et Crise[s] Économique[s]: Esquisses d'une cinématographique wallonne*, Namur: Press Universitaires de Namur/Yellow Now.
Romney, Jonathan (2012), 'La Comédie Humaine', *Sight and Sound*, April, pp. 40–3.
Røssaak, Eivind (2011), 'The Still/Moving Field: An Introduction', in Eivind Røssaak (ed.), *Between Stillness and Motion: Film, Photography and Algorithms*, Amsterdam: Amsterdam University Press, pp. 11–26.
Rosello, Mireille (2014), 'Olivier Masset-Depasse's *Illégal*: How to narrate silence and horror', *SubStance* 43:1, pp. 13–25.
Rouchy, Marie-Elisabeth, (2008), 'Soleil belge', *Le Nouvel Observateur (TéléObs)*, 19 June.
Rouyer, Philippe and Tobin, Yann (2011), 'Entretien entre Jean-Pierre and Luc Dardenne: Une histoire qu'on n'avait jamais racontée', *Positif* 604, pp. 9–13.
Rouyer, Philippe and Tobin, Yann (2014), 'Entretien avec Jean-Pierre and Luc Dardenne: Trouver le bon rythme', *Positif* 639, pp. 11–15.
Roy, André (2008), 'Eldorado de Bouli Lanners', *24 Images* 140, p. 58.
Ruëll, Niels (2007), 'Why do couples break up?', *Agenda*, pp. 4–5.
Santilli, Paul (2006), 'Cinema and Subjectivity in Krzysztof Kieślowski', *Journal of Aesthetics & Art Criticism* 64:1, pp. 147–56.
Sargeant, Jack and Stephanie Watson (1999), 'Introduction', in Jack Sargeant and Stephanie Watson (eds), *Lost Highways: An Illustrated History of Road Movies*, London: Creation, pp. 5–20.
Sarris, Andrew (1962), 'Notes on the Auteur Theory in 1962', in Leo Braudy and Marshall Cohen (eds), *Film Theory and Criticism*, seventh edition, Oxford: Oxford University Press, pp. 451–4.
Schlesinger, Philip (2000), 'The sociological scope of "national" cinema', in Mette Hjort and Scott Mackenzie (eds), *Cinema and Nation*, London: Routledge, pp. 19–31.
Schwartz, Arnaud (2007), 'Joachim Lafosse, cinéaste. Il porte les espoirs du cinéma belge', *La Croix*, <https://www.la-croix.com/Archives/2007-02-21/Joachim-Lafosse-cineaste.-Il-porte-les-espoirs-du-cinema-belge.-_NP_-2007-02-21-284662> (last accessed 21 June 2016).
Sépul, Réné (2005), 'Premiers Films', *La Libre Belgique*, 5 November, pp. 16–18.
Sépul, Réné (2010), 'Illégal', *La Libre Belgique*, 2 October, pp. 8–10.
Serpieri, Victor (2008), 'Lafosse aux serpents …', *Avant-Scene Cinéma* 576, pp. 98–100.
Shaw, Deborah (2013), 'Deconstructing and Reconstructing "Transnational Cinema"', in Stephanie Dennison (ed.), *Contemporary Hispanic Cinema: Interrogating the Transnational in Spanish and Latin American Film*, Woodbridge: Tamesis, pp. 47–66.
Sojcher, Frédéric (1996), *Cinéma européen et identitiés culturelles*, Brussels: Editions de L'Université de Bruxelles.
Sojcher, Frédéric (1999a), *La Kermesse héroïque du cinéma belge: Le miroir déformant des identités culturelles (1965–1988)*, Paris: L'Harmattan.
Sojcher, Frédéric (1999b), *La Kermesse Héroïque du Cinéma Belge III: Le Carousel Européen (1988–1996)*, Paris: L'Harmattan.
Sojcher, Frédéric (2001), 'Le cinéma: convergence ou divergence culturelle? L'exemple belge', in Soon-Mi Peten, Frédéric Sojcher and Yvon Thiec (eds), *Cinéma, Audiovisuel, Nouveaux Médias: La Convergence: Un Enjeu Européen*, Paris: L'Harmattan, pp. 57–78.
Sotinel, Thomas (2005), 'Ultranova, de Bouli Lanners: Un récit à l'étrangeté charmeuse', *Le Monde*, 11 May.
Smith, Anthony (2000), 'Images of the Nation: Cinema, Art and National Identity', in

Mette Hjort and Scott Mackenzie (eds), *Cinema and Nation*, London: Routledge, pp. 45–59.
Spaas, Lieve (2000), *The Francophone Film: A Struggle for Identity*, Manchester: Manchester University Press.
Steele, Jamie (2016), 'Towards a "transnational regional" cinema: the francophone Belgian case study', *Transnational Cinemas*, 7:1, pp. 50–66, reprinted by permission of the publisher (Taylor & Francis Ltd, http://www.tandfonline.com).
Steele, Jamie (2018a), 'Cross-Border Collaboration: Subnational Film Policies and Cultural Frameworks in Belgium and France', in Nolwenn Mingant and Cecilia Tirtaine (eds), *Reconceptualising Film Policies*, Oxford and New York: Routledge, pp. 168–82.
Steele, Jamie (2018b), 'Cinema Made in Liège: a "hub" of francophone Belgian filmmaking', in Michael Gott and Thibaut Schilt (eds), *Cinéma-Monde: De-centred Perspectives on Global Filmmaking in French*, Edinburgh: Edinburgh University Press.
Steele, Jamie (2018c), 'Diasporic Belgian Cinema: transnational and transcultural approaches to Molenbeek and Matongé in *Black* (Adil El Arbi and Bilall Fallah, 2015)', in James Harvey (ed.), *Nationalism in 21st-century Western European Cinema*, London: Palgrave.
Stevens, Isabel (2014), 'Woman on the verge', *Sight and Sound* 24:9, pp. 65–7.
Stiers, Didier (2007a), 'Le cinéma a changé ma vie', *Zone02*, 17–30 January, p. 6.
Stiers, Didier (2007b), 'Interview: Olivier Masset-Depasse séduit avec *Cages*, "Je voulais que ce soit un film romantique au vrai sens du terme"', *Zone02*, 22 May, pp. 6–7.
Stratton, David (2002), 'On the Run/An Amazing Couple (Un Couple Épatant)/After Life (Après La Vie)', *Variety* 388:6 September, p. 26.
Swiss Films (2013), *Swiss Audiovisual Guide 2013/2014*, <https://web.archive.org/web/20141228024808/http://swiss-audiovisualguide.ch/modules/standard/?page_id=1&lang=1&navTitle=Latest%20edition> (last accessed 11 May 2014).
Taminiaux, Pierre (2013), 'La Francophonitude belge: Du Surréalisme à Cobra', *Francosphères* 2:2, pp. 149–61. DOI: 10.3828/franc.2013.14.
Taxshelter.be (2015), <http://www.taxshelter.be/> (last accessed 21 June 2015).
Télébruxelles (2008), 'Quel développement pour le cinéma à Bruxelles?', <https://web.archive.org/web/20090307124053/http://www.telebruxelles.net/portail/content/view/4576/321/> (last accessed 22 October 2010).
Tesolin, Giorgio and Mélanie Zylberberg (2009), 'Le cinéma belge, un investissement refuge? Panorama du marché tax shelter', *Regards Economiques* 74, October, pp. 1–10.
Tessé, Jean-Philippe (2011), 'Petite fusée', *Cahiers du Cinéma*, May, pp. 20–1.
Thabourey, Vincent (2006), 'La raison du plus faible: Loin, très loin du paradis', *Positif* 545/546, July–August, pp. 130–1.
Thabourey, Vincent (2008), 'Élève libre: De l'initation à la prédation', *Positif* 577, February, pp. 96–7.
Thomas, Paul (1995), *Un Siècle de Cinéma Belge*, Ottignies: Éditions Quorum.
Thomas, Peter (1990), 'Belgium's north–south divide and the Walloon regional problem', *Geography*, 75:1, pp. 36–50.
Thys, Marianne (1996; 1999), *Belgian Cinema/Le Cinéma Belge/De Belgische Film*, Ghent: Ludion.
Tinazzi, Noël (2006), 'La Raison du Plus Faible: un polar social remarquable de Lucas Belvaux', *La Tribune*, 19 July.
Tomasovic, Dirk (1996/1997), 'Le lieu, l'espace, les passages', *Revue Belge du Cinéma* 41, Winter, pp. 57–61.
Trinon, Hadelin (1990), 'Belgique: Entre Flamands et Wallons', in Guy Hennebelle

and Marcel Oms (eds), *Champs-Contrechamps (Le Cinéma Rural en Europe)*, Paris: Éditions du Centre Pompidou, pp. 31–3.
Trumpbour, John (2002), *Selling Hollywood to the World: US and European Struggles for Mastery of the Global Film Industry 1920–1950*, Cambridge: Cambridge University Press.
Turim, Maureen (2014), 'French Neo-Noir: An Aesthetic for the *Policier*', in Homer B. Petty and Robert Barton Palmer (eds), *International Noir*, Edinburgh: Edinburgh University Press, pp. 61–83.
Van Cauwenberghe, Jean-Claude (ed.) (1998), *Oser être Wallon! Ouvrage collectif sur l'identité wallone*, Gerpinnes: Quorum.
Van de Craen, Piet (2002), 'What, if anything, is a Belgian?', *Yale French Studies* 102, pp. 24–33.
Van den Braembussche, Antoon (2002), 'The Silence of Belgium: Taboo and Trauma in Belgian Memory', *Yale French Studies* 102, pp. 34–52.
Van Ginderachter, Maarten (2012), 'Nationalist Versus Regionalist? The Flemish and Walloon Movements in *Belle Époque* Belgium', in Joost Augusteijn and Eric Storm (eds), *Region and State in Nineteenth-Century Europe*, London: Palgrave, pp. 209–26.
Van Hoeij, Boyd (2010), *10/10*, Brussels: Ministère de la communauté française de Belgique.
Vangoghtoutcourt.be (n.d.), 'Hainaut Cinéma et la dynamique de la création cinématographique en Hainaut', <https://www.evernote.com/shard/s294/sh/374d7688-3994-4a52-8d46-4559c41162a5/f2b162e834e207c1ac78392180976bff> (last accessed 20 April 2016).
Verhaeghe, Marceau (2005), 'Ultranova de Bouli Lanners: Ultra modern solitude', *Cinergie*, 1 April, <http://www.cinergie.be/webzine/ultranova_de_bouli_lanners_2005_04_01> (last accessed 14 February 2017).
Verheul, Jaap (2016), 'Out of Many, One: The Dual Monolingualism of Contemporary Flemish Cinema', in Tijana Mamula and Lisa Patti (eds), *The Multilingual Screen: New Reflections on Cinema and Linguistic Difference*, New York: Bloomsbury Academic, pp. 317–34.
Vincendeau, Ginette (1992), 'Noir is also a French word', in Ian Cameron (ed.), *The Movie Book of Film Noir*, London: Studio Vista, pp. 49–58.
Vincendeau, Ginette (1999), 'Back to the Blackboard', *Sight and Sound*, 7:6, pp. 12–15.
Vincendeau, Ginette (2003), *Jean-Pierre Melville: An American in Paris*, London: BFI.
Vincendeau, Ginette (2007), 'The Right of the Weakest', *Sight and Sound*, December, p. 89.
Vincendeau, Ginette (2008), 'Sons and lovers', *Sight and Sound*, May, pp. 52–3.
Vincendeau, Ginette (2011), 'The Frenchness of French Cinema: The Language of National Identity, from the Regional to the Trans-national', in William Higbee and Sarah Leahy (eds), *Studies in French Cinema: UK Perspectives 1985–2010*, Bristol and Chicago: Intellect, pp. 337–52.
Vincendeau, Ginette (2016), 'French film noir', *Sight and Sound* 26:11, November, pp. 42–9.
Vlaeminckx, Jean-Michel (2002), 'Gros Plan: Joachim Lafosse', *Cinergie.be* <http://www.cinergie.be/webzine/gros_plan_joachim_lafosse> (last accessed 19 July 2016).
Vlaeminckx, Jean-Michel (2003), 'La Raison du plus fort', *Cinergie.be*, 1 January, <http://www.cinergie.be/webzine/la_raison_du_plus_fort> (last accessed 21 September 2016).
Vlaeminckx, Jean-Michel (2004), 'Zoning Lonesome cow-boys', *Le Moniteur du Film en Belgique* 229, June, pp. 16–18.

Vlaeminckx, Jean-Michel (2005), 'Le séquestré d'Eve', *La Libre Belgique*, 7 December.
Vlaeminckx, Jean-Michel and Anne Feuillère (2008), 'Bouli Lanners, Eldorado', *Cinergie*, 9 May, <http://www.cinergie.be/webzine/bouli_lanners_eldorado> (last accessed 14 February 2017).
Von Dassanowsky, Robert and Oliver C. Speck (2011), *New Austrian Film*, New York and Oxford: Berghahn Books.
Wallimage.be (2017), 'Depuis le mois de mars...', Facebook.com, <https://www.facebook.com/WallimageBE/photos/a.145884151769.122965.145874751769/10154582078416770/?type=3> (last accessed 20 June 2017).
Walker, Michael (1992), 'Film Noir: Introduction', in Ian Cameron (ed.), *The Movie Book of Film Noir*, London: Studio Vista, pp. 8–38.
Warehime, Marja (2006), *Maurice Pialat*, Manchester: Manchester University Press.
Weissberg, Jay (2006a), 'Private Property', *Variety* 404, 25 September–1 October, pp. 76–7.
Weissberg, Jay (2006b), 'Cages', *Variety*, 23 October, <http://variety.com/2006/film/reviews/cages-1200512435/> (last accessed 17 July 2017).
Wen, Xianghui (2014), 'The withdrawal of touch in close encounter: The tactility of facial close-ups in Ingmar Bergman's films', *Journal of Scandinavian Cinema*, 4:1, pp. 15–25.
Wheatley, Catherine (2011), 'Unseen/obscene: the (non-) framing of the sexual act in Michael Haneke's *La Pianiste*', in Robert von Dassanowsky and Oliver C. Speck (eds), *New Austrian Film*, New York amd Oxford: Berghahn Books, pp. 177–88.
Williams, James (2013), *Space and Being in Contemporary French Cinema*, Manchester: Manchester University Press.
Wise, Damon (2016), 'New Talent Emerges From Belgian Cinema Scene', *Variety*, 15 May, <http://variety.com/2016/film/spotlight/new-talent-emerges-from-belgian-cinema-scene-1201771914/> (last accessed 9 January 2018).
Wolfreys, Jim (2008), 'Reality Bites', *Socialist Review*, December, <http://www.socialistreview.org.uk/article.php?articlenumber=10633> (last accessed 23 June 2010).
Wong, Cindy Hing-Yuk (2011), *Film Festivals: Culture, People, and Power on the Global Screen*, Piscataway: Rutgers University Press.
Wood, Mary (2007), *Contemporary European Cinema*, London: Hodder Arnold.
Zone02 (2007), 'Pseudo-Psychologie: Cages' (review), 9–22 May, p. 26.

FILMS CITED

38 témoins/One Night, Lucas Belvaux. France/Belgium: Agat Films & Cie, 2012.
À nos amours/To Our Loves, Maurice Pialat. France: Les Films du Livradois, 1983.
À perdre la raison/Our Children, Joachim Lafosse. Belgium/Luxembourg/France/Switzerland: Versus Production, 2012.
Aaltra, Benoît Delépine and Gustave Kervern. Belgium/France: La Parti Productions, 2004.
Aanrijding in Moscou/Moscow, Belgium, Christophe Van Rompaey. Belgium: A Private View, 2008.
Adventures of Tintin, The, Steven Spielberg. United States of America/New Zealand: Columbia Pictures, 2011.
Âge de raison, L': le cinéma des frères Dardenne/The Age of Reason: The Cinema of the Dardenne Brothers, Luc Jabon. Belgium: W.I.P./Novak Production, 2013.
Après la vie/After Life, Lucas Belvaux. France/Belgium: Agat Films & Cie, 2002.
Ariel, Aki Kaurismäki. Finland: Finnish Film Foundation, 1988.
Asphalt Jungle, The, John Huston. United States of America: MGM, 1950.
Astérix et le Domaine des Dieux/Asterix and Obelix: Mansion of the Gods, Louis Clichy and Alexandre Astier. France/Belgium: M6 Studio, 2014.
Au fond du Dutroux, Richard Olivier. Belgium: Olivier Films, 1996.
Australia, Jean-Jacques Andrien. France/Switzerland/Belgium: Les Films de la Drève, 1989.
Autre, L'/The Missing Half, Benoît Mariage. Belgium/France/Switzerland: CAB Productions, 2003.
Baden Baden, Rachel Lang. Belgium/France: Tarantula, 2016.
Bal Masqué/The Masked Ball, Julien Verbos. Belgium: Ma Jolie Maison, 1998.
Banquet des fraudeurs, Le/The Smugglers' Banquet, Henri Storck. Belgium/West Germany: Efilm/Tevefilm, 1952.

Bienvenue chez les Ch'tis/Welcome to the Sticks, Dany Boon. France: Pathé Renn Productions, 2008.
Black, Adil El Arbi and Bilall Fallah. Belgium: A Team Productions, 2015.
Blue Belgium Rob Van Eyck. Belgium: Flemish Film Productions, 2000.
Boerensymfonie/Symphonie paysanne/Peasant Symphony, Henri Storck and Maurice Delattre. Belgium: Cinéma-Edition-Production, 1942–4.
Bonnie and Clyde, Arthur Penn. United States of America: Warner Brothers, 1967.
Bout de la langue, Le/Tip of the Tongue, Xavier Istasse. Belgium: Ambiances Productions, 2015.
C'est arrivé près de chez vous/Man Bites Dog, Rémy Belvaux, André Bonzel and Benoît Poelvoorde. Belgium: Les Artistes Anonymes, 1992.
Ça commence aujourd'hui/It All Starts Today, Bertrand Tavernier. France: Les Films Alain Sarde, 1999.
Ça rend heureux, Joachim Lafosse. Belgium/Italy: Eklektik Productions, 2006.
Cages, Olivier Masset-Depasse. Belgium/France: Versus Production, 2006.
Carlo, Michaël R. Roskam. Belgium: CCCP, 2004.
Cavale/On the Run, Lucas Belvaux. France/Belgium: Agat Films & Cie, 2002.
Cercle Romain, Le, Raymond Haine. Belgium: Belfilm asbl, 1960.
Cercle rouge, Le, Jean-Pierre Melville. France/Italy: Euro International Films, 1970.
Chambre froide/Cold Storage, Olivier Masset-Depasse. Belgium/France: Alexis Films, 2000.
Conte sur moi/The Unexpected Taste of Apple, Jonas Bloquet. France/Belgium: Grand Film Palace, 2015.
Convoyeurs attendent, Les/The Carriers Are Waiting, Benoît Mariage. Belgium/France/Switzerland: K-Star, 1999.
Couperet, Le/The Axe, Costa-Gavras. France/Belgium/Spain: KG Productions, 2005.
Couple épatant, Un/An Amazing Couple, Lucas Belvaux. France/Belgium: Agat Films & Cie, 2002.
Cow-boy, Benoît Mariage. Belgium: K2 SA, 2005.
Daens, Stijn Coninx. Belgium/France/Netherlands: Dérives Productions, 1992.
Dans l'ombre/In the Dark, Olivier Masset-Depasse. Belgium/France/Switzerland: Versus Production, 2004.
Déjà s'envole la fleur maigre/From the Branches Drops the Withered Blossom, Paul Meyer. Belgium: Les Films de l'Eglantine, 1960.
Dekalog/The Decalogue, Krzysztof Kieślowski. Poland/West Germany: Senders Freies Berlin/Telewizja Polska, 1989 [film and television].
De Premier/Prime Minister, Erik Van Looy. Belgium: FBO, 2016.
De rouille et d'os/Rust and Bone, Jacques Audiard. France/Belgium: Why Not Productions, 2012.
Deliverance, John Boorman. United States of America: Warner Brothers, 1972.
Dersu Uzala, Akira Kurosawa. Soviet Union/Japan: Atelier 41, 1975.
Des plumes dans la tête/Feathers in My Head, Thomas De Thier. Belgium: JBA Production, 2003.
Die Hard, John McTiernan. United States of America: Twentieth Century Fox, 1988.
Det sjunde inseglet/The Seventh Seal, Ingmar Bergman. Sweden: Svensk Filmindustri (SF), 1957.
Deux jours, une nuit/Two Days, One Night, Jean-Pierre and Luc Dardenne. Belgium/France/Italy: Archipel 35/Les Films du Fleuve, 2014.
Deuxième Souffle, Le/ Second Wind, Jean-Pierre Melville. France: Les Productions Montaigne, 1966.
Dikkenek, Olivier Van Hoofstadt. France/Belgium: Europacorp, 2006.

Doulos, Le/The Finger Man, Jean-Pierre Melville. France/Italy: Compagnia Cinematografica Champion, 1963.
Down by Law, Jim Jarmusch. United States of America/West Germany: Black Snake, 1986.
Drop, The, Michaël R. Roskam. United States of America: Big Screen Productions, 2014.
Économie du couple, L'/After Love, Joachim Lafosse. France/Belgium: Versus Production/Les Films du Worso, 2016.
Égoïste Nature/Selfish Nature, Joachim Lafosse. Belgium: Eklektik Productions, 2000.
Eldorado, Bouli Lanners. Belgium/France: Casa Kafka Pictures, 2008.
Élève libre/Private lessons, Joachim Lafosse. France/Belgium: Haut et Court, 2008.
Emploi du temps, L'/Time Out, Laurent Cantet. France: Haut et Court, 2001.
Enfants du Borinage, lettre à Henri Storck, Les/The Children of Borinage, A Letter to Henri Stork, Patric Jean. Belgium: Centre du Cinéma et de l'Audiovisuel de la Fédération Wallonie-Bruxelles, 2000.
Eraserhead, David Lynch. United States of America: American Film Institute (AFI), 1977.
Été à Droixhe, Un/A Summer in Droixhe, Richard Olivier. Belgium: Olivier Films, 1996.
Faces, John Cassavetes. United States of America: Walter Reade Organisation, 1968.
Far West, Le/Far West, Jacques Brel. France/Belgium: The International Film Company, 1973.
Fée, La/The Fairy, Dominique Abel, Fiona Gordon and Bruno Romy. France/Belgium: MK2 Productions, 2011.
Femme entre chien et loup/Vrouw tussen hond en wolf/Woman in a Twilight Garden, André Delvaux. Belgium/France: La Nouvelle Imagerie/Les Productions de la Guéville, 1979.
Fidèle, Le/Racer and the Jailbird, Michaël R. Roskam. Belgium/France/The Netherlands: Savage Film, 2017.
Fille inconnue, La/The Unknown Girl, Jean-Pierre and Luc Dardenne. Belgium/France: Les Films du Fleuve, 2016
Film 1, Willem Wallyn. Belgium: Canal+/Luna Films, 1999.
Fils, Le/The son, Jean-Pierre and Luc Dardenne. Belgium/France: Archipel 35/Les Films du Fleuve, 2002.
Folie privée/Private Madness, Joachim Lafosse. Belgium/France: Ryva Production, 2004.
Full Monty, The, Peter Cattaneo. United Kingdom/United States of America: Redwave Films, 1997.
Gangsters, Olivier Marchal. France/Belgium: A.J.O.Z. Films, 2002.
Gamin au vélo, Le/The Kid With a Bike, Jean-Pierre and Luc Dardenne. Belgium/France/Italy: Archipel 35/Les Films du Fleuve, 2011.
Géants, Les/The Giants, Bouli Lanners. Belgium/France/Luxembourg: Versus Production, 2011.
Gueule ouverte, La/A Mouth Agape, Maurice Pialat. France: Lido Films, 1974.
Germania anno zero/Germany Year Zero, Roberto Rossellini. Italy/France/Germany: Tevere Film, 1948.
Grand paysage d'Alexis Droeven, Le/The Wide Horizons of Alexis Droeven, Jean-Jacques Andrien. Belgium: Les Films de la Drève, 1981.
Hiver 60/Winter 60, Thierry Michel. Belgium: CCA, 1983.
Honnête commerçant, Un/Step by Step, Philippe Blasband. Belgium/Luxembourg: Artemis Productions, 2002.

Iceberg, L'/Iceberg, Dominique Abel, Bruno Romy and Fiona Gordon. Belgium: Courage Mon Amour, 2005.
Il a plu sur le Grand Paysage/It Rained on the Great Landscape, Jean-Jacques Andrien. Belgium: Les Films de la Drève, 2014.
Illégal/Illegal, Olivier Masset-Depasse. Belgium/Luxembourg/France: Haut et Court, 2010.
Intouchables/The Intouchables, Olivier Nakache and Éric Toledano. France: Quad Productions, 2011.
Jambon d'Ardenne/Ham and Chips, Benoît Lamy. France/Belgium: Lamy Films/ Reganne Films, 1977.
Je pense à vous/You're On My Mind, Jean-Pierre and Luc Dardenne. Belgium/ Luxembourg/France: Dérives Productions, 1992.
Jour se lève, Le/Daybreak, Marcel Carné. France: Productions Sigma, 1939.
Ladri di biciclette/Bicycle Thieves, Vittorio De Sica. Italy: Produzioni De Sica, 1948.
Last Night on Earth, Giles Daoust. Belgium: Title Films, 2004.
Last Resort, Pawel Pawlikowski. United Kingdom: BBC, 2000.
Le Havre, Aki Kaurismäki. Finland/France/Germany: Sputnik, 2011.
Liaison pornographique, Une/An Affair of Love, Frédéric Fonteyne. France/Switzerland, Belgium/Luxembourg: ARP Sélection, 1999.
Loft, Erik Van Looy. Belgium: Woestijnvis, 2008.
Looking for Eric, Ken Loach. United Kingdom/France/Italy/Belgium/Spain: Sixteen Films/FilmFour, 2009.
Loulou, Maurice Pialat. France: Action Films, 1980.
Ma Loute/Slack Bay, Bruno Dumont. France/Germany/Belgium: 38 Productions, 2016.
Ma petite entreprise/My Little Business, Pierre Jolivet. France: Bac Films, 1999.
Marchienne de Vie, Richard Olivier. Belgium: Olivier Films, 1994.
Mémoires/Memoirs, Jean-Jacques Andrien. Belgium: Les Films de la Drève, 1984.
Misère au Borinage/Poverty in the Borinage, Henri Storck and Joris Ivens. Belgium, 1933.
Mobile Home, François Pirot. Belgium/Luxembourg/France: Tarantula, 2012.
Muno, Bouli Lanners. Belgium: Versus Production, 2001.
Mur, Le/The Wall, Alain Berliner. Belgium/France: Haut et Court, 1998.
My Childhood, Bill Douglas. United Kingdom: BFI, 1972.
Naked City, The, Jules Dassin. United States of America: Hellinger Productions, 1948.
Navets blancs empêchent de dormir la nuit, Les/White Turnips Make it Hard to Sleep, Rachel Lang. Belgium/France: ChevalDeuxTrois, 2011.
Non, Wallonie, ta culture n'est pas morte/No Wallonia, Your Culture is Not Dead, Bouli Lanners. Belgium, 1996.
Nue propriété/Private Property, Joachim Lafosse. Belgium/France/Luxembourg: Haut et Court, 2006.
On the Road Again – Le cinéma de Bouli Lanners/On the Road Again – The Cinema of Bouli Lanners, Benoît Mariage. Belgium: Novak Production, 2011.
Ordinary Man, Vincent Lannoo. Belgium/France: Hélicotronic, 2005.
Part du ciel, Une/A Piece of Sky, Bénédicte Liénard. France/Belgium/Luxembourg: Arte Film Cinema, 2002.
Parfois trop d'amour/'Sometimes There's Too Much Love', Lucas Belvaux. France/ Belgium: Les Films de la Drève, 1992.
Pas son genre/Not My Type, Lucas Belvaux. France/Belgium: Agat Films & Cie, 2014.
Pianiste, La/The Piano Teacher, Michael Haneke. Austria/France/Germany: Arte France Cinéma/MK2 Productions/Wega Film, 2001.
Police, Maurice Pialat. France: Gaumont, 1985.
*Pour que la guerre s'achève, les murs devraient s'écrouler/For the War to End, the

Walls Should Have Crumbled, Jean-Pierre and Luc Dardenne. Belgium: Dérives Productions, 1980.
Pourquoi se marier le jour de la fin du monde?/Why Get Married the Day the World Ends?, Harry Cleven. Belgium/Luxembourg: Artémis Productions, 2000.
Pour rire!/'Gags!', Lucas Belvaux. France: Gemini Films, 1996.
Pour toi je ferai bataille/For You I Will Fight, Rachel Lang. Belgium: Mediadiffusion, 2010.
Premiers, les derniers, Les/The First, the Last, Bouli Lanners. France/Belgium: Versus Production, 2016.
Problemski Hotel, Manu Riche. Belgium/France: Cassette for Timescapes, 2015.
Promesse, La/The Promise, Jean-Pierre and Luc Dardenne. Belgium/France/Luxembourg/Tunisia: Les Films du Fleuve, 1996.
Prophète, Un/A Prophet, Jacques Audiard. France/Italy: Why Not Productions, 2009.
Pure Fiction, Marian Handwerker. Belgium: Alexis Films, 1998.
Quai des Brumes/Port of Shadows, Michel Carné. France: Ciné-Alliance, 1938.
Quand la mer monte/When the Sea Rises, Yolande Moreau and Gilles Porte. Belgium/France: Ognon Pictures, 2004.
Quatre cents coups, Les/The 400 blows, François Truffaut. France: Les Films du Carrosse, 1959.
Raining Stones, Ken Loach. United Kingdom: Channel Four Films, 1993.
Raison du plus faible, La/The Right of the Weakest, Lucas Belvaux. Belgium/France: Agat Films & Cie, 2006.
Raison du plus fort, La/The Right of the Strongest, Patric Jean. France: Lapsus SARL, 2003.
Rapt, Lucas Belvaux. France/Belgium: Agat Films & Cie, 2009.
Regarde Jonathan, Jean Louvet, son oeuvre/Consider Jonathan, Jean Louvet, his work, Jean-Pierre and Luc Dardenne. Belgium: Dérives Productions, 1983.
Régate, La/The Boat Race, Bernard Bellefroid. Belgium/Luxembourg/France: Liaison Cinématographique, 2009.
Rien à déclarer/Nothing to Declare. France: Pathé, 2010.
River, The, Jean Renoir. France/United Kingdom/India/United States of America: Oriental International Films, 1951.
Rosetta, Jean-Pierre and Luc Dardenne. France/Belgium: Les Films du Fleuve, 1999.
Rumba, Dominique Abel, Fiona Gordon and Bruno Romy. France/Belgium: MK2 Productions, 2008.
Rundskop/Bullhead, Michaël R. Roskam. Belgium/The Netherlands: Savage Film/Eyeworks Film & TV Drama, 2011.
Scarface, Joachim Lafosse. Belgium, 2001.
Signaleur, Le/The Signalman, film, Benoît Mariage. Belgium: K2 SA, 1997.
Silence de Lorna, Le/Lorna's Silence, Jean-Pierre and Luc Dardenne. France/Belgium/Italy/Germany: Archipel 35/Les Films du Fleuve, 2008.
Smultronstället/Wild Strawberries, Ingmar Bergman. Sweden: Svensk Filmindustri, 1957.
Strass, Vincent Lannoo. Belgium: Radowsky Films, 2001.
Tendresse, La/Tenderness, Marion Hänsel. Belgium/France/Germany: Asap Films, 2013.
Thanasse et Casimir/Thanasse and Casimir, René Picolo. Belgium: Les Films MG, 1946.
Toto le héros/Toto the hero, Jaco Van Dormael. Belgium/France/Germany: Iblis Films, 1991.
Tout ça (ne nous rendra pas la Belgique)/Bye Bye Belgium, Philippe Dutilleul, Isabelle Christiaens and Nathalie Jacobs. Radio Télévision Belge Francophone (RTBF), 2006 [television].

Travellinckx, Bouli Lanners. Belgium: Latitudes Productions, 1999.
Trêve, La/The Break, Radio Télévision Belge Francophone (RTBF). Belgium: Hélicotronc, 2016– [television series].
Tribu, Joachim Lafosse. Belgium: IAD, 2001.
Trois couleurs: Bleu/Three Colours: Blue, Krzysztof Kieślowski. France/Poland/Switzerland: MK2 Productions, 1993.
Tueurs/Killers, François Troukens and Jean-François Hensgens. Belgium/France: Versus Production, 2017.
Tulitikkutehtaan tyttö/The Match Factory Girl, Aki Kaurismäki. Finland: Esselte Video, 1990.
Ultranova, Bouli Lanners. Belgium: Versus Production, 2005.
Van Gogh, Maurice Pialat. France: Erato Films/Studio Canal, 1991.
Vie d'Adèle, La/Blue is the warmest colour, Abdellatif Kechiche. France/Belgium/Spain: Quat'sous Films/Wild Bunch/France 2 Cinéma, 2013.
Vie de Jésus, La/The Life of Jesus, Bruno Dumont. France: 3B Productions, 1997.
Vie rêvée des anges, La/The Dreamlife of Angels, Erick Zonca. France: Diaphana Films, 1998.
Welcome, Philippe Lioret. France: Nord-Ouest Productions, 2009.
Western, Manuel Poirier. France: Salomé/Diaphana Films, 1997.

INDEX

Note: page numbers in *italics* refer to illustrations; those followed by n refer to notes.

'40 years of small studio or production company filmaking', 2–3
'50 ans de cinéma belge/50 ans de decouvertes', 3, 19–20, 31, 41, 57, 182

'A' - grade film festivals, 4, 41, 83, 107, 162
À perdre la raison/Our Children, 83, 85, 95, 103n, 104n
Aanrijding in Moscou/Moscow, Belgium, 42
Abel, Dominique, 42, 132, 160, 184
'absent presence', 143
Acadèmie des Beaux-Arts, Liège, 130
Adam, Ilke, 9–10, 11
The Adventures of Tintin, 48
'affinity', 180
L'âge de raison, le cinéma des frères Dardenne, 74
Aire-sur-la-Lys, 181
Akerman, Chantal, 20, 31
Alaouié, Hichame, 85
Albert I, King, 10
'aleatory' filmmaking style, 92
Algeria, 38
Alion, Yves, 163
Altman, Rick, 131, 146
'ambiguity', 101, 124, 127, 132
American
   cinema, 112–13
   film culture, 132
   film noir, 121–2, 124, 174
   road movies, 154n
'American format', 151
'anchoring', regional and local, 51, 87, 103n, 113, 160
Anderson, Benedict, 11, 19
André, François, 13, 48, 62–4, 65, 79, 98–9, 147, 166

Andrew, Dudley, 143, 161, 177n
Andrien, Jean-Jacques
   Cinéma Wallonie, 20
   countryside, 88–90
   Les Films de le Dreve, 104n, 176n
   Le grand paysage d'Alexis Droeven, 87
   industry, 135
   and linguistic conflict, 4
   Manifeste pour la culture wallonne, 19, 58
   'nostalgia', 144
Antonioni, Michelangelo, 84
Après la vie/After Life, 155
Arbi, Adil El, 40
Archer, Neil, 133, 146, 147, 152
Ardennes, 145–53
   Belvaux, 157
   CinemaScope, 172
   Folie privée, 98
   holiday-making, 91–2, 145
   Lanners, 23–4, 141, 153
   not 'marked', 148
Argentina, 38
Ariel, 153
Arras, 161
'Arrêté royal du 22 juin 1967 tendant à promouvoir la culture cinématographique', 30
'art cinema', 22, 28, 94, 130, 132, 156, 159, 182
'art film', 43, 49, 112
Arts, 84
ASMCF conference 2013, 81n
The Asphalt Jungle, 122
Astérix et le Domaine des Dieux/Asterix: Mansion of the Gods, 41
Astier, Alexandre, 41
ateliers, 2–3
Aubenas, Jacqueline, 87

213

Audiard, Jacques, 39, 54, 164
Augé, Marc, 67
Auquier, Yves, 115–16
Australia, 135, 144
Australian National Cinema, 109
auteurism
  'approproation', 48
  Belvaux, 155
  Bergman, 120
  Douglas, 118
  in francophone Belgium, 3, 30
  Lafosse, 84–5
  Masset-Depasse, 108, 112
  road movies, 24
  and transnationalism, 158
'autodidacts', 4, 111, 131, 153
'autoproduction' label, 82
L'autre/The Missing Half, 85
L'Avant-Scène Cinéma, 159

Bacon, Francis, 119
Baden Baden, 112
Bailleul, 181
Bajomée, Danielle, 18, 52, 165
Balibar, Étienne, 111
Balkan countries, 28
Balzac, Honoré de, 175
'banal aboutness', 51, 98, 162, 182
'banal nationalism', 11–12, 14–15, 182
Le banquet des fraudeurs/The Smuggler's Banquet, 22, 25n
Barthes, Roland, 94
Basque cinema, 181
Basque country, 28, 36
Bauche, Nicolas, 77, 78, 96–7
Bauman, Zygmunt, 17, 147
Bazin, André, 54, 75–6, 88, 161, 172, 177n
Beauvois, Xavier, 181
becultural.co.uk, 184
Belgian art, 22
Belgian film ecosystem, 26–50
Belgian literature, 12–13, 25n
'Belgian school', 159
Belgique toujours grande et belle, 17
'la belgitude', 15, 25n
Belgium, 66, 107, 157, 159, 164–5, 166, 179, 180–1
'Belgorama', 130
Bellefroid, Bernard, 100
Bellour, Raymond, 93–4, 95, 104n
Belmans, Jacques, 29
Belvaux, Lucas, 155–77
  carnival, 99
  film-school generation, 22
  funding, 4, 36
  genre-based filmmaking, 183

transnationalism, 24
visibility of Belgian cinema, 184
Wallonia 'in crisis', 7
Walloon culture, 9, 88
women, 149
Belvaux, Rémy, 82, 157
Bénézet, Delphine, 55, 87, 99, 140
Benghozi, Pierre-Jean, 83–4
Bergfelder, Tim, 37, 45
Bergman, Ingmar, 84, 112, 113, 120–6, 128
Bergson, Henri, 24, 93–4, 121, 142, 143
Berlin Wall, 16
Berliner, Alain, 16, 45
Besson, Luc, 36
biculturalism, 5
Bienvenue chez les Ch'tis/Welcome to the Sticks, 44, 107, 159, 161
Billig, Michael, 11, 14–15, 15
Black, 25n, 40
Blasband, Philippe, 157
Bloquet, Jonas, 154n
Blümlinger, Christa, 104n
Boerensymfonie/Symphonie paysanne/Peasant Symphony, 87
Bon, François, 65, 66
Bonmariage, Manu, 61, 130, 174
Bonnie and Clyde, 154n
Bonzel, André, 82
Boon, Dany, 41, 44, 159, 161
Boorman, John, 130, 145–6
Bordwell, David, 112, 132, 163, 172–3
Borinage, 109, 115–16, *115*, 168
Bosch, Hieronymus, 119
Bossut, 108
Bouckaert, Peter, 37
boundaries, 102–3
Bourdieu, Pierre, 41, 44, 62, 65, 66
Le bout de la langue/Tip of the Tongue, 7
box office, 41, 44, 44–5, 47, 48, 58
Brabant Walloon, 86, 88, 89, 108
Bradfer, Fabienne, 127, 141
Bredael, Jacques, 29, 32, 36, 50n
Breillat, Catherine, 181
British social realist films, 171
Brittany, 151
Brockart, Jacques-Henri, 154n
Bronckart, Jean-Henri, 105–6, 108
Broquet, Julien, 108, 112
Brunfaut, Jeanne, 183
Brussels
  box office, 48
  'Bruxelles Tournage', 50n
  CCA, 40
  'diversification' of Belgian cinema, 4
  'Dutroux affair', 100

INDEX

film festivals, 42
 'la belgitude', 15
 Lafosse, 85, 86
 Masset-Depasse, 110–11
 Wallonia 'in crisis', 165
Brussels Film Festival, 41, 42
Brussels International Fantastic Film Festival, 42
Brussels Urban Landscape Exhibition, Bozar 2016, 141–2
'Bruxelles Tournage', 32, 50n
Bruxelles-Capitale, 3, 9, 21, 32, 179
Bruxellimage, 35, 50n
Buache, Freddy, 159, 161
'buddy movie', 153
Bullhead, 47
Bullot, Fabienne, 167

Ça commence aujourd'hui/It all Starts Today, 76
Ça rend heureux, 82, 83, 85, 103n
Cages, 7, 23, 105–29, *120*, *124*, *127*, 181, 183
Caillé, 28
Calais, 181
camerawork
 fixed, *143*
 fluidity, 79, 102
 framing, *93*
 handheld, 56, 71
 mobility, 67, 89, *89*, 90
 movement, 59, 72, 78, *138*, 172
 proximity, 63–4, 70, 92–3
 spatial dynamics, 104n, 123–7
Campany, David, 94
Canada, 8, 38
Canadian literature, 20
Cannes film festival
 'art cinema', 28
 Belvaux, 162
 Dardenne brothers, 4, 17, 35, 46, 53, 80
 French film industry, 180
 Lafosse, 83
 'national cinema', 41–2
 realism, 132
Cantet, Laurent, 81n
Carlo, 142
Carné, Marcel, 176
carnival, 14, 51, 53, 99
Cassavetes, John, 84, 103n, 112
casting, 53–4
Catalan independence referendum 2017, 29
Catalonia, 10, 28
Cattaneo, Peter, 171
Cattet, Hélène, 31
Cavale/On the Run, 155, 156, 170, 177n

Central Asian countries, 28
Centre du Cinéma et de l'Audiovisuel (CCA)
 auteurism, 33
 'cultural project tests', 30–1
 decree, 49n
 distribution, 40
 exhibition, 45, 50n
 funding, 21, 160
 promotion, 42–3, 184
 regional cinema, 34–5
 'self-selectivity', 41, 179
 'split screen', 2
 'topical' themes, 183
Centre national du cinéma (CNC), 40
Centre Public d'Action Sociale (CPAS), 66
centre-periphery dynamic, 62
Le cercle Romain, 30
Le cercle rouge, 163, 173
Un Certain Régard, 83
C'est arrivé près de chez vous/Man Bites Dog, 82, 86, 92, 132, 157
Chagoll, Lydia, 130
Chambre froide/Cold Storage, 106, 110, 113, *113*, 115–18, *117*, 123, 128, 152
Chang, Justin, 103
Charleroi, *113*
 Belvaux, 165
 CinemaScope, 173
 Les convoyeurs attendent, 87
 Deux jours, une nuit, 66
 Masset-Depasse, 106, 110, 113–14, 115–17, 119, 128
Charlier, Georges, 142
Charlier, Jacques, 134, 173
Chaumont-Gistoux, Wavre, 86
Christie, Ian, 5–6, 27, 28, 30, 41, 43, 49n
cinéaste, 108
Ciné-Bulles, 73, 144
ciné-club, 159
Cinéfinance, 39
Cinéfondation workshops, 83
Cinema and Landscape, 108
'cinema at the periphery', 5–7, 21, 179, 181, 185
'*cinéma de contrebande*', 164
Cinéma et cetera, 101, 104n
cinéma nordiste, 6–7, 22, 55, 109, 128
'cinema of restraint', 101–2
Cinema of the Low Countries, 16–17
Cinéma Wallonie, 20
'cinéma-monde', 21, 34, 159–60
'cinemas of small nations', 5, 8, 42, 44, 57, 179, 181, 185
CinemaScope, 143–4, 172–3
Cinémathèque Royale, 2–3, 130

Cinémathèque Suisse, 27, 57, 141–2
'Cinematic Reference Points', 80n
'cinematographic fables', 84
Cinergie, 42, 73, 132, 134
Cinévox, 42
Cleven, Harry, 39
Clichy, Louis, 41
CNC (Centre national du cinéma), 40
Coesens, Anne, 112, 122–3
Cohen, Nick, 68
Collard, Christophe, 2
Collins, Richard, 8
colour palette, 88, 117–18, 140, 146, 160, 173–4
comedy, 132, 156
Communaute Française Wallonie-Bruxeles (CFWB), 49n
Congo Holocaust, 14, 99
Coninx, Stijn, 17
Conte sur moi/The Unexpected Taste of Apple, 154n
Contemporary French Cinema, 55
Conversation en Wallonie/Conversations in Wallonia, 13
Les convoyeurs attendent/The Carriers Are Waiting
  camerawork, 123
  carnival, 99
  Charleroi, 87
  CinemaScope, 172–3
  colour palette, 117–18
  filiation, 140
  'national cinema', 132
  slag heaps, 115–16
  spatial dynamics, 183
Costa-Gavras, 163
Cotillard, Marion, 54, 83
countryside, 141–5
Le couperet/The Axe, 163
Un couple épatant/An Amazing Couple, 155, 156
CPAS (Centre Public d'Action Sociale), 66
crime genre, 162, 163
'crisis of masculinity', 149, 163, 166, 166–71
'critical capital', 41
'critical transnationalism', 34, 48, 49
Crofts, Stephen, 21–2, 27–8, 30
Crousse, Nicolas, 145
Cucco, Marco, 47
'cultural capital', 44
'cultural exceptionalism', 36
'cultural project tests', 31
'culture of self-doubt', 146–7
'culture of struggle', 165

Cuppens, Kris, 85, 97
Czach, Liz, 41

Daens, 17
Daewoo, 65, 66
d'Alcantara, Vanja, 31
Dans l'ombre/In the Dark, 110, 127
Danvers, Louis, 145–6
Daoust, Giles, 82
Dardenne, Jean-Pierre, 58, 72, 75, 79, 80n
Dardenne, Luc
  'banality', 52
  capitalism, 68
  casting, 54
  centre-periphery dynamic, 61–2
  film festivals, 46
  Kieślowski, 81n
  'labyrinth', 62–3
  location, 58
  Meuse river, 71–2
  'non-places', 76
  Seraing, 57
  socio-economics, 65–6, 77–8, 80
  spatial dynamics, 59
  video documentaries, 69–70
Dardenne brothers, 51–81
  'art cinema', 28
  and Bazin, 177n
  'Belgian school', 159
  camerawork, 92
  carnival, 99
  colour palette, 174
  editing, 113
  film festivals, 4, 41–3, 184
  funding, 33, 83
  and Lafosse, 84–5
  landscape, 136–7, 154n, 173
  Luxembourg, 38
  paternalism, 116–17
  physical brutality, 100
  'post-Dardenne generation', 179, 182
  regional memories, 135
  'self-selectivity', 9
  Seraing, 22, 59–65, 168
  and social commentary, 169
  'social memory', 121
  'social-realist' films, 123
  socio-economics, 164–5
  socio-political, 163
  spatial dynamics, 139
  synchronicity, 150
  tax shelter, 35
  transnationalism, 39, 46–8, 52–5
  unadorned realism, 132
  'urgent realism', 138
  video documentaries, 98, 133

Wallonia, 86–8
Walloon regionalism, 17–19
women's employment, 136, 149, 166, 177n
Darras, Matthieu, 91, 97
Dassin, Jules, 174
Davay, Paul, 30
De Certeau, Michel, 67
De Cleene, Michiel, 142
De Heusch, Luc, 10, 11, 13–14, 15, 22, 119–20
de Meyst, Emile-Georges, 130
de Poorter, Wim, 29
De Sica, Vittorio, 73, 167
De Thier, Thomas, 57–8, 99, 182
de Welz, Fabrice, 111, 145
Defrance, Léonard, 174
Déjà s'envole la fleur maigre/From the Branches Drops the Withered Blossom, 4, 22, 52, 113, *115*, 116–17, 123, 168, 179
Dekalog/The Decalogue, 81n
Deleuze, Gilles, 29, 93–4, 140, 142
Deliverance, 130
Delon, Alain, 132, 149
Delor, Frédéric, 43, 50n
Delvaux, André, 4, 33, 55, 104n, 118–19
Denis, Fernand, 43, 72, 151, 159, 161
Denmark, 28, 38, 44
Dersu Uzala, 130
Deschouwer, Kris, 9–10, 11, 24n
Destrée, Jules, 10, 25n
Le Deux, 43
Deux jours, une nuit/Two Days, One Night, 51–81, 71, 72
  casting, 83
  distribution, 46
  framing, 173
  funding, 39, 81n
  maternalism, 68
  movement, 170
  transport, 166
  unemployment, 114–15
Le Deuxième Souffle/Second Wind, 175
'devalorisation' of man', 166
'diachronic' approach to film history, 1, 3, 24n, 27, 38
'dialogic partner', 27
Die Hard, 177n
Dikkenek, 54
Dillet, Benoît, 61, 64, 67, 71
Dirkx, Paul, 12–13, 25n
'discourse of victimhood', 99–100
disenfranchisement, 170
distribution, 26–50, 184–5

'diversification' of Belgian cinema, 4
documentary films, 29, 74, 95, 133, 141, 154n, 164, 170, 174; *see also* video documentaries
Dogme 95, 82, 92
Doignon, Geraldine, 31
Domenach, Élise, 85
Doret, Thomas, 53
'double alienation', 172
Douglas, Bill, 118
Douin, Jean-Luc, 73, 119
Le Doulos/The Finger Man, 163, 174–5
Down by Law, 151–2
Droixhe district, 172, 174
The Drop, 47
Drouot, Pierre, 130
Du Welz, Fabrice, 27
dualism, 6–7
Dubois, Jacques, 12, 13, 144
Duculot, Pierre, 110
Dumont, Bruno, 80–1n, 86–8, 103n, 107, 128, 133, 181
Duplat, Guy, 32
durée, 142
Dutch language, 47
'Dutroux affair', 14, 23, 99–100, 104n
Duvivier, Julien, 163
Dyer, Richard, 104n

East Asian Cinema, 156
East Asian filmmaking, 48
L'économie du couple/After Love, 83, 85, 111
The Economist, 81n
'ecosystem', 37, 40
L'Écran Témoin, 101, 104n
L'Écran Total, 41
editing, 112–13, 128n, 131
Edmond, John, 89, 90
Égoïste Nature/Selfish Nature, 85, 94–5
Eldorado, 130–54
  'banal aboutness', 182
  camerawork, *143*
  CinemaScope, 172–3
  countryside, 88
  'devalorisation of man', 166
  film festivals, 42
  fluidity, 126
  genre-based filmmaking, 7
  landscape, 99, 144
  Liège, *149*
  road movies, 24
Élève libre/Private Lessons, 42, 83, 85, 95, 99, 100–3, 154n
Elkington, Trevor, 28
Elle magazine, 108

Elsaesser, Thomas
  'contained', 49
  distribution, 45
  'Euro-puddings', 106
  filiation, 183
  'national cinema', 5–6, 27
  'post-national cinema Europe', 19
  privatisation, 37
  sub-state, 28, 178
L'enfant, 60, 61, 63–4, 72, 76, 77–9, 166, 169
Les enfants du Borinage, lettre à Henri Storck/The Children of Borinage, A Letter to Henri Storck, 164
Engelen, Leen, 40
Ensor, James, 119
Entre Chien et Loup, 160
L'Envers de l'Écran, 159
Eraserhead, 113
Un été à Droixhe/A Summer in Droixhe, 174
EURIMAGES, 35, 38, 103n
'Europe of the Regions', 10–11
European Audiovisual Observatory, 37
European Bank of Investment, 32
'European film', 107
European film festival, Brussels, 83
European Union, 10–11, 35, 37, 178, 179
'Euro-puddings', 39, 106
Everett, Wendy, 38, 146, 147, 148–9
exhibition, 26–50, 106–7, 157, 184, 185n
L'Express, 108
'exteriority/interiority', 113
Ezra, Elizabeth, 5, 20, 25n, 27, 53, 153, 158

Faces, 103n
Fallah, Bilall, 40
'family portraits', 84
'fantastic realism', 118–19
Fassbinder, Rainer Werner, 84, 104n
federalisation, 9–10, 15, 16
Fédération Wallonie-Bruxelles, 43, 183
La Fée/The Fairy, 160
Felperin, Leslie, 88
female body, 57
Festival de Kann, 131
Festival International du Film Francophone, Namur, 42
Festival Scope, 184
fetishisation, 92, 134–6, *135*, 146, 151, 153
Feuillère, Anne, 123
Fevry, Sébastien, 161, 162, 166–7, 170–3, 176, 183
Fichte, Johann Gottlieb, 11
Le Fidèle/Racer and the Jailbird, 47

'Fifty French Filmmakers of the Twenty-first Century', 159
filiation, 99
  aesthetic, 151
  American, 174, 175
  artistic, 140
  painterly, 130–1
  patriarchal, 68
  stylistic, 110–13, 130, 179
  stylistic and thematic, 183
  thematic, 58
La fille inconnue/The Unknown Girl, 46, 54, 80n, 83
film festivals, 27, 40–1, 53, 106, 131, 184
film noir, 126–7, 145, 162, 163
  American, 121–2, 124, 174
  French, 23–4, 166, 175, 177n
'film of the community', 170
'Film productions of the French-speaking Belgian community from Wallonia-Brussels', 42
Film Studies, 185
Les Films de le Drève, 104n, 176n
Les Films du Fleuve, 39
film-school generation, 4, 22, 36
Le fils/The Son, 62, 99, 116
Finland, 44, 150, 153
Flanders
  countryside, 104n
  distribution, 46–7, 48
  'Dutroux affair', 100
  ethnolinguism, 33, 179
  funding, 21, 40
  'la belgitude', 15
  and nationalism, 9–12
  politics, 29
  unemployment, 165
Flanders Image, 42
Flausch, Fernand, 131
Flémalle, 71
Flemish cinema, 46–7, 48, 179
Flemish Community of Belgium, 30
Flemish culture, 15–16
Flemish nationalism, 25n
Flemish painting, 119–20, 121, 128n, 143; *see also* painting
Flemish separatists, 11–12
Flemish-language films, 27
fluidity, 125–7, 147, 148
Folie privée/Private Madness, 82–3, 85–6, 86–93, *93*, 95, 97–9, 103n, 182–3
'folkloric', 172–3
Fontaine, José, 25n, 52, 61, 98, 116
Fonteyne, Frédéric, 26, 38, 45
Fourons villages, 87, 88, 90, *90*, 144, 154n
Fowler, Catherine, 87

fragmentation
  cinema, 54
  distribution, 47, 49
  families, 22–3, 76, 80, 82–104
  framing, 69–70
  linguistic, 8, 11–12, 27
  of nation-state, 179
  transnationalism, 5
  workforce, 66, 68
France
  box office, 48
  casting, 166
  as 'country of culture', 106–7
  'cultural capital', 43–4
  filiation, 73
  film festivals, 184
  'France for French filmmakers', 36
  funding, 30, 33, 39
  identification, 49
  industrialism, 58
  'national cinema', 156
  polars, 157
  sociopolitical issues, 164–5
  transnationalism, 55, 66, 179–81
France, Cécile de, 53–4
France-Soir, 132
'francophone cinema', definition, 34
Francophone literature, 12–13
French Caribbean, 34
French Community of Belgium or Wallonia-Brussels Federation (CBWF), 31, 32
'French film ecosystem', 49n
French film noir, 23–4, 166, 175, 177n
French New Realism, 55, 65, 76, 81n, 133, 137, 152, 163
French New Wave, 30
French Poetic Realism, 54, 175–6
'French Political Cinema', 81n
French star system, 54
Fritzl, Josef, 100
The Full Monty, 171
funding, 32–3, 34–40, 82–3, 148, 155–6

Gabin, Jean, 175
Gabriel, Benoît, 115–16, 117–18, 136, 139, 179
Galicia, 36
Galt, Rosalind, 43
Le gamin au vélo/The Kid With a Bike, 51–81, 74, 78, 81n, 100, 113, 150, 173
Gangsters, 157
Garson, Charlotte, 102
Gauditiaubois, André, 49
Les géants/The Giants, 38, 145–6, 153

Gellner, Ernest, 11, 14
Genappe, Wallonia, 99
Gendron, Nicolas, 144, 148
'Generation 2000', 159
'geographic filmmaker', 160
Gerlache, Alain, 47–8
German Expressionism, 112
German Occupation, 87
Germania anno zero/Germany Year Zero, 54, 73–4
Germanic-language cinema, 9
Germany, 33, 36, 39, 66
Gilliam, Terry, 112
glocal, 26–7
Gordon, Fiona, 31, 42, 132, 160, 184
Gossens, Jan, 12
Gott, Michael, 146, 147–8
Le grand paysage d'Alexis Droeven/The Wide Horizons of Alexis Droeven, 22, 87, 88–90, 90, 144, 154n
Grand-Halleux, Ardennes, 86
Grenoble, 160, 170
Guédiguian, Robert, 84
La gueule ouverte/A Mouth Agape, 89, 90
Guiot, Nicolas, 112

Haenal, Adèle, 54, 83
Hainaut, 109, 110, 116, 122, 174
Hall, Stuart, 17
Hammond, Brady, 109, 121
Haneke, Michael, 101–2, 104n
Hannerz, Ulf, 6, 19, 28, 37, 40, 158, 180
Hänsel, Marion, 31
Hardt, Michael, 67–8
Harper, Graeme, 108, 113, 118, 121, 122
Hayward, Susan
  French film noir, 156, 163, 173, 176
  middlebrow, 176–7
  'national cinema', 5–6
  women, 57, 78–9, 117
Hedling, Erik, 121–2
heists, 155–77
Héliot, Louis, 111
Hensgens, Jean-François, 4
Hep Taxi! 139
Herder, Johann Gottfried, 11
Hermalle-sous-Huy detention centre, Engis, 111
'hermeneutics of noir', 163–4, 175, 176
Herzog, Werner, 83
Heyrendt, Hubert, 1
Higbee, William, 25n, 28, 34, 48, 49, 55, 158
Higson, Andrew, 21–2, 25n, 27–9, 59, 99, 147–8, 158, 181
Hitchcock, Alfred, 129n

219

Hiver 60/Winter 60, 22
Hjort, Mette
   'banal aboutness', 162
   'cinemas of small nations', 5, 6–8, 44
   'marked' transnationalism, 34, 105–6, 109, 128n, 148, 181, 183–4
   'monocultural', 51
   'national cinema', 36
   'shared culture', 28, 55
   'topical' themes, 4, 77, 107
   transnationalism, 39
Hodgin, Nick, 128n
holiday-making, 145
Hollywood
   distribution, 30, 38, 45, 180
   editing, 112–13
   Flemish connection with, 50n
   Lanners, 132
   post-classical, 145–6, 177n
   remakes, 47–8
l'homme fragile et fatigué, 166–71
Un honnête commerêçant/Step by Step, 157
Hooghe, Liesbet, 15–16, 18–19
Hopper, Edward, 131
horror, 145
hors-champs (off-screen space), 101–3, 102, 104n, 152
'hot nationalism', 2
Hugo, Victor, 175
L'Humanite dimanche, 165
humiliation, 167
Huppert, Isabelle, 83
Huston, John, 122, 163, 174

IAD (Institut des arts de diffusion), 84, 112
L'iceberg, 132
'identitarian' cinema, 18, 28, 36, 42
'identitarian nationalism', 36
Illégal/Illegal, 107, 110, 111, 128–9n
Iñárritu, Alejandro González, 155
industrialism, 61, 70–3, 99, *117*, *143*, 168, *168*, 181
Ingberg, Henry, 31, 33, 41, 45
Innen Leben/Insyriated, 184
Les Inrockuptibles, 148, 154n
INSAS (Institut Supérieur des Arts), 84, 85
Institut des arts de diffusion (IAD), 84, 112
Intouchables/The Intouchables, 44
Iordanova, Dina, 6–7, 21, 180
Ireland, 38
Italian Neorealism, 4, 54, 73, 80n, 121–2, 167
Italy, 33, 38
Ivens, Joris, 4, 113, 128n

Jack, Belinda Elizabeth, 12
Jäckel, Anne, 38
Jacobowitz, Florence, 90, 96
Jambon d'Ardenne/Ham and Chips, 91–2, 145
Jarmusch, Jim, 151–2
Jaumain, Michel, 185n
Je pense à vous/You're On My Mind, 51–2, 53, 57, 59, 99, 168, 173, 182
Jean, Patric, 164
Jeancolas, Jean-Pierre, 54
le jeune cinéma, 55, 152, 156, 171, 180
Jimenez, Mary, 31
Jolivet, Pierre, 163
Le jour se lève/Daybreak, 176
journey, 60, 145–53
Jules, Dominique, 104n

Kaganski, Serge, 175
Kahn, Cédric, 156
Kampusch, Natascha, 99–100
Kaplan, Catherine, 145
Kassovitz, Mathieu, 156
Kaurismäki, Aki, 131, 148–9, 151, 153, 154n, 160
Keating, Patrick, 124, 138
Kechiche, Abdellatif, 39
Keiller, Patrick, 142, 154n
Kempenaers, Jan, 142
Kiarostami, Abbas, 84
Kieślowski, Krzysztof, 58, 81n, 155
Klinger, Barbara, 24n
Kurosawa, Akira, 130
KVS theatre (Koninklijke Vlaamse Schouwburg), 12

La Une, 2
'labyrinth', 62–3
Laderman, David, 146, 149
Ladri di biciclette/Bicycle Thieves, 73, 75–6, 167
Lafosse, Joachim, 82–104
   'art cinema', 28
   camerawork, 141
   film festivals, 27, 41–3, 184
   film-school generation, 4, 22
   Flemish painting, 143
   fragmentation, 182–3
   framing, *93*
   and Lanners, 133
   Luxembourg, 38
   and Masset-Depasse, 111
   paternalism, 23
   'post-Dardenne generation', 56–7
   realism, 154n

Wallonia, 157
Walloon culture, 9
Lahire, Bernard, 164
Lamy, Benoît, 18, 25n, 91–2, 145
'Landscapes of Belgium', Musée d'Ixelles, 140, 173
Lang, Fritz, 112
Lang, Rachel, 112
language, 15–16, 98
Lanners, Bouli, 141–5
  'autodidacts', 4
  camerawork, *143*
  CinemaScope, 172
  countryside, 88
  'devalorisation of man', 166
  filiation, 179
  film festivals, 27–8, 41–3, 57–8
  film-school generation, 22
  Flemish painting, 121
  fluidity, 126
  genre-based filmmaking, 183
  landscape, 144
  Luxembourg, 38
  marginality, 164
  regionalism, 16
  road movies, 23–4, 130–54
  slag heaps, 115, 117, 128n
  visibility of Belgian cinema, 184
  Wallonia 'in crisis', 7
  Walloon culture, 9, 18
Lannoo, Vincent, 82
Last Night on Earth, 82
Last Resort, 111
Le Havre, 160, 177n
Le Havre, 160
Ledo, Margarita, 5, 36, 178
Lefebvre, Martin, 113, 142
Lefort, Gérard, 61
'leftover spaces', 61, 64, 67–8, 71
Lesuisse, Anne-Françoise, accent, 60, 61, 63
Une liaison pornographique/An Affair of Love, 38
Libération, 160
Liberski, Stefan, 153
'libre arbitre' (free will), 102
La Libre Belgique, 1, 32, 38, 50n, 86, 133, 134
Liège, 155–77
  Bajomée, 52
  Belvaux, 24
  'culture of struggle', 18
  Dardenne, Luc, 72
  documentary films, 164–5
  filmmaking in, 36, 50n
  Lanners, 133, *135*, 143, 145, 148, *149*, 150–1, 153

Masset-Depasse, 110–11
'particularism', 181
post-industrialism, 133–41, 171–6
La raison du plus faible, 167, 176
Le silence de Lorna, 64, *65*
'Liège film school', 159
Liège-Seraing basin, 59
Liénard, Bénédicte, 149, 166
'lieux', 62
Lille, 68, 181
Lim, Song Hwee
  'critical transnationalism', 34, 48, 49
  'shared culture', 28, 55
  'stillness', 94
  transnationalism, 5, 8, 158
'limiting', 21, 29, 59, 147, 158
linguistic communities, 29–33
Lioret, Philippe, 111
Loach, Ken, 41, 83, 171
'local anchoring', 51, 113
'localised struggles', 133, 137
localism, 41
Locarno film festival, 82, 83, 113, 184
Loft, 47
Loison, Guillaume, 132
'lonesome zonings', 133–41
Looking for Eric, 41
Loopmans, Maarten, 139
Lorfèvre, Alain, 82, 103n, 111–12, 123, *125*
Lorraine, 66
Louvet, Jean, 12, 13, 19
Lovat, Simon, 131
Low Countries, 17, 143, 146–7, 150
Luce, Maximilien, 174
Luxembourg, 38–9, 103n, 107
Lynch, David, 112, 113
Lyons, 165

Ma Loute/Slack Bay, 107
Ma petite entreprise/My Little Business, 163
Machin, Alfred, 179
Maghreb countries, 28
magic realism, 154n
Magritte awards, 42–3, 53, 56, 184
Mahler, Gustave, 89–90
Mai, Joseph, 54, 74, 81n, 177n
Malraux, André, 29
Mandelbaum, Jacques, 132–3, 163
Manifeste pour la culture wallonne, 19, 58
Marchal, Olivier, 157
marginalisation, 51–81
marginality, 80, 179
  accent, 65–79

Mariage, Benoît
  L'autre, 85
  camerawork, 123
  carnival, 99
  filiation, 136
  'post-Dardenne generation', 179
  'regional anchorage', 87
  La revue toudi, 19, 57–8
  slag heaps, 115, 117–18
  sociopolitical issues, 163
  Strip-Tease, 132
  Wallonia 'in crisis', 7
'marked' transnationalism, 5, 34, 45–6, 105–29, 128n, 148, 181, 183
Marseille, 177n
Marshall, Bill, 21, 34, 43, 44, 159–60, 180
Martel, Frédéric, 1, 12, 14, 15, 16
Martinez, Dominique, 160
Martin-Jones, David, 6–7, 21, 180
Marxism, 80n
Masset-Depasse, Olivier, 105–29
  Cages, 23, *124*, 183
  and Dardenne brothers, 133
  filiation, 179
  film festivals, 27, 82, 184
  film-school generation, 4, 22
  and Mariage, 7
  'marked' transnationalism, 181
  paternalism, 152
  Walloon culture, 9
  women, 57
Massey, Doreen, 24, 134, 142, 143, 144, 145
Mathijs, Ernest
  'Belgian disease', 100
  'Dutroux affair', 104n
  filiation, 84
  Low Countries, 4, 146–7, 150
  'national cinema', 16–17
  'particularism', 22, 86
Le Matin, 20, 180–1
Maule, Rosanna, 33
Maystadt, Philippe, 32
Mazierska, Ewa, 24, 146, 147, 148–9, 150, 153, 154n
McTiernan, John, 177n
MEDIA, 38
MEDIA II, 38
Meier, Ursula, 31
Meikle, Jeffery L., 149
Melbye, David, 113–14
Mello, Marie-Hélène, 163, 165
melodrama, 127, 156
Mélon, Marc-Emmanuel, 52, 73, 85, 157–8
Melville, Jean-Pierre
  Belvaux, 177n

colour palette, 168
crime and gangster films, 170
filiation, 166, 174–5, 176
  polars, 23–4, 159, 163–4
Merigeau, Pascal, 171
Meunier, Constantin, 174
Meuse river, 63–4, 71, 72, 74, 78–9, 111, 136, 139
Meyer, Paul, 4, 17, 18, 22, 52, 113–16, 123, 168
Michel, Thierry, 45, 58, 61
Middle Eastern countries, 28
Miller, Richard, 26, 29, 32, 35
Milquet, Joëlle, 183
Ming-Liang, Tsai, 94
Minister of Culture, 32
Minister of Finance, 38
Ministry of Culture, 3, 39, 183
mise-en-scène
  'demi-rupture', 64
  filiation, 151
  fluidity, 79
  industrial architecture, 172
  industrial landscape, 136–7
  Masset-Depasse, 124, *124*, 125
  minimalist, 177n
  and national culture, 57
  noir-ish, 173
  obstacles, 70
  La raison du plus faible, 167
  Seraing, 58
  slag heaps, 115–16, 122
  spatial dynamics, 62
  transnationalism, 181
Misère au Borinage/Poverty in the Borinage, 4, 18, 29, 113, 164, 170, 179
Mobile Home, 38, 148
Mockel, Albert, 17
Le Monde, 16, 66, 73, 108, 163
'monocultural', 51, 52, 80, 99, 182
Mons-Marcinelle, 36
Morin, Edgar, 10, 24–5n
Morocco, 38
La Mort de l'Automobile, 131
Mosley, Philip
  biculturalism, 5
  carnival, 99
  cinéma nordiste, 55
  countryside, 88
  'cultural mode of production', 30
  documentary films, 133
  'Dutroux affair', 100
  filiation, 52, 58, 73, 75
  Flemish language, 3
  Fourons villages, 154n

INDEX

funding, 33
'impersonation', 182
industrialism, 61, 137
Kaurismäki, 149
'la belgitude', 15
magic realism, 132
'monocultural', 51
'national cinema', 16, 27–8
nationalism, 25n
paternalism, 117
public service broadcasting, 2
La raison du plus faible, 175
'responsible realism', 54, 80n
Royal Decree 1952, 29
'small national cinema', 8
social commentary, 169
'social memory', 121, 144
socio-economics, 87
'split', 9, 27
synchronicity, 150
transport, 166
Mouton, Olivier, 104n
Mulvey, Laura, 94
Munich film festival, 82
Le Mur/The Wall, 16
Murat, Pierre, 174
Murnau, F. W., 112
Murphy, David, 13
Murray, Jonathan, 118
My Childhood, 118

Naficy, Hamid, 28, 158
Nakache, Olivier, 44
The Naked City, 174
Namur, 157, 160
'national cinema'
   Besson, 36
   Christie, 41
   Cinematheque Royale and CCA, 2–3
   'community-based' cinema, 7
   distribution, 44–5, 80
   Elsaesser, 27
   exhibition, 46
   Fowler, 87
   France, 156
   funding, 39
   Higson, 178
   Lanners, 132
   Ledo, 5–6
   'limiting', 21–2, 147
   promotion, 42
nationalism, 9–20, 119–20, 153, 178
Nations and Nationalism, 14
Les navets blancs empêchent de dormir la nuit/White Turnips Make it Hard to Sleep, 112

Nazi collaboration, 4, 14
Neale, Steve, 111, 127
Negri, Antonio, 67–8
Nénert, Claire, 83–4
'neo-neo-expressionist' approach, 112
neo-noir, 126–7
Nessolson, Lisa, 172
Nestigen, Andrew, 28
Netherlands, 36–7, 38, 44, 47, 50n, 184
'network narratives', 155
New Austrian film, 100
'New Europe', 111, 147
'New European cinema', 111
The New Face of Political Cinema, 55
'New Francophone Belgian cinema', 28
'New Hollywood', 106
'New Order', 14
Newcraighall, 118
Neyrat, Cyril, 172, 173–4
'noir aesthetic', 157, 163, 173
'non-places', 67, 76
Nord/North, 181
Nord-Pas-de-Calais
   Dumont, 86, 107
   fluidity, 126
   landscape, 120–4, *120*, 148
   'marked' transnationalism, 105–6, 109
   'particularism', 181
   transnationalism, 55, 111
   Wallimage, 33, 50n, 180
   women's employment, 68
North Africa, 28, 34
'northern cinema', 55
Northern France, 87
Norway, 28, 44, 58
'nostalgia', 144
'le nouveau cinéma belge francophone', 27
Nue propriété/Private Property, 38, 41, 83, 85–93, 95–9, *96*, 103n, 104n, 182–3
Nuttens, Jean-Dominique, 70, 104n
N-VA, 11, 29

The Observer, 68
obstacles, 70
Olivier, Richard, 133–4
Olsen, Mark, 170
On the Road Again – Le cinéma de Bouli Lanners, 141, 150, 153
O'Rawe, Des, 92, 104n
Ordinary Man, 82
O'Regan, Tom, 109
Oser être wallon!: ouvrage collectif sur l'identité wallone, 20
Osganian, Patricia, 54
O'Shaughnessy, Martin, 36, 52, 54, 62–6, 69, 81n, 134, 137

Ostend, 160
'Other Belgian Cinema' film festival, Strasbourg, 27
Ozu, Yasujirō, 142

Paasi, Anssi, 14
painting, 24, 116, 119, 130–1, 131, 143–4, 174; *see also* Flemish painting
Palmer, Tim, 49n
Parfait Amour/Perfect Love, 181
Parfois trop d'amour/ Sometimes there's too much love, 156, 176n
Paris, 110, 157–61, 165, 177n, 184
Park, Eun-Jee, 116, 152, 154n
Une part du ciel/A Piece of Sky, 149, 166
'particularism', 22, 23, 51, 52, 64, 86, 146, 181
Pas son genre/Not My Type, 99, 156, 161
paternalism, 23, 78, 117, 152
Pathé, 179
Pawlikowski, Pawel, 111
Pays noir/Black country, 115–16, 117–18
Paysages professionnels du STP 1964–1971, 173
'peasant cinema', 87
Penn, Arthur, 154n
Peru, 184
Petrie, Duncan, 6, 7–8, 44, 181, 183–4
Peugeot plant, Montbéliard, 66–7
photography, 93–9, 104n, 115–18, 134, 142, 173
physical borders, 70
'physical brutality', 100
Pialat, Maurice, 80n, 84, 89, 90, 182
Pialoux, Michel, 66
La Pianiste/The Piano Teacher, 101–2
Picard, Edmund, 10
Picolo, René, 30
Pictanovo, 107
Pirot, François, 38, 84–5
Pirotte, Jean, 10, 14–15, 17
plan séquences, 94–6, 102–3
'plic-ploc', 112, 128n
Pliskin, Fabrice, 181
Pluijgers, Jean-François, 32, 54
Des plumes dans la tête/Feathers in My Head, 98–9, 99, 182
Poelvoorde, Benoît, 82
poetics, 161–2, 166, 171–6
Poirer, Manuel, 151
Poirson-Dechonne, Marion, 166
Poland, 38, 58
polars (thrillers), 156–7, 159, 162–3, 163, 166
Polet, Jacques, 86, 88, 100, 174
'popular aesthetic', 44

Positif, 28, 42, 83, 85, 159
'Post-1995 French Cinema: Return of the Social, Return of the Political?', 55
post-colonialism, 19
'post-Dardenne generation', 55–9
post-industrialism, 133–41, 171–6
'post-national', 6
'post-national cinema Europe', 19
Pour rire!, 156
Pour toi je ferai bataille/For You I Will Fight, 112
Pourquoi se marier le jour de la fin du monde?/Why Get Married the Day the World Ends?, 39
Powrie, Phil, 55, 152, 163, 166
Prédal, René, 156, 160
'pregnant moment', 94, 96
De Premier/Prime Minister, 47
Les premiers, les derniers/The First, The Last, 130
President of the Jury Prize, 82
'private' trilogy, 85, 103, 182–3
privatisation, 37
'problem of identity', 147
production, 26–50
La promesse/The Promise, 38, 52–4, 59–61, 73–4, 80n, 92, 98, 116–17, 154n
promotion, 42–3
Un prophète/A Prophet, 164
'psychological-physical' axis, 113–20, 121–2, 128
Puri, Tara, 61, 64, 67, 71

Le Quai des Brumes/Port of Shadows, 160
Les quatre cents coups/The 400 blows, 73, 94
Quebec, 8, 34, 73
Quinet, Patrick, 26
Quinzaine des réalisteurs/Directors' Fortnight, 83–4

Radio Campus Brussels, 101
Raining Stones, 171
La Raison des plus faibles: Rapport au travail, ecritures domestiques et lectures domestiques et les lectures en milieu populaires, 164
La raison du plus faible/The Right of the Weakest, 7, 24, 149, 156–76, 162, 167, 168, 182
La raison du plus fort/The Right of the Strongest, 164
Rancière, Jacques, 84
Rapt, 156, 160

Rascaroli, Laura, 24, 146, 147, 148–9, 150, 153, 154n
Rayner, Jonathan, 108, 113, 118, 121, 122
realism, 54, 80n, 86
    cinematic, 88
    magic, 154n
    responsible, 54
    sensuous, 54
    unadorned, 132
    urgent, 56, 59, 60, 79, 134, 138
Redmond, Sean, 109, 121
La Régate/The Boat Race, 100
'regional aesthetic', 120
'regional anchorage', 87, 103n
'regional' cinema, 2–3, 28, 42, 44, 59, 66, 80, 178
regionalism, 16, 21
'regionalist cinema', 88
Régnier, Natacha, 166
Renier, Jérémie, 54
Renoir, Jean, 79
Resnais, Alain, 84, 155
'responsible realism', 54
'Responsible Realists', 80n
Reuchamps, Min, 9–10, 24n
Revue Belge, 60
La revue nouvelle, 33
La revue toudi
    Belvaux, 157
    box office, 48
    Dardenne brothers, 65
    fragmentation, 98–9
    Lafosse, 85
    Louvet, 13
    Manifeste pour la culture wallonne, 33
    mise-en-scène, 62
    transnationalism, 73
    Walloon cinema, 7, 57–8
    Walloon regionalism, 18–19, 182
Reynaert, Philippe
    Cannes film festival, 162
    'cinema is an industry', 29
    France, 26, 44–5
    'identitarian' cinema, 36
    Luxembourg, 38
    Ministry of Culture, 32, 39
    Nord-Pas-de-Calais, 107
    Screen Brussels, 50n
    television, 184
Reynders, Didier, 38
Rhône Alps regional film fund, 160
Richard, Salomé, 112
Rien à déclarer/Nothing to Declare, 41
The River, 79
road movies, 23–4, 130–54
    American, 154n

Rochet, Bénédicte, 7, 42
Roekens, Anne, 7, 49n, 173, 183
romantic comedies, 156
Romanticism, 10
Romney, Jonathan, 59
Romy, Bruno, 42, 132, 160, 184
Rongione, Fabrizio, 85
Rosetta
    box office, 48
    camerawork, 63
    Cannes film festival, 4
    centre-periphery dynamic, 61–2
    colour palette, 79
    editing, 113
    exploitation, 61
    female body, 57
    filiation, 54
    framing, 92
    marginality, 75, 154n
    'national cinema', 53, 132
    'nostalgia', 144
    paternalism, 116–17, 152
    regional memories, 135
    social commentary, 169
    socio-economics, 68–9, 165
    transnationalism, 55
    transport, 166
    women's employment, 136, 149
Roskam, Michaël R., 27, 40, 47, 142
Røssaak, Eivind, 94
Rossellini, Roberto, 54, 74
Rouchy, Marie-Elisabeth, 133
De rouille et d'os/Rust and Bone, 39, 54
Rowden, Terry, 5, 20, 25n, 27, 53, 153, 158
Roy, André, 132
Royal Decree 1952, 29
Royal Decree 1967, 179
RTBF (*Radio et Télévision Belge Francophone*), 1–2, 16, 43, 47, 50n, 104n, 159
Rumba, 42, 132
Rundskop/Bullhead, 27, 40
rural setting, 86, 88–90, 99, 104n
Ryva Productions, 84–5

Sargeant, Jack, 131
Sarris, Andrew, 155
Scandinavia, 28, 44
Scarface, 95
SCC (Service de Culture Cinématographique), 2–3
Schlesinger, Philip, 5–6
Les Schtroumpfs/The Smurfs, 184
Sclessin, 71
Scotland, 10, 118

Scottish Gaelic cinema, 181
Scottish independence referendum 2015, 29
Screen Brussels, 31, 32, 35, 50n
Screen Flanders, 35
'self-confirming selectivity', 27, 41
'self-selectivity', 31, 179
'semantic', 131, 146
'sensuous realism', 54
Seraing, 22, 51–81, 65, 134, 154n, 168
'séries C', 38
Serpieri, Victor, 101
Service de Culture Cinématographique (SCC), 2–3
'shared culture', 28, 49, 55
Shaw, Deborah, 52, 156, 158–9
Le silence de Lorna/Lorna's Silence
   Bazin, 177n
   'demi-rupture', 64
   exploitation, 61
   film festivals, 42
   maternalism, 77, 81n
   realism, 80n
   Seraing, 65
   synchronicity, 110–11, 150
   'urgent realism', 60
   women's employment, 177n
Simenon, Georges, 12–13, 25n, 175, 177n
Det sjunde inseglet/The Seventh Seal, 113, 120
Skåne, 122
slag heaps, 105–29, 113, 128n
'small cinema', 5–9
'Small Cinemas' conference, 8th (2017), 26–7
Smith, Anthony, 14, 17, 119
Smulronstället/Wild Strawberries, 113
Les Snuls, 154n
'social cinema', 58
'social memory', 117, 121
'social' thrillers, 161–6
'social-realist' films, 123
'socio-economic decline', 87
Le Soir, 101, 108
Sojcher, Frédéric, 18, 24–5n, 27, 31–2, 35, 47, 183
Sotinel, Thomas, 140
soundtrack, 79, 89–90, 91
Soviet Union, 28
Spaas, Lieve, 8–9, 56, 135, 164
Spain, 38, 39
spatial dynamics, 59–65, 86, 102, 142
Speck, Oliver C., 99–100
Spellbound, 129n
Spielberg, Steven, 48
'split', 2, 5, 9, 27
Staiger, Janet, 163

Steele, Jamie, 25n, 36, 50n
Steeman, Stanislas-André, 177n
'stillness', 93–4, 97, 102, 142, 143, 144
'stills', 82–104
Storck, Henri, 4, 87, 113, 164
Stories We Tell Ourselves event, 49n
Strass, 82
Stratton, David, 177n
Strip-Tease, 132
Sub-Saharan Africa, 34
sub-state, 28–9, 29–33
Sweden, 28, 38, 44
Switzerland
   cinéma-monde, 21
   co-productions, 38, 103n
   distribution, 43–4, 180
   film festivals, 184
   'francophone cinema', 34
   linguistic fragmentation, 8–9
   'national cinema', 36
   Peugeot plant, Montbeliard, 66
'synchronic' approach to film history, 24n, 26
'syntactic', 131, 146

Taminiaux, Pierre, 12, 15
Tavernier, Bertrand, 76
Tax Rebate for International Productions (TRIP), 36
tax shelter, 21, 32, 37–8, 39–40
Téchiné, André, 159
Technicolor, 79
Télébruxelles, 50n
television, 8, 16, 33, 132, 178, 184
Terril de Charbonnage, 174
Tessé, Jean-Philippe, 79
Thabourey, Vincent, 100–1, 161–2, 163, 164
Thanasse et Casimir/Thanasse and Casimir, 30
theatre, 13, 19
thematic filiation, 58
Theunissen, Marianne, 133–4
'third solitudes' model, 20
38 témoins/One Night, 100, 156, 172
Thomas, Paul, 154n
Thompson, Kristin, 163
thrillers (*polars*), 4, 7, 23–4, 155–77
Thys, Marianne, 27, 30
Tintin comic books, 184
Tixhon, Axel, 7, 173, 183
Toledano, Éric, 44
Tomasovic, Dirk, 60
'topical' themes, 4, 80, 107, 128, 138, 180, 181, 183
Toto le héros/Toto the Hero, 132

Tout ça ne nous rendra pas la Belgique/Bye Bye Belgium, 1–2, 8, 178
Transnational Cinema: A Reader, 5
'Transnational Nordic Cinema', 28
transnationalism, 5, 178–82
   'affinitive', 39
   Cages, 23, 111
   'cinema of transvergence', 25n
   co-productions, 37
   'critical', 34, 48, 49
   Dardenne brothers, 59, 80
   Deux jours, une nuit, 66
   European, 148–9
   filiation, 151
   funding, 40
   Le gamin au vélo, 73
   glocal, 26–7
   Lim, 8
   'marked', 105
   modes of narration, 156
   North Africa, 28
   prodution, distribution and exhibition, 21
   'shared culture', 44
transport, 60, 63, 71, 75, 153, 167, *167*
La Trêve/The Break, 145
Tribu, 82, 85
Trier, Joachim, 58
La trilogie, Après la Vie, 156, 159, 160, 177n
TRIP (Tax Rebate for International Productions), 36
Trois couleurs: Bleu/Three colours: Blue, 81n
Troukens, François, 4
Truffaut, François, 73, 84, 94, 176–7n
Tueurs/Killers, 4
Tulitikkutehtaan tyttö/The Match Factory Girl, 149
Turim, Maureen, 164
'Twenty-five Years of French Cinema', 159
'two solitudes', 8

Uccle, 86
Ultranova, 130–54, *138*, *140*
   auteurism, 41
   CinemaScope, 172–3
   countryside, 88
   'devalorisation of man', 166
   fetishisation, *135*
   road movies, 24
   slag heaps, 115, 117, 128n
   Wallonia 'in crisis', 7
unadorned realism, 132
unemployment, *115*, 161–6
United Kingdom, 38, 58, 73

United States of America (USA), 47–9, 66, 68, 73, 180
'urgent realism', 56, 59, 60, 79, 134, 138

VAF (Vlaams Audiovisuel Fonds), 21, 35, 40
Van de Craen, Piet, 10–11, 13, 15, 16, 16–17
Van den Braembussche, Antoon, 11, 12, 14, 15, 23, 119
Van Dormael, Jaco, 132
Van Ginderachter, Maarten, 25n
Van Hoeij, Boyd, 55–6, 112, 125, 128n, 159
Van Holsbeek, Joe, 99
Van Hoofstadt, Olivier, 54
Van Looy, Eric, 47
Van Rompaey, Christophe, 42
Vande Winkel, Roel, 40
Vandenbulcke, Guy, 185n
Venice film festival, 83
Vercruysse, Sophie, 84–5
Verhaeghe, Marceau, 132, 137
Verheul, Jaap, 46–7
Vernet, Marc, 89
Versus Productions, 105–6, 131, 154n
Vidal, Belen, 6–7, 21, 180
video documentaries, 59, 69, 98; *see also* documentary films
La vie d'Adèle/Blue is the warmest colour, 39
La vie de Jésus/The Life of Jesus, 181
La vie rêvée des anges/The Dreamlife of Angels, 62, 68–9, 136, 166, 181
Le Vif/L'Express, 108
Vincendeau, Ginette
   Belvaux, 171, 174–5
   Le cercle rouge, 163
   crime and gangster films, 170
   film festivals, 41
   French film noir, 177n
   glocal, 27
   language and national identity, 34
   Nue propriété, 87–8, 91, 95, 97
   unemployment, 104n, 165
Vlaams Audiovisuel Fonds (VAF), 21, 35, 40
Vlaeminckx, Jean-Michel, 123
Vn Zuylen, Eric, 84–5
von Dassanowsky, Robert, 99–100
Von Dormael, Jaco, 43
VRT (*Vlaams Radio en Televisieomroeporganisatie*), 16

Wagner, Richard, 90
Wald, Micha, 111

Walker, Michael, 163
Wallimage
   Cannes film festival, 162
   'cultural project tests', 31–2
   film festivals, 27
   funding, 4
   polars, 157
   'regional' cinema, 35, 40, 179–80
   tax shelter, 38–9
   Télébruxelles, 50n
   territorialisation, 33
   'topical' themes, 183
Wallimage-Bruxellimage funding line, 32
Wallonia
   'art cinema', 22
   Belvaux, 159–61, 163–4
   box office, 48–9
   Cages, 108–9, 128
   cinéma nordiste, 6–7
   colour palette, 174
   co-productions, 36
   cultural heritage, 17–19
   Dardenne brothers, 56, 58, 80
   Destrée, 25n
   economic crisis, 111
   Eldorado, 143
   'fifty years of Belgian cinema' event, 3
   film festivals, 42
   and Flanders, 104n
   funding, 21
   industrial heritage, 4
   industrialism, 66, 151
   journey, 61
   'la belgitude', 15–16
   Lafosse, 82–104
   Lanners, 23–4
   nationalism, 8–10, 12, 179
   patriarchal society, 152
   polars, 176
   post-industrialism, 71, 74, 133–6, 168
   La raison du plus faible, 157
   'regional' look of, 86
   regionalism, 13
   road movies, 147–8
   'shared concerns', 55
   'social memory', 121–2
   socio-economics, 182–3
   Télébruxelles, 50n
   television, 184
   'topical' themes, 77–8
   transnationalism, 179–80
   unemployment, 52
   Wallimage, 40

La Wallonie, 17
Walloon
   countryside, 141–5
   cultural identity, 19–20, 49n
   culture, 116, 153, 157
   economic crisis, 165, 183
   identity, 70
   nationalism, 15–16, 51, 182
   regionalism, 13, 17–19, 25n
   self-image, 12–13, 133
Walloon cinema, 178, 181
   categorisation, 7
   Dardenne brothers, 57–8
   economic crisis, 173
   funding, 32
   Le grand paysage d'Alexis Droeven, 87
   'identitarian' cinema, 42
   industrial heritage, 113
   Lafosse, Joachim, 85
   mise-en-scène, 61, 62–3
   Royal Decree 1952, 29–30
   synchronicity, 110
War of the Worlds [radio play], 1
Warehime, Marja, 84, 89
Watson, Stephanie, 131
WBI (Wallonie-Bruxelles International), 184
Weight of the World, 65, 66
Weissberg, Jay, 95, 123
Welcome, 111
Welles, Orson, 1
Wen, Xianghui, 125
Wenders, Wim, 82, 131, 148–9, 151
Western, 151, 152
Western Europe, 68
Wheatley, Catherine, 101–2
Willeman, Paul, 181
Williams, James, 67, 88, 102, 103n, 104n, 142, 156
women filmmakers, 19–20, 31
women-led narratives, 57
Wong, Kar-Wai, 112
working class, 59, 60, 68–74, 77, 81n

Yale French Studies, 9
Yernaux, Paul, 49
Yon, François, 111

Zéno, Thierry, 132
Zonca, Erick, 68, 133, 136, 166
Zone02, 129n

EU representative:
Easy Access System Europe
Mustamäe tee 50, 10621 Tallinn, Estonia
Gpsr.requests@easproject.com